MW00612172

A Complete Guide to

Understanding The Dispensationalism Controversy

By
Kerry Trahan

This book is an updated version
of the author's Th. D.
Dissertation, which was
originally submitted to the
faculty of Louisiana Baptist
Theological Seminary February,
2007

Published by:

Disciple of Jesus Ministries, Inc.

Port Neches, Texas

Email: doj@att.net

**All Scripture quotations are
from the King James Version
(KJV) of the Bible.**

© **Copyright 2007 by Kerry Trahan.** All rights
reserved.   This   publication   may   not   be
reproduced in part or in whole by any means
without permission from Kerry Trahan.

ISBN 978-0-9800959-0-6

Library of Congress Control Number: 2007940724

**Printed in the United
States of America**

Acknowledgments

I would like to express my deepest appreciation to those who have contributed so much time and labor to help make this publication possible.

To Jeanne McElwee for her tireless and patient editing.

To Mary Hertel for proofreading.

To my wife Rosetta, who so lovingly compensates for my frequent absences from common life.

To the faithful members of A Church of Jesus, who are so sacrificially dedicated to the service of our Lord.

Table of Contents

Table of Contents
(Cont.)

Endorsement of *Understanding the Dispensationalism Controversy*

By Dr. Thomas Ice

In too many circles the term "dispensationalism" has become a Christian cuss word. Is dispensationalism really as bad as some of its critics contend? Kerry Trahan has written *A complete Guide to Understanding the Dispensationalism Controversy* from a sympathetic perspective.

Dispensationalism has always been a misunderstood theology, partly because of the extreme reactions by many of its critics, who all too often demonize it as a heresy or near-heresy. Dispensationalism has also suffered at the hands of its advocates who sometimes teach things in the name of dispensationalism that are inconsistent with actual tenants of dispensationalism.

Kerry Trahan's book does an excellent job of defining, describing and presenting the essentials of dispensationalism so that a friend or foe of this theology should have a clear grasp of its teachings and characteristics. As a dispensationalist, Trahan demonstrates a clear understanding of this theology and interacts intelligently with the primary and secondary issues relating to dispensationalism. Trahan also interacts with historical issues that often surround dispensationalism.

Trahan and I believe that dispensationalism represents the best attempt by man to state what the Bible, from Genesis to Revelation, is about. Dispensationalism is the outworking of a consistently literal hermeneutic that challenges many of the church's traditional views in the areas of Israelology, ecclesiology, and eschatology. For anyone who would like a reliable source for dispensational theology and its implications, I strongly recommend this important and timely treatment of these issues. Instead of viewing dispensationalism as a roadblock to understanding God's Word, the reader of this book will at least receive a fair and knowledgeable perspective of one of the most popular theologies in our day.

Maranatha,

Thomas Ice
Executive Director
The Pre-Trib Research Center
Liberty University
Lynchburg, Virginia

Forewords

(Alphabetically Sequenced)

"It is a valuable book, very thorough research. Would be best as a teaching tool for pastors, college and seminary students. A good Pastor's book."

Pastor David Brown, PhD
First Baptist Church – Oak Creek
Oak Creek, WI
logosresourcepages.org

~ ~ ~

"Kerry Trahan has brought clarity to a complex and controversial subject with his *Complete Guide to Understanding the Dispensationalism Controversy*. This book is an excellent resource guide for those who want to go deep into the history of Dispensationalism, its terms and definitions, its theological perspectives and the opposing views of non-dispensationalists."

Evangelist Mike Gendron,
Director of Proclaiming The Gospel Ministry

~ ~ ~

"Kerry Trahan does a masterful job of reviving dispensational knowledge in an easy to understand way. I strongly recommend *A Complete Guide to Understanding the Dispensationalism Controversy* to anyone who wants to read and understand the history and prophecies of the Bible from Genesis to Revelation."

Pastor Kevin Lea
Calvary Church
Port Orchard, WA

~ ~ ~

"[This book] is going to be a valuable resource tool. I am just now beginning to teach dispensations in the young adult Sunday School and am sure that I'll be referring to it often. I am impressed with the thoroughness of the work and the way all sides are fairly presented."

Pastor Noel Mayes
Former teacher at New Tribes Bible College in Waukesha, WI
Maple Ridge Bible Church
Boscobel, WI

~ ~ ~

"I am happy for the publication: not enough being written on this most important subject (as I see it, the only way to understand the Bible)… I thought the section on Law-Grace excellent."

Ron Merryman
Merryman Ministries
Casa Grande, AZ

Forewords
(Cont.)

"It is my privilege to recommend the work *A Complete Guide to Understanding the Dispensationalism Controversy*. Kerry Trahan lays a solid foundation for understanding and gives a clear presentation of both the history and concept of Dispensationalism. The author provides a balanced and thorough presentation as the reader is drawn to consider the often-overlooked theological implications of the topic. This book will be a valuable addition to the library of any sincere student of the Word. It is a well-documented, scholarly presentation that consults and thoroughly researches scores of reference works before presenting a clear and biblically based conclusion."

Dr. Bill Sheffield
Dean of Biblical Studies
Louisiana Baptist University

~ ~ ~

"Your book, *A Complete Guide to Understanding the Dispensationalism Controversy*, has presented the subject of dispensational truth in a logical, factual, and Scriptural way that any person who desires to know about the subject can easily understand this teaching. I have read many papers and books on the subject and have not found any that present the subject with such clarity as you have. I highly recommend your work to those having an interest in this subject."

Dr. Roy Wallace
Academic Dean
Louisiana Baptist Theological Seminary

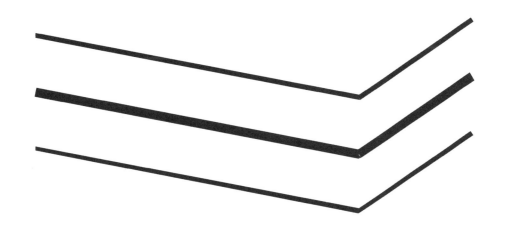

Section One

—Laying a Foundation

CHAPTER ONE
—INTRODUCTION TO PART ONE

Have you ever wondered why our Lord, at one point in time, forbade the disciples to take His message to the Gentiles (Mat 10:5-10), and then later commanded that same group of disciples to go to the Gentiles (Mat 28:19-20)? Even if no other dilemma be cited, this one alone forces the reader to: (1) resort to the *spiritualization* of the plain text of Scripture, or (2) recognize *dispensational distinctions*.

Countless similar Biblical dilemmas could also be cited. For example: Why do most New Testament believers stop short of adopting and adhering to many Old Testament practices? Israel was commanded to slay and destroy certain idolatrous nations/peoples that did not accept and follow Jehovah…. Are Christians to kill those who do not accept Jesus Christ as personal Lord and Savior? Then, there is the issue of sacrificing lambs at the Temple altar. And speaking of the Temple: where *is* the Temple at which Christians should worship and visit three times a year? Are we obligated to go to Jerusalem and build one? Are Christians to appoint a high priest and set up a priestly system after the Levitical pattern? Then, there is the issue of those many Old Testament laws…. Are Christians to execute judgment upon those transgressors who fail to precisely observe all that is written in the Mosaic code? For example: Are those who gather firewood on Saturday to be stoned to death? There are many such laws, the breaking of which demanded punishment by death. Then there is the matter of those very strict dietary laws (e.g., eating no pork, shellfish, etc.). Circumcising all male children (as a religious rite) was also required. In addition, the manner after which the Passover is to be kept is spelled out in great detail. Are the many New Testament churches that are not now practicing the Passover in all of its detail in violation against God and His Holy Word? An almost limitless number of similar requirements might be listed (e.g., the observance of Saturday instead of Sunday as the Sabbath; exacting an eye for an eye, or a tooth for a tooth for law-breakers; certain practices having to do with polygamy; designation of certain cities as *cities of refuge* where any person who kills another may flee for safety; laws pertaining to the avenger of blood; land promises; Jubilee, with laws pertaining to the releasing of those who are in debt; requirements involving an unmarried man marrying the childless widow of his deceased brother; battlements constructed for the roofs of houses; etc.)

A number of other questions arise: Is there any justification for recognizing the time in which a Christian now lives as different from the time in which Adam and Eve lived prior to the fall? And if so, how is it different? The same questions might be asked in regard to other times as well. What about the time prior to Noah's flood? ...The time Israel was in Egypt? ...Israel's conquest of Canaan? ...Israel under the Judges and Kings? ...Daniel's day? ...When Israel was under Babylonian captivity? Etc. Is *some, none,* or *all* of what was written during these periods of time applicable to today's Christian believer? And then there's the matter of the upcoming millennial kingdom! Will things be different then than they are now?

As these questions are considered, it seems that we are left with no choice but to recognize certain distinctions. Hence, serious consideration will be given in the chapters ahead to a system of belief that has come to be known as *dispensationalism.*

It is not the author's intention to cover in any great detail the tenets of dispensationalism. It is rather his purpose to provide certain *theological perspectives* which will greatly assist the reader's understanding of the system of dispensationalism, especially as it relates to other theological systems. These considerations will include such issues as: a general definition of dispensationalism; a basic description of the tenets of dispensationalism; the history and development of dispensationalism; the three principle elements of dispensationalism; interpretation methods; both primary and secondary theological differences between dispensationalism and opposing theological points of view (particularly that of covenant theology); Millennialism and Rapturism; Old Testament vs. New Testament application; the interpretation of prophecy; the significance of prophecy; and perspectives on Law and Grace.

CHAPTER TWO

—DEFINING DISPENSATIONALISM

One of the first things a student must do in order to develop a good understanding of what is meant by the term *dispensation* is to seek out a workable definition. Below, a definition of the term is provided from three sources: first, how the term is defined in the *dictionary;* second, its *Biblical* use; and third, *theological* usages of the term.

DICTIONARY DEFINITION OF 'DISPENSATION'

The word **dispensation** is defined in the *Merriam-Webster's Collegiate Dictionary* as:

1 a : a general state or ordering of things; *specifically*: a system of revealed commands and promises regulating human affairs

b : a particular arrangement or provision especially of providence or nature

2 a : an exemption from a law or from an impediment, vow, or oath

b : a formal authorization

3 a : the act of dispensing

b : something dispensed or distributed [1]

BIBLICAL DEFINITION OF 'DISPENSATION'

The student must also examine how the term ***dispensation*** is used in Scripture. Charles Ryrie writes as follows:

> At least three dispensations (as commonly understood in dispensational teaching) are mentioned by Paul. In Ephesians 1:10 he writes of "an administration [dispensation, KJV] suitable to the fullness of the times," which is a future period. In Ephesians 3:2 he designates the "stewardship [dispensation, KJV] of God's grace," which was the emphasis of the content of his preaching at that time. In Colossians 1:25-26 it is implied that another dispensation preceded the

---

[1] Merriam-Webster, I. *Merriam-Webster's Collegiate Dictionary.* 10th ed. Springfield, Mass., U.S.A.: Merriam-Webster, 1996, c1993.

present one, in which the mystery of Christ in the believer is revealed.[2]

Roy Aldrich presents the Biblical definition of the word as follows:

> The word dispensation is a Scriptural term. It occurs in 1 Corinthians 9:17, Ephesians 1:10, Ephesians 3:2, and Colossians 1:25. The Greek word is *oikonomia*. It is a compound word derived from the words *oikos* (house) and *nomos* (law). The literal meaning is *house* rule and the general meaning is *stewardship, economy,* or *government.* Dispensational truth simply means that God has dealt with the human race or the Jews under different economies or responsibilities.[3]

Robert Lightner writes:

> In scriptural usage the Greek word οἰκονομέω ("dispensation") refers to an administration or stewardship (Luke 16:2–4; 1 Cor. 9:17; Eph. 1:10; 3:2, 9; Col. 1:25; 1 Tim. 1:4). (Cf. the related word οἰκονόμος in Luke 12:42; 16:1, 3, 8; Rom. 16:23; 1 Cor. 4:1–2; Gal. 4:2; Titus 1:7; 1 Pet. 4:10; and the verb οἰκονομέω in Luke 16:2.) Every stewardship, economy, or administration obviously involves and includes time, though that is not necessarily the most important feature of it.[29] [4]

THEOLOGICAL USAGES OF THE TERM

A theological definition of the term **dispensation** must also be sought. As suggested above by Lightner, it will be helpful for the reader to understand that generally the emphasis is intended to fall upon the *responsibility* that God gives rather than the *time period.*

---

[2] Cf. Ryrie, Charles C., *Dispensationalism*, (Chicago: Moody Press, 1995) p. 27.

[3] Aldrich, Roy L., "An Apologetic for Dispensationalism," *Bibliotheca Sacra.* Dallas TX: Dallas Theological Seminary, 1996, c1955-1995.

29 29. Some early dispensational writers, though not all of them, stressed the time aspect. See, for example, Scofield's definition in *The Scofield Reference Bible* (New York: Oxford University Press, 1945), p. 5.

[4] Lightner, Robert P., "Theological Perspectives on Theonomy Part I: Theonomy and Dispensationalism," *Bibliotheca Sacra.* Dallas TX: Dallas Theological Seminary, 1996, c1955-1995.

Lightner derives the following theological usage of the term:

> Building on the above definition of a dispensation, dispensationalism may be defined as that system of theology which interprets the Bible literally—according to normal usage—and places primary emphasis on the major biblical covenants—Abrahamic, Palestinian, Davidic, New—and sees the Bible as the unfolding of distinguishable economies in the outworking of God's major purpose to bring glory to Himself.[5]

The Oxford English Dictionary defines *dispensation* in the following manner:

> A religious order or system, conceived as divinely instituted, or as a stage in a progressive revelation expressly adapted to the needs of a particular nation or period of time, as the patriarchal, Mosaic (or Jewish) dispensation, the Christian dispensation; also the age or period during which such system has prevailed.[6]

According to Aldrich, "It is probable that this definition [listed immediately above] would be generally approved by both modern dispensationalists and nondispensationalists."[7]

The *Funk and Wagnalls New Standard Dictionary* defines dispensation as follows:

> The period during which a particular revelation of God's mind and will has been operative on mankind; as during the Christian dispensation; during the patriarchal dispensation.[8]

Listed below are a number of other theologians, authors, etc.... who have also submitted *theological* definitions of the term *dispensation*:

F. L. Chapell:

> A method of working, an economy or plan...in which God acts according to a certain method.[9]

---

[5] Lightner, Ibid.

[6] *Oxford English Dictionary*, s.v.

[7] Aldrich, Roy L., "A New Look at Dispensationalism," *Bibliotheca Sacra.* Dallas TX: Dallas Theological Seminary, 1996, c1955-1995.

[8] *Funk and Wagnalls New Standard Dictionary*, s.v.

[9] Chapell, F. L., *Biblical and Practical Theology*, p. 22.

Merrill Unger:

> Dispensation (Gr. *oikonomia, management of a household,* hence English *economy*). A dispensation is an era of time during which man is tested in respect to obedience to some definite revelation of God's will...[10]

C. I. Scofield:

> A dispensation is a period of time during which man is tested in respect of obedience to some *specific* revelation of the will of God.[11]

> These periods are marked off in Scripture by some change in God's method of dealing with mankind, or a portion of mankind, in respect of the two questions of sin and of man's responsibility. Each of the dispensations may be regarded as a new test of the natural man, and each ends in judgment— marking his utter failure.[12]

C. McKay Smock:

> A dispensation is a certain period during which God tests man's obedience to a definite, but partial revelation of His will.[13]

H. A. Ironside:

> A dispensation is a stewardship committed to men during a certain age.[14]

> A dispensation then is a period of time in which God is dealing with men in some way in which He was not dealing with them before.[15]

---

[10] Merrill F. Unger, "Dispensations," *Unger's Bible Dictionary.*

[11] Scofield, C. I., Editor, *The Scofield Reference Bible,* p. 5.

[12] Scofield, C. I., *Rightly Dividing the Word of Truth* (Grand Rapids: Zondervan Publishing House, 1965), p. 19.

[13] C. McKay Smock, *God's Dispensations,* p. 9.

[14] Ironside, H.A., Unpublished Class Notes, Dallas Theological Seminary, as cited by Roy Aldrich in "An Apologetic for Dispensationalism," *Bibliotheca Sacra.* Dallas TX: Dallas Theological Seminary, 1996, c1955-1995.

[15] Ironside, H. A., *Wrongly Dividing the Word of Truth,* p. 6.

Alexander Souter:

> Dispensation (Gr. *oikonomia*), household management, stewardship, hence any provision of trust or the duties of that position, provision, arrangement.[16]

John Graber:

> Dispensationalism is that system of Biblical interpretation which interprets the Bible from the viewpoint of designated periods of time during which a particular revelation of God's will and mind is operative, and during which man is tested in relation to that particular revelation.[17]

Michael A. Harbin:

> Dispensationalism is an effort to interpret Scripture on the basis of the distinctives of God's demands for and relationships with mankind. This pertains to man's stewardship toward God.[18]

W. Graham Scroggie:

> The word *oikonomia* bears one significance, and means "an administration," whether of a house, of property, of a state, or a nation, or as in the present study, *the administration of the human race or any part of it, at any given time.* Just as a parent would govern his household in different ways, according to varying necessity, yet every one for one good end, so God has at different times dealt with men in different ways, according to the necessity of the case, but throughout for one great, grand end.[19]

Charles Ryrie:

> A dispensation is a distinguishable economy in the outworking of God's purpose.[20]

---

[16] Souter, Alexander, *A Pocket Lexicon to the Greek New Testament.*

[17] Graber, John, "Ultra-Dispensationalism," p. 5, unpublished Doctor's dissertation, Dallas Theological Seminary, Dallas, Texas, 1949, as quoted by Roy L. Aldrich, in "An Outline Study on Dispensationalism," *Bibliotheca Sacra.* Dallas TX: Dallas Theological Seminary, 1996, c1955-1995.

[18] Harbin, Michael A., "The Hermeneutics of Covenant Theology," *Bibliotheca Sacra.* Dallas TX: Dallas Theological Seminary, 1996, c1955-1995.

[19] Scroggie, W. Graham, *Ruling Lines of Progressive Revelation*, pp. 62–63.

[20] Ryrie, Charles C., "The Necessity of Dispensationalism," *Bibliotheca Sacra.* Dallas TX: Dallas Theological Seminary, 1996, c1955-1995.

CONCLUSION

Based on the information presented above, the student should be able to derive a good understanding of what is meant by the term *"dispensationalism"* as it is commonly used among dispensationalists and non-dispensationalists today.

Concerning this latter (*theological*) usage of the term, some raise the argument that *dispensationalism*, as dispensationalists currently employ the term, is not sufficiently based on the Scripture. Charles Ryrie answers such criticism in the following manner:

> Now the dispensationalist uses the word theologically as a title for the distinctive administrations of God throughout the entire Bible. For instance, under Moses God administered the world in a distinctive way; therefore, he calls that *administration* (not *period* necessarily) the Mosaic dispensation. To say that it is not valid to use the word this way because the Bible never uses it in specific connection with certain of the dispensationalists' dispensations is of no consequence. Do we not use the word *atonement* of the work of Christ on the cross even though it is never used that way in the Bible? Certainly freedom must be granted to use a term theologically which may not be used in that way Biblically as long as the theological use is not un-Biblical.[21]

---

[21] Ryrie, Ibid.

FOR FURTHER STUDY ON THE DEFINITION OF DISPENSATIONALISM

Ryrie, Charles C., *Dispensationalism* (Chicago: Moody Press, 1995) pp. 23-30, 34-38, 47-48, 162-164.

FOR ADDITIONAL STUDY[22] ON THE DEFINITION OF DISPENSATIONALISM

Chapell, F. L., *Biblical and Practical Theology*, p. 22.

Graber, John, "Ultra-Dispensationalism," p. 5, unpublished Doctor's dissertation, Dallas Theological Seminary, Dallas, Texas, 1949.

Ironside, H.A., Unpublished Class Notes, Dallas Theological Seminary.

- - -. *Wrongly Dividing the Word of Truth*, p. 6.

Jamieson, R., A. R. Fausset, A. R. Fausset, D. Brown, & D. Brown. *A Commentary, Critical and Explanatory, on the Old and New Testaments*. Oak Harbor, WA: Logos Research Systems, Inc., 1997. Ge 41:25, Ex 19:16, Ex 25:18, Ex 30:18, Ex 34:33, Le 10:2, 2 Ki 2:1, 2 Ki 20:3, 2 Ch 6:18, Ec 5:8, So 1:13, So 2:8, So 6:11, Is 34:4, Is 58:13, Joe 2:27, Am 9:11, Jn 4:21, 1 Co 1:20, 1 Co 9:17, 1 Co 10:11, Ro 11:35, Eph 1:10, Eph 3:21, Col 1:25, Col 2:17, 1 Ti 1:4, Tit 3:9, Heb 1:2, Heb 6:16, 1 Pe 1:20, 1 Jn 1:1, Re 11:4, and Re 20:12.

Pfeiffer, C. F., & E. F. Harrison. *The Wycliffe Bible Commentary : New Testament*. Chicago: Moody Press, 1962. 1 Co 9:17, Eph 1:10, Eph 3:2, and Col 1:25.

Pieters, Albertus, *A Candid Examination of the Scofield Bible*, p. 14.

Scroggie, W. Graham, *Ruling Lines of Progressive Revelation*, pp. 62–63.

Scofield, C. I., Editor, *The Scofield Reference Bible*, p. 5.

- - -. *Rightly Dividing the Word of Truth* (Grand Rapids: Zondervan Publishing House, 1965), p. 19.

Smock, C. McKay, *God's Dispensations*, p. 9.

Souter, Alexander, *A Pocket Lexicon to the Greek New Testament*.

Unger, Merrill F., "Dispensations," *Unger's Bible Dictionary*.

~

See also all resources under the Bibliography identified by a <~> mark at the beginning of the reference.

---

[22] Note: it is not to be assumed that ALL works suggested by the author for review have been written from a dispensational standpoint.

CHAPTER THREE
—THE BASIC TENETS OF
DISPENSATIONALISM

The purpose of this chapter is to familiarize the reader with the basic tenets of dispensationalism. The arrangement of these tenets, as they are generally recognized today, is not so much the result of a consensus reached among any one group of theologians, but has come about as a product of the employment of a *consistent literal* method of interpreting the Bible. The importance of the effects of a *consistent literal* method of interpreting the Scriptures, a matter that will be covered in much greater detail later, simply cannot be overstated.

In this chapter, our examination of the doctrine will take into account only the **tenets** of dispensationalism as they exist in their current modern form. (The various forms of dispensational tenets which predate our day-in-time are addressed in a later chapter entitled *History and Development of Dispensationalism.*)

Three categories are acknowledged: (1) a basic level of dispensational division which is virtually beyond any reasonable dispute, (2) a more detailed level of dispensational division in which opinions vary—the tenets of which are often subjected to moderate degrees of debate, and (3) an extreme level of dispensational division which are often subjected to controversy and considerable debate.

THE BASIC LEVEL OF
DISPENSATIONAL DIVISION

The basic level of dispensational division can hardly be subjected to legitimate debate—it is virtually indisputable. Clarence Mason expresses what most dispensationalists would agree comprise these basic divisions.

> This writer submits that the dispensational viewpoint is inherent in the facts of the Bible's sequence of events. The line of reasoning goes like this: If the fall of man be accepted as a Biblical fact, all Bible believers of whatever theological bracket recognize that there was an essential difference between the state of man before and after that horrendous event. Again, the Epistle to the Hebrews and other portions of the New Testament labor the distinction between the

condition of things before the cross and what obtained after the cross. Some insist upon a more severe transition than others, but the old and the new are not to be confused without disastrous interpretational results. Further, all chiliasts believe another tremendous transition will take place at the return of the Lord Jesus Christ.

It will be seen, therefore, that we have here at least five different periods with their distinctiveness: (1) Man in a period prior to the fall; (2) man as fallen; (3) man under the old covenant, i.e., precross; (4) man since the historic fact of Christ's cross and resurrection; (5) redeemed man as ruling with Christ over a changed earth. It is relatively unimportant what these periods are named. It is relatively unimportant if one comes up with exactly seven.[23]

Again, one would be hard-pressed to find any sincere Bible-believer who is willing to raise issue against such clear and basic divisions in the Word of God, whether they are called *dispensations* or not. In this sense, every true believer of Bible-truth is a dispensationalist. This holds true (with various exceptions pertaining to the fifth division listed above), even when the kindred camp most sharply contrasted with dispensationalism—namely, covenant theology—is considered. (Covenant theology is a system of theology which will later be identified and further examined; the reader will often find this system of theology referred to in contrast with dispensationalism.) Again, in this sense, every sincere Bible-believer is a dispensationalist. As Lewis Sperry Chafer used to say:

> If one does not bring a lamb to the altar in worshiping God, then he is a dispensationalist. One who worships on Sunday instead of Saturday is also a dispensationalist, because he recognizes the Sabbath was for Israel, not the church (Exod. 20:8–11).[24]

---

[23] Mason, Jr., Clarence E., "A Review of Dispensationalism by John Wick Bowman: Part I," *Bibliotheca Sacra*. Dallas TX: Dallas Theological Seminary, 1996, c1955-1995.

[24] As cited by P. P. Enns in *The Moody Handbook of Theology*. Chicago, Ill.: Moody Press, 1997, c1989.

So "a dispensationalist is simply one who recognizes that God deals differently with people in different ages or economies."[25]

THE SECOND (MODERATE) LEVEL OF DISPENSATIONAL DIVISION

In light of the above, then to what might we attribute the distinctions that exist between those who call themselves *dispensationalists* and those who do not? Charles C. Ryrie is commonly credited[26] for identifying three basic and indispensable essentials commonly referred to as the *sine qua non*[27] (the absolutely indispensable parts) of dispensationalism. These three points are the foundation upon which the theological system of dispensationalism is built (in its contemporary form). They constitute the fundamental distinctions that exist between dispensationalists and non-dispensationalists. Ryrie, in his book entitled *Dispensationalism,* lists these three essentials as follows:

(1) The recognition of a consistent distinction between Israel and the Church

(2) A consistent and regular use of a literal principle of interpretation

(3) A basic and primary conception of the purpose of God as His own glory rather than the salvation of mankind[28]

Perhaps the reader agrees with the divisions described in the first part of this chapter, but has yet to determine in his own mind whether or not he himself is a *dispensationalist.* These three tenets may be considered the deciding factors. A person who adopts these tenets is a

---

[25] Enns, P. P., *The Moody Handbook of Theology.* Chicago, Ill.: Moody Press, 1997, c1989.

[26] See, for example, Bowers, Russell H., Jr., "Dispensational Motifs in the Writings of Erich Sauer," *Bibliotheca Sacra.* Dallas TX: Dallas Theological Seminary, 1996, c1955-1995.

[27] "[Late Latin, without which not]: something absolutely indispensable or essential." (Merriam-Webster, I. [1996, c1993]. *Merriam-Webster's collegiate dictionary.* Includes index. [10th ed.]. Springfield, Mass., U.S.A.: Merriam-Webster.) See Ryrie, Charles C., *Dispensationalism,* (Chicago: Moody Press, 1995) pp. 38-41.

[28] Ryrie, Charles C., *Dispensationalism,* (Chicago: Moody Press, 1995) p. 45. See also Enns, P. P., *The Moody Handbook of Theology,* Chicago, Ill.: Moody Press, 1997, c1989.

"dispensationalist" whether he refers to himself by that designation or not.

The second of these essential elements—a consistent and regular use of a literal principle of interpretation—is the base upon which the other tenets of dispensationalism rest. The method of interpretation employed by those who have adopted this particular system of theology is clearly stated in this point. (The issue of the *consistent literal* method of interpreting the Bible, along with the other tenets of dispensationalism, particularly the two accompanying tenets listed above, will be covered in greater detail in the chapters ahead.)

The Table below (**Table One**) describes the seven dispensations as they have come to be commonly recognized today:

Table One [29]

Name	Scripture	Responsibilities	Judgment(s)
Innocency	Genesis 1:3-3:6	Keep Garden. Do not eat one fruit. Fill, subdue earth. Fellowship with God.	Curses, and physical and spiritual death.
Conscience	Genesis 3:7-8:14	Do good.	Flood.
Civil Government	Genesis 8:15-11:9	Fill earth. Capital punishment.	Forced scattering by confusion of languages.
Patriarchal Rule (formerly *promise*)	Genesis 11:10-Exodus 18:27	Stay in Promised Land. Believe and obey God.	Egyptian bondage and wilderness wanderings.
Mosaic Law	Exodus 19:1-John 14:30	Keep the law. Walk with God	Captivities.
Grace	Act 2:1-Revelation 19:21	Believe on Christ. Walk with Christ.	Death. Loss of rewards.
Millennium	Revelation 20:1-15	Believe and obey Christ and His government.	Death. Great White Throne Judgment.

[29] Cf. Ryrie, Charles C., *Dispensationalism*, (Chicago: Moody Press, 1995) p. 54. Cp. Ryrie, Charles C., *Dispensationalism Today* (Chicago: Moody Press, 1965) pp. 57-64, and Enns, P. P., *The Moody Handbook of Theology*, Chicago, Ill.: Moody Press, 1997, c1989.

It should be pointed out that features from one dispensation are in some cases incorporated into subsequent dispensations; thus, elements from the period of *conscience, government,* and *patriarchal rule* (formerly referred to as *promise*) continue on in subsequent dispensations. It should also be pointed out that God's program for the Church, which occurs during the dispensation of "Grace," is viewed by dispensationalists as *parenthetical.* To put it another way: "God does not count time prophetically when Israel is in a scattered condition and does not exist as a nation in her own land." [30]

At this point, the author seeks to provide an explanation to the reader as to how dispensationalists see the transition from the almost indisputable five divisions listed earlier in this chapter, to the seven listed in **Table One** above, which is the arrangement currently adopted by most modern dispensationalists. Relying on what he calls "a consistently workable definition," [31] Ryrie justifies the two additions in the following manner:

> It is not difficult to justify most of the usual seven dispensations... If one is a premillennialist, then the distinguishable economy of God in the millennium during which Christ is visibly present is easily recognized. This present dispensation whose principal, not exclusive, characteristic is grace also is easily justified... The same is apparent with the Mosaic dispensation of the law, and the point need not be labored. It is the time between the beginning of creation to the giving of the law that gives rise in some minds to the question of the validity of all the dispensations which are said to belong to that period. However, before the fall of man the arrangement was certainly distinguishably different from that after the fall. Already we have accounted for five dispensations: innocence, whatever name should be given to that which obtained after the fall and to the time of Moses, the law, grace, and the millennial kingdom. The very fact that it is difficult to find a suitable name to cover the entire economy from the fall to Moses ought to make one

---

[30] Chapell, F. L., *Biblical and Practical Theology*, p. 301. Also see Ryrie, Charles C., *Dispensationalism*, (Chicago: Moody Press, 1995) pp. 134, 177.
[31] Since Ryrie's definition is deemed critical, the reader is here reminded of it again. Ryrie defines a dispensation as "a distinguishable economy in the outworking of God's purpose."

examine carefully the validity of trying to view that entire period as having only one dispensation operating during it. It should be apparent that up to the time of Abraham God's administration concerned all nations, whereas with Abraham He began to single out one nation, and in the singling out He made a very distinctive covenant with Abraham. Therefore, the distinguishable characteristic of God's dealing with Abraham in promise seems sufficient to delineate the dispensation of promise. The only question that remains is whether or not the dispensations of conscience and government are valid. Suppose there is only one dispensation during this period, what will it be called? If there are two, what are the distinguishing features that justify two? The problem is complicated by the fact that the revelation of Scripture covering this long period is very brief, but from what is revealed we must seek an answer. It seems to this writer that there is sufficient warrant in God's new arrangement for human government in the time of Noah to distinguish a dispensation at that time (*cf.* Gen. 9:6 with Gen. 4:15). If this be agreed with, then there are seven dispensations, and one must admit that the more one studies in the light of a basic definition the conclusion is that there are seven dispensations. It seems to be somewhat fashionable these days to avoid this conclusion or at least to minimize the earlier dispensations, but if one has a consistently workable definition and if one applies it throughout all history, then it seems hard not to conclude that there are seven.[32]

This dispensational scheme (as presented in **Table One** above) will be that which the author is denoting as he uses the term *dispensationalism* throughout this book. This is not to say, however, that no variations among viewpoints exist.

THE THIRD (EXTREME) LEVEL OF DISPENSATIONAL DIVISION

Some dispensational distinctions go beyond those mentioned above and are often subjected to a considerable degree of scrutiny. These include:

---

[32] Ryrie, Charles C., "The Necessity of Dispensationalism," *Bibliotheca Sacra.* Dallas TX: Dallas Theological Seminary, 1996, c1955-1995.

Pre-Adamite. Some teach what is commonly referred to as a *pre-Adamite* era. Those holding such views claim that another earth, an earlier *fully inhabited* earth, existed prior to the events of creation described in the early chapters of Genesis. (This view is not given consideration in this book.)

Ultra-Dispensationalism. Another view that is appropriately placed in the extreme category is a view that has come to be known as *ultra-dispensationalism* (the prefix *ultra* self-categorizes this term as *extreme*). This view suggests that the Church is divided into two groups—one a Jewish Church and the other the body of Christ. (This view is also not brought into consideration in this book.)

Progressive-Dispensationalism. Another view that has recently developed over the last thirty years is that of *progressive-dispensationalism*. (This view will be briefly defined and examined later in this book.)

CHAPTER FOUR

—COVENANT THEOLOGY

This chapter on covenant theology and the following chapter dealing with various views concerning the millennium, rapture, etc., are important here to insure that the reader understands that substantial contrasts exist between dispensationalism and covenant theology. As Michael A. Harbin points out:

> These two schools, popularly known as covenant theology and dispensationalism, are often set at odds with one another.[33]

Although *spiritually* kindred in relationship, many *doctrinal* issues (such as views concerning Israel and the Church, the millennium, the rapture, etc.) set these two opposing *theological* camps apart. The distinctions result primarily from the manner in which each interprets the Bible: the covenant theologian interprets the Scriptures *allegorically*, while dispensationalists on the other hand, employ the *consistent literal* method of interpretation. This results in fundamental differences between these two systems at the foundational level.

In this chapter, the reader is introduced to these foundational differences as they pertain to the manner in which each camp divides up the various ways God has dealt with mankind throughout history, is dealing with mankind today, and will deal with mankind in the future. Upon the completion of this chapter, the reader is advised to compare the viewpoints presented in this chapter introducing a basic description of covenant theology with the dispensational divisions outlined in Table One in the previous chapter.

It has already been presented in summary how dispensationalists arrive at seven distinct periods of *time* (i.e., *stewardships—* dispensations) in which God deals with mankind in various manners in regards to *responsibilities* and pending *judgments* (i.e., *responsibilities* inherent within each particular dispensation; *judgments* for failing to meet the corresponding *responsibilities*). The covenant theologian also recognizes certain distinctions to some

---

[33] Harbin, Michael A., "The Hermeneutics of Covenant Theology," *Bibliotheca Sacra.* Dallas TX: Dallas Theological Seminary, 1996, c1955-1995.

degree, and even goes so far as to use the term *"dispensation"* to describe them; yet he does not classify himself a *dispensationalist*.

First, the reader must become generally acquainted with what covenant theology is. Michael A. Harbin describes it in the following manner:

> Covenant theology is a system developed by two men, Johannes Cocceius (1603–1669) and Hermann Witsius (1636–1708). It was an attempt to tie the Old and New Testaments together by two covenants. The first was called the covenant of works, defined as the covenant instituted by God with Adam after creation. This was abrogated by the Fall and was replaced by the covenant of grace. The covenant of grace is the covenant of salvation, a single covenant for all men after the Fall.[9] Thus the unifying feature of the Bible in this system is God's grace.[34]

Gordon Lewis, pointing out the differences between covenant theology and dispensationalism, describes covenant theology as follows:

> The major unifying concept of Scripture, according to covenant theology, is not divine dispensations, but divine covenants. And the covenants stressed are two: the covenant of works and the covenant of grace (sometimes differently named).[1] The essential elements of the covenants may be seen in the covenant of works and the covenant of grace. Under the covenant of works, God and Adam are the parties involved. The condition for righteousness is obedience, and the reward for disobedience is death. God and Christ for sinners are the parties involved in the execution of the covenant of grace. The condition is faith in Christ for which the reward is eternal life.
>
> Subsumed under the covenant of grace are numerous subordinate covenants, such as those with Abraham and David.[35]

---

9 9. Hermann Witsius, *The Economy of the Covenants* (London: T. Tegg and Sons, 1837). 1:26.

[34] Harbin, Idem.

1 1. Louis Berkhof, *Systematic Theology*, pp. 265, 270.

[35] Lewis, Gordon R., "Theological Antecedents of Pretribulationism," *Bibliotheca Sacra*. Dallas TX: Dallas Theological Seminary, 1996, c1955-1995.

Robert Lightner writes:

> Covenant theology, on which theonomy is solidly based, represents a different system and yields different results. It is that system of theology which places primary emphasis on the theological covenants—redemption, works, grace—viewing the biblical covenants as stages in the development of the covenant of grace for its understanding of Scripture and the accomplishment of God's major purpose, which is redemptive.[36]

Enns, summarizing the points of the "Westminister Confession of Faith," writes the following when identifying covenant theology:

> Man fell from original righteousness and became dead in sin, that sin and death being imputed to all mankind. God originally entered into a covenant of works with Adam, but when he sinned, God enacted the covenant of grace. In his sin man lost all ability to will anything spiritually good.[37]

Clarence E. Mason, Jr., after listing the "five different periods with their distinctiveness" (i.e., those identified in the previous chapter as that "basic level of dispensational division which are virtually beyond any reasonable dispute"), objects to the covenant theologian's two-division position as follows: "It is simply not true that there are only two covenants and thus two ages."[38]

To summarize what has been stated thus far: the primary distinction between covenant theology and dispensationalism (based on the manner in which each interprets the Bible) has to do with how each view the divisions of God's dealings with mankind. Dispensationalists see seven distinct divisions (as previously described) while covenant theologians see only two: (1) *Law* (that period prior to Adam's sin) and (2) *Grace* (this period since Adam's sin). These differences have an enormous bearing on how many other doctrines of the Bible are interpreted and viewed theologically.

---

[36] Lightner, Robert P., "Theological Perspectives on Theonomy Part I: Theonomy and Dispensationalism," *Bibliotheca Sacra*. Dallas TX: Dallas Theological Seminary, 1996, c1955-1995.

[37] Enns, P. P., *The Moody Handbook of Theology*. Chicago, Ill.: Moody Press, 1997, c1989.

[38] Mason, Jr., Clarence E., "A Review of Dispensationalism by John Wick Bowman: Part I," *Bibliotheca Sacra*. Dallas TX: Dallas Theological Seminary, 1996, c1955-1995.

However, Hodge, a prominent *covenant theologian*, in his book entitled *Systematic Theology*, acknowledges a number of other divisions. Even though covenant theologians do not adhere to the dispensational divisions as dispensationalists describe them, it is interesting to note how Hodge often uses the term "dispensation" in his writings. In fact, one of his subtitles is: *"The Identity of the Covenant of Grace under all **Dispensations**."* [39] The content under this subtitle immediately precedes a section in which Hodge presents his views on these divisions. After concentrating heavily upon the issue of salvation, and under the subsequent subtitle *"Different Dispensations,"* Hodge presents his divisions as follows:

First, from Adam to Abraham.

The first dispensation extended from Adam to Abraham...

The Second Dispensation.

The second dispensation extended from Abraham to Moses... distinguished from the former...

The Third Dispensation.

The third dispensation of this covenant was from Moses to Christ...

The Gospel Dispensation.

The gospel dispensation is called new in reference to the Mosaic economy, which was old, and about to vanish away. It is distinguished from the old economy...

- ...It is more spiritual, not only in that the types and ceremonies of the Old Testament are done away...

- ...in the New Testament the gospel greatly predominates over the law. Whereas, under the Old Testament, the law predominated over the gospel.

- The Christian economy is specially the dispensation of the Spirit... the Spirit on all flesh... This was so distinguishing a characteristic of the Messianic period that the evangelist says, "The Holy Ghost was not yet given, because that Jesus was not yet glorified." (John vii. 39.)...

---

[39] Hodge, C., *Systematic Theology*. Oak Harbor, WA: Logos Research Systems, Inc., 1997.

- The old dispensation was temporary and preparatory; the new is permanent... This dispensation is, therefore, the last before the restoration of all things; the last, that is, designed for the conversion of men and the ingathering of the elect. Afterwards comes the end; the resurrection and the final judgment. In the Old Testament there are frequent intimations of another and a better economy, to which the Mosaic institutions were merely preparatory....[40]

Below is a list of several more examples of the manner in which Hodge employs *dispensational-sounding* language in his writings:

"The Christian dispensation"

"The Redeemer is the same under all dispensations."

"There is not a doctrine concerning Christ, taught in the New Testament, which the Apostles do not affirm to have been revealed under former dispensations."

"The Old dispensation was an adumbration [sketchy outline] of the New..."

"These different aspects under which the Mosaic economy..."

"Dispensation of the covenant of grace"[41]

After reviewing the above, one might consider Hodge's position merely another variation of dispensationalism, but this would be a mistake. His frequent use of dispensational terms, phrases, and even dispensationalist-like divisions might somewhat bewilder the researching student. Even so, Hodge's position is not to be mistaken as that of a dispensationalist (more later).

In spite of the language, sharp distinctions exist between the two opposing camps. P. P. Enns, for example, refers to one of these primary distinctions as he contrasts the dispensational position with covenant theology—namely, the distinction which dispensationalists recognize between Israel and the Church:

COVENANT THEOLOGY. A system of theology teaching that God entered into a covenant of works with Adam, who failed, whereupon God entered into a covenant of

---

[40] Hodge, Ibid.
[41] Hodge, Ibid.

grace, promising eternal life to those who believe. Covenant theology affirms there is one people of God called true Israel, the church (in contrast to dispensationalism, which teaches there are two people of God, called Israel and the church).[42]

This, regardless of the often employed dispensationalist-like language, is indeed what Hodge believes. He writes:

> The people of God before Christ constituted a Church, and... the Church has been one and the same under all dispensations.[43]

Karleen points out how covenant theology further misses the mark by placing an unwarranted emphasis upon *two covenants*; this, he says, contradicts the "biblical data":

> Covenant theology, systematized only within the last 350 years, is a theologically conservative approach to the Bible that sees all of God's dealings with humanity as based on two of three covenants, particularly a "covenant of works" and a "covenant of grace." (As promises made by God, covenants *are* found in the Bible. But these are not.)[3] In covenant theology there is one central purpose of God in history, to create through election and the application of the work of Christ one redeemed people, saved through the covenant of grace. This underlying feature of covenant theology, actually a presupposition concerning God's purpose in and beyond history, has plausible elements. God is certainly saving people from all ages, and He does it always through the cross. However, for such a presupposition to be workable it must fit the facts, and this one is too often contradicted by the facts. Its adherents must bend biblical data in order to keep the position alive....[44]

---

[42] Enns, P. P., *The Moody Handbook of Theology*. Chicago, Ill.: Moody Press, 1997, c1989.

[43] Hodge, C., *Systematic Theology*. Oak Harbor, WA: Logos Research Systems, Inc., 1997.

3 3. See Charles C. Ryrie, *Dispensationalism Today* (Chicago: Moody Press, 1965); see also in ch. 1, The Nature of the Bible, on the biblical covenants.

[44] Karleen, P. S., *The Handbook to Bible Study: With a Guide to the Scofield Study System*. New York: Oxford University Press, 1987.

To summarize: covenant theology, though classified as conservative in it beliefs, and though its proponents often use dispensational-like language, stands opposed to the seven-division system as generally adopted by the dispensational theologian (although the covenant theologian does acknowledge certain "dispensational" divisions). The fundamental difference lies in the fact that the covenant theologian asserts that Israel and the Church are to be viewed as one people of God, while dispensationalists recognize a clear distinction between Israel and the Church. This sharp difference arises from how each theological camp interprets the Bible: the covenant theologian resorts to *spiritualization* of the Text; while the dispensationalist adheres to a *normal, literal* method of interpreting the Bible. Clarifying these differences represent a major focus of much of the content ahead.

CHAPTER FIVE

—THE MILLENNIUM AND THE RAPTURE

This chapter has been included to introduce to the reader certain theological terms related to last day events, namely, the *millennium* (premillennialism, amillennialism, postmillennialism) and the *rapture* (pretribulationism, midtribulationism, posttribulationism, and partial rapturism). Listed below is a brief description of these prophecy-related terms. Having a basic knowledge of these theological viewpoints is essential if the subject matter in the upcoming chapters is to be understood.

A DESCRIPTION OF THE TERMS[45]

Millennium. "A thousand years; the name given to the era mentioned in Rev. 20:1–7."[46]

Postmillennialism. Belief that Christ will return after a kingdom, the millennium, has run its course on earth; regards this as a period of success for the gospel before the coming of Christ. The rapture *is not* a significant issue in postmillennialism.

Amillennialism. The view of the plan of God that holds there is no physical/spiritual kingdom on the earth over which Christ reigns visibly and personally; regards the millennium as a symbol of the age of the Church and identifies the binding of Satan [Rev 20:1-10] with Christ's work in the past (Mat 12:29). The rapture *is not* a significant issue in amillennialism.

Premillennialism. The doctrine that Christ will return to establish a literal kingdom on the earth in fulfillment of Old Testament promises; regards the millennium as a period between the second coming of Christ and the last judgment. The rapture *is* a significant issue in premillennialism.

Rapture. "The word popularly applied to the translation of the church at the end of the present age... The central passage dealing

---

[45] See Karleen, P. S., *The Handbook to Bible Study*: With a Guide to the Scofield Study System. New York: Oxford University Press, 1987; and Wood, D. R. W., D. R. W. Wood, & I. H. Marshall. *New Bible Dictionary*. electronic ed. of 3rd ed. Downers Grove: InterVarsity Press, 1996, c1982, c1962. Page 338.

[46] Easton, M., *Easton's Bible Dictionary*. Oak Harbor, WA: Logos Research Systems, Inc., 1996, c1897.

with the rapture is 1 Thess. 4:13–18. The Lord will descend from heaven, the dead in Christ will rise first, then all living believers will be caught up together with them to meet the Lord in the air, to be with Him forever after… The change which is to take place in Christians in the twinkling of an eye at the rapture is described in 1 Cor. 15:35–54." [47] The rapture is a position primarily held by premillennialists.

Pretribulationism. The Church will be taken from the earth by means of the rapture (1Th 4:13-18) before the events of the tribulation begin. Usually, in this view, the events to follow are designed to accomplish the purpose of bringing a large portion of ethnic Israel to Christ. Dispensationalists are generally pretribulationists.

Posttribulationism. The Church will remain on earth throughout the events of the tribulation, and the rapture will occur along with the second advent of Christ. During the tribulation the wrath of God will be experienced by the Church, as well as by Israel and the world.

Partial Rapturism. Only those believers who possess sufficient spirituality and are watching for the coming of Christ will be raptured at the beginning of the tribulation. The rest will go through it as a kind of purgation. This is a view not held by many.

Midtribulationism. Stressing the Biblical distinction between the two halves of the tribulation (three and a half years each), this view sees the Church raptured at the midpoint of the period. This is also a minority view.

THE THEOLOGICAL OUTCOMES

Where one stands relative to these theological distinctions is a direct result of how he or she interprets the Scriptures, particularly those related to prophecy. Generally speaking, though there are exceptions, covenant theologians consider themselves amillennialists (meaning, no millennium) while dispensationalists generally adopt the premillennial point of view. [48] It obviously follows, then, that the

---

[47] Evans, W., & S. M. Coder, *The Great Doctrines of the Bible.* Enl. ed. /. Chicago: Moody Press, 1998, c1974.

[48] It should be pointed out that a broad range of variation concerning dispensational theology exists among some who consider themselves premillennialists: "A dispensation is an era of time during which man is tested in respect to obedience to some definite revelation of God's will. Seven such dispensations are recognized by many premillennialists. Other premillennialists speak of only three or four. Still others prefer not to be classed as dispensationalists at all." (*Unger's Bible*

rapture holds no significance for those who consider themselves amillennialists. This represents a major part of the controversy between covenant theology and dispensationalism.

To put it another way, covenant theologians see in their theology three basic stages: (1) the first covenant (from Adam to the fall), (2) the second covenant (from the fall to the end of this age), and (3) the afterlife. According to this view, mankind is currently abiding in the stage just prior to the afterlife. (Though dispensationalists see these two covenants as artificially imposed upon the Biblical text, they are regarded by covenant theologians as paramount in significance. All perceived "dispensational" divisions are recognized by covenant theologians as merely subsumed under their two-covenant system—this explains Hodge's dispensationalist-like language.)

Dispensationalists, on the other hand, look for an upcoming earthly age beyond the current one; an age referred to as the *millennium*. This view sees as yet future: (1) the rapture of the church, (2) the seven-year tribulation, (3) the second advent of Christ, and (4) the 1,000-year millennial kingdom; *then* (5) the afterlife.

Dictionary, p. 269) as cited by Roy L. Aldrich in "An Outline Study on Dispensationalism," *Bibliotheca Sacra*. Dallas TX: Dallas Theological Seminary, 1996, c1955-1995.

CHAPTER SIX

—HISTORY AND DEVELOPMENT OF DISPENSATIONALISM

In order to arrive at accurate perceptions of the various theological perspectives that pertain to dispensationalism, a good understanding of its *history and development* is necessary. For this reason, a somewhat extensive explanation is offered in this chapter.

Concerning the ***history of dispensationalism***, the following charges are commonly levied against dispensationalism by non-dispensationalists: (1) amillennialism, not premillennialism, has been the dominant (i.e., longest held) view throughout the history of the church, (2) the early fathers of the church were not dispensationalists, and (3) dispensationalism is of relatively recent origin (usually citing Darby as its father).

The information provided in this chapter is meant to test the validity of these charges. Since there are links, it will be beneficial to first briefly address *early premillennialism* and the rise of *amillennialism*.

EARLY PREMILLENNIALISM

Even though amillennialism, not premillennialism, has been the dominant (i.e., longest held) view throughout the history of the church (i.e., Christendom), it is important to understand that premillennialism was the dominant view held by the Christian Church for at least the first two centuries of her existence. As Enns writes:

> The church from the beginning was premillennial in belief. The *Didache* (c. A.D. 100), Clement of Rome (A.D. 96 or 97), the *Shepherd of Hermas* (A.D. 140–150), Ignatius of Antioch (A.D. 50–115?), Papias (A.D. 80–163), Justin Martyr (b. c. A.D. 100), Irenaeus (d. A.D. 200), Tertullian (A.D. 150–225), and other sources indicate that the early church believed in the return of Jesus Christ to personally establish His earthly kingdom.[76] [49]

---

76 76. Charles C. Ryrie, *The Basis of the Premillennial Faith* (Neptune, N.J.: Loizeaux, 1953), pp. 17–26. This is an extremely valuable source in not only tracing the history of premillennialism but also explaining the hermeneutical principles and

Modern dispensationalists draw significant support from the fact that the early Church was predominantly premillennial. It is widely "acknowledge[d] that the early church fathers were strongly chiliastic"[50] (i.e., believed that Jesus will reign on earth for 1,000 years). Even opponents of dispensationalism (and of "modern premillennialism") describe dispensationalism as having been "known anciently as radical chiliasm."[51] It should be pointed out, however, that even though the early Church was predominantly premillennial, it fell woefully short in the area of *eschatological* theological development. Concerning this deficiency Walvoord writes as follows:

> The early church fathers were not clear on many details of their eschatology, and many of them do not speak at all on this subject... they certainly had not worked out the details.[52]

THE RISE OF AMILLENNIALISM

As will be discussed later in sections dealing with interpretation methods, the emergence of the allegorical method of interpretation gave rise to amillennialism. As this infectious disease spread, the fathers began to gradually loosen their grip on premillennialism.

Walvoord sadly notes:

> The early premillennialism of the first two centuries was soon engulfed by the amillennialism which arose in the third and fourth centuries. Amillennialism with its spiritualization of prophecy provided no basis for considering a matter like pretribulationism. It was not until the Protestant Reformation that the authority of Scripture and the imminency of Christ's return were once again firmly recognized. It was not until

---

the biblical foundation of premillennialism in the unconditional covenants of the Old Testament.
[49] Enns, P. P., *The Moody Handbook of Theology*. Chicago, Ill.: Moody Press, 1997, c1989.
[50] Witmer, John A., ed., Rev. of "Joachim of Fiore's Breakthrough to Chiliasm," Robert E. Lemer, *Cristianesimo Nella Storia* 6 (October 1985): 489–512. *Bibliotheca Sacra*. Dallas TX: Dallas Theological Seminary, 1996, c1955-1995.
[51] Cf. John F. Walvoord, Rev. of *Christ's Kingdom And Coming* by Jesse Wilson Hodges. Wm. B. Eerdmans Publishing Co., Grand Rapids, 1957. 247 pp. with indexes. *Bibliotheca Sacra*. Dallas TX: Dallas Theological Seminary, 1996, c1955-1995.
[52] Walvoord, John F., "Posttribulationism Today—Part IV: Futurist Posttribulational Interpretation," *Bibliotheca Sacra*. Dallas TX: Dallas Theological Seminary, 1996, c1955-1995.

premillennialism became a major factor in the church in the nineteenth century that pretribulationism could even be considered.[53]

The informed reader needs no reminding of how *dark* that period was from early in the fourth century up until the time of the Protestant Reformation. It should come as no surprise, then, that while the church (i.e., Christendom, excepting of course those small groups of scarcely recognized, persecuted true believers) abandoned premillennialism early-on and adopted instead amillennialism throughout the majority of its history (i.e., during the dark ages). This adds no legitimacy at all to the arguments raised against dispensationalism on these grounds.[54]

Since most covenant theologians are amillennialists, and are thereby opponents of dispensationalism, it would greatly enhance their position to undermine the link that exists between dispensationalism and these early premillennial (chiliastic) views; but doing so would require furtively calculated intellectual maneuverings.

Even so, though dispensationalism can be considered a further theological development of the premillennialism of the early church (i.e., the anti-Nicene fathers) it would be a mistake to consider it an exact fit. One of the mistakes of historic premillennialism was "its merger of Israel and the church."[55] As a result, it may be observed in history that some were premillennialists but not dispensationalists:

> It is true that many patristic and pre-19th-century premillennialists were nondispensational because they understood the church to take the place of Israel and its promises, which quickly led to historic amillennialism.[56]

Hence:

> Dispensationalism should be considered not a new doctrine, but a refinement of premillennialism such as was

---

[53] Walvoord, Ibid.

[54] For a more detailed defense against this unfounded argument see Charles C. Ryrie, *Dispensationalism* (Chicago: Moody Press, 1995) 70-72.

[55] Walvoord, John F., J. D. Pentecost, ed. Rev of *Dispensationalism In America*, by C. Norman Kraus. John Knox Press, Richmond, 1958. 156 pp. *Bibliotheca Sacra.* Dallas TX: Dallas Theological Seminary, 1996, c1955-1995.

[56] Witmer, John A., "A Review of Wrongly Dividing the Word of Truth—Part 2," *Bibliotheca Sacra.* Dallas TX: Dallas Theological Seminary, 1996, c1955-1995.

held by the early fathers. A similar refinement can be observed in all major doctrines in the history of the church.[57]

Below is a brief examination of this "refinement" as it has occurred throughout the Church's history. Considered first will be the positions held by the early Church fathers. Then the more recent developments of dispensationalism are addressed.

INITIAL DEVELOPMENTS OF DISPENSATIONAL-LIKE THEOLOGY

Ryrie, in his book entitled *Dispensationalism*,[58] delineates four segments of times when treating the history of dispensationalism:

(1) An early period beginning with Justin Martyr (110-165) to Joachim of Fiore (ca. 1135-1202)

(2) A period he refers to as "the Period Before Darby," which spans a period of time from Pierre Poiret (1646-1719) to Isaac Watts (1674-1748)

(3) An era he refers to as "Systematized Dispensationalism" which spans a period of time from Darby (1800-1882) to the 1980s, and

(4) A time since the 1980s in which some, referred to by Ryrie as "neodispensationalists," have introduced significant changes to normative, traditional, dispensationalism

Many dispensational writers (including this author) consider Ryrie's work on this subject the premier of our time.[59]

The following is a list of positions held by a number of early Church fathers which clearly indicate that their thinking was developing along dispensational-like lines. The reader will observe that in the initial stages of dispensational development, there seems to be a self-imposed limit to the number *four* in the minds of some of these early fathers.[60]

---

[57] Walvoord, John F., Rev. of *Backgrounds To Dispensationalism* by Clarence B. Bass. Wm. B. Eerdmans Publishing Company, Grand Rapids, Michigan, 1960. 184 pp. *Bibliotheca Sacra.* Dallas TX: Dallas Theological Seminary, 1996, c1955-1995.

[58] Ryrie, Charles C., *Dispensationalism*, (Chicago: Moody Press, 1995) pp. 61-72.

[59] Much of the subsequent information in this chapter dealing with the history of dispensationalism has been drawn from the information Ryrie presents: cf. *Dispensationalism* (Chicago: Moody Press, 1995) pp. 61-72.

[60] Although this view was primarily held by the early church fathers, more recent signs of this influence have also emerged. F. L. Chapell (??-1901) also limited his

Justin Martyr (A. D. 110-165). Justin Martyr, in the *Dialogue with Trypho,* discussed concepts that revealed his belief that God made distinctions at various times in His dealings with mankind. Even though a period prior to Enoch may be assumed (since he speaks of a time "since Enoch"), Justin Martyr distinguishes only *four* periods. Perhaps this limit was deliberate due to the apparent trend prevalent during his time concerning the number *four.* This may also account for the fact that even though "it is certain that Justin looked for a distinct 1,000-year millennial reign of Christ on earth, he did not discuss it in dispensational terms. He seemed rather to include it under the dispensation of Christ."[61]

The four distinctions made by Justin Martyr are as follows:

I.   A period "since Enoch, Noah with his sons, and all others in similar circumstances, who neither were circumcised nor kept the Sabbath"

II. A period prior to "the giving of the law ... so many generations, ... who lived between the times of Abraham and of Moses ... justified by circumcision and the other ordinances ... (XCII)"

III. A period distinguished "by the giving of the law"

IV. The present dispensation

---

dispensational divisions to four. Speaking of Chapell, George Dollar writes: "He noted that others listed seven dispensations but he preferred four which he designated Patriarchal, Israelitish, Christian, and the Kingdom." Dollar states that F. L. Chapell and A. J. Gordon were the two men responsible for the dispensational doctrines of Gordon College of Theology and Missions in Boston, Massachusetts. Dollar ascribes a good deal of significance to the Prophetic Conference held in 1886, of which Chapell participated, stating the following: "Indeed, no careful student of American fundamentalism and dispensationalism can afford to neglect this all-important conference." According to Dollar, "It is not too much to suppose that Chapell's own thinking was crystallized as far as his dispensational views were concerned by this gathering in Chicago of 1886." Dollar lists others who attended as follows: "Among the great men who participated in this 1886 conference were James H. Brookes, A. J. Gordon, H. M. Parsons, W. G. Morehead, W. J. Erdman, D. W. Whittle, A. J. Frost, Nathaniel West, and George C. Needham, ..." (Dollar, George W., "Early American Dispensationalist:—The Reverend F. L. Chapell," *Bibliotheca Sacra.* Dallas TX: Dallas Theological Seminary, 1996, c1955-1995.)

[61] Crutchfield, Larry V., "Ages and Dispensations in the Ante-Nicene Fathers," *Bibliotheca Sacra.* Dallas TX: Dallas Theological Seminary, 1996, c1955-1995.

Ryrie notes: "Earlier in the same work he spoke of the present dispensation and of its gifts of power (LXXXVII)."[62]

Irenaeus (A. D. 130-200). Irenaeus was clearly a major advocate of the common view held by the early Church fathers that the number *four* was of particular importance, and that its significance was to be considered when determining the division of God's economies. In reference to this aspect of Irenaeus' divisions, Crutchfield states the following:

> The method by which Irenaeus arrived at the number of dispensations is interesting as it is based on quadriplex prototypes, both in nature and in Scripture.[59] He reasoned that the Gospels can be neither greater nor fewer than four in number because of the analogy of the quadriform structure of creation. Irenaeus maintained that there are four zones of the world inhabited by mankind and four principal winds.[63]

Crutchfield goes on to cite Irenaeus' conclusion that:

> While the Church is scattered throughout all the world, and the "pillar and ground" [1 Tim. 3:15] of the Church is the Gospel and the spirit of life; it is fitting that she should have four pillars [1 Tim. 3:15], breathing out immortality on every side, and vivifying men afresh. From which fact, it is evident that the Word, the Artificer of all, He that sitteth upon the cherubim, and contains all things, He who was manifested to men, has given us the Gospel under four aspects, but bound together by one Spirit.[60] [64]

---

[62] Cf. Charles C. Ryrie, *Dispensationalism* (Chicago: Moody Press, 1995) 63

59 59. Irenaeus *Against Heresies* 3. 11. 8–9. In his discussion of "the reason of the truth why the fourth day is called the Tetras," Victorinus of Petau gives a disjointed little discourse on the quadriform nature of certain things. He cites the four elements of which the world is composed, four seasons, four living creatures before God's throne (Rev. 4:6), four Gospels, and four rivers flowing in paradise (Gen. 2:10). He then makes reference without elaboration to "four generations of people from Adam to Noah, from Noah to Abraham, from Abraham to Moses, from Moses to Christ the Lord, the Son of God" (*On the Creation of the World*).

[63] Crutchfield, Idem.

60 60. Irenaeus *Against Heresies* 3. 11. 8–9. Methodius, in following the figure of the four trees in Judges 9:8–15, maintained that "also four Gospels have been given, because God has four times given the Gospel [good news] to the human race and has instructed them by four laws, the times of which are clearly known by the diversity of the fruits" (*Banquet of the Ten Virgins* disc. 10, chap. 2).

[64] Crutchfield, Idem.

Crutchfield further notes:

> Irenaeus developed this reference to Christ sitting on the cherubim (Ps. 80:1) in conjunction with the "four living creatures" of Revelation 4:7. Observing that the cherubim were four-faced,

> Irenaeus contended that "their faces were images of the dispensation of the Son of God"... he saw the dispensational arrangements of God culminating in the final dispensation brought in by Christ.[62] [65]

Based on these notions, Irenaeus wrote: "the gospel is quadriform [so also is]... the course followed by the Lord. ... For this reason were four principal covenants given to the human race...." From this point in his writings, the following divisions of economies can be determined:

I.   A period "prior to the deluge, under Adam"

II. A period "after the deluge, under Noah"

III. A period initiated by "the giving of the law, under Moses"

IV. A period "which renovates man, and sums up all things in itself by means of the Gospel, raising and bearing men upon its wings into the heavenly kingdom." (*Against Heresies*, III, XI.8)[66]

Ryrie points out:

> He [Irenaeus] did not call these periods dispensations in this place, though he often spoke of the dispensations of God and especially of the Christian dispensation (see *Against Heresies*, V, XXVIII.3).[67]

Crutchfield concludes:

> Though some Fathers set forth only four such dispensations, others came very close to making nearly the same divisions modern dispensationalists do. In Irenaeus,

---

[62] 62. Irenaeus believed that all the dispensations culminate in Christ. "For those things which have been predicted by the Creator alike through all the prophets has Christ fulfilled in the end, ministering to His Father's will, and completing His dispensations with regard to the human race" (*Against Heresies* 5. 26. 2).

[65] Crutchfield, Idem.

[66] Cf. Charles C. Ryrie, *Dispensationalism* (Chicago: Moody Press, 1995) 64

[67] Ryrie, Charles C., *Dispensationalism* (Chicago: Moody Press, 1995) 64

Victorinus of Petau, and Methodius the number of dispensations is artificially restricted to four because of the quadriplex types adduced from both nature and Scripture which seemed to require it. Without such an artificially self-imposed constraint, the result is more like that found in Tertullian.[84] [68]

Clement of Alexandria (A. D. 150-220). Clement of Alexandria also proposed a four-division system:

I.   Adam

II.   Noah

III. Abraham

IV. Moses [69]

Augustine (A. D. 354-430). Augustine uses the term "former dispensation" to describe a time in which "sacrifice was suitable… but is not suitable now."[70] He goes on to write that while God is "without any change in Himself…"

> [He] knows infinitely better than man what [change] is fitting for every age, and who is, whether He give or add, abolish or curtail, increase or diminish, … until the beauty of the completed course of time, the component parts of which are the dispensation adapted to each successive age, shall be finished, like the grand melody of some ineffably wise master of song, … (*To Marcellinus,* CXXXVIII, 5, 7).[71]

Joachim of Fiore (ca. 1135-1202). Joachim of Fiore, according to one historian, sets forth the following "tripartite scheme of history"[72]:

---

84 84. Refer to Appendix A. While the absence of this incentive for a fourfold dispensational system allows greater freedom for division along more naturally biblical lines, at least in Tertullian's case, it also results in a system with less well-defined boundaries than those found in Justin Martyr and Irenaeus. As pointed out in note 64, Irenaeus developed a "complete system" (Roberts and Donaldson, ed., *The Ante-Nicene Fathers*), a sevenfold system that closely approximates what is found in contemporary dispensationalism.

[68] Crutchfield, Idem.

[69] Cf. Charles C. Ryrie, *Dispensationalism* (Chicago: Moody Press, 1995) 63-64

[70] Cf. Ryrie, 64

[71] Cf. Ryrie, 64

[72] Paul Boyer, *When Time Shall Be No More* (Cambridge, Mass.: Harvard Univ. Press, 1992), 52 as cited by Charles C. Ryrie in *Dispensationalism* (Chicago: Moody Press, 1995) 65

I.   The age of Law

II. The Age of Grace, and

III. The Future Age of the Spirit and righteousness

Ryrie concludes:

> It is not suggested, nor should it be inferred, that these early Church Fathers were dispensationalists in the later sense of the word. But it is true that some of them enunciated principles that later developed into dispensationalism, and it may be rightly said that they held to primitive or early dispensational-like concepts.[73]

DEVELOPMENTS OF DISPENSATIONAL THEOLOGY PRIOR TO DARBY

Ryrie distinguishes a group of writers who contributed to the development of dispensational thought prior to the time of Darby. These writers are listed as follows:

Pierre Poiret (1646-1719). This French mystic and philosopher wrote a six-volume work entitled *L'OEconomie Divine,* the English version having been published in 1713. In this work the following premillennial and dispensational scheme was presented:

I.   Infancy—to the Deluge

II. Childhood—to Moses

III. Adolescence—to the prophets (about the time of Solomon)

IV. Youth—to the coming of Christ

V.   Manhood—"some time after that"

VI. Old Age—"the time of man's decay" (V and VI seem to be the early and latter part of the Christian dispensation.)

VII. Renovation of all things—the Millennium[74]

---

[73] Ryrie, 65

[74] Peter Poiret, *The Divine OEconomy: or An Universal System of the Works and Purposes of God Towards Men Demonstrated* (London, 1713), as cited by Charles C. Ryrie in *Dispensationalism* (Chicago: Moody Press, 1995) 65

John Edwards (1637-1716). John Edwards published a two-volume work in 1699 entitled *A Compleat History or Survey of All the Dispensations* in which the following dispensational scheme was presented:

I.   Innocency and Felicity, or Adam created upright

II.   Sin and Misery, Adam fallen

III.   Reconciliation, or Adam recovered, from Adam's redemption to the end of the world

    A. Patriarchal economy

        1. Adamical, antediluvian

        2. Noahical

        3. Abrahamick

    B. Mosaical

    C. Gentile (concurrent with A and B)

    D. Christian or Evangelical

        1. Infancy, primitive period, past

        2. Childhood, present period

        3. Manhood, future (millennium)

        4. Old age, from the loosing of Satan to the conflagration [75]

Isaac Watts (1674-1748). Isaac Watts was a notable hymn writer and theologian. Watts's extensive writings represent a period in which "there was significant thinking and considerable literature on the subject of God's dealings with mankind throughout the ages. This was a period of developing dispensationalism."[76]

Ryrie lists Watts's dispensational outline as follows:

I.   The Dispensation of Innocency, or the Religion of Adam at first

II.   The Adamical Dispensation of the Covenant of Grace, or the Religion of Adam after his Fall

---

[75] John Edwards, *A Compleat History or Survey of All the Dispensations and Methods of Religion* (London, 1699), 1:v., as cited by Charles C. Ryrie in *Dispensationalism* (Chicago: Moody Press, 1995) 66
[76] Ryrie, Charles C., *Dispensationalism* (Chicago: Moody Press, 1995) 67

III. The Noahical Dispensation, or the Religion of Noah

IV. The Abrahamical Dispensation, or the Religion of Abraham

V. The Mosaical Dispensation, or the Jewish Religion

VI. The Christian Dispensation[77]

In reference to this outline, and in defense of the charge that dispensationalism is of relatively recent origin (usually citing Darby as the father), Ryrie emphasizes the following point:

> Except for the exclusion of the Millennium (he did not consider it a dispensation), this outline is exactly like that in the *Scofield Reference Bible,* and it is Watts's outline, not Darby's![78]

SYSTEMATIZED DISPENSATIONALISM —DARBY TO THE 1980S

John Nelson Darby (1800-1882). John Darby was a leader among the Plymouth Brethren. Having abandoned a legal career in order to commit himself to the service of our Lord, Darby became instrumental in converting many Roman Catholics to the Protestant faith. He indeed had much to do with the systematization and promotion of dispensationalism, but, as is obvious from that which has already been pointed out above, did not originate the concept.

Ryrie lists Darby's dispensational scheme as follows:

I. Paradisaical state to the Flood

II. Noah

III. Abraham

IV. Israel

    A. Under the law

    B. Under the Priesthood

    C. Under the kings

V. Gentiles

VI. The Spirit

VII. The Millennium[79]

---

[77] As cited by Charles C. Ryrie in *Dispensationalism* (Chicago: Moody Press, 1995) 67

[78] Ryrie, 67

[79] The *Collected Writings of J. N. Darby* (London: G. Morrish, 1867), 2:568-73, as cited by Charles C. Ryrie in *Dispensationalism* (Chicago: Moody Press, 1995) 68

Again, Ryrie refutes the common misperception that "dispensationalism originated with Darby." Ryrie also addresses another misperception that "Darby's system was taken over and popularized by Scofield"; Ryrie states that this perception "is not historically accurate."[80]

C. I. Scofield (1843-1921). The *Scofield Reference Bible* certainly was a major contributing factor to the widespread popularity of dispensationalism. In this work, Scofield, also formerly a lawyer, presents the following dispensational scheme:

I.   Man Innocent (from creation to expulsion from Eden)

II.   Man Under Conscience (from Eden to the Flood)

III.   Man in Authority Over the Earth (Noah to Abraham)

IV.   Man Under Promise (Abraham to Moses)

V.   Man Under Law (Moses to Christ)

VI.   Man Under Grace (death of Christ to the rapture)

VII. Man Under the Personal Reign of Christ (millennial reign of Christ)

Scofield identifies these seven dispensations as follows:

> These periods are marked off in Scripture by some change in God's method of dealing with mankind, or a portion of mankind, in respect to the two questions: of sin, and of man's responsibility. Each of the dispensations may be regarded as a new test of the natural man, and each ends in judgment— marking his utter failure in every dispensation.[81]

Others. P. P. Enns points out that Scofield's influence extended to two other figures that should be mentioned when speaking of the history and development of dispensationalism. Enns credits these men with having made a "notable impact in their time":

> James H. Brookes (1830–1897), a Presbyterian pastor from St. Louis and a popular conference speaker, and James

---

[80] Ryrie, 69

[81] C. I. Scofield, *Rightly Dividing the Word of Truth* (New York: Loizeaux, 1896), p. 12, as cited by P. P. Enns in *The Moody Handbook of Theology.* Chicago, Ill.: Moody Press, 1997, c1989.

M. Gray (1851–1935), who became president of Moody Bible Institute...[82]

In addition, a new edition of Scofield's work published in 1967 under the chairmanship of E. Schuyler English, as Enns states, includes contributions made by a number of other outstanding dispensational scholars:

> Frank E. Gaebelein (Stony Brook School), William Culbertson (Moody Bible Institute), Charles L. Feinberg (Talbot Seminary), Allan A. Mac Rae (Faith Seminary), Clarence E. Mason (Philadelphia College of Bible), Alva J. Mc Clain (Grace Seminary), Wilbur M. Smith (Trinity Evangelical Divinity School), and John F. Walvoord (Dallas Seminary).[83]

After pointing out the following commonly shared position that "Charles Ryrie's *Dispensationalism Today* is undoubtedly the premier defense of dispensationalism," Enns presents the following noteworthy list of dispensational scholars/writers and schools:

> J. Dwight Pentecost's *Things to Come* and the eschatological writings of John F. Walvoord (principally *The Millennial Kingdom* and the trilogy *Israel in Prophecy, The Church in Prophecy,* and *The Nations in Prophecy*) have ably set forth the dispensational position. Charles L. Feinberg's *Millennialism: Two Major Views* has equally defended this system. Lewis Sperry Chafer's august *Systematic Theology* sets forth dispensationalism in a comprehensive manner.
>
> Among the schools that are avowedly dispensational are: Dallas Theological Seminary, Grace Theological Seminary, Talbot Theological Seminary, Western Conservative Baptist Seminary, Multnomah School of the Bible, Moody Bible Institute, Philadelphia College of the Bible, and many others.[84]

---

[82] Enns, P. P., *The Moody Handbook of Theology*. Chicago, Ill.: Moody Press, 1997, c1989.

[83] Enns, Ibid.

[84] Enns, Ibid.

Ryrie charts the dispensational schemes presented above as follows:

REPRESENTATIVE DISPENSATIONAL SCHEMES *

Pierre Poiret 1646-1719	John Edwards 1639-1716	Isaac Watts 1674-1748	J.N. Darby 1800-1882	James H. Brookes 1830-1897	James M. Gray 1851-1935 (Pub. 1901)	C.I. Scofield 1843-1921 (Pub. 1909)
Creation to the Deluge (Infancy)	Innocency	Innocency	Paradisaical state (to the Flood)	Eden	Edenic	Innocency
	Adam fallen Antediluvian	Adamical (after the Fall)		Antediluvian	Antediluvian	Conscience
Deluge to Moses (Childhood)	Noahical	Noahical	Noah	Patriarchal	Patriarchal	Human Government
	Abrahamick	Abrahamical	Abraham			Promise
Moses to Prophets (Adolescence)	Mosaical	Mosaical	Israel——under law -under Priesthood -under kings	Mosaic	Mosaic	Law
Prophets to Christ (Youth)						
Manhood and Old Age	Christian	Christian	Gentiles	Messianic	Church	Grace
			Spirit	Holy Ghost		
Renovation of All Things			Millennium	Millennial	Millennial	Kingdom
					Fullness of times	
					Eternal	

*Charles C. Ryrie, *Dispensationalism* (Chicago: Moody, 1995), p.71.

Recent NeoDispensationalism—From the 1980s to Present

It is also worth pointing out that Ryrie distinguishes another period "beginning in the 1980s." In this period, referred to as "Recent Neodispensationalism," Ryrie speaks of "a group from within the dispensational camp [who] have been promoting significant changes in normative, or traditional, dispensationalism." Ryrie lists these newly introduced tenets as follows:

I.   The kingdom of God is the unifying theme of biblical history

II.   Christ has already inaugurated the Davidic covenant and is now reigning in heaven on the throne of David (right hand of the Father = the throne of David)

III. The concept of two purposes and two peoples of God (Israel and the church) is not valid, thus

IV.   The church is not a separate group of redeemed people, nor was it unrevealed in the Old Testament (just unrealized)

V.   There is one divine plan of holistic redemption for all people and all areas of human life (personal, societal, cultural, and political)[85]

Ryrie, drawing from a work by Craig A. Blaising and Darrel L. Bock[86] entitled *Progressive Dispensationalism* (Wheaton, Ill.: Victor, 1993), p. 123, writes the following: "this new teaching proposes four primary dispensations in biblical history and charts them as follows":

I.   Patriarchal to Sinai

II.   Mosaic to Messiah's Ascension

III. Ecclesial to Messiah's Return

IV.   Zionic

    A. Millennial

    B. Eternal[87]

---

[85] Cf. Craig A. Blaising, "Contemporary Dispensationalism," *Southwester Journal of Theology* 36, vol. 2 (Spring 1994): 11-13, as cited by Charles C. Ryrie in *Dispensationalism* (Chicago: Moody Press, 1995) 69

[86] Blaising and Bock have had considerable influence on the doctrinal positions of Dallas Theological Seminary.

[87] Cf. Charles C. Ryrie, *Dispensationalism* (Chicago: Moody Press, 1995) 69-70

As the title of the work from which this outline has been taken indicates, this (the positions now promoted by men such as Blaising and Bock) has come to be known as "progressive dispensationalism." Concerning this "new departure" (i.e., a departure from normative dispensationalism) Ryrie writes:

> Progressives wish to call their teachings "developments" within dispensationalism so that they can still call themselves dispensationalists, but they clearly seem to include changes (that is, essential differences from dispensationalism).[88]

Such proposed "significant changes" constitute a "departure" which has caused considerable concern among a number of today's normative dispensationalists.

SIGNS OF HOPE FOR TODAY

Today, there is a growing number adopting, developing and promoting normative dispensationalism. Among the more notable movements is that of the Pre-Trib Study Group headed up by Drs. Thomas Ice and Tim LaHaye. The author's alma maters, Louisiana Baptist University and Louisiana Baptist Theological Seminary, are also to be included. Others might be listed as well.[89]

~ ~ ~

This concludes the section entitled "Laying a Foundation." Undertaken in the upcoming section is an examination of "Ryrie's *Sine Qua Non*."

---

[88] Ryrie, 70

[89] Though the author is not wholly familiar with all listed below, it is his understanding that the following schools are among those (in addition to those listed above in the last paragraph on page 55) which adopt and promote dispensationalism: Baptist Bible College, Franklin, MO.; Boston Baptist College, Boston, MA.; Temple Baptist Seminary, Chattanooga, TN.; Pensacola Christian College, Pensacola, FL.; Heartland Baptist College, Oklahoma City, OK; Washington Bible College/Capital Bible Seminary, Lanham, MD.; Maranatha Baptist Bible College, Watertown, WI.; Northland Baptist Bible College, Dunbar, WI.; Emmaus Bible College, Dubuque, IA.; Chafer Theological Seminary, Albuquerque, NM.; New Tribes Bible Institute, Waukesha, WI./Jackson, MI.; and others.

FOR FURTHER STUDY ON THE HISTORY AND DEVELOPMENT OF DISPENSATIONALISM

Aldrich, Roy, "A New Look at Dispensationalism," *Bibliotheca Sacra* 120 (January-March 1963).

Bowers, Russell H., Jr., "Dispensational Motifs in the Writings of Erich Sauer," *Bibliotheca Sacra*, 1996, c1955-1995.

Burns, J. Lanier. Rev. of *Evangelical Dictionary of Theology*. Edited by Walter A. Elwell. Grand Rapids: Baker Book House, 1984. xxi + 1204 pp. *Bibliotheca Sacra*, 1996, c1955-1995.

**Crutchfield, Larry V., "Ages and Dispensations in the Ante-Nicene Fathers," *Bibliotheca Sacra*, 1996, c1955-1995.

- - -. "Israel and the Church in the Ante-Nicene Fathers," *Bibliotheca Sacra*, 1996, c1955-1995.

Deibler, E. C. Rev. of *Evangelicalism and Anabaptism*. Edited by C. Norman Kraus. Scottdale, PA: Herald Press, 1979. 190 pp. *Bibliotheca Sacra*, 1996, c1955-1995.

*Dollar, George W., "Early American Dispensationalist:—The Reverend F. L. Chapell," *Bibliotheca Sacra*, 1996, c1955-1995.

*Enns, P. P. *The Moody Handbook of Theology*. Chicago, Ill.: Moody Press, 1997, c1989.

Geisler, Norman L., "A Premillennial View of Law and Government," *Bibliotheca Sacra*, 1996, c1955-1995.

Hannah, John D., "The Early Years of Lewis Sperry Chafer," *Bibliotheca Sacra* 144 (January-March 1987).

Harbin, Michael A., "The Hermeneutics of Covenant Theology," *Bibliotheca Sacra*, 1996, c1955-1995.

Houghton, George G., "Lewis Sperry Chafer, 1871–1952," *Bibliotheca Sacra*, 1996, c1955-1995.

Ice, Thomas D., "An Evaluation of Theonomic Neopostmillennialism," *Bibliotheca Sacra*, 1996, c1955-1995.

Lightner, Robert P. Rev. of *The Origins of Dispensationalism* by Larry Crutchfield. Lanham, MD: University Press of America, 1992. 236 pp. *Bibliotheca Sacra*, 1996, c1955-1995. (Oct 1992A).

*Mason, Jr., Clarence E., "A Review of Dispensationalism by John Wick Bowman: Part I," *Bibliotheca Sacra*, 1996, c1955-1995.

Pentecost, J. Dwight, "Salvation in the Tribulation," *Bibliotheca Sacra*, 1996, c1955-1995.

*Richard, Ramesh P., "Premillennialism as a Philosophy of History— Part I: Non-Christian Interpretations of History," *Bibliotheca Sacra*, 1996, c1955-1995.

*- - -. "Premillennialism as a Philosophy of History—Part II: Elements of a Biblical Philosophy of History," *Bibliotheca Sacra*, 1996, c1955-1995.

*- - -. "Premillennialism as a Philosophy of History—Part III: The Premillennial Interpretation of History," *Bibliotheca Sacra*, 1996, c1955-1995.

**Ryrie, Charles C., *Dispensationalism* (Chicago: Moody Press, 1995) pp. 11, 13-19, 23, 46, 61-72, 75, 145-146, 154, 162, 191.

**- - -. *The Basis of the Premillennial Faith* (Neptune, N.J.: Loizeaux, 1953) pp. 17-26.

- - -. Rev. of *A Bibliographic History Of Dispensationalism*. Compiled by Arnold D. Ehlert. Grand Rapids: Baker Book House, 1965. 110 pp. *Bibliotheca Sacra*, 1996, c1955-1995.

- - -. "The Necessity of Dispensationalism," *Bibliotheca Sacra*, 1996, c1955-1995.

*Walvoord, John F., J. D. Pentecost, ed. Rev. of *Dispensationalism In America* by C. Norman Kraus. John Knox Press, Richmond, 1958. 156 pp. *Bibliotheca Sacra*, 1996, c1955-1995.

*- - -. Rev. of *Backgrounds To Dispensationalism* by Clarence B. Bass. Wm. B. Eerdmans Publishing Company, Grand Rapids, Michigan, 1960. 184 pp. *Bibliotheca Sacra*, 1996, c1955-1995.

- - -. Rev. of *Christ's Kingdom And Coming* by Jesse Wilson Hodges. Wm. B. Eerdmans Publishing Co., Grand Rapids, 1957. 247 pp. with indexes. *Bibliotheca Sacra*, 1996, c1955-1995.

- - -. Rev. of *Contemporary Options in Eschatology: A Study of the Millennium* by Millard J. Erickson. Grand Rapids: Baker Book House, 1977. 197 pp. *Bibliotheca Sacra*, 1996, c1955-1995.

- - -. Rev. of *Dispensationalism Today* by Charles C. Ryrie. Chicago: Moody Press, 1965. 221 pp. *Bibliotheca Sacra*, 1996, c1955-1995.

- - -. Rev. of *Fundamentalism And The Missouri Synod* by Milton L. Rudnick. St. Louis, Missouri: Concordia Publishing House, 1956. 152 pp. *Bibliotheca Sacra*, 1996, c1955-1995.

- - -. Rev. of *Jesus Christ And History* by George Eldon Ladd. Chicago: Inter-Varsity Press, 1963. 62 pp. *Bibliotheca Sacra*, 1996, c1955-1995.

*- - -. "Posttribulationism Today—Part IV: Futurist Posttribulational Interpretation," *Bibliotheca Sacra*, 1996, c1955-1995.

Witmer, John A., ed. Rev. of "Joachim of Fiore's Breakthrough to Chiliasm" by Robert E. Lemer, *Cristianesimo Nella Storia* 6 (October 1985): 489–512. *Bibliotheca Sacra*, 1996, c1955-1995.

*- - -. "A Review of Wrongly Dividing the Word of Truth—Part 1," *Bibliotheca Sacra*, 1996, c1955-1995.

*- - -. "A Review of Wrongly Dividing the Word of Truth—Part 2," *Bibliotheca Sacra*, 1996, c1955-1995.

- - -. ed. Rev. of "Dividing the Word of Truth: An Examination of Dispensationalism" by Stuart A. Frayne, Theodolite 7 (1984): 3–15. *Bibliotheca Sacra*, 1996, c1955-1995.

*- - -. ed. Rev. of "Trying The Spirits—Dispensationalism" by R. C. Harbach, The Standard Bearer, XLII (April 1, 1966), 302. *Bibliotheca Sacra*, 1996, c1955-1995.

*- - -. ed. Rev. of "Toward A Historical Interpretation Of The Origins Of Fundamentalism" by Ernest R. Sandeen, *Church History,* March, 1967, pp. 66–83. *Bibliotheca Sacra*, 1996, c1955-1995.

- - -. Rev. of *The Johannine Logos* by Gordon H. Clark. Nutley, NJ: Presbyterian and Reformed Publishing Company, 1972. 90 pp. *Bibliotheca Sacra*, 1996, c1955-1995.

Zuck, Roy. B. Rev. of *Dispensationalism* by Charles C. Ryrie. Chicago: Moody Press, 1995. 224 pp. *Bibliotheca Sacra*, 1996, c1955-1995.

FOR ADDITIONAL STUDY[90] ON THE HISTORY AND DEVELOPMENT OF DISPENSATIONALISM

Bass, Clarence B., *Backgrounds to Dispensationalism* (Grand Rapids: Baker Book House, 1960).

Blaising, Craig A., "Development of Dispensationalism by Contemporary Dispensationalists," *Bibliotheca Sacra*, 1996, c1955-1995.

- - -. "Doctrinal Development in Orthodoxy," *Bibliotheca Sacra*, 1996, c1955-1995.

Crutchfield, Larry V., "The Doctrine of Ages and Dispensations as Found in the Published Works of John Nelson Darby (1800–1882)" (PhD diss., Drew University, 1985).

Ehlert, Arnold D., *A Bibliographic History of Dispensationalism* (Grand Rapids: Baker Book House, 1966).

J. F. Bethune-Baker, *An Introduction to the Early History of Christian Doctrine* (London: Methuen & Co., 1942).

Kraus, C. Norman, *Dispensationalism in America* (Richmond, VA: John Knox Press, 1958).

Lowith, Karl, *Meaning in History.*

McClain, Alva J., "A Premillennial Philosophy of History," *Bibliotheca Sacra,*"3:113–14, April-June, 1956.

Philip Schaff and Henry Wace, ed., *Nicene and Post-Nicene Fathers,* second series, 14 vols. (Grand Rapids: Wm. B. Eerdmans Publishing Co., n.d.).

---

[90] Note: it is not to be assumed that ALL works suggested by the author for review have been written from a dispensational standpoint.

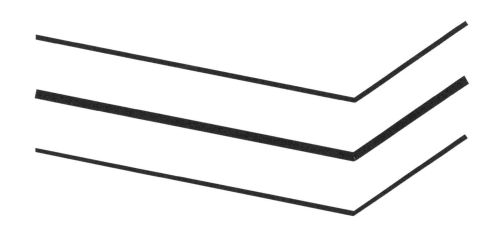

Section Two

—Ryrie's Sine Qua Non

CHAPTER SEVEN

—INTRODUCTION TO RYRIE'S SINE QUA NON

At this point we begin an examination of the three points of Ryrie's *sine qua non*. Due to their significance, these points are again listed:

(1) The recognition of a consistent distinction between Israel and the Church

(2) A consistent and regular use of a literal principle of interpretation

(3) A basic and primary conception of the purpose of God as His own glory rather than the salvation of mankind [91]

These three points are considered the primary factors that distinguish a *dispensationalist* from a *nondispensationalist*. The term *sine qua non* indicates that they are the basic and **indispensable essentials** of dispensationalism.

---

[91] Ryrie, Charles C., *Dispensationalism*, (Chicago: Moody Press, 1995) p. 45. See also Enns, P. P., *The Moody Handbook of Theology,* Chicago, Ill.: Moody Press, 1997, c1989.

CHAPTER EIGHT

—GOD'S PRIMARY PURPOSE IN SCRIPTURE

The focus of this chapter is that of *God's primary purpose* in Scripture. An answer to the following question is sought: Is God's primary purpose in Scripture *soteriological* (pertaining to salvation) as covenant theologians claim? ... Or is it *the glory of God*, as dispensationalists claim?

It is worth noting that the answers to some questions are not quite so black and white. For example: Is God *gracious?* ... Or is God *wrathful?* The answer, of course, is that God is both *gracious* and *wrathful*. So the question at hand is not whether God reveals *a* purpose in Scripture which relates to salvation and/or *another* purpose that relates to His own glory, but whether either of these constitutes His **primary** purpose.

Approaching the matter from an entirely different angle might also help. Consider which of the following could more feasibly be taken away: (1) God's revealed plan concerning man's salvation... or (2) God's glory. Even if God's redemptive plan could be removed from the picture, God would still be glorious. God's glory, on the other hand, is an entirely different matter. It would be impossible to remove God from His glory or vice versa. God is simply a glorious God! He always has been; He always will be! This would be true even if He had never chosen to redeem fallen mankind from his deplorably miserable condition.

DESCRIPTION OF THE DEBATE/ARGUMENT

The excerpts listed below from various authors describe the nature of the debate. As usual, the controversy is framed by examining the positions of the two primary opposing camps— covenant theology and dispensationalism.

Charles Ryrie writes:

> The covenant theologian, in practice, believes this purpose to be salvation (although covenant theologians strongly emphasize the glory of God in their theology), and the

dispensationalist says the purpose is broader than that; namely, *the glory of God.*

...

To the normative dispensationalist, the soteriological, or saving, program of God is not the only program but one of the means God is using in the total program of glorifying Himself. Scripture is not man-centered as though salvation were the main theme, but is God-centered because His glory is the center. The Bible itself clearly teaches that salvation, important and wonderful as it is, is not an end in itself but is rather a means to the end of glorifying God (Eph. 1:6, 12, 14).[92]

John F. Walvoord writes:

The larger purpose of God is the manifestation of His own glory.[93]

Elsewhere, Walvoord writes:

All the events of the created world are designed to manifest the glory of God. The error of covenant theologians is that they combine all the many facets of divine purpose in the one objective of the fulfillment of the covenant of grace. From a logical standpoint, this is the reductive error—the use of one aspect of the whole as the determining element.[94]

P. S. Karleen also addresses the nature of the debate:

The amillennialist has hypothesized as an overall statement about the Bible that the purpose of God is to take out of mankind a people who will be recipients of special blessings, particularly the enjoyment of Him. This sounds very reasonable. However, when it is allowed to reshape the data rather than *being reshaped* by the data of the Bible, then it becomes a prejudice.[95]

---

[92] Ryrie, Charles C., *Dispensationalism* (Chicago: Moody Press, 1995) p. 40

[93] John F. Walvoord, "Review of Crucial Questions About the Kingdom of God, by George E. Ladd," *Bibliotheca Sacra* 110 (January 1953): 3-4, as cited by Charles C. Ryrie in *Dispensationalism* (Chicago: Moody Press, 1995) p. 40

[94] John F. Walvoord, *The Millennial Kingdom* (Findlay, Ohio: Dunham, 1959), 92, as cited by Charles C. Ryrie in *Dispensationalism* (Chicago: Moody Press, 1995) p. 41, 93

[95] Karleen, P. S., *The Handbook to Bible Study: With a Guide to the Scofield Study System.* New York: Oxford University Press, 1987.

Elsewhere, Karleen writes:

> In covenant theology there is one central purpose of God in history, to create through election and the application of the work of Christ one redeemed people, saved through the covenant of grace. This underlying feature of covenant theology, actually a presupposition concerning God's purpose in and beyond history, has plausible elements. God is certainly saving people from all ages, and He does it always through the cross. However, for such a presupposition to be workable it must fit the facts, and this one is too often contradicted by the facts. Its adherents must bend biblical data in order to keep the position alive.[96]

THE PURPOSE OF GOD IN RELATION TO THE BASIC DEFINITION OF DISPENSATIONALISM

W. Graham Scroggie draws attention to "one great, grand end" in his definition of what a dispensation is:

> Just as a parent would govern his household in different ways, according to varying necessity, yet ever for one good end, so God has at different times dealt with men in different ways, according to the necessity of the case, but throughout for one great, grand end.[97]

Concerning God's designed purpose in the overall dispensational scheme, Ryrie quotes the 1883 hermeneutics of Milton Terry:

> With each new series of generations some new promise is given, or some great purpose of God is brought to light.[98]

In reference to this statement Ryrie writes:

> It is the marking off of these stages in the revelation of the purpose of God that is the basis for the dispensational approach to the interpretation of the Scriptures.[99]

Having such thoughts in mind, Ryrie incorporates the idea of God's primary purpose directly into his "concise definition" of

---

[96] Karleen, Ibid.
[97] W. Graham Scroggie, *Ruling Lines of Progressive Revelation* (London: Morgan & Scott, 1918), 62-63, as cited by Charles C. Ryrie in *Dispensationalism* (Chicago: Moody Press, 1995) p. 30
[98] Milton S. Terry, *Biblical Hermeneutics* (Grand Rapids: Zondervan, n.d.), 568.
[99] Ryrie, 31

dispensationalism; he is careful to point out that he is presenting "a definition, not a description":

> A concise definition of a dispensation is this: *A dispensation is a distinguishable economy in the outworking of God's purpose.*[100]

And this purpose, according to normative dispensational interpretation, is the *glory of God.*

THE PURPOSE OF GOD IN RELATION TO BIBLICAL UNITY

The argument is often framed under the heading of "Biblical unity." Non-dispensationalists accuse dispensationalists of undermining the *unity* of the Bible by distinguishing the economies. One such claim is that dispensationalists' insistence that the primary purpose of God in Scripture as His own glory rather than the salvation of man, undermines the importance of God's plan of salvation. This misperception has resulted in the extreme view held by some that dispensationalists teach more than one way of salvation. This, of course, is not true. Ryrie points out that the problem arises from a failure to understand that "unity and distinction are not necessarily contradictory concepts."[101] To further clarify this point Ryrie presents the following argument: "the human body is not disunited because the hand is distinct from the ear, [nor is a building disunited because] distinctions [exists] between the iron and wood that go into it."[102] Ryrie then refers to the ultimate rationale to validate his argument, namely, "the unity of the Trinity ... [pointing out that even the] opponents of dispensationalism... are very careful to maintain distinctions in the three Persons comprising the Godhead!"[103]

Ryrie further writes:

> What is this unity that is supposedly destroyed? It is, in the nondispensationalist's opinion, the unity of the overall purpose of redemption. The so-called covenant of grace is the governing category by which all Scripture is to be understood. God's purpose in the world is to redeem, and men have been,

---

[100] Ryrie, 28
[101] Ryrie, 92
[102] Ryrie, 92
[103] Ryrie, 92

are, and will always be redeemed in the same manner throughout all time.

...

The covenant theologian is so focused on making all of Scripture fit into the restriction superficially imposed by his covenant of grace, he is forced to make all of it align with the outworking of a single purpose—the salvation of man.[104]

To emphasize this "aspect" (error) of covenant theology, Ryrie quotes the covenant writer Roderick Campbell as follows:

Everything in history and life is subservient to spiritual redemption.[105]

Ryrie concludes:

No dispensationalist minimizes the importance of God's saving purpose in the world. But whether it is God's total purpose, or even His principal purpose, is open to question. The dispensationalist sees a broader purpose in God's program for the world than salvation, and that purpose is His own glory. For the dispensationalist the glory of God is the governing principle and overall purpose, and the soteriological program is one of the principal means employed in bringing to pass the greatest demonstration of His own glory. Salvation is part and parcel of God's program, but it cannot be equated with the entire purpose itself.

...

Thus... the unifying principle of covenant theology is, in practice, soteriological. The unifying principle of normative dispensationalism is doxological, or the glory of God, for the dispensations reveal the glory of God as He manifests His character in the differing stewardships given to man.[106]

The "unity" connection is also emphasized by P.P. Enns. He writes the following under a subheading entitled "Biblical unity":

Dispensationalists emphasize that the unifying theme of the Bible is the glory of God. In contrast to covenant

---

[104] Ryrie, 93

[105] Campbell, Roderick, *Israel and the New Covenant* (Philadelphia: Presbyterian Board of Christian Education, 1936), p. 14, as cited by Charles C. Ryrie in *Dispensationalism* (Chicago: Moody Press, 1995) 93.

[106] Ryrie, 93-94

theology, which emphasizes salvation as the unifying theme, dispensationalists see salvation as man-centered and simply one aspect of God's glory. "Scripture is not mancentered as though salvation were the main theme, but it is God-centered because His glory is the center."[14] In every age or dispensation God has revealed His glory, which is the unifying theme of Scripture.... its focus on the glory of God rather than the salvation of man as the objective of all things. It centers on God, not man.[107]

Ryrie concludes:

> The economies, stewardships, or dispensations [are] stages... in the unfolding of [God's] purpose. Dispensationalism, therefore, recognizes both the unity of His purpose and the diversity in the unfolding of it. ... Only dispensationalism can maintain unity and diversity at the same time and offer a consistent system of interpretation.[108]

THE ISRAEL AND CHURCH CONNECTION

The student will find that when any one particular view is adopted, it generally leads to the adoption of a number of other kindred views, and these kindred views lead to the adoption of additional kindred views... and so on. In other words, it will be found that from the fundamental doctrines of covenant theology emerge a number of other doctrines that are also at odds with dispensationalism. (This holds true for all systems of theology. This is why it is so critical to have a good foundation.) Such interdependencies among doctrines can clearly be seen in covenant theology's interpretation of Israel and the Church being one-and-the-same, and their associated belief that God's primary purpose in Scripture is the salvation of man rather than to reveal His (God's) own glory.

In fact, God reveals a number of secondary purposes in Scripture. In reference to this multiplicity of God's purposes, Ryrie, criticizing Daniel Fuller for not consistently applying, as he claims to, the

---

14 14. Ryrie, Charles, *Dispensationalism Today*, p. 46.

[107] Enns, P. P., *The Moody Handbook of Theology*. Chicago, Ill.: Moody Press, 1997, c1989.

[108] Ryrie, Charles C., *Dispensationalism* (Chicago: Moody Press, 1995) 33.

"inductive method of Bible study [pertaining to] Israel [and the] church," writes the following:

> The dispensationalist believes that God has two distinct purposes—one for Israel and one for the church.[109]

So again, the point is not to ascertain the many purposes of God, for God obviously has many, not the least of which is the salvation of man. The point is rather to ascertain God's *primary* purpose.

When narrowing his focus to the *primary* purpose of God, Ryrie later clarifies:

> It is not a matter of superimposing a dual purpose of God on the Scriptures, but it is a matter of recognizing that in the New Testament the word *Israel* does not mean the church and vice versa.[110]

Karleen also points out the relation of God's primary purpose to Israel and the Church:

> Since God's purpose, according to covenant theology, is singular, there can be no room for separate tracks of sidings....[111]

Karleen continues:

> It is especially in the area of the purpose of God during this and coming ages that the covenant theologian runs into difficulty. He cannot account for the very distinctive present-day works of the Holy Spirit, for much teaching concerning the nature of the universal Church and the local church, and for much of the biblical revelation concerning unfulfilled prophecy. It is no accident that these three areas are affected, for they are connected, and in order to lay them out fully one must note distinctions that the Bible makes. For example, the very practice... of seeing the Church in the Old Testament and confusing Israel and the Church in the New Testament clearly flies in the face of biblical evidence. Yet, unfortunately, presupposition is allowed to take precedence over biblical data.[112]

---

[109] Ryrie, 85
[110] Ryrie, 90
[111] Karleen, P. S., *The Handbook to Bible Study: With a Guide to the Scofield Study System.* New York: Oxford University Press, 1987.
[112] Karleen, Ibid.

Lightner sums up the matter by referring to the inexorable connection between the three points of Ryrie's *sine qua non:*

> A consistently literal or normal hermeneutic brings one to see distinctions in God's program with Israel and His program with the church, and that underscores the theological rather than the soteriological nature of God's primary purpose in the world.[37] [113]

DISTINGUISHED FROM PROGRESSIVES' VIEWS ALSO

A difference of viewpoint also exists between normative dispensationalists and the more recent views introduced by progressive dispensationalists concerning the purpose of God. Progressives identify:

> The goal and purpose of history as Christological in contrast to normative dispensationalism's focus on the glory of God. ... [This] goes hand in hand better with the Messianic, eschatological, unified kingdom emphasis.[114]

CONCLUDING ARGUMENTS

The dispensational viewpoint involves a developing/increasing revelation of God's purpose, not equally discernable in every stage. Along these lines of thought, Calvin appropriately wrote:

> In like manner, if a householder instructs, rules, and guides his children one way in infancy, another way in youth, and still another in young manhood, we shall not on this account call him fickle and say that he abandons his purpose. Why, then, do we brand God with the mark of inconstancy...[115]

Ryrie fits this idea into what he refers to as the "spiral concept":

> Dispensationalism reveals the outworking of God's plan in the historical process in a progressive revelation of His glory.[116]

---

[37] 37. Ryrie, Charles, *Dispensationalism Today*, pp. 43–47.

[113] Lightner, Robert P., "Theological Perspectives on Theonomy Part I: Theonomy and Dispensationalism," *Bibliotheca Sacra.* Dallas TX: Dallas Theological Seminary, 1996, c1955-1995.

[114] Ryrie, Charles C., *Dispensationalism* (Chicago: Moody Press, 1995) 165.

[115] John Calvin, *Institutes of the Christian Religion* (London: Wolfe & Harison, 1561), II, XI, 13, as cited by Ryrie, p. 36.

[116] Ryrie, 37

Later Ryrie begins an excellent summary of arguments by first posing the following question:

> How do we know that the glory of God is the purpose of God above and beyond His saving purpose? [117]

Ryrie answers this question as follows:

> First, the plain statement of Scripture declares that salvation is to the praise of God's glory, which simply means that redemption is one of the means to the end of glorifying God (Eph. 1:6, 12, 14). Salvation, for all of its wonder, is but one facet of the multifaceted diamond of the glory of God. Second, all theologians of whatever persuasion realize that God has a plan for the angels. It does not involve redemption, for the elect angels do not experience it and the nonelect angels cannot. And yet for the angels God has a distinct program—a distinct purpose—and it is not soteriological. Third, if one is a premillennialist (not even necessarily of the dispensational variety) he recognizes that in the kingdom program God has a purpose that, though it involves salvation, is not confined to redemption. Obviously God has other purposes in this world besides the redemption of mankind, though with our man-centered perspective we are prone to forget that fact. [118]

Ryrie later adds to this list: "the glory of God revealed through nature." [119]

Ryrie further expounds the argument:

> There is nothing wrong with God's having a purpose for Israel and a purpose for the church and letting these two purposes stand together within His overall plan. After all, God has a purpose for angels, for the unsaved, and for nations that are different from His purpose for Israel and the church. Yet no antidispensationalist worries about a "dichotomy" there. The unifying principle of Scripture is the glory of God as revealed in the variegated purposes revealed and yet to be revealed. To pick out one of these purposes and force everything else into its mold is to warp the revelation of God. That is the error of the nondispensationalist. [120]

---

[117] Ryrie, 94
[118] Ryrie, 94
[119] Ryrie, 213
[120] Ryrie, 142

FOR FURTHER STUDY ON GOD'S PRIMARY PURPOSE

Ryrie, Charles C., *Dispensationalism* (Chicago: Moody Press, 1995) pp. 28-31, 33, 36-37, 39, 40-41, 45, 85, 90-95,129, 135, 142, 164-165, 213.

FOR ADDITIONAL STUDY[121] ON GOD'S PRIMARY PURPOSE

Dollar, George W., "Early American Dispensationalist:—The Reverend F. L. Chapell," *Bibliotheca Sacra*. Dallas TX: Dallas Theological Seminary, 1996, c1955-1995.

Enns, P. P. The Moody Handbook of Theology. Chicago, Ill.: Moody Press, 1997, c1989.

Feinberg, John, "Salvation in the Old Testament," in *Tradition and Testament*, ed. John S. Feinberg and Paul D. Feinberg (Chicago: Moody, 1981).

Karleen, P. S. *The Handbook to Bible Study: With a Guide to the Scofield Study System*. New York: Oxford University Press, 1987.

Lightner, Robert P., "Theological Perspectives on Theonomy Part I: Theonomy and Dispensationalism," *Bibliotheca Sacra*. Dallas TX: Dallas Theological Seminary, 1996, c1955-1995.

Mason, Jr., Clarence E., "A Review of Dispensationalism by John Wick Bowman: Part II," *Bibliotheca Sacra*. Dallas TX: Dallas Theological Seminary, 1996, c1955-1995.

---

[121] Note: it is not to be assumed that ALL works suggested by the author for review have been written from a dispensational standpoint.

CHAPTER NINE

—ISRAEL AND THE CHURCH

In the last chapter, one of the three points of Ryrie's *sine qua non* was briefly examined—namely, God's primary purpose in Scripture. Contemplated in this chapter is a matter of even greater significance when it comes to the variances that exist between dispensationalists and nondispensationalists—namely, how Israel and the Church are to be viewed. Ryrie points out how crucial a matter this is:

> This is probably the most basic theological test of whether or not a person is a dispensationalist, and it is undoubtedly the most practical and conclusive. The one who fails to distinguish Israel and the church consistently will inevitably not hold to dispensational distinctions; and one who does will.[122]

So the purpose at hand is to discover whether the New Testament Church has replaced Israel (the nondispensational position), or whether the Church and Israel are to be considered entirely separate entities altogether (the dispensational position). The perception one comes away with as these questions are contemplated has an enormous bearing on how he or she will understand the Scriptures. Or, perhaps better stated, how one understands (interprets) the Scriptures has an enormous bearing on how he or she will perceive the answers to these questions. (The issue of *interpretation methods* will be considered in detail over the remaining chapters of this section.)

When comparing theological systems one soon discovers that the lines are often blurry when it comes to Israel and the Church—the solid stance that normative dispensationalists maintain concerning this issue being the exception. The disagreements, sometimes disparagements, span from the early Church fathers up to the recently introduced positions espoused by today's *neo-dispensationalists* (often referred to as *progressive* dispensationalists).

We begin by identifying the debate. The issue is then described from both the non-dispensational and dispensational points-of-view.

---

[122] Ryrie, Charles C., *Dispensationalism* (Chicago: Moody Press, 1995) p. 39.

The chapter is then concluded with summarizing excerpts from Charles Ryrie's book entitled *Dispensationalism.*

IDENTIFYING THE DEBATE

The student is faced with two diametrically opposed views, only one of which can possibly be right. Walvoord describes these two views as follows:

> One of the definitive questions is whether the New Testament church fulfills Israel's prophetic programs. Here, among conservative interpreters at least, are two distinct schools of thought: (a) the teaching that Israel has a special program of God, beginning with Abraham and continuing on into eternity to come, and (b) the teaching that the programs of God for Israel and the church are essentially one and consist in the fact that both are the recipients of God's salvation.[123]

In other words, nondispensationalists (although exceptions exist)[124] make little or no distinctions between Israel and the Church. Dispensationalists, on the other hand, firmly recognize a clear distinction between the two, and claim that *Israel* is always to be understood as *Israel* and the *Church* is always to be understood as the *Church;* no merge at all between the two is considered viable (with the exception of the fact that today a saved Jew becomes part of the Church). Both views are presented below. Each section contains a number of quotes from representatives of each respective camp.

---

[123] Walvoord, John F., "Does the Church Fulfill Israel's Program? - Part 1," *Bibliotheca Sacra.* Dallas TX: Dallas Theological Seminary, 1996, c1955-1995.

[124] Walvoord notes both historic and "modern" inconsistencies exist; even Hodge's abandonment of the position: "The idea that Israel means Israel, not the church as such, however, did not originate in Darby, nor is it confined to dispensationalism or premillennialism. Charles Hodge, who was a postmillenarian, insisted that Israel always means the nation Israel, and is not a synonym for the church. He further showed that the nation Israel is due a future conversion (cf. Rom. 11:26). Hodge included Israel in the church, but opposed Calvin's idea that Israel was to be interpreted in a spiritualized sense as embracing all the elect. That Darby made new distinctions is correct; that such distinctions are completely novel is a factual error (cf. Charles Hodge, *Epistle to the Romans,* 1955, p. 374). Many modern scholars who are not dispensationalists have abandoned the equation of Israel and the church, much as Hodge did a century ago." (Walvoord, John F., A review of *Backgrounds To Dispensationalism,* by Clarence B. Bass. Wm. B. Eerdmans Publishing Company, Grand Rapids, Michigan, 1960, 184 pp. *Bibliotheca Sacra.* Dallas TX: Dallas Theological Seminary, 1996, c1955-1995.

A Brief Description of the Nondispensational View of Israel and the Church

We begin by pointing out that, according to Ryrie, "All nondispensationalists blur to some extent the distinction between Israel and the church. Such blurring fails to recognize the contrast that is maintained in Scripture between Israel, the Gentiles, and the church."[125]

Charles Hodge states his nondispensational position as follows:

> There is no authorized definition of the Church, which does not include the people of God under the Mosaic law.[126]

Hodge continues under the subheading *"The Church under the New Dispensation is identical with that under the Old"*:

> It is not a new Church, but one and the same. It is the same olive-tree. (Rom. xi. 16, 17.) It is founded on the same covenant, the covenant made with Abraham.
>
> ...
>
> The conclusion is that God has ever had but one Church in the world.[127]

Later, Hodge continues under the subheading *"The Promise of Eternal Life made before the advent"*:

> The covenant of grace, or plan of salvation, being the same in all its elements from the beginning, it follows, first, in opposition to the Anabaptists, that the people of God before Christ constituted a Church, and that the Church has been one and the same under all dispensations. It has always had the same promise, the same Redeemer, and the same condition of membership, namely, faith in the Son of God as the Saviour of the world.[128]

Later still, Hodge presents to his readers the following comments under the subheading *"Are the Jews to be restored to their own Land?"*:

---

[125] Ryrie, Charles C., *Dispensationalism* (Chicago: Moody Press, 1995) 127

[126] Hodge, C., *Systematic Theology*. Oak Harbor, WA: Logos Research Systems, Inc., 1997.

[127] Hodge, Ibid.

[128] Hodge, Ibid.

There could not be a more distinct assertion that all difference between the Jew and Gentile has been done away within the pale of the Christian Church. This, however, is not a mere matter of assertion, it is involved in the very nature of the Gospel. Nothing is plainer from the teachings of Scripture than that all believers are one body in Christ, that all are the partakers of the Holy Spirit, and by virtue of their union with Him are joint and equal partakers of the benefits of his redemption; that if there be any difference between them, it is not in virtue of national or social distinctions, but solely of individual character and devotion. That we are all one in Christ Jesus, is a doctrine which precludes the possibility of the preeminence assigned to the Jews in the theory of which their restoration to their own land, and their national individuality are constituent elements.

The Apostles uniformly acted on this principle. They recognize no future for the Jews in which the Gentile Christians are not to participate. As under the old dispensation proselytes from the heathen were incorporated with the Jewish people and all distinction between them and those who were Jews by birth, was lost, so it was under the Gospel. Gentiles and Jews were united in undistinguished and undistinguishable membership in the same Church. And so it has continued to the present day; the two streams, Jewish and Gentile, united in the Apostolic Church, have flowed on as one great river through all ages. As this was by divine ordinance, it is not to be believed that they are to be separated in the future.[129]

This same concept can be noted in the manner in which Jamieson employs the use of the term "true Israel" when referring to the Church:

> Ye were once aliens from the commonwealth *of Israel* (in the time of her *Old Testament prophets*), but now ye are members of the true Israel, built upon the foundation of her New Testament apostles and Old Testament prophets.[130]

---

[129] Hodge, Ibid.

[130] Jamieson, R., A. R. Fausset, A. R. Fausset, D. Brown, & D. Brown. *A Commentary, Critical and Explanatory, on the Old and New Testaments*. Oak Harbor, WA: Logos Research Systems, Inc., 1997. Eph 2:20.

Such use of the term (and/or the concept) "true Israel" is common to covenant theology. In light of such statements, this system of theology clearly stands in direct contradistinction to dispensationalism. Enns writes:

> Covenant theology affirms there is one people of God called true Israel, the church (in contrast to dispensationalism, which teaches there are two people of God, called Israel and the church).[131]

Most covenant theologians are amillennialists. Amillennialists, as Karleen points out, staunchly adhere to the idea that Israel and the Church are one and the same:

> Since God's purpose is not, in their view, to work with separate peoples through history, but rather to establish one people, there is no essential difference between Israel and the Church here, and the future of Israel does not involve national regathering, regeneration, and enjoyment of the land. The land blessings, which from the Old Testament alone may reasonably be interpreted as physical, earthly and visible, are viewed by the amillennialist as absorbed by the Church, part of the same people as Israel. Thus, the land and other promises were supposedly never meant to be fulfilled physically. This amounts to a reinterpretation of the Old Testament by the New Testament.[132]

Gordon Lewis writes:

> Covenant theologians generally think they are justified in interpreting all the promises to Israel as fulfilled in the church, and often do not anticipate a historical millennium.... the differences between national Israel and institutional churches are not duly acknowledged.[133]

At this point, the reader is introduced to the term "replacement theology." As Robert Pyne notes:

> Paul clearly recognized the narrowing of the promise even in Genesis (Rom. 9:6–7), and his point is that it has now

---

[131] Enns, P. P., *The Moody Handbook of Theology*. Chicago, Ill.: Moody Press, 1997, c1989.
[132] Karleen, P. S., *The Handbook to Bible Study: With a Guide to the Scofield Study System*. New York: Oxford University Press, 1987.
[133] Lewis, Gordon R., "Theological Antecedents of Pretribulationism," *Bibliotheca Sacra*. Dallas TX: Dallas Theological Seminary, 1996, c1955-1995.

narrowed to Christ and those who believe in Him. Does this mean that God has set aside ethnic Israel? On the basis of these statements some have supported a "replacement theology," which makes the church the new Israel.[134]

This is, of course, the inevitable outcome of the theological positions described above which fail to make the appropriate *Biblical* distinctions between Israel and the Church.

Another unavoidable result pertains to how one must interpret Scripture. Again, in order to remain consistent with the theological positions described above, *spiritualization* of the Scriptures becomes a necessity; such *spiritualization* of Scripture is the observation made by Charles Ryrie, as can be seen in his following comments concerning Ladd's position:

> For example, Ladd in order to add support to his posttribulational view is forced to regard the 144,000 of Revelation 7 as referring not to literal Israel but to spiritual Israel or the church.[135]

George W. Dollar notes the same as he cites Chapell:

> The contention is made that the promises to Israel have been greatly misunderstood for they have been "spiritualized and made to refer to the church, a method of interpretation, which, if generally applied, would make the Bible a very untrustworthy Book."[23] The mischief of this very all-too-common interpretation "lies in saying these prophecies do not primarily and finally have a literal application to Israel."[24] [136]

Much more on the severity of this error (i.e., inappropriate interpretation methods) will be covered in the chapters immediately ahead.

---

[134] Pyne, Robert A., "The 'Seed,' the Spirit, and the Blessing of Abraham," *Bibliotheca Sacra*. Dallas TX: Dallas Theological Seminary, 1996, c1955-1995. Pyne notes that this idea is implied in Herman Ridderbos, *Paul: An Outline of His Theology*, trans. J. R. DeWitt (Grand Rapids: Eerdmans, 1975), 333–41.

[135] Ryrie, Charles C., "The Necessity of Dispensationalism," *Bibliotheca Sacra*. Dallas TX: Dallas Theological Seminary, 1996, c1955-1995, referring to George E. Ladd, *The Blessed Hope*, p. 126.

23 23. F. L. Chapell, *Biblical and Practical Theology*, p. 213.

24 24. F. L. Chapell, *Biblical and Practical Theology*, p. 214.

[136] Dollar, George W., "Early American Dispensationalist:—The Reverend F. L. Chapell," *Bibliotheca Sacra*. Dallas TX: Dallas Theological Seminary, 1996, c1955-1995.

A Brief Description of the Dispensational View of Israel and the Church

In direct contrast to the nondispensational position presented above, "The contemporary dispensational position on the relationship between Israel and the church is succinctly stated by Walvoord as follows":

> As related to premillennial interpretation, normative dispensationalism tends to emphasize certain important distinctives. One of the most significant is the contrast provided between God's program for Israel and God's present program for the church. The church composed of Jew and Gentile is considered a separate program of God which does not advance nor fulfill any of the promises given to Israel.
>
> The present age is regarded as a period in which Israel is temporarily set aside as to its national program. When the church is translated, however, Israel's program will then proceed to its consummation.[137]

Walvoord's points are to be carefully considered. Emphasizing the significance of the "contrast... between God's program for Israel and God's present program for the church," Walvoord points out that the Church "does not advance nor fulfill any of the promises given to Israel." As noted above, nondispensationalists strongly disagree. The points of disagreement that emerge from such diametrically opposed "contrasts" are numerous. Karleen touches on some very significant outcomes of these differences as he speaks of the idea of the *kingdom* and the *promises* given to Israel in the Old Testament:

> We have already mentioned that the amillennialist asserts that the Bible does not teach that there will be a physical kingdom on the earth over which Christ will reign. Hence, Israel will not experience fulfillment of the Old Testament promises of national blessing. The premillennialist believes that there will be a physical kingdom on the earth, involving the fulfillment of national promises to Israel, with Christ present as King. The postmillennialist holds that there will be an earthly kingdom, but without the visible presence of Christ.

---

[137] Walvoord, John F., "Dispensational Premillennialism," *Christianity Today*, September 15, 1958, p. 13, as cited by Larry V. Crutchfield in "Israel and the Church in the Ante-Nicene Fathers," *Bibliotheca Sacra*. Dallas TX: Dallas Theological Seminary, 1996, c1955-1995.

This view sees Scripture as teaching that Christ will return to earth after the kingdom has been inaugurated by human beings and has run its course. This kingdom is to be equated roughly with some period of blessing in the present age between the two advents of Christ.[138]

Agreement exists concerning the clear distinction between Israel and the Church, even when speaking of some dispensationalists who are not always classified in the mainstream of normative dispensationalism. Blaising, for example, appears to endorse Darby's position on the matter when he writes:

The absolute distinction between Israel and the church. The ecclesiological-eschatological synthesis of Darby was his genius and the dominating conceptual center of modern dispensationalism. The most determinative portion of Scripture for him was Paul's letter to the Ephesians and particularly the description of the οἰκονομία, the dispensation, in Ephesians 1:9–10. In the future Christ will unite all things in Himself, including both heavenly and earthly spheres. The nature of the heavenly sphere is especially elaborated in Ephesians. Jesus Christ has been exalted above it already. Spiritual powers and forces of wickedness presently inhabit it, bringing misery on the earth. But the victory over them has already been won by Christ. On the earth, since the time of Christ's ascension, He has been forming a composite people (believing Jews and Gentiles with equal standing) to inhabit these heavenly regions as His body and bride. The wicked angelic hosts will be displaced, the church (those called out from the earth) will take the ruling position in the heavenlies, and the angels, who are now being educated in these things, will be subordinate to them. With Christ the church will rule the creation from the heavenlies, mediating the blessings of God on the earth (replacing thus the present flow of misery out of those places from deviate angelic hosts). When this happens, altered conditions on the earth will ensue.

This then is synthesized with the eschatological expectations of the Old Testament. Israel and the nations will have a future in an earthly kingdom-empire. The church and

---

[138] Karleen, P. S., *The Handbook to Bible Study: With a Guide to the Scofield Study System.* New York: Oxford University Press, 1987.

the church's future, however, is completely different from that of Israel and the Gentiles. The church is a heavenly people emerging on the earth now, but called out of the earthly entities of Israel and the Gentiles, having come into being since the ascension of Christ. Israel and the Gentiles are earthly people and have a future on the earth. Since history and prophecy concern the earth and earthly people, they do not concern the church. This means that the tribulation and the millennial kingdom concern earthly people only. Therefore they do not concern the church. The church's entrance into her destiny, the heavens, is not the subject of Old Testament prophecy. That entrance will take place by the rapture. The rapture is an event unrelated to earthly prophetic events, including the return of Christ to the earth before the millennium. In the future Christ will unite all things in Himself. The heavenly people will share His glory in the heavens; the earthly people will receive glory from the heavens as it shines on them and they will share in that glory on the earth.[139]

Another of Walvoord's points to be considered is the fact that this "present age is [to be] regarded as a period in which Israel is temporarily set aside as to its national program." Most dispensationalists view this as a "parenthetical" period. Again, these views constitute the major points at which the two opposing theological camps collide. Nondispensationalists, of course, deny any such "setting aside" (parenthesis) of Israel inasmuch as they see Israel entirely merged with the Church and the Church entirely merged with Israel—i.e., one-and-the-same.

Unfortunately, however, *progressive*[140] dispensationalists appear to be drifting further in their already compromised position on this issue. Robert Saucy, for example, writes the following:

---

[139] Blaising, Craig A., "Development of Dispensationalism by Contemporary Dispensationalists," *Bibliotheca Sacra.* Dallas TX: Dallas Theological Seminary, 1996, c1955-1995. Blaising notes that "Some of the best essays on this are in Darby's *Collected Writings,* vols. 2 and 11. Some suggestions are 'Divine Mercy in the Church and toward Israel,' 2:122–64, esp. pp. 122–23, 127; 'The Purpose of God,' 2:266–77, esp. 266–67, 271–72; 'The Hopes of the Church of God,' 2:278–383, esp. 288–89, 376–78; and 'Elements of Prophecy, in Connection with the Church, the Jews, and the Gentiles,' 11:41–54, esp. 41–47."

[140] The term "progressive dispensationalists" is not to be confused with the concept of *progressive revelation.* "Dispensationalists all recognize that there is the element

Instead of a strict parenthesis that has no relation with the messianic kingdom prophecies of the Old Testament, many dispensationalists [Saucy included] now acknowledge the present age of the church as the first-stage partial fulfillment of these prophecies. Israel and the church are no longer viewed as representing two different purposes and plans of God, as some earlier dispensationalists taught; they are now seen as sharing in the same messianic kingdom of salvation history (p. 9).[141]

Speaking of these "progressive dispensationalists," Robert Lightner writes:

A clear and consistent distinction between God's program with Israel and His program with the church, is denied, or at least toned down, by progressive dispensationalists. Similar to Ladd, they hold that the present position of Christ at the Father's right hand is a partial fulfillment of the messianic kingdom age.[142]

Pyne points out that Saucy acknowledges "that these developments move progressive dispensationalists closer to nondispensational systems."[143]

Nevertheless, those adhering to the *normative* dispensational system have remained unwavering in their position—namely, that

---

of progressive revelation throughout Scripture, and in fact this is inherent in and emphasized by dispensational interpretation…. The issue accordingly is not progressive revelation versus nonprogressive revelation, but rather whether in progressive revelation there is contradiction or correction [in the New Testament] of what was commonly assumed to be the main tenor of Old Testament revelation." (Walvoord, John F., "Does the Church Fulfill Israel's Program? - Part 1," *Bibliotheca Sacra.* Dallas TX: Dallas Theological Seminary, 1996, c1955-1995.)

[141] As cited by Robert A. Pyne, Williams, Lin M., ed., *Bibliotheca Sacra.* Dallas TX: Dallas Theological Seminary, 1996, c1955-1995 in his review of *The Case for Progressive Dispensationalism: The Interface Between Dispensational and Non-Dispensational Theology* by Robert L. Saucy. Grand Rapids: Zondervan Publishing House, 1993. 336 pp.

[142] Lightner, Robert P., A review of *The Origins of Dispensationalism* by Larry Crutchfield, Lanham, MD: University Press of America, 1992. 236 pp. *Bibliotheca Sacra.* Dallas TX: Dallas Theological Seminary, 1996, c1955-1995 (Oct 1992A).

[143] Pyne, Robert A., Williams, Lin M., ed., A review of *The Case for Progressive Dispensationalism: The Interface Between Dispensational and Non-Dispensational Theology* by Robert L. Saucy, Grand Rapids: Zondervan Publishing House, 1993. 336 pp. *Bibliotheca Sacra.* Dallas TX: Dallas Theological Seminary, 1996, c1955-1995.

Israel and the Church are strictly distinct, and the temporary postponement of God's dealings with Israel is to be considered "parenthetical." Concerning this Ryrie writes as follows:

> Classic dispensationalism used the words *parenthesis* or *intercalation* to describe the distinctiveness of the church in relation to God's program for Israel. An intercalation is an insertion of a period of time in a calendar, and a parenthesis in one sense is defined as an interlude or interval (which in turn is defined as an intervening or interruptive period). So either or both words can be appropriately used to define the church age if one sees it as a distinct interlude in God's program for Israel (as clearly taught in Daniel's prophecy of the seventy weeks in 9:24-27).[144]

Roy Zuck summarizes Ryrie's answer to "progressives" in the following manner:

> Ryrie points out that a clear distinction between Israel and the church seems to be minimized because progressives have given little attention to the prophecy of the 70 weeks in Daniel 9:24–27 in which there is an interval between the 69th and 70th weeks, which points to the church as a parenthesis in God's program for Israel.[145]

For clarity's sake, the normative dispensational position is here again expressed by quoting the following comments by P. P. Enns:

> Dispensationalism builds on the fact that God has given unconditional promises to Israel, such promises as the Abrahamic Covenant (Gen. 12:1–3). In that one God promised a land and a physical posterity to Abraham, wherein He would bless the descendants of Abraham. Dispensationalists believe these promises will be fulfilled

---

[144] Ryrie, Charles C., *Dispensationalism* (Chicago: Moody Press, 1995) 134. (See also p. 177.) In reference to the issue of "parenthesis," Ryrie directs his readers to the following: "L. S. Chafer, *Systematic Theology* (Dallas: Seminary Press, 1948), 4:41; H. A. Ironside, *The Great Parenthesis* (Grand Rapids: Zondervan, 1943); Walvoord, *The Millennial Kingdom*, 227-30; and J. Randall Price, "Prophetic Postponement in Daniel 9 and Other Text," in *Issues in Dispensationalism*, ed. Wesley R. Willis and John R. Master (Chicago: Moody, 1994), 141-50."

[145] Zuck, Roy. B., A review of *Dispensationalism* by Charles C. Ryrie, Chicago: Moody Press, 1995, 224 pp. *Bibliotheca Sacra.* Dallas TX: Dallas Theological Seminary, 1996, c1955-1995.

literally in the future with Israel. Nondispensationalists spiritualize the prophecies and relegate them to the church.

...

Church uniqueness. Dispensationalists emphasize that Israel always denotes the physical posterity of Jacob and is never to be confused with the church. A concordance study of the term *Israel* indicates it is always used to denote Jacob's physical descendants and is never used in a "spiritualized" sense to refer to the church.[12] Although nondispensationalists frequently refer to the church as "the new Israel," it is an unwarranted designation.

Dispensationalists teach that God has a distinct program for Israel and a distinct program for the church. The commands given to one are not the commands to the other; the promises to the one are not the promises to the other. God calls on Israel to keep the Sabbath (Exod. 20:8–11), but the church keeps the Lord's Day (1 Cor. 16:2). Israel is the wife of Yahweh (Hos. 3:1), but the church is the Body of Christ (Col. 1:27).

First Corinthians 10:32 is important in noting that a distinction is maintained between Israel and the church *after* the birth of the church (Acts 3:12; 4:8, 10; 5:21, 31; Rom. 10:1; 11:1–29). In Romans 11 Paul discusses extensively the future when Israel will be saved, emphasizing a distinctive future hope for Israel as a nation. The chapter sets Israel in contrast with the Gentiles—who are coming to faith until the fullness of the Gentiles, when Israel will be saved.[13]

...

Church. Dispensationalism is nowhere more distinctive than in its doctrine of the church. Dispensationalists hold that the church is entirely distinct from Israel as an entity. This is argued from several points. (1) The church was a mystery, unknown in the Old Testament (Eph. 3:1–9; Col. 1:26). (2) The church is composed of Jews and Gentiles; the Gentiles

---

12 12. The singular passage that is referred to by nondispensationalists is Galatians 6:16 where it is suggested that "Israel of God" may refer to the church. However, the Greek word *kai* (and) is probably used epexegetically in this case, that is, peace and mercy come upon the true Israel of God—Israelites who walk by faith, not the Judaizers.

13 13. See Ryrie, *Dispensationalism Today*, pp. 132–55, for a helpful discussion noting the distinction of the church from Israel.

being fellow-heirs with Jews without having to become Jewish proselytes—something that was not true in the Old Testament (Eph. 3:6). This issue was resolved in Acts 15 when the Judaizers attempted to put Gentiles under the law. (3) The church did not begin until Acts 2. It is the baptizing work of the Holy Spirit that unites believers with Christ and one another, making up the church (1 Cor. 12:13). That work was still future in Acts 1:5, but in Acts 11:15 it is clear that it began in Acts 2, establishing the birth of the church. Dispensationalists also believe that the church will conclude its existence upon the earth at the rapture, prior to the Tribulation (1 Thess. 4:16). (4) The church is consistently distinguished from Israel in the New Testament (1 Cor. 10:32).

...

Distinction between Israel and the church. The term *Israel* always refers to the physical posterity of Jacob; nowhere does it refer to the church.[78] Although nondispensationalists frequently refer to the church as the "new Israel," there is no biblical warrant for doing so. Many passages indicate Israel was still regarded as a distinct entity after the birth of the church (Rom. 9:6; 1 Cor. 10:32). Israel was given unconditional promises (covenants) in the Old Testament that must be fulfilled with Israel in the millennial kingdom. The church, on the other hand, is a distinct New Testament entity born at Pentecost (1 Cor. 12:13) and not existing in the Old Testament, nor prophesied in the Old Testament (Eph. 3:9). It exists from Pentecost (Acts 2) until the rapture (1 Thess. 4:13–18). Herein lies the reason for belief in the pretribulation rapture: the purpose of the Tribulation is to judge unbelieving Gentiles and to discipline disobedient Israel (Jer. 30:7); the church does not have purpose or place in the Tribulation.

...

The marriage has reference to the church and takes place in heaven, whereas the marriage supper has reference to Israel

---

78 78. [Again] The only passage that is somewhat debatable is Galatians 6:16. The Greek *kai* should probably be understood epexegetically as "even." Israel of God thus refers to believing Israelites who walk by faith and not as the legalistic Judaizers.

and takes place on earth in the form of the millennial kingdom.[146]

It should be pointed out that the Church's duration upon this earth from the time of inception (Pentecost) until the time of departure (rapture) is a time in which particular attention must be given to the role of the Holy Spirit.

CONCLUSION

The following excerpt, found on page 85 of Charles Ryrie's book entitled *Dispensationalism*, serves as an appropriate conclusion to this chapter:

> The amillennialist's hermeneutics allow him to blur completely the meanings of the two words [Israel and church] in the New Testament such that the church takes over the fulfillment of the promises to Israel. In that view true Israel is the church. The covenant premillennialist goes halfway. The church and Israel are somewhat blended, though not amalgamated in this age (they are kept distinct in the Millennium). The dispensationalist studies the words in the New Testament, finds that they are kept distinct always, and therefore concludes that when the church was introduced God did not abrogate His Promises to Israel or enmesh them into the church. That is why the dispensationalist recognizes two purposes of God and insists on maintaining the distinction between Israel and the church. And all of this is built on an induction study of the use of two words, not a scheme superimposed on the Bible. In other words, it is built on a consistent use of the literal, normal, or plain method of interpretation without the addition of any other principle that will attempt to give respectability to some preconceived conclusions.[147]

---

[146] Enns, P. P., *The Moody Handbook of Theology*. Chicago, Ill.: Moody Press, 1997, c1989.

[147] Ryrie, Charles C., *Dispensationalism* (Chicago: Moody Press, 1995) 85. Ryrie attaches the following note: "For such an inductive study of the meaning of the words *Israel* and *church*, see Charles Ryrie, *The Basis of the Premillennial Faith* (New York: Loizeaux Bros., 1953), 62-70. Most nondispensationalist make no such study. Also see, Arnold G. Fruchtenbaum, "Israel and the Church," in *Issues in Dispensationalism*, ed. Wesley R. Willis and John R. Master (Chicago: Moody, 1994), 113-29."

FOR FURTHER STUDY ON ISRAEL AND THE CHURCH

Ryrie, Charles C., *Dispensationalism* (Chicago: Moody Press, 1995) pp. 16, 20, 37, 39-41, 43 (fn 43), 45, 51, 69, 74, 85-86, 89-90, 95, 105, 123-144, 147-148, 163-165, 172, 174-176, 197, 213.

Walvoord, John F., "Does the Church Fulfill Israel's Program? - Part 1," *Bibliotheca Sacra.* Dallas TX: Dallas Theological Seminary, 1996, c1955-1995.

FOR ADDITIONAL STUDY[148] ON ISRAEL AND THE CHURCH

Barker, Kenneth L., "The Scope and Center of Old and New Testament Theology and Hope," in *Dispensationalism, Israel and the Church,* 293–328.

Battle, John A., Jr., "Paul's Use of the Old Testament in Romans 9:25–26," *Grace Theological Journal* 2 (1981).

Bauer, Walter, Arndt, William F., and Gringrich, F. Wilbur, *A Greek-English Lexicon of the New Testament and Other Early Christian Literature,* rev. F. Wilbur Gingrich and Frederick W. Danker (Chicago: University of Chicago Press, 1979), 218.

Berkhof, Louis, *Systematic Theology* (Grand Rapids: Wm. B. Eerdmans Publishing Co., 1941), p. 570–71.

Blaising, Craig A., Ibach, Robert D., Jr., Ed. *Bibliotheca Sacra. Dallas TX: Dallas Theological Seminary, 1996, c1955-1995.* A review of "Revelation and the Hermeneutics of Dispensationalism," William H. Shepherd, Jr., *Anglican Theological Review* 71 (1989): 281–99.

Bock, Darrell L., "The Reign of the Lord Christ," esp. 37–67.

Brookes, *Israel and the Church,* pp. 7, 12–15; "*Till He Come,*" p. 95; and *Maranatha,* pp. 393, 401–2, 521–23.

Brown, David, *Christ's Second Coming,* pp. 167–173.

Bruce, *The Epistle of Paul to the Romans,* 196.

Burns, J. Lanier, "The Future of Ethnic Israel in Romans 11," *Dispensationalism, Israel and the Church,* 188–229.

Campbell, Donald K., "The Church in God's Prophetic Program," in *Essays in Honor of J. Dwight Pentecost,* pp. 149–50, 158-61.

Chafer, Lewis Sperry, *Systematic Theology* (Dallas, TX: Dallas Seminary Press, 1947–48), 1:5; 4 and 7:98–99.

Chapell, F. L., *Biblical and Practical Theology,* pp. 22, 28-29 (cf. pp. 300-3).

---

[148] Note: it is not to be assumed that ALL works suggested by the author for review have been written from a dispensational standpoint.

Chisholm, Robert B., *Interpreting the Minor Prophets* [Grand Rapids: Zondervan, 1990], 24.

Cook, W. Robert, *The Theology of John* (Chicago: Moody Press, 1970), pp. 90, 237, and n. 35.

Cranfield, *A Critical and Exegetical Commentary on the Epistle to the Romans,* 500.

Cyprian, *Epistles of Cyprian* Ep. 69. 3; Ep. 72. 7; *Treatises of Cyprian* Treat. 2. 10; and Treat. 9. 9.

Denton, R.C. as cited by Enns, P. P. (1997, c1989). *The Moody handbook of theology.* Chicago, Ill.: Moody Press. 29.

Dunn, James, *Romans,* Word Biblical Commentary, 2 vols. [Dallas, TX: Word, 1988], 2:693.

Feinberg, Paul D., "Hermeneutics of Discontinuity," in *Continuity and Discontinuity,* ed. John S. Feinberg (Westchester, IL: Crossway, 1988), 109–28.

Feinberg, Charles L., *Millennialism* (1980) p. 232.

Fuller, Daniel P., *Gospel and Law: Contrast or Continuum?* [Grand Rapids: William B. Eerdmans Publishing Co., 1980], pp. 130–34.

Glenny, W. Edward, "The Israelite Imagery of 1 Peter 2," in *Dispensationalism, Israel and the Church: The Search for Definition,* ed. Craig A. Blaising and Darrell L. Bock (Grand Rapids: Zondervan, 1992), esp. 37–67, 163–68, and 156–87.

- - -. "The 'People of God' in Romans 9:25–26," *Bibliotheca Sacra,* Dallas TX: Dallas Theological Seminary, 1996, c1955-1995.

Hays, Richard B., *Echoes of Scripture in the Letters of Paul* [New Haven, CT: Yale University Press, 1989], 63–70.

Hendriksen, William, *"And So All Israel Shall Be Saved"* (Grand Rapids: Baker's Book Store, 1945).

Henry, Carl F. H., ("The Concerns and Considerations of Carl F. H. Henry: An Interview," *Christianity Today,* March 13, 1981, p. 22).

Hodge, Charles, *Commentary on the Epistle to the Romans* (Philadelphia: H. B. Garner, 1883), pp. 462–602.

Hoehner, Harold W., *Chronological Aspects of the Life of Christ* (Grand Rapids: Zondervan, 1977), pp. 115–39.

- - -. "Ephesians," in *The Bible Knowledge Commentary, New Testament,* ed. John F. Walvoord and Roy B. Zuck (Wheaton, IL: Victor, 1983), 629.

Hoekema, Anthony, *The Bible and the Future* [Grand Rapids: Eerdmans, 1979], 144–45.

Hoyt, Herman A., "A Dispensational Premillennial Response," in *The Meaning of the Millenium,* 41–46, esp. 43.

Hughes, Philip Edgcumbe, *A Commentary on the Epistle to the Hebrews* (Grand Rapids: Wm. B. Eerdmans Publishing Co., 1977), p. 496.

Irenaeus, *Against Heresies* 3. 1. 1; 3. 3. 2–3; 5. 34. 1; 5. 32. 2.

Johnson, S. Lewis, "Evidence from Romans 9–11," in *A Case for Premillenialism: A New Consensus,* ed. Donald K. Campbell and Jeffrey L. Townsend [Chicago: Moody, 1992], 199–223.

Justin, *Dialogue* chap. 135.

Käsemann, Ernst, *Commentary on Romans,* trans. and ed. Geoffrey W. Bromiley [Grand Rapids: Eerdmans, 1980], 270, 274.

Ladd, George Eldon., *Crucial Questions about the Kingdom of God* (Grand Rapids: Eerdmans, 1952), 98.

- - -. "Historic Premillenialism," in *The Meaning of the Millenium,* ed. Robert G. Clouse (Downers Grove, IL: InterVarsity, 1977), 23.

Liddon, H. P., *Explanatory Analysis of St. Paul's Epistle to the Romans* (1899; reprint, Minneapolis: James and Klock, 1977), 171–72.

Lord, David N., *The Coming and Reign of Christ.* New York, 1808.

Master, John R., "The New Covenant," in *Issues in Dispensationalism,* ed. John R. Master and Wesley R. Willis [Chicago: Moody, 1994], 98.

McClain, Alva J., *Daniel's Prophecy of the Seventy Weeks* (Grand Rapids: Zondervan, 1940).

- - -. *The Gospel of God's Grace* (Chicago: Moody, 1973), 183.

- - -. *The Greatness of the Kingdom* (Chicago: Moody, 1959), pp. 135–254, 511–15.

Moo, Douglas, *Romans 1–8,* Wycliffe Exegetical Commentary [Chicago: Moody, 1991], 567.

Morris, *The Epistle to the Romans,* 369.

Payne, J. Barton, *The Theology of the Older Testament* [Grand Rapids: Zondervan Publishing House, 1962], p. 91.

Pentecost, *Things to Come,* pp. 546, 561–62, 574–77.

Pieters, Albertus, *The Seed of Abraham* (Grand Rapids: Wm. B. Eerdmans Publishing Co., 1950).

Poythress, *Understanding Dispensationalists,* 40.

Richard, Ramesh P., "Selected Issues in Theoretical Hermeneutics, Part 4: Application Theory in Relation to the Old Testament," *Bibliotheca Sacra* 143 (October-December 1986): 307–10.

Ridderbos, Herman, *Paul: An Outline of His Theology,* ed. John Richard DeWitt (Grand Rapids: Eerdmans, 1975), 197–204.

Ryrie, Charles C., *Basic Theology* (Wheaton, IL: Victor, 1986), 306.

Ryrie, Charles C., *The Ryrie Study Bible* [Chicago: Moody, 1978], 1951.

Saucy, Robert L., *The Case for Progressive Dispensationalism,* 50–57, 187–218.

- - -. "The Church as the Mystery of God," in *Dispensationalism, Israel and the Church,* 127–55.

- - -. "The Relationship of Dispensationalism to the Eternal Purpose of God" (Th.D. diss., Dallas Theological Seminary, 1961), pp. 18–19.

Sauer. Eric, *From Eternity to Eternity* (Grand Rapids: Wm. B. Eerdmans Publishing Co., 1972), p. 193.

Schmidt, Karl Ludwig, *Theological Dictionary of the New Testament,* 2:370.

Seiss, Joseph A., *The Last Times and the Great Consummation.* Philadelphia and London, 1860.

Stuart, *Hosea-Jonah,* 36; 41-42.

Tertullian *On Prescription against Heretics* chap. 20.

Waltke, Bruce K., "A Response," in *Dispensationalism, Israel and the Church,* 349, n. 2.

Walvoord, John F., *Israel in Prophecy* (Grand Rapids: Zondervan Publishing House, 1962).

Walvoord, John F., *The Church in Prophecy* (Grand Rapids: Zondervan Publishing House, 1964), pp. 154–65.

Witmer, John A., ed., *Bibliotheca Sacra.* Dallas TX: Dallas Theological Seminary, 1996, c1955-1995. A review of "The Revival of Apocalyptic in the Churches," George Eldon Ladd, Review and Expositor 72 (Summer 1975): 263–70. "The Eschatology of Hal Lindsey," Dale Moody, Review and Expositor 72 (Summer 1975): 271 -78.

- - -. Ibach, Robert D., ed., *Bibliotheca Sacra.* Dallas TX: Dallas Theological Seminary, 1996, c1955-1995. A review of "Covenant Conditionality and a Future for Israel," Ronald W. Pierce, *Journal of the Evangelical Theological Society* 37 (March 1994): 27–38.

- - -. "Romans," in *The Bible Knowledge Commentary, New Testament,* ed. John F. Walvoord and Roy B. Zuck (Wheaton, IL: Victor, 1983), 478–79.

Wright, Christopher J. H., ("The Use of the Bible in Social Ethics: Paradigms, Types, and Eschatology," *Transformation* 1 [January/March 1984]:11–20).

~

See also all resources under the Bibliography identified by a <#> mark at the beginning of the reference.

CHAPTER TEN

—INTRODUCTION TO
INTERPRETATION METHODS

Briefly examined in the previous two chapters were the first and third points of Ryrie's *sine qua non*—namely, (1) "a basic and primary conception of the purpose of God as His own glory rather than the salvation of mankind," and (3) "the recognition of a consistent distinction between Israel and the Church." Beginning at this point, the remaining point (i.e., the second point) of Ryrie's *sine qua non* is taken into consideration, namely: (2) the fact that *only* dispensationalists employ "a consistent and regular use of a literal principle of interpretation" when interpreting the Bible.

The matter of **interpretation methods** may rightly be considered the *root* of what causes a person to become either a dispensationalist or a nondispensationalist. When the Bible is interpreted *literally*, it has a profound affect on a number of theological issues. A *thorough* understanding of this subject is therefore most beneficial to the serious student. Throughout the next several chapters, the subject of *interpretation methods* is covered somewhat extensively in regards to its beginning, history, development, nature, and various related theological outcomes. The main focus will be on how each of these fields of study relate to the literal method of interpretation. Also examined are the various *challenges* dispensationalists face within their own camp, as well as some of the *charges* raised against dispensationalism by non-dispensationalists. In light of the importance of this subject, the reader is encouraged to read these upcoming chapters carefully and prayerfully. (Note: the overall content of these upcoming chapters on interpretation methods is condensed and summarized in a concluding chapter entitled "Summary and Conclusions to Interpretation Methods.")

Determining which *method of interpretation* is to be employed as the Bible is read is a matter of paramount importance, one which must be settled at the outset of one's theological journey. Again, this factor plays an extremely critical role in distinguishing a dispensationalist from a nondispensationalist. It is the *key* factor in explaining how the borders of a number of the various theological camps have become defined. This plays a particularly critical role in the area of prophecy (as will be discussed later). It is essential that each person make a firm decision to accept what the Bible plainly says about doctrine, or they will surely find themselves, at least to some degree, taking one of two dangerous and delusional positions, namely: (1) that doctrine does not really matter, or (2) formulating some sort of a method to reinterpret the plain language of Scripture in order to make it say what they think it ought to say. Those who adopt the former soon find themselves free-falling headlong into some form of apostasy (i.e., any form of religion that betrays the truth). Those who adopt the latter inevitably become victimized by the encroachment of serious doctrinal error. In either case, the Christian faith becomes, for all practical purposes, a fatally flawed and utterly unreliable religion in which multi-faceted confusion and chaos abounds.

It is the author's opinion that few matters compare to, and none exceed in importance to, the *method* with which one interprets the Bible. Two basic methods in which the Bible may be interpreted will be examined and compared, namely: (1) the *literal* method and (2) the *allegorical* method.

CHAPTER ELEVEN

—TWO METHODS OF
INTERPRETATION TO CHOOSE FROM

Virtually every prominent representative from each of the theological camps acknowledges the fundamental need of determining a method of interpretation. As mentioned in the previous chapter, there are two basic methods to choose from—the *literal* and the *allegorical*.[149] Even amillennialists, who typically adhere to the *allegorical* method of interpretation rather than the *literal* method generally adopted by premillennialists, admit the fundamental importance of one's interpretation method. One such example is Allis (referred to by some as "a champion of amillennialism") who writes as follows: "The question of literal versus figurative interpretation is… one which has to be faced at the very outset."[150] Pentecost (a premillennialist) also writes in similar fashion: "The fact that the Word of God cannot be correctly interpreted apart from a correct method of and sound rules for interpretation gives the study its supreme importance."[151] So we begin our study with the firm conviction that the method which a believer adopts in interpreting the Scriptures is of the utmost importance in his search to know and understand God, God's Word, and God's will. These two basic methods of interpretation are now briefly examined and compared.

THE ALLEGORICAL METHOD

First, the Allegorical method of interpretation is briefly examined. Ramm defines this method as follows: "Allegorism is the method of interpreting a literary text that regards the literal sense as the vehicle

---

[149] Pentecost points out that there have been "many diverse methods of interpreting the Scriptures… during the course of the history of interpretation, … but two methods of interpretation… have a vital effect on Eschatology: the allegorical and the grammatical-historical methods. The literal method is generally held to be synonymous with the grammatical-historical method." (Pentecost, J. Dwight, *Things To Come*. Grand Rapids, MI.: Zondervan publications, 1958, p. 4). Cf. also Milton S. Terry, *Biblical Hermeneutics*, pp. 163-74, where such methods as the Halachic, Hagadic, Mystical, Accommodation, Moral, Naturalistic, Mythical, Apologetic and Dogmatic, besides the Allegorical and Grammatico-historical, are also traced.

[150] Allis, Oswald T., *Prophecy and the Church*, p. 17.

[151] Pentecost, J. Dwight, *Things To Come*. Grand Rapids, MI.: Zondervan publications, 1958, p. 3.

for a secondary, more spiritual and more profound sense."[152] This, as Angus-Green write, adds to "the literal meaning of the terms employed a moral or spiritual one."[153] Allis, in an effort to defend his allegorical system of belief that many of the "types" contained in the Old Testament are merely "figures of speech... and cannot be understood literally," says that these types have "a special significance and importance... *a deeper and far more wonderful meaning...* than, taken in their Old Testament context and connection, they seem to contain"[154] (italics and bold added).

1) **The dangers of the allegorical method.** The dangers of the allegorical method should be obvious to most readers. Fritsch notes the inevitable consequences: "the literal and historical sense of Scripture is completely ignored, and every word and event is made an allegory of some kind either to escape theological difficulties or to maintain certain peculiar religious views..."[155] Pentecost expresses the same concern, pointing out that this has the potential to "pervert the true meaning of Scripture... under the guise of seeking a deeper or more spiritual meaning."[156] Pentecost further states: "The allegorical method, which depends on the rationalistic approach of the interpreter, or conformity to a predetermined theological system, leaves one without a basic authoritative test."[157]

Terry warns that this "give[s] wing to all manner of fanciful speculation. It does not draw out the legitimate meaning of an author's language, but foists into it whatever the whim or fancy of an interpreter may desire."[158] Angus-Green agree: "There is... unlimited scope for fancy... in the mind of the expositor."[159] Ramm says that accepting this "second-sense meaning" of the Bible, and thereby adopting such a "spiritualizing" method of interpretation, "is to open the door to almost uncontrolled speculation and imagination."[160]

---

[152] Ramm, Bernard, *Protestant Biblical Interpretation*, p. 21.
[153] Angus, Joseph, and Green, Samuel G., *The Bible Handbook*, p. 220.
[154] Allis, Oswald T., *Prophecy and the Church*, pp. 17-18.
[155] Fritsch, Charles T., "Biblical Typology," *Bibliotheca Sacra*, 104:216, April, 1947.
[156] Pentecost, p. 4.
[157] Pentecost, p. 12.
[158] Terry, Milton S., *Biblical Hermeneutics*, p. 224.
[159] Angus, Joseph, and Green, Samuel G., *The Bible Handbook*, p. 220.
[160] Ramm, Bernard, *Protestant Biblical Interpretation*, p. 65.

Even staunch advocates of the allegorical method of interpretation are forced to admit:

> If it [the figurative or "spiritual" interpretation of a given passage] is used to empty words of their plain and obvious meaning, to read out of them what is clearly intended by them, then allegorizing or spiritualizing is a term of reproach which is well merited.[161]

Pentecost points out the inevitable second danger to which this error leads: "the basic authority in interpretation ceases to be the Scriptures, but the mind of the interpreter."[162] Farrar concurs, stating that this undermining of the Bible's authority would "corrupt the meaning of Scripture…, making Scriptural mysteries out of our own imaginations."[163]

2) **The result of the allegorical method:** Those who adopt this method of interpretation are left with a Bible that has been "reduced… to what seems reasonable to the interpreter, and, as a result, makes true interpretation of Scripture impossible."[164] Karleen notes: "In allegorical interpretation it is quite easy to impose any preconceptions on Scripture, since the most evident meaning is tossed aside in favor of one that is actually arrived at subjectively."[165] This puts the reader in a very vulnerable position, since he can be sure of absolutely nothing. As will be seen shortly, this is what opened the door to the horrible abuses that occurred in the history of the church during *the Dark Ages*.

THE LITERAL METHOD

As noted above, "the literal method is generally held to be synonymous with the grammatical-historical method." [166] "It is called the grammatical-historical method to emphasize the fact that the meaning is to be determined by both grammatical and historical considerations."[167] The literal method is "in direct opposition to the

---

[161] Allis, Oswald T., *Prophecy and the Church*, p. 18.
[162] Pentecost, p. 5.
[163] Cf. F. W. Farrar, *History of Interpretation*, p. 232.
[164] Pentecost, p. 6.
[165] Karleen, P. S., *The Handbook to Bible Study: With a Guide to the Scofield Study System*. New York: Oxford University Press, 1987.
[166] Pentecost, p. 4.
[167] Pentecost, p. 9. Cf. Thomas Hartwell Horne, *An Introducotn to the Critiacl Study and Knowledge of the Holy Scriptures,* I, 322.

allegorical method of interpretation."[168] "To interpret literally means nothing more or less than to interpret in terms of *normal, usual, designation.*"[169] It "gives to each word the same exact basic meaning it would have in normal, ordinary, customary usage, whether employed in writing, speaking or thinking."[170] Rather than forcing a mystical secondary meaning into the primary position, based on the perception that there is a deeper meaning hidden within the text, the literalist handles the secondary meaning in a much different manner, namely, "All secondary meanings of documents, parables, types, allegories, and symbols, depend for their very existence on the previous literal meaning of the terms…"[171]

This is hardly out of the ordinary—it is clearly the commonly accepted practice of interpreting other literature—as Ramm points out: "The literal meaning of sentences is the normal approach in all languages…" He is careful to put the secondary sense in its proper place: "The literalistic approach does not blindly rule out figures of speech, symbols, allegories, and types; but if the nature of the sentence so demands, it readily yields to the second sense." (Figures of speech, allegories, etc. will also be covered in greater detail later.) "This method [i.e., the literal approach]," Ramm writes, "is the only sane and safe check on the imaginations of man."[172]

---

[168] Pentecost, p. 9.
[169] Ramm, Bernard, *Protestant Biblical Interpretation*, p. 64.
[170] Pentecost, p. 9. Cf. Ramm, Bernard, *Protestant Biblical Interpretation*, p. 53.
[171] Ramm, Bernard, *Protestant Biblical Interpretation*. One of several points listed "In defence of the literal approach…" cf. pp. 54 ff.
[172] Ramm, cf. pp. 54 ff.

CHAPTER TWELVE

—THE HISTORY OF INTERPRETATION

The two basic hermeneutical[173] methods of interpretation—the literal and the allegorical—can be better understood by observing both the history and development of interpretation methods. Pentecost, in chapter two of his book entitled *Things to Come,* outlines seven stages in the history of interpretation:

I.   The Beginning of Interpretation

II. Old Testament Jewish Interpretation

III. Literalism in the Time of Christ

IV. The Rise of Allegorism

V.   The Dark Ages

VI. The Reformation Period

VII. The Post-Reformation Period[174]

Each of these seven stages is briefly covered below:

The Beginning of Interpretation. Denoting when the hermeneutical concept of interpretation began, Pentecost writes:

> It is generally agreed by all students of the history of hermeneutics that interpretation began at the time of the return of Israel from the Babylonian exile under Ezra as recorded in Nehemiah 8:1-8.[175]

This became necessary for two reasons: (1) "The discovery of the forgotten 'book of the law' by Hilkiah," and (2) "because the Jews had replaced their native tongue with Aramaic while in exile. Upon their return the Scriptures were unintelligible to them."[176]

Old Testament Jewish Interpretation. Jerome, who rejected the strict literal method of interpretation, "calls the literal interpretation 'Jewish.'"[177] "It would seem," therefore, as Pentecost points out, that

---

[173] Hermeneutics is defined as: "the study of the methodological principles of interpretation (as of the Bible)." (Merriam-Webster, I. *Merriam-Webster's Collegiate Dictionary.* 10th ed. Springfield, Mass., U.S.A.: Merriam-Webster, 1996, c1993.)

[174] Pentecost, J. Dwight, *Things To Come.* Grand Rapids, MI.: Zondervan publications, 1958. pp. 16-33.

[175] Pentecost, p. 16.

[176] Pentecost, p. 16. Cf. Bernard Ramm, *Protestant Biblical Interpretation,* p. 27.

[177] Farrar, F. W., *History of Interpretation,* p. 232.

in Jerome's mind, "the literal method and Jewish interpretation were synonymous."[178] It is well documented by others as well that Rabbinism did not employ the allegorical method, but the literal method of interpretation.[179] Pentecost therefore concludes, that "in spite of all the fallacies of the Rabbinism of the Jews… they followed a literal method of interpretation."[180]

Literalism in the Time of Christ. Literalism in the time of Christ can be seen on two fronts: (1) literalism among the Jews, and (2) literalism among the apostles.

The literalism among the Jews in the time of Christ was, of course, a carry over from the literalism that existed in Rabbinism prior to His appearance. Although the Jews had "warped" the Scriptures by a "hyper-literalistic"[181] application of the method,[182] it is clear that they employed the literal method. Pentecost points out, however, that, "It was not the method that was at fault, but rather the misapplication of it."[183] Perhaps Paul had this error in mind when he issued the following warning to the Corinthians: "[God] …hath made us able ministers of the new testament; not of the letter, but of the spirit: for the letter killeth, but the spirit giveth life" (2Co 3:6).[184] In any event, New Testament believers are clearly warned against making the same "hyper-literalistic" mistakes that the Jews made.

The exclusive use of the literal method of interpretation among the Jews can be partly explained by the fact that allegorism had not yet arisen as an alternative method of interpretation. As Horne states:

---

[178] Pentecost, p. 17.

[179] Cf. F.W. Farrar, *History of Interpretation*, pp. 60-61.

[180] Pentecost, p. 17.

[181] It is important to understand that "Literal hermeneutics does not mean literalistic." (Blaising, Craig A., "Development of Dispensationalism by Contemporary Dispensationalists," *Bibliotheca Sacra*. Dallas TX: Dallas Theological Seminary, 1996, c1955-1995.)

[182] Cf. Bernard Ramm, *Protestant Biblical Interpretation,* p. 28.

[183] Pentecost, p. 19.

[184] Pfeiffer, on the other hand, presents the following view of this verse: "The contrast between **the letter killeth** and **the spirit giveth life** is not a contrast between extreme literalism and a free handling of Scripture (as in the allegorical method of interpretation); the contrast is rather between the Law as a system of salvation requiring perfect obedience (cf. Rom 3:19, 20; 7:1-14; 8:1-11; Gal 3:1-14) and the Gospel as God's gift of grace in Christ." (Pfeiffer, C. F., & E. F. Harrison. *The Wycliffe Bible Commentary: New Testament*. Chicago: Moody Press, 1962. 2 Co 3:6.)

"The allegorical interpretation of the sacred Scriptures cannot be historically proved to have prevailed among the Jews from the time of the captivity ... Philo of Alexandria was distinguished among those Jews who practices this method; and he defends it as something ***new and before unheard of***, and for that reason opposed by the other Jews."[185] (Emphasis added.) "No one would argue," Pentecost writes, "that the literalism of the Jewish interpreters was identical with present day grammatical-historical interpretation."[186]

The literalism among the apostles was the carry over to be expected from the literalism that existed among the Jews—from whence the apostles emerged; the Scriptures provide no indication that a change in method was called for at their conversion (other than, as mentioned above, to avoid the errors of legalism).

Concerning this issue Girdlestone has written:

> We are brought to the conclusion that there was one uniform method commonly adopted by all the New Testament writers in interpreting and applying the Hebrew Scriptures. It is as if they had all been to one school and had studied under one master. But was it the Rabbinical school to which they had been? Was it to Gamaliel, or to Hillel, or to any other Rabbinical leader that they were indebted? negative... The Lord Jesus Christ, and no other, was the original source of the method.[187]

Pentecost concludes: "It was not necessary for the apostles to adopt another method to rightly understand the Old Testament, but rather to purify the existing method from its extremes."[188]

The Rise of Allegorism. Farrar traces the rise of allegorism back to Aristobulus. He writes: "He [Aristobulus] is one of the precursors whom Philo used though he did not name, and he is the first to enunciate two theses which were destined to find wide acceptance, and to lead to many false conclusions in the sphere of exegesis."[189] Pentecost states that Philo's purpose in adopting "this concept of

---

[185] Horne, Thomas Hartwell, *And Introduction to the Critical Study and Knowledge of the Holy Scriptures,* I, 324.
[186] Pentecost, p. 19.
[187] Girdlestone, R. B., *The Grammar of Prophecy,* p. 86. Cf. also Charles Augustus Briggs, *General Introduciton to the Study of Holy Scripture,* p. 443.
[188] Pentecost, p. 20.
[189] Farrar, p. 129.

Aristobulus" was to "reconcile Mosaic law and Greek philosophy so that the Mosaic law might become acceptable to the Greek mind."[190] "The influence of Philo was most keenly felt in the theological school of Alexandria."[191] This influence found its way into the thinking of Pantaenus, the first teacher of the school of Alexandria. Pantaenus "was succeeded by *Clement of Alexandria,* who, believing in the divine origin of Greek philosophy, openly propounded the principle that all Scripture must be allegorically understood."[192]

This leads us to Origen. Origen is perhaps the most influential character among those responsible for bringing about the development of allegorism. In the Alexandrian school, Origen developed his allegorical method of interpreting the Scriptures. Schaff states that Origen developed "a formal theory of interpretation," attributing "to the Scriptures a threefold sense." He summarizes Origen's threefold development as follows:

1. A somatic, literal, or historical sense, furnished immediately by the meaning of the words, but only serving as a veil for a higher idea.

2. A psychic or moral sense, animating the first, and serving for general edification.

3. A pneumatic or mystic and ideal sense, for those who stand on the high ground of philosophical knowledge.[193]

Origen's influence was considerable—he is recognized as a chief among the fathers of allegorical thought. Farrar states that Origen was the foremost exponent of one of the "three diverse exegetical schools in the late Patristic period." Farrar identifies these three schools as follows:

1. The Literal and Realistic (Tertullian)

2. The Allegorical (Origen)

3. The Historical and Grammatical (Theodore of Mopsuestia)[194]

---

[190] Pentecost, p. 21. Cf. also George Holley Gilbert, *The Interpretation of the Bible,* pp. 37 ff.

[191] Pentecost, p. 22.

[192] Farrar, pp. 182-83.

[193] Schaff, Philip, *History of the Christian Church,* II, 521.

The Historical-Grammatical school, which flourished chiefly in Antioch,[195] was directly antithetical to the school in Alexandria. These opposing camps were represented respectively by, Tertullian and Irenaeus on the one hand, and Clement and Origen on the other.[196]

The disastrous effect that the Alexandrian school has had on interpretation is ongoing and can hardly be measured. Case points out that "...Ever since Origen's day certain interpreters of Scripture have sought to refute millennial expectations by affirming that even the most striking statements about Jesus' return are to be understood figuratively..."[197] Besides the obvious effect on such matters as prophecy, equally dreadful was the effect this corrupt method of interpretation had on the developing ecclesiastical system of Origen's time. This development resulted in a number of evils, not the least of which was the misinterpretations the church began to adopt concerning its own authority. Those seduced by the Alexandrian school's influence began to twist and skew the Scriptures in order to accommodate their error; the Word of God had to be force-fitted into the church's misaligned claims of authority. Augustine[198] became a key player in this horrible error. Farrar points out:

> The exegesis of St. Augustine is marked by the most glaring defects... He laid down the rule that the Bible must be interpreted with reference to Church Orthodoxy, and that no Scriptural expression can be out of accordance with any

---

[194] Cf. F. W. Farrar, *History of Interpretation*, p. 177. Farrar also states on pages 213-15 that *Theodore of Mopsuestia* was "the ablest, the most decided, and the most logical representative of the School of Antioch."

[195] For more on the school of Antioch see Pentecost, p. 24-25.

[196] Cf. F. W. Farrar, *History of Interpretation*, pp. 182-83.

[197] Case, Shirley Jackson, *The Millennial Hope,* pp. 214-16.

[198] Concerning Augustine and the effects he had on "the institutional church," Harbin writes the following: "Protestantism has three controls... The first is the testimony of the Holy Spirit in the believer (John 14:26; 1 John 2:27)... A second control is the combined testimony of the body of believers... A third control is the literal method of interpretation. This is the most reliable of the three, since it is the least dependent on frail human instruments. This is the method adopted by the church in the Reformation. This is not to say that it was not an accepted method before that time. In actuality it dates back to the early church (cf. Acts 17:11). *The loss of this control at the time of Augustine led to the institutional church considering itself the final control.*" (Bold and italics added.) (Harbin, Michael A., "The Hermeneutics of Covenant Theology," *Bibliotheca Sacra.* Dallas TX: Dallas Theological Seminary, 1996, c1955-1995.)

other... everything in Scripture which appeared to be unorthodox or immoral must be interpreted mystically...[199]

Farrar continues:

...When once the principle of allegory is admitted, when once we start with the rule that whole passages and books of Scripture say one thing when they mean another, the reader is delivered bound hand and foot to the caprice of the interpreter. He can be sure of absolutely nothing except what is dictated to him by the Church...[200]

Farrar then laments the fact that:

Unhappily for the Church, unhappily for any real apprehension of Scripture, the allegorists, in spite of protest, were completely victorious.[201]

The Dark Ages. As the description implies, there is unfortunately not much to present in the way of exegesis in the period referred to as the Dark Ages. This is due to the fact, as stated above, that "the interpretation of the Bible had to adapt itself to tradition and to the doctrine of the Church."[202]

Farrar summarizes the lacking exegetical contributions of the period as follows:

During the Dark Ages, from the seventh to the twelfth century, and during the scholastic epoch, from the twelfth to the sixteenth, there are but a few of the many who toiled in this field who add a single essential principle, or furnished a single original contribution to the explanation of the Word of God... not one writer in hundreds showed any true conception of what exegesis really implies.[203]

The Reformation Period. The Reformation era can be described as a breath of fresh air in a number of ways; this certainly holds true concerning the issue of sound exegesis. Pentecost attributes: "The whole Reformation movement may be said to have been activated by a return to the literal method of interpretation of the Scriptures." He states that "the translators, who did so much to stir up the flame of

---

[199] Farrar, pp. 236-37.
[200] Farrar, p. 238.
[201] Farrar, p. 238.
[202] Berkhof, Louis, *Principles of Biblical Interpretation,* p. 23.
[203] Farrar, p. 245.

Reformation, were motivated by the desire to understand the Bible literally."[204]

The translators form a bridge from the treacherous time of the Dark Ages to the desperately needed light of the Reformation. Farrar likens the phases of this transition period to a chain with a number of notable links. Referring to one of the "chief links" of this chain in its beginning stages, he states the following: "Valla, a Canon of St. John Lateran... had... learnt from the revival of letters that Scripture must be interpreted by the laws of grammar and the laws of language."[205]

Next mentioned is Erasmus. He, as Pentecost points out, "laid the foundation for the grammatical interpretation of the Word of God."[206]

Another translator mentioned is Wiclif (Wyclif). He remarked that, "the whole error in the knowledge of Scripture, and the source of its debasement and falsification by incompetent persons, was the ignorance of grammar and logic."[207]

Next came Tyndale. Briggs quotes Tyndale as saying:

> The Scripture hath but one sense, which is the literal sense. And that literal sense is the root and ground of all, and the anchor that never faileth, whereunto if thou cleave, thou canst never err or go out of the way. And if thou leave the literal sense, thou canst not but go out of the way.[208]

This long overdue return by the translators to the integrity of sound exegesis laid the foundation for the Reformation period. Of this period, two names stand out: Luther and Calvin. "Both of these are marked by their strong insistences on the literal method of interpretation."[209]

Concerning these two men Ramm writes:

> *Exegesis did not start in earnest till the church was a millennium and a half old.* With the literalism of Luther and Calvin the light of Scripture literally flamed up...[210]

---

[204] Pentecost, p. 26.

[205] Farrar, pp. 312-13.

[206] Pentecost, p. 26. Cf. F. W. Farrar, *History of Interpretation*, p. 320.

[207] Cited by F. W. Farrar, *History of Interpretation*, pp. 278-79.

[208] Briggs, Charles Augustus, *General Introduction to the Study of Holy Scripture*, pp. 456-57.

[209] Pentecost, p. 27.

[210] Ramm, Bernard, *Protestant Biblical Interpretation*, pp. 62-63.

Farrar says that, "Luther... lays down what he [Luther] conceives to be the true rules of Scripture interpretation." These rules can be summarized as follows:

(1) The necessity for grammatical knowledge

(2) The importance of taking into consideration times, circumstances, and conditions

(3) The observance of the context

(4) The need of faith and spiritual illumination

(5) Keeping what he [Luther] called "the proportion of faith"

(6) The reference of all Scripture to Christ[211]

A number of Luther's other teachings are also to be noted:

- The supreme and final authority of Scripture, the *sufficiency* of Scripture, that each passage has one clear, definite, and true sense of its own

- Rejection of the validity of allegory

- Maintenance of the *perspicuity* of Scripture (i.e., the Bible is to be interpreted like any other book)

- The absolute indefeasible *right of private judgment* for all Christians, who have been made by God a spiritual priesthood.[212]

Calvin, as does Luther, holds a unique place in the history of interpretation. Schaff refers to him as "the founder of the grammatico-historical exegesis."[213]

Pointing out Calvin's rejection of the "allegorical interpretation as something peculiarly satanic," Gilbert writes the following: "One must go back to the best work of the school of Antioch to find so complete a rejection of the method of Philo as is furnished by Calvin."[214]

Perhaps no better explanation can be given for the remarkable success of the Reformation in breaking free from the horrible darkness that the Dark Ages imposed upon them than the fact that

---

[211] Farrar, pp. 331-32.

[212] Cf. Farrar, pp. 325-30.

[213] Philip Schaff, cited by Gerrit H. Hospers, *The Principle of Spiritualization in Hermeneutics*, p. 12

[214] Gilbert, George Holley, *The Interpretation of the Bible*, p. 209.

faithful men such as these, as well as many others not mentioned, "made the Bible accessible to all."[215] The reformers illustrated both by word, deed, and much sacrifice that interpreting the Scriptures literally was indeed the proper way to interpret them—the way God intended them to be interpreted.

The Post-Reformation Period. The good influences of the reformers made way for the rise of a number of other notable defenders of the faith. Farrar lists a few of them as follows: "Oecolampadius (1581), Bucer (1551), Brenz (1570), Bugenhagen (1558). Musculus (1563), Camerarius (1574), Bullinger (1575), Chemnitz (1586), and Beza (1605)."[216] In spite of their general agreement in such matters as the principles of interpretation, and rejection of the longstanding abuses of the church in the area of authority and tradition, their progress was limited against the dominance of the opposing mammoth religious system. In spite of such tremendous opposition, however, a number of defenders of the faith emerged. Pentecost lists a few of them as follows: John Koch (1669), John James Wetstein (1754), John Albert Bengel (1752). Others listed include: Lightfoot, Westcott, Ellicott, and John Augustus Ernesti.[217]

Reflecting on this critically trying time, and drawing into focus our own generation, Harbin writes the following:

> The question of authority is probably the key question of this generation. Conservative Christianity has struggled to resist numerous attempts to erode the base of authority rediscovered during the Reformation, when the Reformers proclaimed *Sola Scriptura,* rather than the pope, as the base of authority.
>
> Following this standard, the Reformers built on the principle of a literal interpretation of Scripture.[1] This hermeneutical principle is more than just a guideline for Bible study. It is also a powerful control on what Scripture may or may not be construed to say. In other words the principle of

---

[215] Farrar, p. 357.
[216] Farrar, p. 342.
[217] Cf. Pentecost, p. 31.
1 1. Bernard L. Ramm, *Protestant Biblical Interpretation* (Grand Rapids: Baker Book House, 1970), pp. 51–59.

literal interpretation is what makes Scripture, and not some interpreter, the authority.[218]

A Summary of the History of interpretation. Pentecost concludes his treatment of the history of interpretation as follows:

> As this history of interpretation is summarized, it is to be noted that all interpretation began with the literal interpretation of Ezra. This literal method became the basic method of Rabbinism. It was the accepted method used by the New Testament in the interpretation of the Old and was so employed by the Lord and His apostles. This literal method was the method of the Church Fathers unto the time of Origen when the allegorical method, which had been devised to harmonize Platonic philosophy and Scripture, was adopted. Augustine's influence brought this allegorizing method into the established church and brought an end to all true exegesis. This system continued until the Reformation. At the Reformation the literal method of interpretation was solidly established and, in spite of the attempts of the church to bring all interpretation into conformity to an adopted creed, literal interpretation continued and became the basis on which all true exegesis rests.
>
> It would be concluded, then, from the study of the history of interpretation that the original and accepted method of interpretation was the literal method, which was used by the Lord, the greatest interpreter, and any other method was introduced to promote heterodoxy. Therefore, the literal method must be accepted as the basic method for right interpretation in any field of doctrine today.[219]

---

[218] Harbin, Michael A., "The Hermeneutics of Covenant Theology," *Bibliotheca Sacra.* Dallas TX: Dallas Theological Seminary, 1996, c1955-1995.
[219] Pentecost, pp. 32-33.

CHAPTER THIRTEEN

—ALLEGORIES, TYPES, SYMBOLS, AND PARABLES

"AN ALLEGORY" IN THE NEW TESTAMENT

The New Testament *does* employ the use of the term "an allegory" in Galatians 4:24 (cf. vv. 21-31). Those who wish to argue on behalf of the allegorical method of interpretation often refer to this passage in order to justify their position. What are literalists to make of this? Though the term *allegory* "is unknown to the other Apostles, and is never sanctioned by Christ,"[220] and Paul's use of the term occurs *only* in this one place in the New Testament, literalists are nonetheless obliged to give the issue due consideration—a response becomes necessary.

It will soon be made clear to the reader that this particular New Testament use of "an allegory" does not strengthen the argument in the manner in which the allegorist hopes. Pentecost is careful to point out that "the use of allegories is not a justification for the allegorical method of interpretation."[221] The question we seek to answer, then, is to what extent and in what manner does the use of "allegories" apply?

Farrar, concurring with Pentecost's position on the matter, writes as follows:

> The occurrence of one such allegory in the Epistle of St. Paul no more sanctions the universal application of the method than a few New Testament allusions to the Haggada compel us to accept the accumulations of the Midrashim; or a few quotations from Greek poets prove the divine authority of all Pagan literature.... [222]

Those attempting to justify the allegorical method of interpretation mistakenly apply this single occurrence as an occasion to railroad-in their entire erroneous method. They proceed to apply

---

[220] Farrar, F. W., *History of Interpretation*, p. 217.

[221] Pentecost, J. Dwight, *Things To Come*. Grand Rapids, MI.: Zondervan publications, 1958, p. 8.

[222] Farrar, p. 23.

this method to all areas of Scripture according to their own whims and fancies. In response to this notion the words of Tyndale, as quoted by Briggs, apply. (Briggs, by the way, is no advocate of the literal method of interpreting the Scripture.) He quotes Tyndale as saying:

> Neverthelater, the Scripture useth proverbs, similitudes, riddles, or allegories, as all other speeches do; but that which the proverb, similitude, riddle, or allegory signifieth, is over the literal sense, which thou must seek out diligently...[223]

ALLEGORIES, TYPES, SYMBOLS, AND PARABLES

As the previous quote of Tyndale makes clear, it would be a mistake to assume that the literal method of interpretation does not permit the legitimate use of types, figures, symbols,[224] and parables. This may seem to weaken the position of the literalists in the face of his opposer,[225] but it will be clearly seen in the following paragraphs that the attacks levied against the literalist by allegorists are baseless and warrant no fear or abandonment.

The student might be a bit surprised to find that literalists do not by any means deny the legitimate use of figurative language in Scripture (whether it be a single use, a dozen uses, or hundreds of uses). Pentecost states the position clearly and in no uncertain terms as follows: "Scriptures abounds in allegories, whether types, symbols, or parables. These are accepted and legitimate media of communication of thought."[226] This position, however, is in no way

---

[223] Briggs, Charles Augustus, *General Introduction to the Study of Holy Scripture,* pp. 456-57.

[224] "This is the type of philosophical idealism which is at the heart of the movement, rather than a correct application of biblical symbolism. As Johnson states, 'The concept of 'literal interpretation' affirms that the meaning of a symbol is determined by textual and contextual considerations. It may appear that such a method would exclude figures and symbols altogether,' but it does not." (Ice, Thomas D., "An Evaluation of Theonomic Neopostmillennialism," *Bibliotheca Sacra.* Dallas TX: Dallas Theological Seminary, 1996, c1955-1995.) Ice's reference is to Elliott E. Johnson, "Apocalyptic Genre in Literal Interpretation," in *Essays in Honor of J. Dwight Pentecost,* ed. Stanley D. Toussaint and Charles H. Dyer (Chicago: Moody Press, 1986), pp. 204–5. See the essay for specific examples.

[225] Cf. Oswald T. Allis, *Prophecy and the Church,* p. 21.

[226] Pentecost, p. 7. See also Terry, *Biblical Hermeneutics,* p. 243; R.B. Zuck's review of *Hermeneutics: Principles and Processes of Biblical Interpretation* by Henry A. Virkler. Grand Rapids: Baker Book House, 1981. 255 pp. *Bibliotheca*

to be taken as a blurring of the distinctions that exist between the *allegorical* and the *literal* methods of interpretation. As Rollin T. Chafer points out, "there is all the difference possible in interpreting a Scripture allegory, on the one hand, and the allegorizing of a plain Scripture on the other hand." [227]

Such responses do not seem to appease the allegorizers much; they continue to present the accusation that because the literalist interprets *types*, it must be concluded that by doing so he employs the *allegorical* method of interpretation. In the face of such accusations literalists such as Ryrie repeatedly respond: "Symbols, figures of speech and types are all interpreted plainly in this method and they are in no way contrary to literal interpretation." [228]

Harbin contributes the following to the debate:

> The point these writers make is that the interpretation of figurative speech requires something other than an explicit, straightforward, dictionary meaning of each word. A figure, in whatever sense, requires recognition of the fact that it is a figure, and that its interpretation transcends the explicit word value. This would seem to imply that the interpretation of figurative language is beyond the scope of the literal method of interpretation.
>
> Historically, however, scholars have allowed figures of speech as an integral part of the historical-grammatical, or literal, method. This is true, no matter which view one takes of the interpretation of prophecy... [229]

Pentecost explains:

> The efficacy of the type depends on the literal interpretation of the literal antecedent. In order to convey truth concerning the spiritual realm, with which realm we are not familiar, there must be instruction in a realm with which

---

Sacra. Dallas TX: Dallas Theological Seminary, 1996, c1955-1995; and R. B. Zuck's review of *The Interpretation of Prophecy* by Paul Lee Tan. Winona Lake, IN: BMH Books, 1974. 435 pp. *Bibliotheca Sacra.* Dallas TX: Dallas Theological Seminary, 1996, c1955-1995.

[227] Chafer, Rollin T., *The Science of Biblical Hermeneutics.* p. 80.

[228] Ryrie, Charles C., *Dispensationalism Today* (Chicago: Moody Press, 1965) p. 87.

[229] Harbin, Michael A., "The Hermeneutics of Covenant Theology," *Bibliotheca Sacra.* Dallas TX: Dallas Theological Seminary, 1996, c1955-1995.

we are familiar, so that, by a transference of what is literally true in the one realm, we may learn what is true in the other realm. There must be a literal parallelism between the type and the antitype for the type to be of any value. The individual who allegorizes a type will never arrive at a true interpretation. The only way to discern the meaning of the type is through a transference of literal ideas from the natural to the spiritual realm.... It is concluded, then, that the Scriptural use of types does not give sanction to the allegorical method of interpretation.[230]

LITERALISTS CONDONE THE USE OF FIGURATIVE/METAPHORICAL LANGUAGE

Literalists, then, far from denying the legitimate use of figurative language, fully condone its use. How can he not? ...the Bible often uses such language! John the Baptist, for example, referred to Jesus as *"the Lamb of God, which taketh away the sin of the world"* (Joh 1:29). The Psalmist writes: *"Keep me as the apple of the eye, hide me under the shadow of thy wings"* (Psa 17:8). The Psalmist again writes: *"He shall cover thee with his feathers, and under his wings shalt thou trust: his truth shall be thy shield and buckler"* (Psa 91:4). An enormous number of similar passages could be cited.

It is upon these types of verses that the allegorist relies for his arguments, since he is aware that figurative language in cases such as these is permitted by the literalist. He contends that the literalist must admit that he is, in essence, adopting the allegorical method of interpretation. He earnestly believes his argument is irrefutable. He believes that this forces the literalist to admit that his strict adherence to the *literal* method requires that he interpret such passages as though Jesus is a literal *lamb*; that God bears the form of some sort of *a feathered creature with wings* having an *apple* in His eye, etc.

Pentecost, again, well states the position: "figures of speech are used as means of revealing literal truth. What is literally true in one realm, with which we are familiar, is brought over, literally, into another realm, with which we may not be familiar, in order to teach us truths in that unfamiliar realm."[231]

---

[230] Pentecost, pp. 8-9.
[231] Pentecost, p. 12.

CLARIFYING THE TERMS

Clarifying certain terms used by each of the two camps is critical. It is in the area of terminology that the allegorist seriously misses the mark. He mistakenly sees as synonymous the terms *spiritualize* and *allegorize*. This leads him to the false conclusion that he is on the right track. In regard to this error Pentecost remarks as follows: "The fact that God is spiritual does not demand allegorical interpretation. One must distinguish between what is spiritual and what is spiritualized."[232]

Craven adds further clarity, and well points out that what is currently intended by the terms *literal* and *spiritual* (as in *spiritualize*) would be better conveyed by the terms *normal* and *mystical*. He sets the record straight in the following manner:

> Literal is not opposed to *spiritual* but to figurative; *spiritual* is an antithesis on the one hand to *material*, and on the other to *carnal* (in a bad sense). The *Literalist* (so called) is not one who denies that *figurative* language, that *symbols*, are used in prophecy, nor does he deny that great *spiritual* truths are set forth therein; his position is, simply, that the prophecies are to be *normally* interpreted (i.e., according to the received laws of language) as any other utterances are interpreted—that which is manifestly literal being regarded as literal, and that which is manifestly figuratively being so regarded. The position of the *Spiritualists* (so called) is not that which is properly indicated by the term. He is one who holds that whilst certain portions of the prophecies are to be *normally* interpreted, other portions are to be regarded as having a *mystical* (i.e. involving some secret meaning) sense. The terms properly expressive of the schools are *normal* and *mystical*.[233]

So it is contended that the terms *normal* and *mystical* would much better convey the ideas intended, since the terms *literal* and *spiritual* fail to adequately describe the true positions of each camp. These

---

[232] Pentecost, p. 14.

[233] Lange, John Peter, *Commentary on the Holy Scriptures: Revelation,* p. 98, as cited by Dwight J. Pentecost in *Things To Come.* (Grand Rapids, MI.: Zondervan publications) 1958, p. 13; and Roy L. Aldrich in "An Apologetic for Dispensationalism," *Bibliotheca Sacra.* Dallas TX: Dallas Theological Seminary, 1996, c1955-1995.

latter terms, however, continue to be commonly employed. It is therefore imperative that a clear distinction be made as to what is meant by them.

Perhaps the following illustration will help further clarify these distinctions. A person attending a baseball game later describes his experience as follows: "The game was a real war! The very first batter knocked the cover off the ball. When the double-play was called in the fourth inning, the coach blew his stack and really began to chew on the players. A few others became hotter than firecrackers. It was a nightmare! The crowd raised the roof as these gladiators spilled their blood and guts on the field. The losers went home with their tails tucked between their legs." The literalists would interpret this explanation, though replete with colorful and assorted *figurative* language, to indeed be signifying a *real* ball game. What the allegorists do, on the other hand, is somewhat akin to claiming that no ballgame actually occurred at all, but that some sort of a cosmic spiritual battle in the heavens is being *allegorically* referenced.

In light of these arguments, one should clearly be able to see the difference between *literal* (normal) and *spiritual* (mystical). There is a huge difference in taking the *literal* signification of a text, even when figurative language is employed, as opposed to reading into the text some *hidden* or *mystical* meaning. Pentecost, along with a number of other literalists,[234] draws the following clear conclusion:

> It will thus be observed that the literalist does not deny the existence of figurative language. The literalist does, however, deny that such figures must be interpreted so as to destroy the literal truth intended through the employment of the figures.[235]

---

[234] For example, Enns writes: "Although the term *literal* may raise questions in some quarters, it should be understood as the normal, customary approach to any literature—the way all language is commonly understood. *Literal*, when describing hermeneutical approach, refers to interpretive method, *not* to the kind of language used in the interpreted literature. Literal *interpretation* recognizes both literal and figurative language." (Enns, P. P., *The Moody Handbook of Theology*. Chicago, Ill.: Moody Press, 1997, c1989). And Ramesh writes: "However, what is *not* meant by literal interpretation is the attempt to circumvent the plain teaching of Scripture." (Richard, Ramesh P., "Methodological Proposals for Scripture Relevance—Part I: Selected Issues in Theoretical Hermeneutics," *Bibliotheca Sacra*. Dallas TX: Dallas Theological Seminary, 1996, c1955-1995). Etc.

[235] Pentecost, p. 13.

Chapter Fourteen
—Rules and Reasons

According to John Bright, "If the Bible is to be normative in matters of faith and practice, it must be the Bible rightly interpreted."[236] But having the correct method of interpretation does not necessarily insure that proper interpretation will follow; Pentecost verifies this fact by referring the reader to the errors of Rabbinism.[237] Since the literal method allows for legitimate use of figurative and symbolic expressions of speech, the reader may find it difficult to detect where to draw the lines. It will therefore be prudent to establish and adopt certain sound and proven **rules** when it comes to interpreting the Scriptures. In the latter portion of the chapter, **reasons for rejecting** the allegorical method of interpretation and **reasons for accepting** the literal method of interpretation are considered.

RULES OF INTERPRETATION

The following Ten Basic Laws have been compiled and adopted by a number of current and/or recent authors[238] as the general rules for understanding and interpreting the Bible:

1. **The Law of Actual Meaning.**

   When the plain sense of Scripture makes common sense, seek no other sense; therefore take every word at its primary, ordinary, literal meaning, unless the immediate context, studied in the light of axiomatic and fundamental truths, indicates a figurative or symbolic meaning.

---

[236] Bright, John, *The Authority of the Old Testament* (Nashville: Abingdon Press, 1967), p. 41, as cited by Ramesh P. Richard, in "Methodological Proposals for Scripture Relevance—Part I: Selected Issues in Theoretical Hermeneutics," *Bibliotheca Sacra.* Dallas TX: Dallas Theological Seminary, 1996, c1955-1995.

[237] Pentecost, J. Dwight, *Things To Come* (Grand Rapids, MI.: Zondervan Publications, 1958) p. 34.

[238] See Combs, Jim, *What on Earth is a Dispensation?* (Springfield, MO.: Tribune Publishers) 1994, pp. 37-38; also see Wallace, Roy, *Studies in Systematic Theology*, (Shreveport, La.: LinWel, 2001) pp. 62-64. Wallace states that this list was compiled by James O. Combs and sent to the subscribers of the *Baptist Bible Tribune*. Combs gives credit as follows: "These concepts have been drawn from the writings of David L. Cooper, Arthur T. Pierson, James R. Graves and many others, who approach the Bible logically, literally and intelligently to see what it specifically says and what it stresses and how it applies truth to the human need."

Corollary: The Bible means what it says and says what it means. It is to be understood literally except when obvious figures of speech (metaphors, similes, etc.) or indicated (in Scripture) types are used.

Corollary: This does not preclude careful study of original language Greek or Hebrew words for clarity of meaning.

2. **The Law of Contextual Meaning.**

Every Scripture must be interpreted in its historical setting and in its grammatical context with attention to who is speaking, to whom the message is given, and under what conditions.

Corollary: Every verse should be considered in the context of its paragraph (pericope) and in the section or chapter where it appears, within the book or in the division of Scripture where it is recorded.

3. **The Law of First Mention.**

We may expect the first mention of a subject or truth to forecast its treatment throughout the Scriptures.

4. **The Law of Full Mention.**

We may expect a rather full and complete treatment of every subject vitally connected with basic doctrine and consecrated living in a major passage or section of Scripture: in some place in the Word, God reveals His full mind on any one subject. [That is to say, as much as He intends to reveal to man—cf. Deu 29:29, etc.]

5. **The Law of Progressive Mention.**

From the first mention of a subject to the last mention there is a progress of doctrine; yet the first and last mention indicate what is between, and the intermediate matter is found to be fitly joined together.

6. **The Law of Comparative Mention.**

To compare Scripture with Scripture is vital to understanding everything about a given truth; all occasions in Scripture where a subject is mentioned should be considered to arrive at the total truth.

7. **The Law of Illustration.**

For most truths God gives one classic illustration to carry the truth home to the heart and mind of the believer.

8. **The Law of Double Reference.**

The Law of Double Reference is the principle of associating similar ideas which are usually separated from one another by long periods of time, but may be blended into a single picture initially (the sufferings of Christ and the glory that should follow), and in which historical past event may illustrate a future prophetic event.

9. **The Law of Spiritual Application.**

Since the timeless Word of God is filled with truth, principles and ideas that were originally relevant to other ages and dispensations may be applied to people today, since "whatsoever was written aforetime was written for our learning that we through patience and comfort of the Scriptures might have hope."

10. **The Law of the Master Key.**

Christ Himself is the Master Key to understanding Scripture, for He is the Supreme subject in fact, symbol, history and prophecy for all the Word of God; therefore expect to find Him in all Scripture.

As a further guide in the employment of the literal method of interpretation, presented below are additional rules[239] for interpreting the Scriptures. Many of these rules may also be found to be valuable guides in the common approach towards the proper interpretation of all literature.

1. Words ought to generally be understood in their usual sense and meaning.

2. The meaning of words is to be determined by the typical linguistic usage, at the time they were written, in the original language. It must be kept in mind that the meaning of some words changes over time.

---

[239] These demands on the exegete are modified excerpts from many of the authors herein quoted, combined with the author's own interpolation. The reader is referred again to the first 64 pages of *Things To Come* by Dwight J. Pentecost, particularly to chapter III, "General Considerations in Interpretation" pp. 34-44.

3. The context is absolutely critical in understanding any given text.

4. The significations of words that have two or more meanings are to be determined by their context.

5. The author's character, parentage, culture,[240] frame of mind, place in time, circumstances under which the book was composed, sentiments, temperament, purpose, etc. must be carefully considered.[241]

6. The original intended reader must be considered.

7. Geographical considerations often assist the exegete.

8. The reader must take from the text what is actually there, being careful not to read into the text notions, ideas, etc. prompted by his own presuppositions or tainted by his own biases, wishes, emotions, circumstances, etc.

9. A transition to a new thought or idea should not be made, except that the language, context, or remaining consistent with the overall clear teaching of Biblical doctrine warrants such a transition; otherwise the reader must remain with the obvious intentions of the writer, as it relates to the context.

10. No parenthesis should be interposed without sufficient reason.

11. A text must be considered against its proper historical background: customs, morals, religion(s), etc.

12. Although there may be a number of applications of any given segment of Scripture, there is only *one* correct interpretation.

---

[240] "Both Testaments need to be studied in their own contexts first—cultural, social, theological, and historical." (Richard, Ramesh P., "Methodological Proposals for Scripture Relevance—Part I: Selected Issues in Theoretical Hermeneutics," *Bibliotheca Sacra*. Dallas TX: Dallas Theological Seminary, 1996, c1955-1995.)

[241] "That the Bible is a human book argues for literal or normal interpretation that seeks to bridge the gaps of culture, grammar, and literature. The divine nature of the Bible demands the recognition of the inerrancy, authority, unity, and mystery of the Bible. ("Mystery" is a term used for miracles, prophecy, and doctrine.) *Interpretation* is seen as the essential and determinative step between observation and application." (Bailey, Mark L. Rev. of *Basic Bible Interpretation* by Roy B. Zuck. Wheaton, IL: Victor Books, 1991. 324 pp. *Bibliotheca Sacra*. Dallas TX: Dallas Theological Seminary, 1996, c1955-1995.)

13. Scripture does not contradict itself. Any interpretation that is not consistent with the overall teaching of Scripture is obviously being interpreted improperly.

14. Scripture is its own best commentary. All interpretations are to be balanced by an exhaustive, concordance type study of the doctrine being developed.

Adherence to the above listed rules, as the Holy Spirit guides the believer into a study of God's Word, will result in productive Biblical studies and lead to proper interpretation.

~ ~ ~

In addition to rules, *reasons* are also important to consider. Listed below are a number of *reasons* why the student should utterly reject the allegorical method of interpretation, and why the literal method should be adopted as the method of choice.

REASONS NOT TO ADOPT THE ALLEGORICAL METHOD

1. "The allegorical method, which depends on the rationalistic approach of the interpreter, or conformity to a predetermined theological system, leaves one without a basic authoritative test."[242]

2. The allegorical method requires dependency upon intellectual training or abilities, or mystical perception, rather than understanding what is written in its generally accepted sense.[243]

3. Not only does this method result in divisions between those who adopt this method of interpretation and those adhering to the literal method of interpretation, but it also insures division within its own camp (since everyone must derive their own conclusions according to their own imagination, after the secondary or spiritualized sense).

4. The method gives rise to uncontrolled and limitless fanciful speculations according to the interpreter's imagination.

5. This method fails to draw out from the author's language his original intent and meaning.

---

[242] Pentecost, p. 12.
[243] Cf. Pentecost, p. 12.

6. The interpreter's presuppositions[244] are bound to come into play; these are limitless. The Scriptures become reduced to what seems reasonable to the interpreter.

7. This method provides a means whereby the reader can escape theological difficulties or add credence to certain peculiar religious views.

8. This method empties words of their plain and obvious meaning.

9. This method perverts Scripture under the guise of seeking a deeper or more spiritual meaning.

10. This method transfers basic authority from the Scripture to the mind of the interpreter.

11. This method makes true interpretation of Scripture impossible.

12. The rise of allegorism is the result of the philosophies of Aristobulus, Philo, Augustine, and Origen (the method is not found prior to their existence); thereby, its negative effect can be clearly traced in the history of the church by simply observing the fruits of their influences (see next point).

13. This method was the interpretation method that led to the Dark Ages.

---

[244] It is incumbent upon the reader to discern the problems that presumptions, presuppositions and preunderstandings might present in the proper understanding of Scripture; these issues can be both subtle and very serious. It is helpful to realize this ahead of time, and be prepared to deal with them appropriately. Concerning this, Blaising writes the following, "Turner, focusing attention on the problem of the exegetical-theological-hermeneutical-cultural preunderstandings, points out that differences are often a case of 'conflicting preunderstandings.'" (Blaising, Craig A., "Development of Dispensationalism by Contemporary Dispensationalists," *Bibliotheca Sacra.* Dallas TX: Dallas Theological Seminary, 1996, c1955-1995. Cf. also David Turner, "The Continuity of Scripture and Eschatology: Key Hermeneutical Issues," *Grace Theological Journal* 6 [Fall 1985]: 275–87.) Zuck, in his review of *The Psychology of Biblical Interpretation* by Cedric B. Johnson points out how these problems can become associated with a number of other problems, such as subjective biases, social pressures, insecurities, etc. He writes: "Of course, understanding why a person approaches the Bible with certain presuppositions and other elements of subjectivity is beneficial. This helps explain why some differing viewpoints exist." (Zuck, R. B. Rev. of *The Psychology of Biblical Interpretation,* by Cedric B. Johnson. Grand Rapids: Zondervan Publishing House, 1983. 119 pp. *Bibliotheca Sacra.* Dallas TX: Dallas Theological Seminary, 1996, c1955-1995.)

14. This method causes believers to be certain of nothing, which opens the door for them to become forced to have dictated to them by the church what the Scriptures say.

REASONS TO ADOPT THE LITERAL METHOD

1. "The fact that the Scriptures continually point to literal interpretations of what was formerly written adds evidence as to the method to be employed in interpreting the Word... When the Old Testament is used in the New it is used only in a literal sense."[245]

2. "It gives us a basic authority by which interpretations may be tested."[246]

3. This method interprets Scripture in a normal, usual, customary designation.

4. Literalism was the method of interpretation of Rabbinism at the time of Christ's first coming, and He issued no correction against it.

5. Literalism was the undisputed method of the Apostles.

6. Jesus took the Old Testament literally.

7. This method led to and was the interpretation method of the Reformers.

8. "One need only study the prophecies which were fulfilled in the first coming of Christ, in His life, His ministry, and His death, to establish the fact. No prophecy which has been completely fulfilled has been fulfilled any way but literally."[247]

~ ~ ~

---

[245] Pentecost, p. 10.
[246] Pentecost, pp. 11-12.
[247] Pentecost, pp. 10-11. Cf. also Charles L. Feinberg, *Premillennialism or Amillennialism,* p. 39.

Dispensationalists consistently adopt the *literal* method of interpreting the Scriptures. This fact is briefly expounded upon in the upcoming chapter.

CHAPTER FIFTEEN

—DISPENSATIONALISM ADOPTS A CONSISTENT LITERAL METHOD OF INTERPRETATION

When one attempts to identify, define, or describe dispensationalism, it is imperative that it be discussed in connection with the literal, historical-grammatical method of interpretation—a method of interpretation absolutely fundamental to dispensationalism. Ramm and Virkler describe this relationship in the following manner:

> Dispensationalism is an effort to interpret Scripture on the basis of the distinctives of God's demands for and relationships with mankind. This pertains to man's stewardship toward God. A basic corollary of this is the assumption of the same literal, historical grammatical method of interpretation followed by many other schools of thought in evangelical Christianity.[248]

Radmacher (also singling out this second point of Ryrie's *sine qua non*) likewise identifies hermeneutics as *the primary* aspect by which dispensationalism is defined. He writes as follows:

> It is so utterly fundamental to understand that the foundational premise of dispensationalism is not theological but hermeneutical.[249]

Walvoord states the link as follows:

> Dispensationalism... is not a premise seized on arbitrarily but a result of the application of literal interpretation of Scripture which all conservatives recognize is the norm for interpreting the Bible.[250]

---

[248] Ramm, *Protestant Biblical Interpretation*, pp. 53, 126; Milton Terry, *Biblical Hermeneutics* (Grand Rapids: Zondervan Publishing House, 1974), p. 173; and Henry A. Virkler, *Hermeneutics: Principles and Processes of Biblical Interpretation* (Grand Rapids: Baker Book House, 1981), p. 73. Cf. Harbin, Michael A., "The Hermeneutics of Covenant Theology," *Bibliotheca Sacra.* Dallas TX: Dallas Theological Seminary, 1996, c1955-1995.

[249] Radmacher, Earl D., "The Current Status of Dispensationalism and Its Eschatology," in *Perspectives on Evangelical Theology,* p. 166.

[250] Walvoord, John F., "Posttribulationism Today—Part IV: Futurist Posttribulational Interpretation," *Bibliotheca Sacra.* Dallas TX: Dallas Theological Seminary, 1996, c1955-1995.

It is far from sufficient, however, to merely state that the dispensational system is founded upon "the *literal* method" of interpretation; as Blaising points out: "literalism is not sufficient by itself to describe the dispensational hermeneutic."[251] The reader is again reminded of the fact that Rabbinism, in spite of their adoption of a strict literal method of interpretation, nevertheless erred. (It may be well to point out here, that not all who have adopted the literal method of interpretation are dispensationalists, but all who are dispensationalists have adopted the literal method of interpretation.) A key word to note in this second of Ryrie's three essentials is the word *"consistent."* It is critical to make the point clear early-on: dispensationalism is a system of belief founded upon a *"consistent"* literal hermeneutic.

Elsewhere Ryrie states:

> **Consistently** literal or plain interpretation is indicative of a dispensational approach to the interpretation of the Scriptures.[252] (Emphasis added.)

Blaising observes:

> For Ryrie... the issue is not simply literal hermeneutics but the *consistent* practice of the same.[253]

This constitutes a fact which simply cannot be overstated: the most fundamental principle of the dispensational system is the adoption of a **consistent** literal method of interpreting the Scriptures. The reader will see that *consistent literalism*, coupled with logically applied rules and guidelines, such as those previously listed, make up the foundational principles of the theological system of dispensationalism. Upon such foundational principles the other tenets of dispensationalism rest. Again, *consistent literalism* is **the** primary element that sets dispensationalism apart from other theological

---

[251] Blaising, Craig A., Ibach, Robert D., Jr., Ed. Rev. of "Revelation and the Hermeneutics of Dispensationalism," by William H. Shepherd, Jr., *Anglican Theological Review* 71 (1989): 281–99. *Bibliotheca Sacra.* Dallas TX: Dallas Theological Seminary, 1996, c1955-1995.

[252] Ryrie, Charles C., *Dispensationalism Today* (Chicago: Moody Press, 1965), p. 46.

[253] Blaising, Craig A., "Development of Dispensationalism by Contemporary Dispensationalists," *Bibliotheca Sacra*, 1996, c1955-1995. Dallas TX: Dallas Theological Seminary.

systems that have failed to adopt such a sound system of Biblical interpretation.

Enns writes of this primary principle as he compares dispensationalism to covenant theology:

> Hermeneutically, dispensationalism follows a *consistently* literal approach to Scripture. Other systems like covenant theology freely admit to fundamental hermeneutical changes within their interpretations of the Bible.[254]

Ryrie, contrasting the *literal* method with the *allegorical* method, emphasizes that the *consistent* literal method "will of necessity," and exclusively, make one a dispensationalist.

> It is not within the scope of this article to rediscuss the entire matter of allegorical and literal interpretation. It must suffice to show that only dispensationalism consistently employs the principles of literal interpretation... If literal interpretation is the only valid hermeneutical principle and if it is consistently applied it will cause one to be a dispensationalist. As basic as one believes literal interpretation to be, to that extent he will of necessity become a dispensationalist.
>
> ...
>
> Only dispensationalism provides the key to consistent literalism, and properly defined it becomes the only valid system of Biblical interpretation.[255]

---

[254] Enns, P. P., *The Moody Handbook of Theology*. Chicago, Ill.: Moody Press, 1997, c1989.

[255] Ryrie, Charles C., "The Necessity of Dispensationalism," *Bibliotheca Sacra*. Dallas TX: Dallas Theological Seminary, 1996, c1955-1995.

CHAPTER SIXTEEN

—THE EFFECTS INTERPRETATION
METHODS HAVE ON HOW ISRAEL AND
THE CHURCH ARE PERCEIVED

Another critically important matter which must be considered is the *effect* the literal method of interpretation (as only dispensationalists *consistently* apply it) has on one's understanding of what the Scriptures teach concerning Israel and the Church. Blaising, referring to the second point of Ryrie's *sine qua non*, the literal method of interpretation, notes that: "The distinction of Israel and the church grows out of this [second point]."[256]

Walvoord likewise relates the first and second points of Ryrie's *sine qua non*, pointing out that the position dispensationalists hold concerning Israel (as distinguished from the Church) results directly from their employment of *consistent literalism*:

> The first tenet of dispensationalism is to interpret the Bible literally, especially as this refers to the nation Israel. Only recently have those who are not adherents to dispensationalism given adequate attention to this distinctive aspect of dispensationalism which is brought out clearly in Charles C. Ryrie's *Dispensationalism Today* (Chicago: Moody Press, 1965).[257]

Again, it is not the author's intention to describe and/or analyze in any *detail* the Biblically supportable distinctions that exist between Israel and the Church; rather to briefly observe the effect that the literal method of interpretation brings to the fore.

---

[256] Blaising, Craig A., "Development of Dispensationalism by Contemporary Dispensationalists," *Bibliotheca Sacra.* 1996, c1955-1995. Dallas TX: Dallas Theological Seminary. See also Russell H. Bowers, Jr., "Dispensational Motifs in the Writings of Erich Sauer," *Bibliotheca Sacra*, Dallas TX: Dallas Theological Seminary, 1996, c1955-1995.

[257] Walvoord, John F. Rev. of *Contemporary Options in Eschatology: A Study of the Millennium,* by Millard J. Erickson. Grand Rapids: Baker Book House, 1977. 197 pp. *Bibliotheca Sacra.* Dallas TX: Dallas Theological Seminary, 1996, c1955-1995.

P. P. Enns writes of how a "consistent literal [method of] interpretation" comes critically to bear on this distinction:

> Dispensationalists attempt to be consistent in literal interpretation; therefore, the Old Testament prophecies concerning Israel are taken seriously. Furthermore, those prophecies pertain to Israel, the descendants of Jacob, not the church. The unconditional covenants of the Old Testament were given to Israel: the Abrahamic Covenant (Gen. 12:1–3) promised Israel a land, a posterity, and blessing; the Palestinian Covenant (Deut. 30:1–10) promised Israel would return to the land; the Davidic Covenant (2 Sam. 7:12–16) promised Israel that Messiah would come from Judah and have a throne and a kingdom, ruling over Israel; the New Covenant (Jer. 31:31–34) promised Israel the spiritual means whereby the nation would enter into blessing and receive forgiveness.
>
> If these covenants are understood literally and unconditionally, then Israel has a future that is distinct from the church. On this basis dispensationalists subscribe to a literal millennium for Israel, which Messiah will establish at His Second Advent (Rev. 19:11–19). But before Israel will enter into blessing the nation must repent and recognize Jesus as the Messiah; a major purpose of the Tribulation is to discipline Israel to bring the nation to faith in Messiah (Jer. 30:7; Ezek. 20:37–38; Dan. 9:24). The Tribulation, thus, will have no reference point for the church, which will be raptured prior to the Tribulation (Rom. 5:9; 1 Thess. 5:9; Rev. 3:10). The *purpose* of the Tribulation pertains to Israel, not the church. This is a major reason why dispensationalists hold to a pretribulation rapture.[258]

Saucy, a *progressive* dispensationalist, also notes that the distinction between Israel and the Church, as recognized by dispensationalists, is a direct result of their refusal to forsake the literal method of interpretation:

> There are types and shadows of realities which later Scriptures reveal as outmoded, but it is the position of

---

[258] Enns, P. P., *The Moody Handbook of Theology*. Chicago, Ill.: Moody Press, 1997, c1989.

dispensationalism that the New Testament does not *reinterpret* the meaning of the nation of Israel as much of church interpretation has done throughout its history.[259]

Concerning this distinction, Lightner, in his review of Fruchtenbaum, exhibits his clear position on the matter:

> Fruchtenbaum… insists that a person is not a dispensationalist unless he keeps distinct God's program with Israel and His program with the church (p. 324). He believes this distinction, based on a literal or normal interpretation of Scripture, is the essence of dispensationalism.[260]

Lightner, reviewing Crutchfield, writes:

> Darby did stress a literal hermeneutic which led to a clear and continued distinction between God's program with Israel and His program with the church.[261]

Lightner, in the first of three excellent articles entitled "Theological Perspectives on Theonomy Part I: Theonomy and Dispensationalism," writes the following:

> Friends and foes of dispensationalism must agree that the all-determinative conviction without which one cannot be a dispensationalist is the distinction between God's program for Israel and His program for the church. This distinction is based solidly on the literal (or as many dispensationalists prefer to call it, the normal) interpretation of Scripture. A consistently literal or normal hermeneutic brings one to see distinctions in God's program with Israel and His program with the church…[262]

---

[259] Saucy, "Contemporary Dispensationalist Thought," p. 11 (italics added).

[260] Lightner, Robert P. Rev. of *Israelology: The Missing Link in Systematic Theology,* by Arnold G. Fruchtenbaum. Tustin, CA.: Ariel Ministries Press, 1989. *Bibliotheca Sacra.* Dallas TX: Dallas Theological Seminary, 1996, c1955-1995 (Jan 1994A).

[261] Lightner, Robert P. Rev. of *The Origins of Dispensationalism,* by Larry Crutchfield. Lanham, MD: University Press of America, 1992. 236 pp. (cf. p.206). *Bibliotheca Sacra.* Dallas TX: Dallas Theological Seminary, 1996, c1955-1995 (Oct 1992A).

[262] Lightner, Robert P., "Theological Perspectives on Theonomy Part I: Theonomy and Dispensationalism," *Bibliotheca Sacra.* Dallas TX: Dallas Theological Seminary, 1996, c1955-1995. Lightner refers the reader to Ryrie, *Dispensationalism Today*, pp. 43–47.

In a subsequent article, Lightner presents as a strong supporting point the fact that: "the law of Moses [was] given to Israel, not to the Church." Note again that this distinction is directly attributable to "interpreting the Bible literally." He writes as follows:

> The fact that God gave the Law to the people of Israel and not to the church is the beginning point for dispensationalism's difference with theonomy. All other points of disagreement stem from this one. In fact the same difference exists between dispensationalism and Reformed theology. Based on dispensationalism's insistence on interpreting the Bible literally (i.e., according to the received laws of language), it holds that God's program for and with Israel is distinct from His program for and with the church.[30] This is not to say that there are not points of similarity and concurrence between the two programs. But Reformed theology and theonomy in particular do not distinguish between the two programs. All the redeemed of all ages are viewed as the covenanted community. On the basis of this assumption, the fact that the Law was given to Israel is not determinative for theonomists, whereas for dispensationalists it is highly significant.[263]

(Note: This "highly significant" issue of "the Law," when contrasting dispensationalists with "Reformed theology and theonomy in particular," will be taken up and considered again in the last section of this book.)

George Dollar, referring to a work by F. L. Chapell entitled *Biblical and Practical Theology*, also points out that this is a key element that distinguishes dispensationalism from "the Reformed line of thought." Note again that "literal" is contrasted to "spiritualizing

---

30 30. "The *Literalist* (so-called) is not one who denies that *figurative* language, that *symbols*, are used in prophecy, nor does he deny that great *spiritual* truths are set forth therein: his position is, simply, that the prophecies are to be *normally* interpreted (i.e. according to the received laws of language) as any other utterances are interpreted—that which is manifestly literal being regarded as literal, that which is manifestly figurative being so regarded" (John Peter Lange, *The Revelation of John*, A Commentary on the Holy Scriptures [New York: Charles Scribner, 1872], p. 98).

[263] Lightner, Robert P., "Theological Perspectives on Theonomy Part III: A Dispensational Response to Theonomy," *Bibliotheca Sacra*. Dallas TX: Dallas Theological Seminary, 1996, c1955-1995.

and allegorizing"—the method of interpretation which these other theological systems out of necessity are forced to adopt:

> In this respect, as in many, Chapell does not follow the Reformed line of thought of Christ's rule over the church now. In fact, he held that "the kingship of Christ has been greatly neglected, confused, and obscured in the past and needs in our day an earnest, honest, and careful recognition" [p. 83]. He saw it was more literal than it had been taught, in stark contrast to the spiritualizing and allegorizing of most of the theologians and Bible teachers. The most serious aspect in this confusion was the failure to pinpoint the return of the Jews to their land and the establishment of their city as the religious capital on earth (Isa. 66:22–23; Zech. 14:16; Matt. 5:35).[264]

Walvoord also notes the same distinction in regard to interpretation:

> Among these problems, one of the definitive questions is whether the New Testament church fulfills Israel's prophetic programs. Here, among conservative interpreters at least, are two distinct schools of thought: (a) the teaching that Israel has a special program of God, beginning with Abraham and continuing on into eternity to come, and (b) the teaching that the programs of God for Israel and the church are essentially one and consist in the fact that both are the recipients of God's salvation.
>
> . . .
>
> Ladd is correct that the issue in interpretation is whether Israel has a special program as contrasted to the program of God for the church, but the contrast is misstated as a contrast for or against progressive revelation. Dispensationalists all recognize that there is the element of progressive revelation throughout Scripture, and in fact this is inherent in and emphasized by dispensational interpretation. The difference between the dispensational interpretation and the nondispensational interpretation is not an affirmation or denial

---

[264] Dollar, George W., "Early American Dispensationalist:—The Reverend F. L. Chapell," *Bibliotheca Sacra*. Dallas TX: Dallas Theological Seminary, 1996, c1955-1995.

of progressive revelation, but rather is the contrast between literal versus nonliteral interpretation. It seems quite clear to most observers of the history of doctrine that prior to the writings of the New Testament, prophets as well as ordinary people in the Old Testament understood that God had a special program for Israel, and that this had its consummation in the coming of their Messiah and in their repossession of the promised land. The golden age predicted in the Old Testament for Israel anticipated a literal fulfillment.

...

The difference in interpretation originates when amillenarians and some premillenarians interpret the New Testament as contradicting or amending this concept to the extent of substituting a nonliteral fulfillment of these hopes voiced in the Old Testament. The issue accordingly is not progressive revelation versus nonprogressive revelation, but rather whether in progressive revelation there is contradiction or correction of what was commonly assumed to be the main tenor of Old Testament revelation. Accordingly the issue is whether the Old Testament teaches a literal fulfillment of specific promises for Israel and whether the New Testament contradicts or supports literal interpretation. Here is the major issue between amillennialism and premillennialism, and also the issue between dispensational premillennialism and nondispensational premillennialism as these terms are commonly used today.

...

Accordingly the principle of literal interpretation is supported, but proper distinctions do not blur the clear lines of demarcation among (a) the nation as a whole, (b) spiritual Israel or believing Israelites, and (c) the church composed of Jews and Gentiles.

...

As will be seen in the study of the promises concerning the land beginning in Genesis 12:7, it is demonstrable that these promises are to be interpreted literally to the physical descendants of Abraham and are never transferred to Gentiles. The same is true for other promises that relate to the nation of Israel as a whole, and the promises in regard to the Davidic kingdom again concern the physical descendants of Abraham, excluding Gentiles....

...

It is most significant that some amillenarians and postmillenarians concede that the word *Israel* normally means Israel.[11] [265]

Enns also directly links Ladd's faulty conclusions, as Walvoord points out above, to his departure from the consistent literal method of interpretation:

The hermeneutical system of historic premillennialism distinguishes it from dispensational premillennialism. In historic premillennialism a distinction between Israel and the church is not maintained nor is a consistently literal interpretive method demanded.[56] Ladd suggests that in its setting, Isaiah 53 is not a prophecy of Messiah yet is seen as such in the New Testament, therefore, the "literal hermeneutic does not work."[57] Furthermore [according to Ladd], "the New Testament applies Old Testament prophecies to the New Testament church and in so doing identifies the church as spiritual Israel."[58] An example of this is Romans 9:25–26, which cites Hosea 1:9,10; 2:23. In the Old Testament citation it refers to Israel, whereas in the New Testament citation it has reference to the church. Other examples of this "spiritualizing hermeneutic" are Romans 2:28–29; 4:11, 16 and Galatians 3:7, 29. The application of the New Covenant of Jeremiah 31:33–34 to the church in Hebrews 8 is a further example. Ladd concludes that "Paul sees the church as spiritual Israel."[59] [266]

---

11 11. Charles Hodge, *Commentary on the Epistle to the Romans* (Philadelphia: H. B. Garner, 1883), pp. 462–602.

[265] Walvoord, John F., "Does the Church Fulfill Israel's Program? - Part 1," *Bibliotheca Sacra.* Dallas TX: Dallas Theological Seminary, 1996, c1955-1995.

56 56. George E. Ladd, "Historic Premillennialism," in *The Meaning of the Millennium*, pp. 19–27.

57 57. Ibid, p. 23.

58 58. Ibid

59 59. Ibid., p. 25.

[266] Enns, P. P., *The Moody Handbook of Theology.* Chicago, Ill.: Moody Press, 1997, c1989.

Walvoord clarifies:

> A literal interpretation of passages dealing with the church and passages dealing with Israel indicate a distinct program, even though there are some similarities...
>
> ...
>
> While it has not been possible to deal with all of Ladd's arguments in support of his conclusions, it is a fair judgment to say that his opposition to dispensationalism is a major cause for his posttribulational view, and that this is normally the case for most posttribulationists. If his premise is correct—that dispensationalism which distinguishes Israel and the church is not a biblical method of interpretation—then Ladd may also be correct in arriving at his posttribulational conclusion. Pretribulationism, however, is clearly based on literal interpretation, which holds that God's program for Israel and His program for the church are not identical.[267]

~ ~ ~

At this point the reader should be able to clearly distinguish that if the Bible is *consistently* interpreted literally, a distinction between Israel and the Church will be clearly seen. In order for an interpreter to arrive at any other conclusion, the *consistent* literal method of interpreting the Bible must be abandoned.

---

[267] Walvoord, John F., "Posttribulationism Today—Part IV: Futurist Posttribulational Interpretation," *Bibliotheca Sacra*. Dallas TX: Dallas Theological Seminary, 1996, c1955-1995.

CHAPTER SEVENTEEN

—INTERPRETATION METHODS AND THE PRIMARY PURPOSE OF GOD IN SCRIPTURE

Another matter of controversy that arises between dispensationalists and non-dispensationalists has to do with Ryrie's third essential element—a basic and primary conception of the purpose of God as His own glory rather than the salvation of mankind. In this chapter, a brief examination of this point is undertaken from a dispensational standpoint, again narrowing the focus to how one's applied method of interpretation comes to bear on this issue.

Russell Bowers, in an article entitled "Dispensational Motifs in the Writings of Erich Sauer," points out that this issue (interpretation method) becomes a distinguishing factor (as it does on the dispensational position concerning Israel and the Church) between dispensationalism and covenant theology.

> Ryrie's third element in his *sine qua non* is the doxological goal of God's workings in history. Sauer affirms this focus. "Everything that God does has Himself eternally as its goal; it comes to pass 'for *his* name's sake' (Psa. 23:3), for *Himself* throughout (Eph. 5:27), 'to the praise of *his* glory' (Eph. 1:6, 12, 14), so that '*God* may be all in all' (1 Cor. 15:28)."[35] But his characterization of Scripture as "the record of salvation"[36] and his repeated references to the history of salvation make it clear that, in his thinking, the provision of salvation for humankind is one of the chief ways by which that glory is revealed. Here again is a rapprochement between what Ryrie held to be distinctive dispensational and covenantal themes.[268]

Here is seen another of the primary divisions between covenant theology and dispensationalism, namely, what God's primary purpose in Scripture is: to the dispensationalist it is "the glory of God"; to the covenant theologian it is "man's salvation." The roots of these

---

35 35. Sauer, *The Dawn of World Redemption,* p. 23.
36 36. Ibid., p. 34.
[268] Bowers, Russell H., Jr., "Dispensational Motifs in the Writings of Erich Sauer," *Bibliotheca Sacra.* Dallas TX: Dallas Theological Seminary, 1996, c1955-1995.

differences are again traceable to the different methods of interpretation adopted by each of these two groups.

It is interesting to note, as Michael Harbin records of Rogers-McKim below, that Calvin saw the matter differently than Ryrie:

> Calvin said the revelation of Christ for man's salvation is the purpose of Scripture. "Calvin cautioned that we must not interpret Scripture as having any other purpose than of revealing Christ for our Salvation."[29] [269]

Harbin, in an article entitled "The Hermeneutics of Covenant Theology," settles on "the glory of God" as the more plausible position after first discussing these two primary possibilities of God's purposes in Scripture in the context of "a broad spectrum of [other] suggestions":

> Milton saw charity as "the end of all Scripture." On this basis, he built "an extraordinarily flexible hermeneutical principle."[32]

> Luther said that Christ as Judge and Savior was his criterion for interpretation.[33] Berkhof suggested that a possible foundation for interpretation is Matthew 21:43,[34] in which Jesus stated that the kingdom of God would be given to a "nation producing the fruit of it." This is the principle, he said, that the church has replaced the nation of Israel in God's program.

> Van der Waal cites both the covenants and the confessions of the Reformation. To him these two seem to be synonymous or at least closely related.[35] MacKay suggested that dispensationalism "proposes the glory of God as the all-inclusive principle for the divine activities."[36]

This is a broad spectrum of suggestions. Two major purposes of Scripture held today are "salvation by Christ" and

---

29 29. Rogers and McKim, *The Authority and Interpretation of the Bible*, p. 107.
[269] Harbin, Michael A., "The Hermeneutics of Covenant Theology," *Bibliotheca Sacra.* Dallas TX: Dallas Theological Seminary, 1996, c1955-1995.
32 32. John R. Knott, *The Sword of the Spirit: Puritan Responses to the Bible* (Chicago: University of Chicago, 1980), pp. 115–16.
33 33. Rogers and McKim, *The Authority and Interpretation of the Bible*, p. 85.
34 34. Berkhof, *Systematic Theology*, p. 699.
35 35. Van der Waal, *Hal Lindsey and Biblical Prophecy*, pp. 51, 68.
36 36. MacKay, *Countdown to Eternity*, p. 13.

"the glory of God." The former is held predominantly by covenant theologians, and the latter predominantly in dispensational circles. Which of these two is appropriate?

Salvation is certainly a major theme throughout the Bible, appearing first after the Fall in the protevangelium (Gen. 3:15), and continuing up to the removal of the curse (Rev. 22:3). However, the glory of God is also emphasized throughout Scripture.

The salvation or redemption of the world by Christ could be subsumed under the subject of the glory of God. For an overriding purpose of the Scriptures, salvation is too narrow a theme, for several reasons.

First, some passages of Scripture (e.g., some of the psalms) do not fit into the theme of salvation. Calvin observed this and rejected Luther's contention that Christ could be found everywhere in Scripture.[37]

Second, because of this difficulty, certain portions of Scripture have been interpreted nonliterally to seek to relate them to the salvation theme. One such portion is the Song of Solomon, which has often been construed as an extended allegory representing the relationship of Christ and His church. The problem is that this approach is not presented in the book itself. Instead the book is written as a straightforward love relationship between a man and a woman. Any allegorical interpretation of the Song of Solomon has no controls. Who decides which details do or do not represent "spiritual" values? When two commentators disagree on a given allegorical interpretation, how does a person decide which one to follow?

Third, this view does not take into account God's role as Judge (Matt. 7:23; 25:41; 2 Cor. 5:10; Rev. 20:11; etc.).

Therefore a more appropriate theme is the glory of God, which is suggested by Hebrews 1:1–3. Interestingly this theme fits well with Westminster standards. It is seen in the *Westminster Confession* in 1.6; 4.1; 6.1; and 18.1. It is also seen in the Westminster catechisms. The first answer in the

---

37 37. Virkler, *Hermeneutics*, p. 67.

Larger Catechism is "Man's chief and highest end is to glorify God and fully to enjoy Him forever." The first answer of the Shorter Catechism says essentially the same thing.[270]

Finally, Lightner links the two dispensational essentials together—i.e., (1) a distinction between Israel and the Church, and (2) that God's primary purpose in Scripture has to do with His own glory rather than the salvation of man. He sees "God's program with Israel" as a key factor, if the "literal or normal" method of interpretation is applied, that steers the interpreter away from drawing the conclusion that the "soteriological" aspect is to be taken as "God's primary purpose in the world":

> A consistently literal or normal hermeneutic brings one to see distinctions in God's program with Israel and His program with the church, and that underscores the theological rather than the soteriological nature of God's primary purpose in the world.[271]

---

[270] Harbin, Michael A., "The Hermeneutics of Covenant Theology," *Bibliotheca Sacra.* Dallas TX: Dallas Theological Seminary, 1996, c1955-1995.

[271] Lightner, Robert P., "Theological Perspectives on Theonomy Part I: Theonomy and Dispensationalism," *Bibliotheca Sacra.* Dallas TX: Dallas Theological Seminary, 1996, c1955-1995. Lightner refers the reader to Ryrie, *Dispensationalism Today*, pp. 43–47.

CHAPTER EIGHTEEN

—CHALLENGES TO LITERALISM
WITHIN THE DISPENSATIONAL CAMP

It would not be accurate to leave the reader with the impression that the adoption of the literal method has resolved all problems, even among conservative dispensationalists. In this chapter a number of problems faced within the camp of dispensational literalism are examined.

MINOR PROBLEMS EXIST IN DEFINING
WHAT IS MEANT BY "LITERALISM"

As previously pointed out, *consistent literalism* in hermeneutics is the method that represents the mainstream view of dispensationalism. Ryrie maintains the narrowness of this distinction by the terms *consistently* and *all*:

> Of course literal interpretation is not the exclusive property of dispensationalists.... The difference [between dispensationalists and nondispensationalists] lies in the fact that the dispensationalist claims to use the normal principle of interpretation *consistently* in *all* his study of the Bible.[272] (Italics added.)

However, what exactly is meant by the term *"literal interpretation"* is an issue not fully resolved among all dispensationalists. Johnson, under a section entitled "Hermeneutical Principles," points out that the *grammatical-historical* has become the most widely accepted, but notes further distinctions within the camp:

> The dispensational tradition is known for its literal interpretation. Ryrie says literal interpretation is part of the *sine qua non* of dispensationalism.[1] But what is meant by "literal" interpretation? Some like Ryrie stress the "plain sense," while others such as Walvoord stress the "literal"

---

[272] Ryrie, Charles C., *Dispensationalism Today* (Chicago: Moody Press, 1965), p. 89.
1 1. Charles C. Ryrie, *Dispensationalism Today* (Chicago: Moody, 1965), 45.

reference.[2] Still others stress "normal language" usage. The most widely accepted understanding of literal interpretation among dispensationalists today is grammatical, historical interpretation. However, this is not distinctive to dispensationalism. Grammatical, historical interpretation is shared broadly by evangelicals.[273]

More extreme examples of disharmony among dispensationalists, however, do exist. Erich Sauer, as Russell Bowers points out, represents one of the more extreme examples. Bowers states that Sauer:

> ...moderates older "mainline" dispensational thinking... In holding to literal interpretation, Sauer does not eliminate the use of spiritualization. He himself "spiritualizes" perhaps more than many other dispensationalists. But he clearly warns that "*mere* spiritualizing is a dangerous circumventing of the simplest meaning of Scripture."[21] ...While holding to literal interpretation and insisting on fulfillment of kingdom promises to national Israel on earth after the second coming of Christ to the earth, Sauer allows for a broad spectrum of typical or "spiritual" interpretations of Old Testament passages. He sees symbolical significance in God's covenant with Abraham in Genesis 15.[23] He sees the Song of Songs as depicting God's love for Israel.[24] At times he goes so far in his symbolism that he seems to violate his own principle of following literal interpretation. For example he says that the dimensions of the New Jerusalem in Revelation 21 "are to be taken as symbolic"[25] and are "not to be taken literally."[26] [274]

2 2. John F. Walvoord, "The Theological Context of Premillennialism," *Bibliotheca Sacra* 108 (July-September 1951): 272–74, 276. He also does talk about "grammatical, historical" interpretation.

[273] Johnson, Elliott E., "Hermeneutical Principles and the Interpretation of Psalm 110," *Bibliotheca Sacra*. Dallas TX: Dallas Theological Seminary, 1996, c1955-1995.

21 21. Sauer, *The Triumph of the Crucified*, p. 146.

23 23. Sauer, *The Dawn of World Redemption*, p. 98.

24 24. Sauer, *The Triumph of the Crucified*, p. 86.

25 25. Sauer, *From Eternity to Eternity*, p. 188.

26 26. Sauer, *From Eternity to Eternity*, p. 193.

[274] Bowers, Russell H., Jr., "Dispensational Motifs in the Writings of Erich Sauer," *Bibliotheca Sacra*. Dallas TX: Dallas Theological Seminary, 1996, c1955-1995.

Bowers goes on to explain how Sauer attempts to justify his mixture of *literalizing* and *spiritualizing*:

> *"Correct exegesis of prophecy and the method of spiritualizing can logically unite only upon the basis of a certain acknowledgment of Higher Criticism."*[32] [275]

It is clear that Sauer departs from the dispensational main stream and seeks to find a solution to the *Old Testament relevance* problem (a problem which deserves separate discussion) by modifying the generally accepted definitions of "literal interpretation." His blend of "spiritualizing" exceeds beyond the ambit of that which may be identified as *minor discrepancies*. Although Sauer denies that the Scriptures err, this unfortunate compromise has apparently moved him to a dangerous reliance upon the fickle source of *"Higher Criticism."*

Again, the above example represents a more extreme case. Focusing again upon the more moderate discrepancies, Bowers proceeds to point out the following:

> The question, of course, is whether any two interpreters, without some clearer predetermined principles, will totally agree on what is "plain," "normal," or in line with "common sense." Nor are they always likely to concur on which statements are to be taken literally and which ones figuratively.[276]

In addition to the above mentioned discrepancies, it is also found that not all dispensational writers apply the same weight to the distinguishing powers of the *"consistently literal"* method. Blaising, for example, states the following:

> Today, for many scholars, to say the difference is simply between literal and spiritual exegesis is not accurate and is in fact misleading.[277]

---

[32] 32. Sauer, *From Eternity to Eternity,* p. 125. (Italics his.)

[275] Cf. Bowers, loc. cit.

[276] Bowers, Idem.

[277] Blaising, Craig A., "Development of Dispensationalism by Contemporary Dispensationalists," *Bibliotheca Sacra.* Dallas TX: Dallas Theological Seminary, 1996, c1955-1995.

He goes on to quote Turner's position as follows:

> He also points out that the differences will not be resolved at the general level of hermeneutical rules but only in the exegesis of specific passages.[278]

Drawing what appears to be a different conclusion than Ryrie's, Blaising writes:

> In conclusion it can be seen that consistently literal exegesis is inadequate to describe the essential distinctive of dispensationalism.[279]

By the few above listed comments and quotes, it should be evident to the reader that not all the details having to do with the consistent literal method of interpretation have been worked out— variations and discrepancies in the area of hermeneutics do indeed exists among dispensationalists. But again, most of these deficiencies are relatively minor by way of comparison. (As far as this author can gather, these minor deficiencies pertain to matters such as: clarification of definitions, sorting out some of the confusion caused by semantics and usage of certain terms, refinement and standardization of the rules of interpretation, etc.)

Such minor discrepancies continue to undergo development and refinement by today's dispensational theologians. With prayer, diligence in Biblical studies, the grace of God, and the leading of the Holy Spirit, dispensationalism will hopefully gain acceptance in the hearts and minds of sincere students of the Word of God (and extend to more conservative Christian seminaries and colleges as well). In the final analysis, there is but one question that needs to be answered: Do the *Scriptures* indeed support this system (dispensationalism) as God's divine arrangement?

---

[278] Turner, David, "The Continuity of Scripture and Eschatology: Key Hermeneutical Issues," *Grace Theological Journal* 6 (Fall 1985): 275–87, as cited by Craig A. Blaising in "Development of Dispensationalism by Contemporary Dispensationalists," *Bibliotheca Sacra.* Dallas TX: Dallas Theological Seminary, 1996, c1955-1995.

[279] Blaising, Craig A., "Development of Dispensationalism by Contemporary Dispensationalists," *Bibliotheca Sacra.* Dallas TX: Dallas Theological Seminary, 1996, c1955-1995.

CHAPTER NINETEEN

—CHARGES RAISED BY NON-DISPENSATIONALISTS AGAINST DISPENSATIONAL LITERALISM

In addition to the *challenges* listed in the previous chapter, which remain to be worked out among dispensationalists, non-dispensationalists have raised a number of *charges* against dispensational literalism.

When faced with such opposition, dispensationalists must keep in mind God's omnipotent nature; neither God nor His Word requires the defense of man. It remains incumbent upon dispensationalists, however, to deal with the matters at hand as clearly and as honestly as possible. As in any case in which opposing forces are prone to collide, it is imperative that the participants seek discernment concerning their opponent's strategies, and make diligent efforts to understand their arguments. These principles certainly apply as one enters the debate concerning which method of interpretation is the proper one to apply when interpreting the Scriptures. Hopefully, each aspirant will keep in mind the importance of the outcome—i.e., the spiritual welfare, perhaps even the eternal state, of the souls of men. It is also important to keep in mind that the opponents faced, in most cases, and this applies to both sides of the aisle, are fellow Christians. It will perhaps be helpful for each contender to consider the arena in which the negotiations are to take place as a *conference table* rather than a *battlefield.* No one ought to be scorned for presenting his case firmly, as long as he is doing so in a fair and honest manner, and is sincerely motivated by the love of Christ.

It will be helpful for the reader to keep in mind the role of Augustine at the origin of the problems pertaining to interpretation. Edwin Blum points out the following:

> A warning needs to be sounded that not everything in Augustine's philosophy or theology can be accepted as biblical. He was a child of his age and some of his views led the church into serious errors. His Neo-Platonism affected his anthropology. His amillennialism and allegorical interpretations were adopted by the medieval church.

Premillennialism and dispensationalism have had to fight his influence.[280]

The criticisms which dispensationalism currently faces can generally be traced back to, via one avenue or another, that which has developed down through the history of the Church as a result of the influence of Augustine.

Critics of dispensationalism continue to emerge and are hardly shy in their challenges. Since a *consistent literal* method of interpretation is the primary foundational principle of dispensationalism, it is not surprising to find their attacks concentrated in this vital area.

Presented below are a number of the various issues raised by those who oppose dispensational literalism. A full rebuttal of these challenges is not intended in this context. The reader can rest assured, however, that these issues have been competently defeated by many of the dispensational writers herein quoted, along with others not mentioned. (The reader may wish to refer to the footnotes for a few brief and general rebuttals provided by selected dispensational authors.)

The purpose in this context is to merely introduce to the reader some of the main components of the debate. The author hopes to stir the student's interest and to provoke him to seek out the matter for himself in further study and thereby derive solid discriminations in his own mind, thus becoming able to prove out the credence or fallacy of one position over another. The student will gradually increase the depth of his understanding regarding the nature of the controversy; his convictions will no doubt become firmer as he continues to study this vital subject. It is important to remember that the Bible is what it is and will remain so forever; let the reader anchor his heart, mind and soul in the depths of its wisdom and wealth.

ATTACKS AND ACCUSATIONS AGAINST CONSISTENT DISPENSATIONAL LITERALISM

1) Dispensationalists are accused of flopping back and forth in an antithetical and contradictory manner between two

---

[280] Blum, Edwin A., "Augustine: The Bishop and Theologian," *Bibliotheca Sacra.* Dallas TX: Dallas Theological Seminary, 1996, c1955-1995.

equally deplorable extremes of interpretation—the literal and the typological.[281]

2) Scofield (a primary proponent of the dispensational system) is accused of being *a heretic* for, among other things, an insistence on the literal interpretation of Scripture... and the validity of Scriptural typology.[282]

3) It is claimed that the Song of Solomon is often viewed by dispensationalists as an allegorical or typological picture of Christ's love for His Church.[283]

4) Difficulties are pointed out in harmonizing dispensational literalism with the exegetical problems of Ezekiel's temple vision in Ezekiel 40–48 (temple, sacrifices, ceremonial law).[284]

---

[281] Cf. Mason, Jr., Clarence E., "A Review of Dispensationalism by John Wick Bowman: Part II," *Bibliotheca Sacra.* Dallas TX: Dallas Theological Seminary, 1996, c1955-1995. Mason states that, "Bowman professes to be amazed that they [these two equally deplorable extremes, in Bowman's opinion] are found in the same strange mind." He notes Bowman's conclusion: "It must suffice here to remark that to the spiritually minded center within the evangelical tradition of the Christian church both methods are wrong and to about the same degree."

[282] Cf. Rand, James F., ed. Rev. of "The Bible and Modern Religions. II. Dispensationalism," *Interpretation,* 10:170–87 by John Wick Bowman, April, 1956. *Bibliotheca Sacra.* Dallas TX: Dallas Theological Seminary, 1996, c1955-1995.

[283] Cf. Howe, Fred R., F. Duane Lindsey, Ed. Rev. of *Christian Theology.* Vol. 3. by Millard J. Erickson. Grand Rapids: Baker Book House, 1985. 444 pp. *Bibliotheca Sacra.* Dallas TX: Dallas Theological Seminary, 1996, c1955-1995. Howe points out, however, that, "no documentation is offered" by Erickson to support his claim. Howe responds as follows: "Obviously he [Erickson] needed to check S. Craig Glickman's definitive work on this very book, *A Song for Lovers* (Inter-Varsity Press), which is written by a dispensational scholar and assuredly does not teach an allegorical view of this book."

[284] Cf. Curtis Crenshaw, *Dispensationalism Today, Yesterday, and Tomorrow* (Memphis: Footstool, 1989), 238.; Floyd Hamilton, *The Basis of Millennial Faith* (Grand Rapids: Eerdmans, 1942), 40, 42.; Archibald Hughes, *A New Heaven and a New Earth* (London: Marshall, Morgan & Scott, 1958), 157.; and Hullinger, Jerry M., "The Problem of Animal Sacrifices in Ezekiel 40–48," *Bibliotheca Sacra.* Dallas TX: Dallas Theological Seminary, 1996, c1955-1995. Hullinger, referring to attacks against dispensationalism by opponents such as Allis, states that, "Dispensationalists have wrongly been put on the defensive regarding this passage.
Nondispensationalists have as much difficulty harmonizing this passage with their theological schemes, for if they reject a literal interpretation of these chapters, they are unable to offer any real exegesis of the texts. Beasley-Murray explains, 'To tackle the vision verse by verse and try to take symbolically thirteen cubits, hooks a handbreadth long, the sixth part of an ephah, place names like Berothat and Hauran,

5) Referring to various connections to fundamentalism, it is claimed that dispensationalists take a "defensive, separatistic, and anti-intellectual stance." [285]

6) Dispensationalism is referred to as "the height of speculative nonsense." [286]

7) Dispensationalism has been described as "the method of deciding in advance which Scriptures deal with the Church and which Scriptures have to do with Israel, and then to interpret the passages concerned in the light of this 'division' of the Word." [287]

8) Dispensationalism has been further described as "an entirely unjustified method of interpretation and is superimposed upon the Scripture arbitrarily." [288]

9) Some opponents of dispensationalism, rejecting the conservative doctrine of verbal inspiration, deny that the view of the Prophet Samuel, "that God delighted in

---

is out of the question, to contradict all reason' (G. R. Beasley-Murray, "Ezekiel," in *The New Bible Commentary,* ed. Donald Guthrie and J. A. Motyer, 3d ed. [Grand Rapids: Eerdmans, 1970], 663)."

[285] Cf. Cook, Stuart S. Rev. of *Looking Both Ways: Exploring the Interface between Christianity and Sociology,* by Richard Perkins. Grand Rapids: Baker Book House, 1987. 189 pp. *Bibliotheca Sacra.* Dallas TX: Dallas Theological Seminary, 1996, c1955-1995.

[286] Ladd, *The Hope of Christ's Second Coming,* p. 130. Cf. the note below.

[287] Ibid. Cf. the following note.

[288] Cf. Walvoord, John F., "A Review of The Blessed Hope by George E. Ladd," *Bibliotheca Sacra.* Dallas TX: Dallas Theological Seminary, 1996, c1955-1995. Walvoord's response (which occurs in the context of the preceding two points also) is presented as follows: "This, of course, is not true, nor is it fair to define dispensationalism in this summary manner. The dispensational interpretation of Scripture is rather the outgrowth of literal interpretation inasmuch as there are differing rules of life in different periods of the progressive revelation of God. Rather than spiritualize these differences, dispensationalists regard them as being pertinent to the age in which they belong. Thus a Jew under the Mosaic covenant was commanded to bring his lamb of sacrifice, something a Christian never has to do who has the one sacrifice in Christ. Under the law, Sabbath breakers were to be stoned, while under the present dispensation no one would think of stoning one guilty of misusing the Lord's day. Dispensationalism is a method of solving these primary problems of interpretation and is far from an arbitrary assumption." For more on Ladd's controversy against dispensationalism, see Walvoord, John F., "Posttribulationism Today—Part IV: Futurist Posttribulational Interpretation," *Bibliotheca Sacra.* Dallas TX: Dallas Theological Seminary, 1996, c1955-1995.

wholesale and unprovoked massacre," could have been inspired by God.[289]

10) Some opponents of dispensationalism deny "that dispensationalism is an adequate explanation of the diversity of Scripture and finds solution instead in the concept that inspiration came through imperfect men whose imperfections are imparted to the Scripture."[290]

11) Dispensationalism is accused of neglecting the life and teaching of Jesus as related to the Church as a result of their method of interpretation.[291]

12) Dispensationalism is accused of being found lacking in social and political interest as a result of their method of interpretation.[292]

13) Dispensationalism is accused of being a recent innovation.[293]

14) Dispensationalism is accused of being a major heresy.[294]

15) Dispensationalism is accused of being a product of "wooden literalism."[295]

---

[289] Walvoord, John F. Rev. of *The Unity Of The Bible* by H. H. Rowley. The Westminster Press, Philadelphia, 1955. 201 pp. *Bibliotheca Sacra*. Dallas TX: Dallas Theological Seminary, 1996, c1955-1995.

[290] Ibid.

[291] Cf. the following note.

[292] Cf. Walvoord, John F., J. D. Pentecost, ed. Rev. of *Dispensationalism In America* by C. Norman Kraus. John Knox Press, Richmond, 1958. 156 pp. *Bibliotheca Sacra*. Dallas TX: Dallas Theological Seminary, 1996, c1955-1995. Walvoord responds as follows: "...the selective principle under which he arranged his material has an underlying fallacy... His real objection to literalism is that dispensationalists interpret literally promises which he would prefer to spiritualize. He admits that literalism is often valid and makes no attempt to justify the criticism. ... The charge that the life and teaching of Jesus are lost to the church in dispensationalism is not true. Dispensationalists recognize that Jesus taught much about the church, especially in the Gospel of John, and are guided by the contextual principle that the subject of each utterance should determine its application. The lack of social and political interest which he lays at the doorstep of dispensationalism is also an inaccurate charge. Any system which emphasizes eternal values will exalt this above the temporal. In the main, it is not a bona fide criticism of dispensationalism."

[293] Cf. Walvoord, John F. Rev. of *Dispensationalism Today* by Charles C. Ryrie. Chicago: Moody Press, 1965. 221 pp. *Bibliotheca Sacra*. Dallas TX: Dallas Theological Seminary, 1996, c1955-1995.

[294] Cf. Ibid.

[295] Cf. Ibid. Walvoord responds: "Although such charges are seldom documented, they have become convincing by mere repetition."

16) Liberals have attacked dispensationalism because of its belief in the inerrant Word of God.[296]

17) Liberals have attacked dispensationalism because... dispensationalists are invariably opposed to liberalism.[297]

18) Amillenarians have opposed dispensationalists because dispensationalists are always premillennial.[298]

19) It is claimed that "Dispensationalists will not interpret the obviously literal as literal, and the obviously symbolical as symbolical. Everything must be literal."[299]

20) The following is claimed: "When the principle of literalness, however, is pressed in a rigid and unyielding manner upon every Scripture, this very principle, which is the natural one to be employed, actually perverts the meaning of the text. Dispensationalism does this to the extreme."[300]

21) It is claimed that the "conviction" which dispensationalists apply in "their literal methods of interpreting the Bible... can lead to a spiritual arrogance bordering on a feeling of

---

[296] Cf. Walvoord, John F. Rev. of *Dispensationalism Today* by Charles C. Ryrie. Chicago: Moody Press, 1965. 221 pp. *Bibliotheca Sacra.* Dallas TX: Dallas Theological Seminary, 1996, c1955-1995.
[297] Cf. Ibid.
[298] Cf. Ibid.
[299] Cf. Walvoord, John F. Rev. of *Backgrounds To Dispensationalism* by Clarence B. Bass. Wm. B. Eerdmans Publishing Company, Grand Rapids, Michigan, 1960. 184 pp. *Bibliotheca Sacra.* Dallas TX: Dallas Theological Seminary, 1996, c1955-1995. Walvoord responds: "Such a sweeping statement must certainly have scholarly proof. Bass does not cite a single dispensationalist in support of his contention that 'everything must be literal.' The reviewer knows of no dispensationalist, Darby, Scofield, Chafer, or even an extremist like Bullinger, of whom this is true. The author's statement is misrepresentation and unsupportable." It should be noted that, "Saucy and John S. Feinberg have noted that many nondispensationalists deny that their hermeneutic is nonliteral or that it is inconsistent." (Robert L. Saucy, "The Critical Issue between Dispensational and Non-Dispensational Systems," John S. Feinberg, "Salvation in the Old Testament," in *Tradition and Testament: Essays in Honor of Charles Lee Feinberg,* ed. John S. Feinberg and Paul D. Feinberg [Chicago: Moody Press, 1981], p. 45. [This quote was taken from Blaising, Craig A., "Development of Dispensationalism by Contemporary Dispensationalists," *Bibliotheca Sacra.* Dallas TX: Dallas Theological Seminary, 1996, c1955-1995])
[300] Cf. Ibid. Walvoord responds: "The reviewer would challenge the author to cite one dispensationalist, however 'extreme,' who fulfills this supposedly 'unbiased' definition of dispensationalism. No dispensationalist insists that every verse in Scripture should be interpreted in a literal way."

infallibility," and that "Scofield and his followers exercise a kind of papal infallibilism."[301]

22) Dispensationalists' citations of scriptural proof texts to support their teachings, has been sarcastically dubbed "spooftexting." This is described as "the cumulative effect of massive citation" and is referred to as a "vice" to be distinguished from "the virtue of proper proof-texting."[302]

23) Dispensationalists are accused of being "ready to settle for the mere occurrence of certain terms as proof of a great deal more than the mere terms necessarily signify."[303]

24) Contrary to the dispensational position, it is proclaimed as a "fact... that there is not only no clear evidence of a millennium in Scripture, but there is no evidence."[304]

25) Dispensationalism is thought of as theological error and "false doctrine."[305]

26) Dispensationalists are said to have left "the pathway of legitimate grammatical-historical interpretation of Scripture... in their insistence upon a strictly literal interpretation of the prophecies of the Old and New Testaments."[306]

27) It is claimed that dispensationalists deny the recognition of figurative language in Scripture, and identify the allegorical or spiritualizing method of interpreting prophecy used by

---

[301] Witmer, John A. Rev. of *Wrongly Dividing the Word of Truth: A Critique of Dispensationalism* by John Gerstner. Brentwood, TN: Wolgemuth & Hyatt, 1991, pp. 85, 252. "A Review of Wrongly Dividing the Word of Truth—Part 1," *Bibliotheca Sacra.* Dallas TX: Dallas Theological Seminary, 1996, c1955-1995.

[302] Ibid. Gerstner, pp. 83, 99–100.

[303] Ibid. Gerstner, p. 17.

[304] Ibid. Gerstner, p. 91. Witmer responds to this preposterous claim by Gerstner as follows: "This not only flies in the face of the repetition of the phrase 'thousand years' six times in Revelation 20:1–7 (which Gerstner obviously also spiritualizes), but ignores the repeated teaching of Scripture concerning the future kingdom for Israel and its character (e.g., Isa. 2:1–5; 4:2–6; 9:6–7; 11:1–12:6; 14:1–3; Zech. 8:1–8; 14:1–21; Acts 1:6–7; 3:20–21; 1 Cor. 15:20–26)."

[305] Witmer, John A., ed. Rev. of "Principles of Interpretation in Regard to Prophecy with Special Reference to Millennialism," C. Kuehne, *The Journal of Theology* 21 (December 1981): 2–28, p. 25. *Bibliotheca Sacra.* Dallas TX: Dallas Theological Seminary, 1996, c1955-1995.

[306] Ibid. Kuehne, p. 6.

amillennialists as nothing more than the recognition of the "figurative-literal sense" of words.[307]

28) Of Dispensationalists it is said: "It seems therefore that the torch of the literalist is an 'ignis fatuus,' leading those who follow it, they know not whither."[308]

29) Against dispensational literalism the following is argued: "The literal interpretation of the Old Testament prophecies relating to the restoration of Israel and the future kingdom of Christ, cannot by possibility be carried out; and if abandoned in one point, it cannot be pressed in regard to others."[309]

~ ~ ~

While this list can hardly be considered exhaustive, it should give the reader examining the controversy levied against dispensationalism a good idea of the characteristics and nature of the debate. This partially describes the arena into which the dispensationalist has been summoned.

Regardless of both the *internal divarications* among dispensationalists (as denoted in the previous chapter) as well as these above-listed examples of *external attacks* by non-dispensationalists, the author is convinced that an honest-hearted investigation will bring the Bible reader to the conclusion that the *consistent literal* approach, as employed by mainstream dispensationalists, is the *only* viable method of interpreting the Scriptures. Failure to adopt this clear and consistent exegetical theological system will most certainly result in confusion and chaos in matters of Biblical exposition.[310] A failure in this critical area—i.e., *consistently* interpreting the Bible according to the *literal* method—has the potential to lead to a discrediting of both the Bible's authority and accuracy. When this occurs, blatantly

---

[307] Ibid. Kuehne, p. 6. In answer to both of these accusations Witmer responds as follows: "[these accusations are] simply not true. The prophecies which have been fulfilled throughout subsequent biblical history either near or remote have all been fulfilled literally and set the pattern for the prophecies which still remain to be fulfilled. Kuehne fails to consider that significant principle of the interpretation of prophecy."

[308] Hodge, C., *Systematic Theology.* Oak Harbor, WA: Logos Research Systems, Inc., 1997.

[309] Ibid.

[310] Cf. Ryrie, Charles, C. Rev. of *The Church In God,* by Harold J. Ockenga. Fleming H. Revell Company, Westwood, New Jersey, 1956. 350 pp. *Bibliotheca Sacra.* Dallas TX: Dallas Theological Seminary, 1996, c1955-1995.

erroneous interpretations of it become inevitable. Such errors have inevitably spawned a multitude of these types of attacks against dispensationalism, as well as against the fundamental doctrines they adopt.[311]

As illustrated above, the challenges to dispensationalism are clear. It should be obvious that the hand of the dispensationalist must be steady, his heart full of courage, his mind clear and sharp, and his pen ready. Men like Charles Ryrie, and the late John Walvoord, as well as a number of others, have set about to answer these challenges with unparalleled eloquence.

At this point the following words of Walvoord, taken from his review of *Dispensationalism Today*[312] by Charles Ryrie, are most appropriate:

> A comprehensive and scholarly discussion of dispensationalism by one thoroughly familiar with its tenets has long been overdue. Most recent discussions on the subject have been attacks on dispensationalism which have been more emotional than factual. Dispensationalism has been charged with an assortment of uncomplimentary qualities such as being a recent innovation, a major heresy, and a product of "wooden literalism." Although such charges are seldom documented, they have become convincing by mere repetition. The resulting confusion and misunderstanding could only be countered by a calm, factual appraisal of what dispensationalism really is and teaches. This has been supplied by Dr. Ryrie.
>
> Dispensationalism has often been accepted in the best circles of evangelicalism, and only in recent days has it been subject to sharp criticism. Sources of criticism have been many. ... Those seeking favor and recognition as intellectuals in the theological world have found by attacking dispensationalism that they had the approval both of the liberals and the amillenarians.

---

[311] Cf. Ryrie, Charles, C., "A Trilogy of Theology," *Bibliotheca Sacra.* Dallas TX: Dallas Theological Seminary, 1996, c1955-1995.

[312] Note: since the time Dr. Walvoord wrote this review, Ryrie has twice updated his book. The title of the new work is simply *Dispensationalism* (Chicago: Moody Press, 1995 & 2007)

The discussion by Dr. Ryrie is designed to accomplish, first, a correction of widespread misconceptions about dispensationalism. Second, he provides a comprehensive treatment of the basic principles of normal, contemporary dispensationalism. He demonstrates that charges against dispensationalism are often either false or misleading and that even capable scholars have been unusually remiss in careful research.[313]

Again, it is beyond the author's current intention to present in any detail rebuttals to the above-listed charges against dispensationalism. The reader may rest assured, however, that dispensationalists, as a minimal amount of research will reveal, have well answered all such charges as those exemplified above.

Dispensationalists, of course, do not draw back from confronting their critics; they see their system as both a sound and positive method of Biblical interpretation. Dispensationalists maintain that the application of their hermeneutical principles resolve a number of otherwise unsolvable interpretation problems.[314]

And, as far as countercharges go, suffice it here to say that dispensationalists "charge... that non-dispensationalists use a mystical system of interpretation of Scripture"[315]; they further contend that "the non-dispensational movement is negative [and that] it has failed to produce a satisfactory positive system of Biblical interpretation."[316]

If the reader has yet to settle these issues in his own heart, it is recommended that he carefully review the three points of Ryrie's *Sine Qua Non* on page 65, and examine again **Table One** located on page 26. Then determine to keep these tenets in mind as he sets sail on his next voyage from Genesis to Revelation.

---

[313] Walvoord, John F. Rev. of *Dispensationalism Today* by Charles C. Ryrie. Chicago: Moody Press, 1965. 221 pp. *Bibliotheca Sacra.* Dallas TX: Dallas Theological Seminary, 1996, c1955-1995.

[314] In the context of a personal conversation the author and his wife had the privilege of sharing with Ron Merryman about this issue over breakfast in March 2004 in Colorado Springs, CO., Ron stated the following: "It is absolutely impossible for a person to understand their Bible any other way than by interpreting it according to the principles, divisions and basic tenets of dispensationalism."

[315] Aldrich, Roy L., "An Apologetic for Dispensationalism," *Bibliotheca Sacra.* Dallas TX: Dallas Theological Seminary, 1996, c1955-1995.

[316] Aldrich, Ibid.

CHAPTER TWENTY

—THE EFFECTS INTERPRETATION METHODS HAVE ON PROPHECY

INTRODUCTION

How one positions himself in regard to the essentials of dispensationalism (particularly the first two of Ryrie's *sine qua non*[317]) has a significant bearing on a number of other important theological viewpoints as well, not the least of which are those issues having to do with the manner in which prophecy is to be interpreted. This, of course, has particular significance in the area of eschatology. Eschatology is defined in *The American Heritage Dictionary* as "The branch of theology that is concerned with the end of the world or of humankind. A belief or a doctrine concerning the ultimate or final things."[318]

It will be beneficial in this context to first briefly note again the following three prophecy-related subjects: (1) the millennium, (2) premillennialism, and (3) amillennialism. Then our study is extended to two additional divisions, namely: (4) amillennialism and covenant theology, and (5) amillennialism and the Reformers. The final division considered is: (6) the development and explanation of several prophecy-related theological viewpoints. This latter division is taken up separately in the next chapter.

THE MILLENNIUM

Concerning the millennium, Enns writes the following:

> The word *millennium* comes from the Latin *mille*, meaning "thousand," and relates to the statement in Revelation 20:4, "They came to life and reigned with Christ for a thousand years."[319]

---

[317] Cf. Ryrie, Charles C., *Dispensationalism*, (Chicago: Moody Press, 1995) p. 45.

[318] *The American Heritage Dictionary,* 3rd Ed., CD-Rom, Ver. 3.5, 1994.

[319] Enns, P. P., *The Moody Handbook of Theology*. Chicago, Ill.: Moody Press, 1997, c1989.

Enns then raises the following important question:

> Should this statement be understood literally or symbolically? ... The answer determines in part one's doctrine of last things.[320]

The connection is clear: one of the very first things the student of prophecy must come to understand is that his views concerning the *millennium* will be directly determined by which method of interpretation he chooses to adopt—the literal or the symbolic.

PREMILLENNIALISM

Dispensationalists adopt the premillennial view of prophecy. This view is directly linked to the literal method of interpretation.

Houghton, in connection with the dispensationalist's position on literalism and their insistence on making a clear distinction between Israel and the Church, notes the importance of dispensationalism's "premillennial understanding of prophecy":

> Chafer taught the importance of understanding the divine program of the ages. This includes all that is involved in the dispensational understanding of Scripture. The literal interpretation of the Bible, recognition of the Church as the body of Christ which is distinct from national Israel, and the premillennial understanding of prophecy are all implied in dispensationalism.[321]

Zuck, as Bailey points out in his review, also makes the connection between *consistent literalism* and prophecy:

> The book affirms an evangelical commitment to the verbal inspiration and inerrancy of the Scriptures. Dispensational premillennialism is seen as the natural result of following a consistent literal approach to prophetic Scriptures.[322]

---

[320] Enns, Ibid.

[321] Houghton, George G., "Lewis Sperry Chafer, 1871–1952," *Bibliotheca Sacra*. Dallas TX: Dallas Theological Seminary, 1996, c1955-1995.

[322] Bailey, Mark L. Rev. of *Basic Bible Interpretation* by Roy B. Zuck. Wheaton, IL: Victor Books, 1991. 324 pp. *Bibliotheca Sacra*. Dallas TX: Dallas Theological Seminary, 1996, c1955-1995.

AMILLENNIALISM

Amillennialism (*no millennium*) is directly antithetical to premillennialism (a belief in a literal millennial kingdom). As Enns points out, amillennialism is one of three major views within conservative theology:

> In conservative theology there are three major views concerning last things: amillennialism, postmillennialism, and premillennialism.[323]

Dispensationalists, as a result of interpreting the Scriptures literally, adopt the premillennial view. Amillennialism, on the other hand, requires the abandonment of the literal method of interpretation.

AMILLENNIALISM AND COVENANT THEOLOGY

Differences in methods of interpretation have resulted in a number of clearly defined opposing theological views concerning the eschatological implications of prophecy. For example, as a result of employing the allegorical method of interpretation, covenant theology has adopted a much different view of prophecy.[324] Ryrie points out that it is their method of interpretation which underlies their viewpoint:

> Covenant theologians are well known for their stand on allegorical interpretation especially as it relates to the prophetic Word, and they are equally well known for their amillennialism which is only the natural outcome of allegorizing.[325]

---

[323] Enns, P. P., *The Moody Handbook of Theology*. Chicago, Ill.: Moody Press, 1997, c1989.

[324] For more on the effect that the allegorical interpretation has had on prophecy (a significant factor in the history of amillennialism—influencing Origen, Clement, and Augustine), see John F. Walvoord, "Posttribulationism Today," *Bibliotheca Sacra* 132 (1975):17.

[325] Ryrie, Charles C., "The Necessity of Dispensationalism," *Bibliotheca Sacra.* Dallas TX: Dallas Theological Seminary, 1996, c1955-1995. Karleen, referring among other things to amillennialism, points out how "this [is] relevant to theology and the interpretation of figurative language." (Karleen, P. S., *The Handbook to Bible Study: With a Guide to the Scofield Study System.* New York: Oxford University Press, 1987.) Also Evan-Coder note, "The amillennial view rejects the literal meaning of the Bible text. The premillennial view accepts kingdom prophecies as literal, placing the return of Christ before the millennium is

AMILLENNIALISM AND
THE REFORMERS

Harbin notes, "...the literal method of interpretation... is the method adopted by the church in the Reformation."[326] The following question will no doubt arise in the student's mind: Why did the reformers fail to actively protest amillennialism, especially in light of the fact that the Reformation Movement was primarily initiated by a return to the literal method of interpretation?

At first, the contemplation of this question appears to be a bit perplexing, but it is explainable. The mammoth apostate religious organization (the Roman church) of which they (the reformers) were formerly a part, due to the allegorizing influences of Augustine and others, held to the amillennial point of view. The reformers quite naturally, and with the utmost sincerity, held this belief at the time the Holy Spirit surgically removed them from this corrupt organization. In order for one to come to an understanding of what happened from that point, the following must be kept in mind: the Holy Spirit's main objective was (and is) the salvation of the souls of men. Souls were being devoured by the droves due to the predatory appetites of this despicably wicked and apostate religious system (the Roman church). One can hardly doubt that this (i.e., salvation) was the main priority of the Holy Spirit, and constituted the *first light* given to the reformers.

The narrowness of this primary focus in the minds of the reformers can easily be seen; they were virtually exclusively fixed upon soteriological issues. We must keep in mind that many of the reformers were martyred for their refusal to abandon the *simplest* tenets of the Christian faith. Why would the Holy Spirit, at that time, go beyond the witness that this standoff demonstrated? Wouldn't a debate over the more detailed theological issues pertaining to eschatology, or any number of other theological issues, only have served to cloud the more critical matters pertaining to salvation? Surely men can be in error concerning their eschatological viewpoints and still go to heaven; the same cannot be said, however, for those harboring duplicities concerning the fundamentals of the gospel! A

---

established." (Evans, W., & S. M. Coder, *The Great Doctrines of the Bible*. Enl. ed. /. Chicago: Moody Press, 1998, c1974.)
[326] Harbin, Michael A., "The Hermeneutics of Covenant Theology," *Bibliotheca Sacra*. Dallas TX: Dallas Theological Seminary, 1996, c1955-1995.

man's eternal destiny hinges upon his belief in, acceptance of, and unqualified committal to such fundamental tenets of the Christian faith. These brave men defended these basic tenets with their very lives.

Furthermore, it must also be recognized that it is impossible for dead men to personally develop in their cause; the less critical theological issues were never reached in their time. In light of these things, it must therefore be concluded that the manner and nature after which the Reformation occurred was no doubt in perfect accord with the will and design of the only wise God, "Who will have all men to be saved, and to come unto the knowledge of the truth" (1 TI 2:4).[327]

---

[327] For a brief summary of the ammillenial position held by the Reformers see Robert G. Clouse, *The Meaning of the Millennium* (Downers Grove, IL: InterVarsity, 1977), 910.

CHAPTER TWENTY ONE

—THE DEVELOPMENT AND EXPLANATION OF SEVERAL PROPHECY-RELATED THEOLOGICAL VIEWPOINTS

The subject matter of this chapter is the last of the six points listed in the previous chapter. Certain eschatological and prophecy-related matters and their relation to *interpretation methods* are taken into consideration. The points examined in this chapter include:

1. The premillennial view was first on the scene.

2. An amillennialism engulfment of premillennialism began in the third and fourth centuries.

3. Premillennialism is clearly based on the literal method of interpretation.

4. Amillennialism is clearly based on the allegorical method of interpretation.

5. Dispensational pretribulationism is an outgrowth of early premillennialism.

6. The premillennial-pretribulational-dispensational position concerning prophecy is clearly based on the literal method of interpretation.

7. A failure to hold to Biblical inerrancy causes discrepancies.

8. Amillennialists admit that if they adopted the literal method of interpretation, they too would have to become premillennial.

9. Misconceptions concerning these issues have led some to the preposterous and confusing claim that prophecy requires some special or different form of interpretation than the rest of the Scriptures.

10. Prophecy pertains to Israel's future.

Again, it is not within the scope of this book to discuss these subjects in detail. The main purpose here is to note their relation to interpretation methods.

1. THE PREMILLENNIAL VIEW WAS
FIRST ON THE SCENE

Pointing out the early roots of premillennialism under a section entitled "History of the Premillennial View," Norman Geisler writes the following:

> The extrabiblical roots of premillennialism go back to the first century. "Among earlier writers the belief was held by the authors of the Epistle of Barnabas [4, 15], the Shepherd, the Second Epistle of Clement, by Paptas, Justin, and by some of the Ebionites, and Cerinthus."[2] There are no references to the millennial belief in the writings of Clement of Rome, Ignatius, Polycarp, Tatian, Athenagoras, or Theophilus. But even Bethune-Baker admits that "we are not justified in arguing from their silence that they did not hold it."[3]
>
> The premillennial view was also shared by Irenaeus, Melito, Hippolytus, Tertullian, and Lactantius.[4] [328]

2. AN AMILLENNIALISM ENGULFMENT
OF PREMILLENNIALISM BEGAN IN THE
THIRD AND FOURTH CENTURIES

Walvoord writes:

> The early premillennialism of the first two centuries was soon engulfed by the amillennialism which arose in the third and fourth centuries.[329]

As noted earlier, *amillennialism* came about as a direct result of *allegorizing* the Scriptures.[330]

---

2 2. J. F. Bethune-Baker, *An Introduction to the Early History of Christian Doctrine* (London: Methuen & Co., 1942), p. 69.

3 3. Ibid.

4 4. Ibid., p. 70.

[328] Geisler, Norman L., "A Premillennial View of Law and Government," *Bibliotheca Sacra*. Dallas TX: Dallas Theological Seminary, 1996, c1955-1995. Cf. Walvoord, John F., "Posttribulationism Today—Part IV: Futurist Posttribulational Interpretation," *Bibliotheca Sacra*. Dallas TX: Dallas Theological Seminary, 1996, c1955-1995.

[329] Walvoord, John F., "Posttribulationism Today—Part IV: Futurist Posttribulational Interpretation," *Bibliotheca Sacra*. Dallas TX: Dallas Theological Seminary, 1996, c1955-1995.

[330] Note: in an earlier chapter in this book entitled "The History of Interpretations," under the heading "The Rise of Allegorism," the history of allegorizing the

3. PREMILLENNIALISM WAS (AND IS) CLEARLY BASED ON THE LITERAL METHOD OF INTERPRETATION

Early Christians were premillennialists. This was due to the fact that they adhered to the literal method of interpretation. The allegorical method of interpretation did not arrive on the scene until the third and forth centuries. Note the unanimity of the following authors.

Dwight Pentecost states:

> The basic differences between the premillennial and amillennial schools and between the pretribulation and posttribulation rapturists are hermeneutical, arising from the adoption of divergent and irreconcilable methods of interpretation.[331]

Oswald Allis, an amillennialists, admits:

> One of the most marked features of Premillennialism in all its forms is the emphasis which it places on the literal interpretation of Scripture.[332]

Floyd Hamilton, an amillennialist, writes:

> Now we must frankly admit that a literal interpretation of the Old Testament prophecies gives us just such a picture of an earthly reign of the Messiah as the Premillennialist pictures. ...The Jews were looking for just such a kingdom as that expected by those premillennialists...[333]

Charles Feinberg writes:

> It can be shown that the reason the early Church was premillennial was traceable to its interpretation of the Word in a literal manner, whereas the cause of the departure from this view in later centuries of the history of the Church is directly attributable to a change in method of interpretation beginning with Origen in particular.[334]

Scriptures is traced to Aristobulus' influence on Philo; then to Pantaenus, the first teacher of the school of Alexandria; to Clement; to Origen; and then to Augustine.

[331] Pentecost, J. Dwight, *Things To Come*. Grand Rapids, MI.: Zondervan publications, 1958, p. 1.

[332] Allis, Oswald T., *Prophecy and the Church*, p. 17.

[333] Hamilton, Floyd E., *The Basis of Millennial Faith*, pp. 38-39.

[334] Feinberg, Charles L., *Premillennialism or Amillennialism*, p. 51.

Thomas Ice writes:

> Literal interpretation includes the development of symbols and themes which yield a rich premillennial theology.[335]

Gordon Lewis writes:

> According to many contemporary theologians, Biblical statements on Christ's second coming do not refer to the future of the world, but to the present inner experience of individuals. For evangelicals, on the other hand, Christ's return to earth is future and literally understood.
>
> …
>
> So from such a literal perspective premillennialists establish a future, personal reign of Christ on earth.[336]

John Hannah concludes:

> In the last analysis, premillennialism must be seen as an authentic part of the conservative evangelical movement at the end of the nineteenth century that gained popularity among those conservatives who favored a rather literalistic interpretation of Scripture, and who recognized in premillennialism a way to remain both biblical and evangelical under difficult circumstances.[69] [337]

4. AMILLENNIALISM IS CLEARLY BASED ON THE ALLEGORICAL METHOD OF INTERPRETATION

As pointed out above, "The early premillennialism of the first two centuries was soon engulfed by the amillennialism which arose in the third and fourth centuries."[338] This newly formed belief was (and is) directly attributable to the allegorical method of interpretation. To

---

[335] Ice, Thomas D., "An Evaluation of Theonomic Neopostmillennialism," *Bibliotheca Sacra.* Dallas TX: Dallas Theological Seminary, 1996, c1955-1995.
[336] Lewis, Gordon R., "Theological Antecedents of Pretribulationism," *Bibliotheca Sacra.* Dallas TX: Dallas Theological Seminary, 1996, c1955-1995.
69 69. Timothy Weber, *Living in the Shadow of the Second Coming, 1875–1982* (Grand Rapids: Zondervan Publishing House, 1983), p. 42.
[337] Hannah, John D., "A Review of The Incredible Scofield and His Book," *Bibliotheca Sacra.* Dallas TX: Dallas Theological Seminary, 1996, c1955-1995.
[338] Walvoord, John F., "Posttribulationism Today—Part IV: Futurist Posttribulational Interpretation," *Bibliotheca Sacra.* Dallas TX: Dallas Theological Seminary, 1996, c1955-1995.

establish this point, we again refer the reader to the unanimous voice of a variety of authors.

John Walvoord writes:

> Amillennialism with its spiritualization of prophecy provided no basis for considering a matter like pretribulationism.[339]

P. S. Karleen writes:

> The history of amillennialism is significant. It can be traced to the Church Fathers, and particularly the approaches to Scriptures of Origen and Clement of Alexandria, who believed that the Bible was to be interpreted allegorically, with the true meaning discovered beneath the surface. Augustine applied this especially to prophecy.[1] [340]

Norman Geisler writes:

> Caius, Origen, and Dionysius, all… engaged in allegorical interpretation of the Bible.[341]

Roy Aldrich writes:

> Thus Floyd Hamilton frankly admits that his amillennialism is based on a symbolic interpretation of Old Testament prophecies. He says, "We believe that the prophecies of the Old Testament were intended to picture the future in symbolic language, under the only religious symbolism that the people of that time would have understood, namely a picture of a restored theocracy, with the Holy City as the capital, and the temple with the sacrificial system as the center of all religious worship. That symbolism is full of spiritual teaching for us today, but is not intended to teach literal restoration of the old theocracy."[13] [342]

---

[339] Walvoord, Ibid.

1 1. John F. Walvoord, "Posttribulationism Today," *Bibliotheca Sacra* 132 (1975):17.

[340] Karleen, P. S., *The Handbook to Bible Study: With a Guide to the Scofield Study System.* New York: Oxford University Press, 1987.

[341] Geisler, Norman L., "A Premillennial View of Law and Government," *Bibliotheca Sacra.* Dallas TX: Dallas Theological Seminary, 1996, c1955-1995.

13 13. Floyd Hamilton, *The Basis of Millennial Faith*, p. 144.

[342] Aldrich, Roy L., "An Apologetic for Dispensationalism," *Bibliotheca Sacra.* Dallas TX: Dallas Theological Seminary, 1996, c1955-1995.

5. DISPENSATIONAL PRETRIBULATIONISM IS AN OUTGROWTH OF EARLY PREMILLENNIALISM

John Walvoord points out how pretribulationism came about:

> Pretribulationism arose as a refinement of premillennialism based on literal interpretation of prophecy which made it difficult to harmonize the doctrine of the rapture with the second coming of Christ to set up His kingdom.[343]

R. B. Zuck, in his review of *The Interpretation of Prophecy* by Paul Lee Tan, writes:

> From time to time, the author shows that the logical conclusion of approaching prophecy literally (while allowing for a full range of figures of speech) leads to belief in a pretribulational rapture.[344]

John Walvoord offers the following response to George Ladd's confusing position on how pretribulational teaching has come about:

> A better explanation is that the rise of futurism and the return to solid Biblical studies and literal interpretation of prophetic Scriptures, which characterized the Brethren movement, led to the pretribulational teaching.
>
> ...
>
> The fact is ignored by the author [Ladd] that the real reason for pretribulationism is the rise of literal and futuristic interpretation of prophecy. He himself admits plainly that the historical argument is by no means final, but that the real question is what the Bible teaches.
>
> An entire chapter is devoted to the dispensational problem, and the statement made is correct, that pretribulationism is an outgrowth of dispensationalism.[345]

---

[343] Walvoord, John F., "Posttribulationism Today—Part IV: Futurist Posttribulational Interpretation," *Bibliotheca Sacra*. Dallas TX: Dallas Theological Seminary, 1996, c1955-1995.

[344] Zuck, R. B. Rev. of *The Interpretation of Prophecy* by Paul Lee Tan. Winona Lake, IN: BMH Books, 1974. 435 pp. *Bibliotheca Sacra*. Dallas TX: Dallas Theological Seminary, 1996, c1955-1995.

[345] Walvoord, John F., "A Review of The Blessed Hope by George E. Ladd," *Bibliotheca Sacra*. Dallas TX: Dallas Theological Seminary, 1996, c1955-1995.

6. THE PREMILLENNIAL–PRETRIBULATIONAL–DISPENSATIONAL POSITION CONCERNING PROPHECY IS CLEARLY BASED ON THE LITERAL METHOD OF INTERPRETATION

We find that the division between premillennial–pretribulational–dispensationalism and amillennialism is directly attributable to the method of interpretation adopted. Those adopting the allegorical method, as opposed to the literal method adopted by dispensationalists, generally find themselves adhering to amillennialism. On the other hand, those who *consistently* interpret the Scriptures literally, thereby adopting both the premillennial and pretribulational views, invariably find themselves numbered among dispensationalists. Those few premillennialists who do not consider themselves dispensationalists (George Ladd, for example) are forced, at least to some degree, to depart from the literal method of interpretation.[346]

Concerning these conclusions Ryrie comments:

> In relation to the present discussion, the question relates to literal or allegorical interpretation, for if literalism is the valid hermeneutical principle then that is an approach to the Scriptures which if consistently applied can only lead to dispensational theology.[347]

Aldrich concurs:

> Dispensationalists are said to use a literal system of prophetic interpretation... Our conclusion is that the normal method of Bible interpretation results in premillennial dispensationalism.[348]

As Enns points out, dispensationalists are able to remain true to their method even when it comes to interpreting prophecy:

> *Literal interpretation.* Dispensationalists follow a consistently literal method of interpretation, which extends to eschatological studies... apply[-ing] the literal scheme of

---

[346] Cf. Ryrie, Charles C., "The Necessity of Dispensationalism," *Bibliotheca Sacra.* Dallas TX: Dallas Theological Seminary, 1996, c1955-1995.

[347] Ryrie, Charles C., "The Necessity of Dispensationalism," *Bibliotheca Sacra.* Dallas TX: Dallas Theological Seminary, 1996, c1955-1995.

[348] Aldrich, Roy L., "An Apologetic for Dispensationalism," *Bibliotheca Sacra.* Dallas TX: Dallas Theological Seminary, 1996, c1955-1995.

interpretation to all the disciplines of theology... insist[-ing] on literal *interpretation* for prophetic Scriptures even though they abound with figurative *language*...

[Concerning prophecy] Dispensationalists attempt to be consistent in literal interpretation...[349]

Elsewhere Enns affirms the same:

> **Interpretation.** ... Literal interpretation refers to "normal" interpretation—understanding words and statements in their normal, customary way.[77] Because prophecies concerning Christ's first coming were fulfilled literally, it makes good sense to expect the prophecies concerning His second coming to be interpreted literally. Furthermore, if prophecy can be spiritualized, all objectivity is lost. Dispensational premillennialists emphasize consistency in interpretation by interpreting prophecy literally.[350]

7. A FAILURE TO HOLD TO BIBLICAL INERRANCY CAUSES DISCREPENCIES

John Walvoord, in his review of *Jesus Christ And History* by George Eldon Ladd, holds a failure to hold to Biblical inerrancy responsible for the extant discrepencies:

> If one accepts the inerrancy of Scripture, it is almost inevitable that he will accept a Biblical eschatology which views the second coming of Christ as a personal future event. Invariably, those who deny this concept also deny the inerrancy of Scripture.[351]

Walvoord, in his review of *The Hope Of Glory* by Dale Moody, speaks of Moody's unfortunate decision to depart from orthodox premillennialism accompanied by his acceptance of the findings of "higher criticism" concerning Biblical inerrancy:

---

[349] Enns, P. P., *The Moody Handbook of Theology*. Chicago, Ill.: Moody Press, 1997, c1989.

77 77. See Charles C. Ryrie, *Dispensationalism Today* (Chicago: Moody, 1965), pp. 86–98; and Bernard Ramm, *Protestant Biblical Interpretation*, 3rd ed. (Grand Rapids: Baker, 1970), pp. 119–27.

[350] Enns, Idem.

[351] Walvoord, John F. Rev. of *Jesus Christ And History* by George Eldon Ladd. Chicago: Inter-Varsity Press, 1963. 62 pp. *Bibliotheca Sacra*. Dallas TX: Dallas Theological Seminary, 1996, c1955-1995.

Dr. Moody began his career with orthodox premillennialism, but later turned to amillennialism, neo-orthodoxy, and existentialism with its accompanying destructive criticism of Biblical inerrancy. The work is accordingly a curious combination of clinging to the past and abandonment to the present. The author holds no brief for Scriptural inerrancy and accepts the findings of higher criticism. He implies doubt concerning the historicity of Adam and Eve. Sometimes, however, he quotes Scripture as authoritative, when it suits his purpose, like a fundamentalist. He interprets Scripture with literalness, as in such a significant passage as Revelation 20:4 (p. 100), or with complete spiritualization, as when discussing Israel's future (p. 156).

...

The fallacy of this volume as well as the whole existential approach to the Bible is that it fails to recognize that hope not based on the inerrant Word is without foundation. Scriptures which are authoritative only when they commend themselves as true to contemporary man's intellectualism have no more authority than the human intellect that labels them as true. This volume, which is the theological autobiography of a scholar at war with himself, is symptomatic of modern theology trying to build certainty on the uncertainties of human judgment.[352]

8. AMILLENNIALISTS ADMIT THAT IF THEY ADOPTED THE LITERAL METHOD OF INTERPRETATION, THEY TOO WOULD HAVE TO BECOME PREMILLENNIAL

P. S. Karleen writes:

It is of great significance that some amillennialists have admitted that if they took prophetic Scripture at face value they would have to be premillennialists.[4] [353]

---

[352] Walvoord, John F. Rev. of *The Hope Of Glory* by Dale Moody. Grand Rapids: William B. Eerdmans Publishing Company, 1964. 300 pp. *Bibliotheca Sacra*. Dallas TX: Dallas Theological Seminary, 1996, c1955-1995.
4 4. See ch. 1, The Nature of the Bible, concerning Oswald Allis.

The reverse, of course, may also be considered true: if a premillennialist adopts the allegorical method of interpretation, he could easily find palatable something other than premillennialism. As Walvoord points out, this is exactly what Augustine did:

> As the dispensational literature... plainly states, the issue between the dispensationalist and the nondispensationalist lies in the dual hermeneutics of Augustine... Following this dual form of interpretation, Augustine abandoned premillennialism for amillennialism.[354]

9. Misconceptions Concerning These Issues Have Led Some to the Preposterous and Confusing Claim That Prophecy Requires Some Special or Different Form of Interpretation Than the Rest of the Scriptures

P.P. Enns provides the following observation:

> *Many conservative non-dispensationalists interpret the Bible literally with the exception of prophecy;* dispensationalists apply the literal scheme of interpretation to all the disciplines of theology.... Dispensationalists insist on literal *interpretation* for prophetic Scriptures even though they abound with figurative *language.* One reason for this, besides consistency, is the demonstrable literalness of prophecies already fulfilled in Christ's first coming.[11] There is every reason to expect the fulfillment of the prophecies concerning Christ's second coming to be literal as well.[355] (Italics and bold type added.)

Enns further observes:

> In this premillennialists criticize conservative amillennialists and postmillennialists for changing their

---

[353] Karleen, P. S., *The Handbook to Bible Study: With a Guide to the Scofield Study System.* New York: Oxford University Press, 1987.
[354] Walvoord, John F. Rev. of *Backgrounds To Dispensationalism* by Clarence B. Bass. Wm. B. Eerdmans Publishing Company, Grand Rapids, Michigan, 1960. 184 pp. *Bibliotheca Sacra.* Dallas TX: Dallas Theological Seminary, 1996, c1955-1995.
11 11. Ryrie, *Dispensationalism Today*, pp. 86–98; see also Bernard Ramm, *Protestant Biblical Interpretation*, 3d ed. (Grand Rapids: Baker, 1970), pp. 119–27.
[355] Enns, P. P., *The Moody Handbook of Theology.* Chicago, Ill.: Moody Press, 1997, c1989.

methodology in hermeneutics by interpreting literally *except in the case of prophecy.*[356] (Italics and bold type added.)

Walvoord explains:

The famous Bishop of Hippo held that while the normal grammatical and historical interpretation was proper in Scripture as a whole, *prophecy was a special case requiring allegorical or spiritualized interpretation rather than literal.* Following this dual form of interpretation, Augustine abandoned premillennialism for amillennialism.

The issue then is not whether all Scripture should be interpreted literally as no one, even the most extreme of dispensationalists attempts to be literal in every instance. Rather *the question is whether prophecy should be interpreted with the same degree of literalness as other forms of divine revelation.* The dispensationalist insists on a single hermeneutics which treats the interpretation of prophecy just as it does other Scripture, interpreting some expressions literally and others as legitimate figures of speech. In attempting to saddle the dispensationalist with a method of interpretation which requires that everything be taken literally, Bass is guilty of setting up a straw man. If in this essential of dispensationalism a scholar cannot comprehend the basic premise of a system, he is in no wise qualified to discuss the subject as a whole.[357] (Italics and bold type added.)

Ice, leading up to his conclusion of the prophecies of the millennial kingdom, writes:

It is wrong, however, to argue against literalness simply because there is a symbolic aspect in some sentences. True, the serpent is a symbol of evil throughout history, but this does not rule out the presence of a literal serpent in the Garden of Eden. Forty connotes the idea of testing, but this does not rule out the fact that Christ was literally tempted in the wilderness for 40 literal days. Mountains often symbolicly

---

[356] Enns, Ibid.

[357] Walvoord, John F. Rev. of *Backgrounds To Dispensationalism* by Clarence B. Bass. Wm. B. Eerdmans Publishing Company, Grand Rapids, Michigan, 1960. 184 pp. *Bibliotheca Sacra.* Dallas TX: Dallas Theological Seminary, 1996, c1955-1995.

suggest rulership, but that does not mean the mountains mentioned in connection with rule in Scripture are not literal (e.g., Mount Zion is a real mountain, even though there is much theology attached to this theme). Therefore the 1,000 years of Revelation 20 can rightly be taken as literal (which some postmillenarians have held).[358]

10. PROPHECY PERTAINS TO ISRAEL'S FUTURE

Concerning prophecy as it pertains to Israel's future, Enns writes:

> *Prophecy.* Dispensationalists attempt to be consistent in literal interpretation; therefore, the Old Testament prophecies concerning Israel are taken seriously. Furthermore, those prophecies pertain to Israel, the descendants of Jacob, not the church.[359]

The following quote bears repeating. Walvoord, pointing out the effects of the abandonment of Scriptural inerrancy, speaking of Moody (a premillennialist who later turned to amillennialism), and pertaining to Israel's future, writes as follows:

> Sometimes... he [Dr. Moody] quotes Scripture as authoritative, when it suits his purpose, like a fundamentalist. ... [But] Scriptures which are authoritative only when they commend themselves as true to contemporary man's intellectualism have no more authority than the human intellect that labels them as true.[360]

In keeping with the first point in Ryrie's *sine qua non,* in an article entitled "Does the Church Fulfill Israel's Program?" John Walvoord identifies four headings under "which the Old Testament specifically prophesies a special program for Israel." He lists these four headings as follows: (a) predictions concerning Abraham, (b) predictions concerning the nation Israel, (c) predictions concerning the land, and (d) predictions concerning the kingdom. These four are directly related and inseparably connected. If it can be illustrated that

---

[358] Ice, Thomas D., "An Evaluation of Theonomic Neopostmillennialism," *Bibliotheca Sacra.* Dallas TX: Dallas Theological Seminary, 1996, c1955-1995.
[359] Enns, P. P., Idem.
[360] Walvoord, John F. Rev. of *The Hope Of Glory* by Dale Moody. Grand Rapids: William B. Eerdmans Publishing Company, 1964. 300 pp. *Bibliotheca Sacra.* Dallas TX: Dallas Theological Seminary, 1996, c1955-1995.

literal fulfillment applies to any one of them, its bearings in relation to the other three must be recognized as well.

Pertaining to the first of these four headings—predictions concerning Abraham—Walvoord points out the following: "As far as the Old Testament is concerned, the promises given to Abraham were literally fulfilled." This carries particular significance, of course, in regards to the soteriological aspects of Jesus' first advent. No one would be foolish enough to deny that this "has been fulfilled literally."

Pertaining to the third heading—predictions concerning the land—Walvoord writes:

> The crux of the question of literal interpretation is found in the many promises given in the Old Testament concerning the land of Israel. Amillenarians are forced to adopt one of two explanations: either that the promises are not literal but refer to heaven, or that the promises are literal but are conditional and Israel failed to meet the condition.
>
> A study of the promises to Israel concerning the land demonstrate that both of these explanations are without support in the Old Testament.
>
> ...It is obvious that God is not talking about heaven, but about a literal land.[361]

Referring the reader to a couple of selected passages (namely, Deuteronomy 28:63–68 and Daniel 9:1–19), Walvoord summarizes as follows:

> In summary, the Scriptures predicted that Abraham's people would leave the land promised to them, and that was literally fulfilled in their bondage in Egypt. It was also predicted they would come back to the literal land, and they did. The Assyrian and Babylonian captivities were predicted, and they were literally fulfilled. It was predicted that Israel would come back to the land, and this again was literally fulfilled.
>
> Subsequent to the life, death, and resurrection of Christ, Jerusalem was destroyed in A.D. 70, and the people of Israel were indeed scattered throughout the whole world. All of this illustrates and supports the pattern of literal fulfillment in

---

[361] Walvoord, John F., "Does the Church Fulfill Israel's Program? - Part 1," *Bibliotheca Sacra.* Dallas TX: Dallas Theological Seminary, 1996, c1955-1995.

relation to a literal land for a literal nation Israel. The only real question which remains is whether the Bible predicts that they will come back to the land a third time and possess it forever.[362]

For the Scriptural answer to this question, Walvoord refers his readers to Jeremiah 16:14–16 and Jeremiah 30:1–7. In these passages (as in many others) "The LORD" plainly states that He "will bring [Israel] again into their land that [He] gave unto their fathers" (Jer 16:15).

Pertaining to the fourth heading—predictions concerning the kingdom—Walvoord writes the following:

> According to 2 Samuel 7 and 1 Chronicles 17, David was promised that his kingdom would continue forever....
>
> ...
>
> All conservative interpreters recognize that the prophecy is ultimately to be fulfilled by Jesus Christ as the Son of David. The difference in point of view, however, is whether it will be a spiritual reign in the hearts of believers or a literal reign on earth.
>
> ...
>
> This is brought out in Isaiah 9:6–7... as brought out in Jeremiah 23:7–8... The promise is repeated so often and in such similar terms that it is amazing that anyone would attempt to spiritualize it and find other than a literal fulfillment.[363]

~ ~ ~

The author hopes this overview has helped the reader's understanding concerning the numerous effects and ramifications the various methods of interpretation impose upon one's theological perspectives. The next chapter summarizes and concludes this rather extensive subject matter.

---

[362] Walvoord, Ibid.
[363] Walvoord, Ibid.

CHAPTER TWENTY TWO

—SUMMARY AND CONCLUSIONS OF INTERPRETATION METHODS

The purpose at hand is to briefly summarize the previous chapters on interpretation methods. Every person who opens the Bible brings to the experience certain hindrances brought about by human weaknesses and imperfections. These hindrances result in numerous faulty understandings of God's Word. These faulty understandings create divisions among Christian believers. Many of our theological differences can be attributed to the flaws that exist in each and every one of us. Even in cases where Christians maintain the best of exegetical intentions, these differences are not easily resolved (they obviously await the Christian's upcoming resurrection experience for their complete remedy).

Among the primary causes for most divisions is the *method* in which each Christian *interprets* that which he reads in the Scriptures. Two basic methods exist: (1) the *literal*, and (2) the *allegorical*. Deciding which *interpretation method* one ought to employ can easily be determined by common sense, logic, and practical rules of normative literary procedure. Therefore, the divisions that improper hermeneutical choices cause ought to be more easily remedied than those problems which arise as a result of fallen human nature. *Christians are dutifully bound to arrive at proper conclusions concerning the matter of interpreting the Bible.*

Since the *allegorical* method can be shown to have arrived on the scene at a later date—for the purpose of appeasing the philosophical wishes of a few men in the early stages of the development of the Church (i.e., in an effort to make Greek philosophy compatible with the beliefs of the Church)—it must be rejected as a legitimate method of interpretation. This conclusion can be further validated and confirmed by the fact that Rabbinism, Jesus, and the Apostles did not employ the allegorical method of interpretation.

In contrast to the *allegorical* method of interpretation stands the *literal* method of interpretation. Again, this was the method employed by Rabbinism as well as by Jesus at the time of His first advent. It was also the method employed by the Apostles and was in no way undermined by the rest of the New Testament writers. It therefore must be accepted as the only legitimate method of interpretation.

The fact that literalists acknowledge the legitimate use of allegorical and figurative language must not be taken as adding credence to the arguments made by the allegorists—namely, that the allegorical method must be adopted. All literalists acknowledge the fact that figures, symbols, and types are a legitimate means of communication. The problems arise as a result of the efforts on the part of the allegorists to undermine the plain literal sense of the Scriptures by displacing it with unsupportable hidden *mystical* meaning, which is wrongfully identified as the *spiritual* sense.

To validate this point further, one need only observe the history of interpretation methods and the resulting effects which each of the methods under consideration have had: first, as it pertains to the errors of the Roman Catholic church; and second, as can be seen in the testimony of the lives of past heroes of the faith and a host of other witnesses. These heroes exemplified glorious light, particularly during the Reformation period.

Another important point to consider is the fact that all prophecies that have thus far been fulfilled have been fulfilled in a *literal* sense. There can be no doubt, then, that the rest of Scripture is to be taken in the same *plain* and *literal* manner.

The most notable outcome of the consistent literal method of interpretation is a system of theology that has come to be known as *dispensationalism.* Charles Ryrie has summarized what has generally become accepted as the three essential points of dispensationalism: (1) the recognition of a consistent distinction between Israel and the Church, (2) a consistent and regular use of a literal principle of interpretation, and (3) a basic and primary conception of the purpose of God as His own glory rather than the salvation of mankind. (The first and third points stem from the second. The rest of the tenets of dispensationalism are also grounded upon this second point.)

It is not sufficient to merely say that the hermeneutics of dispensationalism is a derivative of the literal method of interpretation; the key word *consistency* must not be overlooked. *Consistent* literalism is primarily what sets dispensationalism apart from other theological systems (most notably among conservatives from covenant theology). It is hard to imagine a person adopting a *consistent* literal method of interpreting the Scriptures not becoming a dispensationalist.

How one views Israel and the Church is directly related to the method of interpretation he has chosen to adopt; the *consistent* literal method of interpretation produces a clear distinction between Israel and the Church, whereas the non-literal method of interpretation does not. The outcome is primarily hinged upon how the Old Testament covenants and prophecies concerning Israel are interpreted. All non-dispensationalists are forced, in one manner or another, to see the New Testament as somehow making void, abrogating, or otherwise changing the plain meaning of the Old Testament prophecies pertaining to Israel. This has been a critical flaw in interpretation throughout most of the Church's history.

When examining the history of interpretation in the Church, it is necessary to distinguish between "historic premillennialism" and "dispensational premillennialism." In *historic premillennialism* a distinction between Israel and the Church is not maintained. (Note: this was a lagging issue for the reformers, whose focus was primarily upon soteriological issues.) This was due to the fact that the church did not maintain a consistently literal method of interpretation. These factors, more than anything else, have resulted in a distinction between dispensationalism and other systems of theology such as covenant theology and theonomy. The following conclusion can be drawn: if the Bible is consistently interpreted literally, a clear distinction will be seen between Israel and the Church. In order for an interpreter to derive any other conclusion, the literal method of interpretation must be abandoned.

Another distinction between dispensationalists and non-dispensationalists pertains to what *God's primary purpose* is in the Scriptures. For the dispensationalist it is the glory of God. For the covenant theologian it is man's salvation. It is concluded that the salvation of man is indeed *a primary and essential* revelation in the Scriptures, but is subsumed under *the overall purpose* of God in the Scriptures—namely, His own glory.

A number of minor problems concerning interpretation methods have yet to be fully resolved among dispensationalists. Not all have settled on exactly what is meant by the term *consistent literal interpretation.* Some stress the "plain sense," while others stress the "literal" reference. Still others stress "normal language" usage.

However, extreme differences having to do with interpretation are rare among dispensationalists (though some do exist). The most widely accepted method today among dispensationalists is the *grammatical, historical interpretation.*

In addition to the minor *challenges* which have yet to be worked out among dispensationalists, there exist a number of *charges* raised by non-dispensationalists against dispensational literalism. The criticisms that dispensationalists currently endure can be traced to Augustine's departure from literalism which led to his adoption of the allegorical method of interpretation.

When faced with any challenge, it is imperative that the participants know their opponent's strategies and understand their arguments. Some of the criticisms which have emerged by non-dispensationalists are preposterous. Dispensational scholars have successfully answered these criticisms by presenting the principles of dispensationalism as the only sound and positive system of Biblical interpretation. It is maintained that the application of these principles serves to resolve a number of otherwise unsolvable interpretation problems.

As consistently pointed out throughout this book, that system of theology referred to as *covenant theology* adopts the allegorical method of interpretation. It has been consistently presented as an opposing view to dispensationalism, which adopts the consistent literal method. Again, two entirely different methods of interpretation underlie the clear distinctions that exist between these two conflicting theological systems.

As a result of adopting an entirely divergent interpretation method, covenant theology has developed entirely different views concerning each of the basic tenets adopted by dispensationalism. The covenant theologian does not see, as do dispensationalists, a distinction between Israel and the Church. Nor do they see God's primary purpose in Scripture as the glory of God; rather, they recognize it as pertaining to the salvation of man. The covenant theologian also, by adhering to the allegorical method of interpretation, derives an entirely different set of views concerning prophecy. The covenant theologian generally adopts the amillennialist view; whereas dispensationalists unanimously adopt the premillennial view. A number of subordinate issues stem from these differences. One of the primary distinctions between these two systems of theology has to do with the manner in which they each divide up the ages (past, present, and future). Another important outcome of these divisions has to do with how each perceives the issue of *Law* and *Grace* (a matter addressed in detail later in this book—cf. Chapters 26–29 and the Appendix).

Craig Blaising, in an otherwise unfavorable review of William Shepherd, points out that he (Shepherd), when "summarizing [the] main tenets" of dispensationalism, correctly notes this "law and grace" issue as a "fundamental division" between covenant theology and dispensationalism.[364] Based on their view of the covenants, man's history is basically seen by covenant theology as divided into two parts: *law* and *grace* (although sub-divisions are recognized). Dispensationalists, on the other hand, see a sevenfold division. As with the other noted distinctions between these two systems of theology, this difference also is directly attributable to the opposing interpretation methods adopted by each camp.

In addition to Ryrie's three essentials of dispensationalism, *consistent literalism* also has a significant bearing on a number of other issues. Among the most critical of these is the effect that the literal method of interpretation has on how *prophecy* is to be interpreted. This, along with the aforementioned *Law-Grace* issue, is to be listed among the major and significant distinctions that exist between dispensationalism and covenant theology.

Concerning the eschatological implications of *prophecy*, it can generally be stated that dispensationalists adopt the premillennial view, while covenant theologians hold to the amillennial view.

When examining *prophecy* in relation to *interpretation methods,* the following related eschatological issues emerge:

1) The premillennial view was first on the scene.

2) An amillennialism engulfment of premillennialism began in the third and fourth centuries.

3) Premillennialism is clearly based on the literal method of interpretation.

---

[364] See Blaising, Craig A., Ibach, Robert D., Jr., Ed. Rev. of "Revelation and the Hermeneutics of Dispensationalism" by William H. Shepherd, Jr., *Anglican Theological Review* 71 (1989): 281–99. *Bibliotheca Sacra.* Dallas TX: Dallas Theological Seminary, 1996, c1955-1995.

4) Amillennialism is clearly based on the allegorical method of interpretation.

5) Dispensational pretribulationism is an outgrowth of early premillennialism.

6) The premillennial-pretribulational-dispensational position concerning prophecy is clearly based on the literal method of interpretation.

7) A failure to hold to Biblical inerrancy causes discrepancies.

8) Amillennialists admit that if they adopted the literal method of interpretation, they too would have to become premillennial.

9) Misconceptions concerning these issues have led some to the preposterous and confusing claim that prophecy requires some special or different form of interpretation than the rest of the Scriptures.

10) Prophecy pertains to Israel's future.

Concerning the prophecies that "pertain to Israel's future," one need only observe the prophecies that have been fulfilled pertaining to Israel's *past;* they have all been fulfilled literally. It is inconsistent and unsupportable, therefore, to consider anything other than a *literal "future"* fulfillment of those prophecies that have yet to be fulfilled.

Considered in the upcoming section are certain related *secondary theological outcomes* as they are viewed by the various camps. The section concludes with a focus on issues which pertain to *Law* and *Grace*.

~ ~ ~

FOR FURTHER STUDY ON INTERPRETATION METHODS

Ryrie, Charles C., *Dispensationalism*. Chicago: Moody Press, 1995, pp. 12, 19, 20, 40, 41, 43, 45, 57, 74, 79-91, 95, 96, 98-101, 130, 142, 146, 147, 157, 158, 164, 174, 175, 177, 191, 192, 197, 213.

Pentecost, J. Dwight, *Things to Come: A Study in Biblical Eschatology*. Grand Rapids, MI.: Zondervan Publishing House, 1980, c1958, pp. 1-64.

FOR ADDITIONAL STUDY[365] ON INTERPRETATION METHODS

Aldrich, Roy L., "An Apologetic for Dispensationalism," *Bibliotheca Sacra*. Dallas TX: Dallas Theological Seminary. 1996, c1955-1995.

Bailey, Mark L. Rev. of *Basic Bible Interpretation,* by Roy B. Zuck. Wheaton, IL: Victor Books, 1991. 324 pp. *Bibliotheca Sacra*. Dallas TX: Dallas Theological Seminary. 1996, c1955-1995.

Blaising, Craig A., "Development of Dispensationalism by Contemporary Dispensationalists," *Bibliotheca Sacra*. Dallas TX: Dallas Theological Seminary. 1996, c1955-1995.

- - -. Ibach, Robert D., Jr., Ed. Rev. of "Revelation and the Hermeneutics of Dispensationalism," by William H. Shepherd, Jr., *Anglican Theological Review* 71 (1989): 281–99. *Bibliotheca Sacra*. Dallas TX: Dallas Theological Seminary. 1996, c1955-1995.

Blum, Edwin A., "Augustine: The Bishop and Theologian," *Bibliotheca Sacra*. Dallas TX: Dallas Theological Seminary. 1996, c1955-1995.

Bock, Darrell L., "The Son of David and the Saints' Task: The Hermeneutics of Initial Fulfillment," *Bibliotheca Sacra*. Dallas TX: Dallas Theological Seminary. 1996, c1955-1995.

- - -. Rev. of *The Uses of the Old Testament in the New,* by Walter C. Kaiser, Jr. Chicago: Moody Press, 1985; *Bibliotheca Sacra*. Dallas TX: Dallas Theological Seminary. 1996, c1955-1995— Jul 1986.

Bowers, Russell H., Jr., "Dispensational Motifs in the Writings of Erich Sauer," *Bibliotheca Sacra*. Dallas TX: Dallas Theological Seminary. 1996, c1955-1995.

Cook, Stuart S. Rev. of *Looking Both Ways: Exploring the Interface between Christianity and Sociology,* by Richard Perkins. Grand Rapids: Baker Book House, 1987. 189 pp. *Bibliotheca Sacra*. Dallas TX: Dallas Theological Seminary. 1996, c1955-1995.

Dollar, George W., "Early American Dispensationalist:—The Reverend F. L. Chapell," *Bibliotheca Sacra*. Dallas TX: Dallas Theological Seminary. 1996, c1955-1995.

Deibler, E. C. Rev. of *Evangelicalism and Anabaptism*. Edited by C. Norman Kraus. Scottdale, PA: Herald Press, 1979. 190 pp. *Bibliotheca Sacra*. Dallas TX: Dallas Theological Seminary. 1996, c1955-1995.

Geisler, Norman L., "A Premillennial View of Law and Government," *Bibliotheca Sacra*. Dallas TX: Dallas Theological Seminary. 1996, c1955-1995.

---

[365] Note: it is not to be assumed that ALL works suggested by the author for review have been written from a dispensational standpoint.

Harbin, Michael A., "The Hermeneutics of Covenant Theology," *Bibliotheca Sacra*. Dallas TX: Dallas Theological Seminary, 1996, c1955-1995.

Hannah, John D., "A Review of The Incredible Scofield and His Book," *Bibliotheca Sacra*. Dallas TX: Dallas Theological Seminary, 1996, c1955-1995.

Houghton, George G., "Lewis Sperry Chafer, 1871–1952," *Bibliotheca Sacra*. Dallas TX: Dallas Theological Seminary, 1996, c1955-1995.

Hullinger, Jerry M., "The Problem of Animal Sacrifices in Ezekiel 40–48," *Bibliotheca Sacra*. Dallas TX: Dallas Theological Seminary, 1996, c1955-1995.

Ice, Thomas D., "An Evaluation of Theonomic Neopostmillennialism," *Bibliotheca Sacra*. Dallas TX: Dallas Theological Seminary, 1996, c1955-1995.

Johnson, Elliott E., "Hermeneutical Principles and the Interpretation of Psalm 110," *Bibliotheca Sacra*. Dallas TX: Dallas Theological Seminary, 1996, c1955-1995.

Lewis, Gordon R., "Theological Antecedents of Pretribulationism," *Bibliotheca Sacra*. Dallas TX: Dallas Theological Seminary, 1996, c1955-1995.

Lightner, Robert P. Rev. of *Israelology: The Missing Link in Systematic Theology,* by Arnold G. Fruchtenbaum. Tustin, CA.: Ariel Ministries Press, 1989., *Bibliotheca Sacra*. Dallas TX: Dallas Theological Seminary, 1996, c1955-1995. (Jan 1994A).

- - -. Rev. of *Essentials of Evangelical Theology,* Vol. 2. By Donald G. Bloesch. San Francisco: Harper & Row, 1979. *Bibliotheca Sacra*. Dallas TX: Dallas Theological Seminary, 1996, c1955-1995. (Jul 1980A).

- - -. Rev. of *The Origins of Dispensationalism,* by Larry Crutchfield. Lanham, MD: University Press of America, 1992. 236 pp. *Bibliotheca Sacra*. Dallas TX: Dallas Theological Seminary, 1996, c1955-1995. (Oct 1992A).

- - -. "Theological Perspectives on Theonomy Part I: Theonomy and Dispensationalism," *Bibliotheca Sacra*. Dallas TX: Dallas Theological Seminary, 1996, c1955-1995.

- - -. "Theological Perspectives on Theonomy Part II: Nondispensational Responses to Theonomy," *Bibliotheca Sacra*. Dallas TX: Dallas Theological Seminary, 1996, c1955-1995.

- - -. "Theological Perspectives on Theonomy Part III: A Dispensational Response to Theonomy," *Bibliotheca Sacra*. Dallas TX: Dallas Theological Seminary, 1996, c1955-1995.

Mason, Jr., Clarence E., "A Review of Dispensationalism by John Wick Bowman: Part I," *Bibliotheca Sacra*. Dallas TX: Dallas Theological Seminary, 1996, c1955-1995.

- - -. "A Review of Dispensationalism by John Wick Bowman: Part II," *Bibliotheca Sacra*. Dallas TX: Dallas Theological Seminary, 1996, c1955-1995.

Pyne, Robert A. Rev. of "The Law of Moses and the Christian: A Compromise," by David A. Dorsey, *Journal of the Evangelical Theological Society* 34 (September 1991): 321–34. *Bibliotheca Sacra. Dallas TX:* CD-ROM. Dallas Theological Seminary, 1996, c1955-1995.

Richard, Ramesh P., "Methodological Proposals for Scripture Relevance—Part I: Selected Issues in Theoretical Hermeneutics," *Bibliotheca Sacra.* Dallas TX: Dallas Theological Seminary, 1996, c1955-1995.

- - -. "Methodological Proposals for Scripture Relevance—Part IV: Application Theory in Relation to the Old Testament," *Bibliotheca Sacra.* Dallas TX: Dallas Theological Seminary, 1996, c1955-1995.

- - -. "Soteriological Inclusivism and Dispensationalism," *Bibliotheca Sacra.* Dallas TX: Dallas Theological Seminary, 1996, c1955-1995.

Ryrie, Charles C., "A Trilogy of Theology," *Bibliotheca Sacra.* Dallas TX: Dallas Theological Seminary, 1996, c1955-1995.

- - -. Rev. of *Is The Rapture Next?* by Leon J. Wood. Zondervan Publishing House, Grand Rapids, 1956. 120 pp. *Bibliotheca Sacra.* Dallas TX: Dallas Theological Seminary, 1996, c1955-1995.

- - -. Rev. of *The Church In God,* by Harold J. Ockenga. Fleming H. Revell Company, Westwood, New Jersey, 1956. 350 pp. *Bibliotheca Sacra.* Dallas TX: Dallas Theological Seminary, 1996, c1955-1995.

- - -. "The Necessity of Dispensationalism," *Bibliotheca Sacra.* Dallas TX: Dallas Theological Seminary, 1996, c1955-1995.

Rand, James F., ed. Rev. of "The Bible and Modern Religions. II. Dispensationalism," *Interpretation*, 10:170–87, by John Wick Bowman, April, 1956. *Bibliotheca Sacra.* Dallas TX: Dallas Theological Seminary, 1996, c1955-1995.

Walvoord, John F., "A Review of The Blessed Hope by George E. Ladd," *Bibliotheca Sacra.* Dallas TX: Dallas Theological Seminary, 1996, c1955-1995.

- - -. Rev. of *The Unity Of The Bible,* by H. H. Rowley. The Westminster Press, Philadelphia, 1955. 201 pp. *Bibliotheca Sacra.* Dallas TX: Dallas Theological Seminary, 1996, c1955-1995.

- - -. J. D. Pentecost, ed. Rev. of *Dispensationalism In America,* by C. Norman Kraus. John Knox Press, Richmond, 1958. 156 pp. *Bibliotheca Sacra.* Dallas TX: Dallas Theological Seminary, 1996, c1955-1995.

- - -. Rev. of *Contemporary Options in Eschatology: A Study of the Millennium,* by Millard J. Erickson. Grand Rapids: Baker Book House, 1977. 197 pp. *Bibliotheca Sacra.* Dallas TX: Dallas Theological Seminary, 1996, c1955-1995.

- - -. Rev. of *Dispensationalism Today,* by Charles C. Ryrie. Chicago: Moody Press, 1965. 221 pp. *Bibliotheca Sacra.* Dallas TX: Dallas Theological Seminary, 1996, c1955-1995.

- - -. Rev. of *Backgrounds To Dispensationalism,* by Clarence B. Bass. Wm. B. Eerdmans Publishing Company, Grand Rapids, Michigan, 1960. 184 pp. *Bibliotheca Sacra.* Dallas TX: Dallas Theological Seminary, 1996, c1955-1995.

- - -. "Does the Church Fulfill Israel's Program? - Part 1," *Bibliotheca Sacra.* Dallas TX: Dallas Theological Seminary, 1996, c1955-1995.

- - -. Rev. of *Jesus Christ And History,* by George Eldon Ladd. Chicago: Inter-Varsity Press, 1963. 62 pp. *Bibliotheca Sacra.* Dallas TX: Dallas Theological Seminary, 1996, c1955-1995.

- - -. Rev. of *The Hope Of Glory,* by Dale Moody. Grand Rapids: William B. Eerdmans Publishing Company, 1964. 300 pp. *Bibliotheca Sacra.* Dallas TX: Dallas Theological Seminary, 1996, c1955-1995.

- - -. "Posttribulationism Today—Part IV: Futurist Posttribulational Interpretation," *Bibliotheca Sacra.* Dallas TX: Dallas Theological Seminary, 1996, c1955-1995.

Witmer, John A., "A Review of Wrongly Dividing the Word of Truth—Part 1," *Bibliotheca Sacra.* Dallas TX: Dallas Theological Seminary, 1996, c1955-1995.

- - -. "A Review of Wrongly Dividing the Word of Truth—Part 2," *Bibliotheca Sacra.* Dallas TX: Dallas Theological Seminary, 1996, c1955-1995.

- - -. ed. Rev. of "Toward A Historical Interpretation Of The Origins Of Fundamentalism," Ernest R. Sandeen, *Church History,* March, 1967, pp. 66–83. *Bibliotheca Sacra.* Dallas TX: Dallas Theological Seminary, 1996, c1955-1995.

- - -. ed. Rev. of "Principles of Interpretation in Regard to Prophecy with Special Reference to Millennialism," C. Kuehne, *The Journal of Theology* 21 (December 1981): 2–28. *Bibliotheca Sacra.* Dallas TX: Dallas Theological Seminary, 1996, c1955-1995.

Zuck, Roy. B. Rev. of *The Psychology of Biblical Interpretation,* by Cedric B. Johnson. Grand Rapids: Zondervan Publishing House, 1983. 119 pp. *Bibliotheca Sacra.* Dallas TX: Dallas Theological Seminary, 1996, c1955-1995.

- - -. Rev. of *Hermeneutics: Principles and Processes of Biblical Interpretation,* by Henry A. Virkler. Grand Rapids: Baker Book House, 1981. 255 pp. *Bibliotheca Sacra.* Dallas TX: Dallas Theological Seminary, 1996, c1955-1995.

- - -. Rev. of *The Interpretation of Prophecy,* by Paul Lee Tan. Winona Lake, IN: BMH Books, 1974. 435 pp. *Bibliotheca Sacra.* Dallas TX: Dallas Theological Seminary, 1996, c1955-1995.

- - -. Rev. of *Daniel: An Introduction and Commentary.* The Tyndale Old Testament Commentaries, by Joyce G. Baldwin. Downers Grove, IL: InterVarsity Press, 1978. 210 pp. *Bibliotheca Sacra.* Dallas TX: Dallas Theological Seminary, 1996, c1955-1995.

- - -. Rev. of *Dispensationalism,* by Charles C. Ryrie. Chicago: Moody Press, 1995. 224 pp. *Bibliotheca Sacra.* Dallas TX: Dallas Theological Seminary, 1996, c1955-1995.

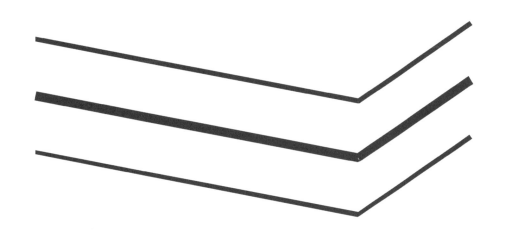

Section Three

—Secondary Theological Outcomes

CHAPTER TWENTY THREE

—INTRODUCTION TO SECONDARY THEOLOGICAL OUTCOMES

It cannot be over emphasized just how important it is to settle in one's heart those matters addressed in the previous section having to do with the *sine qua non* of dispensationalism—especially that which pertains to *interpretation methods*. Many doctrinal differences among even conservative Christians can be traced to variances on these *primary* principles. And, as might be expected, a whole host of *secondary* doctrinal issues emerge as a direct result of where one positions himself on these *fundamentals*. It stands to reason that if there is no agreement at the fundamental level, the secondary doctrines developed will also be at odds. How can it be otherwise? These contrary doctrinal positions, then, result in a number of various forms of divisions among Christians, who are otherwise intended by God to be in unified agreement. The differences, in some cases, are so acute, it almost leaves one with the impression that certain groups referring to themselves as "Christians" hardly even belong to the same body of believers.

Though an almost endless number could be listed for review, the primary focus of this section is to examine several of the secondary doctrinal outcomes which *divide* Christians, primarily as a result of the failure to interpret the Bible according to the *consistent literal* method. Before undertaking that rather arduous task, however, considered first will be those doctrines which are generally held in *agreement* by all conservative camps. Then those doctrines which represent the *divisions* will be taken into consideration.

CHAPTER TWENTY FOUR
—COMMON ESCHATOLOGY

Relatively speaking, only recently has there been any significant level of theological development in the field of eschatological studies (the study of *last things*). It is clear that the position one takes on those matters discussed in the preceding chapters concerning interpretation methods has an enormous bearing on one's views concerning the *millennium*. It is equally clear, in turn, that the varying positions held on the *millennium* (i.e., premillennialism, amillennialism, and postmillennialism) have a profound effect on a number of other doctrines having to do with *last things*.

Before moving on to a more detailed examination of the critical matters pertaining to the millennium (and other *distinguishing* doctrines affected) which *divide* Christians, we first lend consideration to those doctrines having to do with *"last things"* as they are generally held in *common* by most orthodox Christians—dispensationalists and non-dispensationalists alike. Below is a summary of such *common* views as P. P. Enns lists them in an article entitled "Eschatology: Doctrine of Last Things."[366]

Common Factors in Eschatology

DEATH

"Death may be thus defined as the end of physical life through the separation of soul and body (cf. James 2:26)."[367] In other words, death does not result in the annihilation of the soul or the spirit. This holds true for both believers and nonbelievers alike: each continues to exist as a conscience being in one of two conditions—saved or lost. Furthermore, virtually all Christians understand death as a result of the sin Adam committed in the garden—the consequence that fell upon the entire human race.

---

[366] Enns, P. P., *The Moody Handbook of Theology*. Chicago, Ill.: Moody Press, 1997, c1989.

[367] Enns, Ibid. Cf. Louis Berkhof, *Systematic Theology* (Grand Rapids: Eerdmans, 1941), p. 668; and Millard J. Erickson, *Christian Theology*, 3 vols. (Grand Rapids: Baker, 1985), 3:1169.

HEAVEN

The word *heaven* is generally understood to mean "that which is above."[368] It is used three ways in the Bible.[369]

(1) ***The atmospheric heaven***. This space surrounding the earth extending to a height of approximately six miles. From the atmospheric heaven the earth receives dew, frost, rain, snow, wind, and thunder.

(2) ***The celestial heaven***. In this realm abides the sun, moon, stars, and planets.

(3) ***The dwelling place of God***. This is the place where God abides, sitting upon His throne. A number of things occur in this realm which has to do with man: from this place God renders judgment, looks down upon His people, and hears their prayers. When He sends His blessings upon man, this is the place from whence they are sent. Today, when a believer passes from this life to the next, he is immediately transported to this glorious dwelling place to enjoy intimate personal fellowship with God forevermore.

HELL

Another matter which is held in general agreement among orthodox Christianity is that which pertains to the subject of *hell*. There are a number of Hebrew and Greek words that have been translated as *"hell"* in our English Bibles (especially in the KJV[370]). Below, these words are listed in their original language along with their various meanings:

- ***Sheol***. The word *sheol* occurs sixty-five times in the Old Testament and is translated by words like "grave," "hell," "pit," and "sheol." This word is used to signify the grave

---

[368] Wilbur M. Smith, *The Biblical Doctrine of Heaven* (Chicago: Moody, 1968), p. 27.

[369] P. P. Enns refers his reader to the excellent article by Wilbur M. Smith, "Heaven" in Merrill C. Tenney, ed., *The Zondervan Pictorial Encyclopedia of the Bible*, 5 vols. (Grand Rapids: Zondervan, 1975), 3:60–64. See also his important work *The Biblical Doctrine of Heaven*. This is undoubtedly the most important book on the subject.

[370] The KJV Bible uses the English word *hell* 54 times; considerably more than any other English translation (with the exception of *The Message: The Bible in Contemporary Language* by E. H. Peterson, Colorado Springs, Colo.: NavPress, 2003, which translates the word hell 59 times).

where the bodies (not the souls) of the dead go; this includes the bodies of all people—both good and bad. Believers are rescued from sheol.

- **Hades.** The word *hades* is used in the New Testament as an equivalent to the Hebrew term *sheol.* Some, based on Ephesians 4:9–10 and 1 Peter 3:19, have developed the theory that *hades,* as an intermediate holding place, has two compartments, a place of torments for the wicked and a place of bliss for the righteous. Not everyone agrees with this theory, however. The New Testament refers to *hades* as both a *place* (of punishment) and a *state* (of death).

- **Gehenna.** The word *gehenna* is derived from the Valley of Hinnom, a place where infants were sacrificed in fire to the god Molech. The prophet Jeremiah associated *gehenna* with the judgment of God; it also was the place where the bodies of animals and criminals were burned. Hence, it became synonymous with eternal punishment, the fire of hell.

- **Tartaroo.** *Tartaroo* conveys the idea of a doleful and dark subterranean region. Though ancient Greeks regarded it as the abode of the wicked dead, according to its single New Testament use (2Pe 2:4), it appears to be connected with an intermediate place for the punishment of fallen angels as they are *held* (i.e., "reserved"), pending the judgment of God.

- **Abyss.** *Abyss,* meaning "bottomless," is the prison for demons over which Satan is king. From the *abyss* demons will be released during the Tribulation (Rev 9:1 ff.). It is the place where Satan, at the second advent of Jesus, will be bound and confined for a thousand years (Rev 20:1-3).

- **Other Terms.** A number of other terms are used in the New Testament to describe the place where unbelievers will live in torment throughout eternity. These include: "the lake that burns with fire and brimstone" (Rev 21:8), "lake of fire" (Rev 19:20; 20:10, 14-15), "unquenchable fire" (Mat 3:12; Mar 9:43, 48), "eternal fire" (Mat 25:41), "furnace of fire" (Mat 13:42, 50), and "outer darkness" (Mat 8:12; 22:13; 25:30).

THE RETURN OF CHRIST

The return of Christ, although many evangelicals disagree over the details, is a highly cherished and comforting hope of believers everywhere. Christ's return is literal; He will physically return in the same manner in which He departed (Act 1:11). Upon returning, He will take believers back with Him to His Father's home (Joh 14:1–3); at which point the mortal bodies of believers will be transformed into immortal ones. Then, they shall take up their promised place of citizenry with God in heaven (Phi 3:20–21; 1Jo 3:2). This great hope and consolation applies not only to living believers but also to believers who have already departed from this life.

RESURRECTION OF THE DEAD

The return of Christ can scarcely be contemplated without considering the hope of bodily resurrection. Both the Old Testament and the New Testament are replete with references to this foundational tenet of the Christian faith. In 1Corinthians chapter fifteen, for example, Paul presents a detailed defense and explanation of the resurrection. Verse seventeen of this chapter is a key verse: "And if Christ be not raised, your faith is vain; ye are yet in your sins." Christ's resurrection is the primary basis for the Christian hope. The New Testament climaxes with a description of an event referred to as "the first resurrection" (Rev 20:4-5).

THE JUDGMENTS

It stands to reason, as Enns puts it, "Because God is holy, He must judge all that is unholy or He would no longer be holy."[371] That judgment will be recompensed upon all people has been a truth recognized by God's people throughout all ages. God's judgments are applicable to the past, present, and future.

- *Past.* The Old Testament records past acts of God's judgments upon Lucifer, fallen angles, heathen nations, Israel, and individuals. Judgments are found in the New Testament as well: for example, judgment fell upon Ananias and Sapphira, members of the early church (Act 5:1-11).

---

[371] Enns, P. P., *The Moody Handbook of Theology*. Chicago, Ill.: Moody Press, 1997, c1989.

- **Present.** The New Testament makes it clear that judgment is active in this present age: *"The wrath of God is revealed from heaven against all ungodliness"* (Rom 1:18).

- **Future.** It is generally recognized that unbelievers will appear before the great white throne to be judged by God (Rev 20:11–15). At this judgment, it is generally agreed, God will prove the guiltiness of those who have rejected God's truth, at which time they will be sentenced to eternal damnation in the lake of fire (Rev 20:15).

Another pending judgment has to do with the devil and all his demons. At the end of this age, they, together with the beast and the false prophet, will be cast into the lake of fire (Rev 20:10).

All of God's judgments are true, fair, just, without bias, and according to perfect righteousness.

THE ETERNAL STATE

It is also generally agreed among evangelicals that the souls of men will live forever in one of two states: either in (1) eternal torments, punishment, and suffering in hell, or (2) in eternal bliss and fellowship with God.

(1) *The State of eternal torments, punishment, and suffering.* In this never-ending state of "punishment" and "torments" the inhabitants are described as spending their time "weeping and gnashing [their] teeth" (Mat 8:12; 13:42, 50; 22:13; 24:51; 25:30; Luk 13:28). Those sentenced to such agony are the rejecters of God (such as the rich man who mistreated Lazarus in this life [Luk 16:19-31]), the devil, the beast, and the false prophet. Some see Luke 12:47–48 as teaching that there will be varying degrees of punishment in hell. Regardless, it is clear that the Bible teaches that these unfortunate souls "will be tormented day and night forever and ever" (Rev 20:10).

Berkhof provides the following description of hell:

> (a) a total absence of the favor of God; (b) an endless disturbance of life as a result of the complete domination of sin; (c) positive pains and sufferings in body and soul; and (d) such subjective punishments as pangs of conscience, anguish, despair, weeping, and gnashing of

> teeth, Matt. 8:12; 13:50; Mark 9:43–44, 47–48; Luke 16:23, 28; Rev. 14:10; 21:8.[372]

(2) *The State of eternal bliss and fellowship with God.* On the other hand, the future is much brighter for believers: they are promised a time of never-ending joy, happiness, fellowship, and bliss. The object and source of this indescribable state is the presence of Almighty God, Jesus Christ, and the Holy Spirit, for in His "presence is fulness of joy... [and at His] right hand there are pleasures for evermore" (Psa 16:11). Those granted this wonderful privilege are the angels (i.e., those that did not fall), New Testament believers (identified as the "church of the firstborn" [Heb 12:23; cf. Col 1:18]), and Old Testament believers (identified as "spirits of just men made perfect" [Heb 12:23]). The place of habitation, New Jerusalem, is described in detail in the New Testament (Mat 8:11; Joh 14:2; Heb 12:22-29; 2Pe 3:10; Rev 21:1–22:5; cf. Isa 65:17).

~ ~ ~

Again, these are the fields of eschatology which find *common* acceptance among most orthodox Christians. In the upcoming chapter, a more detailed examination of the critical matters pertaining to the millennium and other affected doctrines which *divide* many Christians are examined.

---

[372] Berkhof, *Systematic Theology*, p. 736, as cited by P. P. Enns, *The Moody Handbook of Theology*. Chicago, Ill.: Moody Press, 1997, c1989.

FOR FURTHER STUDY ON COMMON ESCHATOLOGY

Ryrie, Charles C., *Dispensationalism* (Chicago: Moody Press, 1995) pp. 18-19, 145-158.

Enns, P. P., "26 ESCHATOLOGY: DOCTRINE OF LAST THINGS: Common Factors in Eschatology," *The Moody Handbook of Theology*. Chicago, Ill.: Moody Press, 1997, c1989.

Pentecost, J. Dwight, *Things To Come*. (Grand Rapids, MI.: Zondervan publications) 1958.

~ ~ ~

P. P. Enns, at the bottom of his article entitled "Eschatology: Doctrine of Last Things: Common Factors in Eschatology," suggest the following reading on the subject of...

HEAVEN AND HELL:

** Colin Brown, ed. *The New International Dictionary of New Testament Theology*, 4 vols. Grand Rapids: Zondervan, 1976. See the articles "Heaven," 2:184–96 and "Hell," 2:205–10.

* J. D. Douglas, ed. *The New Bible Dictionary*. Grand Rapids: Eerdmans , 1962. pp. 510, 518–19.

* Walter A. Elwell, ed.*Evangelical Dictionary of Theology*. Grand Rapids: Baker, 1984. Consult the various articles on "Heaven," "Hell," "Hades," "Sheol," and "Gehenna."

** Millard J. Erickson.*Christian Theology*, 3 vols. Grand Rapids: Baker, 1985. 3:1225–41.

** R. Laird Harris. "Sheol." In *Theological Wordbook of the Old Testament*, 2 vols., edited by R. Laird Harris, Gleason L. Archer, Jr., and Bruce K. Waltke. Chicago: Moody, 1980. 2:892–93.

** Gerhard Kittel and Gerhard Friedrich, eds. *Theological Dictionary of the New Testament*, 10 vols. Translated by Geoffrey W. Bromiley. Grand Rapids: Eerdmans, 1964–1967. See the articles on "Hades," 1:146–49, and "Heaven," 5:497–536.

** Wilbur M. Smith. *The Biblical Doctrine of Heaven*. Chicago: Moody, 1968. This outstanding work ought to be consulted for a definitive discussion of heaven. An extensive bibliography is included.

** William G. T. Shedd. *Dogmatic Theology*, 3 vols. Reprint. Nashville: Nelson, 1980. 2:667–754.

* Merrill C. Tenney, ed. *The Zondervan Pictorial Encyclopedia of the Bible* , 5 vols. Grand Rapids: Zondervan, 1975. See the various articles on "Heaven," "Hell," "Hades," "Sheol," and "Gehenna."

* Merrill F. Unger.*Unger's Bible Dictionary.* Chicago: Moody, 1961. pp. 462–64, 467.

CHAPTER TWENTY FIVE

—MILLENNIALISM AND RAPTURISM

By far, the most significant theological outcomes pertaining to the *sine qua non* of dispensationalism have to do with *eschatology*. As briefly discussed in the previous chapter, there is *general agreement* concerning many aspects of *eschatological* studies among the various camps of conservative evangelicals. It is also true that within this particular field of study some of the most *pronounced differences* are found. That which lies at the heart of most of these differences has to do with how each view the millennium. As pointed out previously, the basic differences are categorized according to the three major opposing points-of-view, namely, *premillennialism, amillennialism,* and *postmillennialism.* The purpose of this chapter is to further develop our examination of these three theological points-of-view, along with certain related views which pertain to the *rapture.* These dissimilar views are then compared side-by-side.

Charles Ryrie, in his book entitled *Dispensationalism,* in a chapter entitled "Dispensational Eschatology," describes a five-point trail which leads up to two primary differences that exist between dispensationalist and non-dispensationalist—i.e., the *rapture* and the *millennium.*[373] Ryrie's five-point trail can be summarized as follows:

1. ***The Hermeneutical Principle.*** Under this point Ryrie underscores the often repeated argument that "consistent literalism is at the heart of dispensational eschatology."

2. ***Fulfillment of Old Testament Prophecies.*** "The literal interpretation of Scripture leads naturally to [this] second feature…. In other words, the literal picture of Old Testament prophecies demands either a future fulfillment or a nonliteral fulfillment. If they are to be fulfilled in the future, then the only time left for that fulfillment is the Millennium. If they are not to be fulfilled literally, then the church is the only kind of fulfillment they receive, but that is not a literal one."

3. ***A Clear and Consistent Distinction between Israel and the Church.*** "This understanding of the fulfillment of Old Testament prophecies quite naturally leads to [this] third feature… which is a vital part of dispensationalism. All other

---

[373] Cf. Ryrie, Charles C., *Dispensationalism* (Chicago: Moody Press, 1995) pp. 145-149.

views bring the church into Israel's fulfilled prophecies except dispensationalism. ... The understanding of the how and when of the fulfillment of Israel's prophecies is in direct proportion to one's clarity and consistency in distinguishing between Israel and the church."

4. *Pretribulation Rapture.* "The distinction between Israel and the church leads to the belief that the church will be taken from the earth before the beginning of the Tribulation (which in one major sense concerns Israel). Pretribulationalism has become a part of normative dispensational eschatology."

5. *The Millennial Kingdom.* "A millennial kingdom fully integrated into the whole theological system is a feature of normative dispensational premillennialism."

Again, points four and five will be the primary subject matter of this chapter.

RAPTURE

The word *rapture* is not found in the Bible. It is a term from the Latin translation meaning to be "caught up" (cf. 1Th 4:17). There are basically three views[374] as to the time the rapture occurs: (1) pretribulation rapture, (2) midtribulation rapture, and (3) posttribulation rapture. Posttribulationalists suggest that the Tribulation is not a time of God's wrath but rather of Satan's wrath.

Gordon Lewis places extreme importance in the rapture question in regards to one's overall view of eschatology. He also emphasizes how directly related this matter is when it comes to distinguishing covenant theology from dispensationalism:

> Because last things succeed past and present things, one's whole Biblical perspective of human history is involved in the rapture question. Pretribulationalism is associated with a dispensational system of theology. Midtribulationalism and posttribulationalism are often at least suspected of some measure of alignment with covenant theology. In the interest of clarity, discussions of the rapture must consider something of the relationship between covenant theology and dispensationalism. We may then be in a position to assess the theological context of pretribulationalism in premillennialism and dispensational premillennialism.[375]

---

[374] Some hold to a fourth view—the partial-rapture theory.
[375] Lewis, Gordon R., "Theological Antecedents of Pretribulationism," *Bibliotheca Sacra.* Dallas TX: Dallas Theological Seminary, 1996, c1955-1995.

Lewis continues:

> Covenant theologians generally think they are justified in interpreting all the promises to Israel as fulfilled in the church, and often do not anticipate a historical millennium.[376]

MILLENNIUM

As is the case with the word *rapture*, the word *millennium* is also not found in the English Bible. It comes from the Latin word *mille*, which means "thousand." A key verse which lies at the heart of the controversy over the millennium is Revelation 20:4:

> "And I saw thrones, and they sat upon them, and judgment was given unto them: and I saw the souls of them that were beheaded for the witness of Jesus, and for the word of God, and which had not worshipped the beast, neither his image, neither had received his mark upon their foreheads, or in their hands; **and they lived and reigned with Christ** *a* ***THOUSAND years***." (Emphasis added.)

A question arises: Is this verse to be taken literally or symbolically? How one answers this question directly affects where he ends up in his eschatology. (It should be noted that the Greek word *chilioi* [hence, *chiliasm*], translated in the above verse as "thousand," is used six times in the context [cf. Rev 20:2-7].)

As explained earlier in this book: but one view was held by the Church for the first two centuries of her existence, namely, that which is currently referred to as *historic premillennialism*. As theological systems developed, three clearly definable positions concerning the millennium emerged: (1) amillennialism, (2) postmillennialism, and (3) dispensational premillennialism. Though not addressed in this chapter, it should also be pointed out that at least two other positions have emerged which represent exceptions to these three points-of-view. These include: (4) the nondispensational premillennial position (such as espoused by George Ladd and J. Barton Payne), and (5) the progressive dispensational position (such as held by Craig A. Blaisings and Darrel L. Bock). These two latter views, in one fashion or another, present variations and/or mixtures of the various aspects of the former three more easily definable positions.

In an article entitled "Eschatology: Doctrine of Last Things," under the subheading "Controversial Factors In Eschatology," P. P. Enns presents the helpful chart below summarizing four theological positions concerning the millennium:

---

[376] Lewis, Ibid.

VIEWS CONCERNING LAST THINGS				
Categories	Amillennialism	Postmillennialism	Historic Pre-millennialism	Dispensational Pre-millennialism
Second Coming of Christ	Single event; no distinction between rapture and second coming; Introduces eternal state.	Single event; no distinction between rapture and second coming; Christ returns after Millennium.	Rapture and second coming simultaneous; Christ returns to reign on earth.	Second coming in two phases: rapture for church; second coming to earth 7 years later.
Resurrection	General resurrection of believers and unbelievers at second coming of Christ.	General resurrection of believers and unbelievers at second coming of Christ.	Resurrection of believers at beginning of Millennium. Resurrection of unbelievers at end of Millennium.	Distinction in resurrections: 1. Church at rapture. 2. Old Testament/ Tribulation saints at second coming. 3. Unbelievers at end of Millennium.
Judgments	General judgment of all people.	General judgment of all people.	Judgment at second coming. Judgment at end of Tribulation.	Distinction in judgment: 1. Believers works at rapture; 2. Jews/ Gentiles at end of Tribulation. 3. Unbelievers at end of Millennium.
Tribulation	Tribulation is experienced in the present age.	Tribulation is experienced in this present age.	Posttrib view: church goes through the future Tribulation.	Pretrib view: church is raptured prior to Tribulation.
Millennium	No literal Millennium on earth after second coming. Kingdom present in church age.	Present age blends into Millennium because of progress of gospel.	Millennium is both present and future. Christ is reigning in heaven. Millennium is not necessarily 1,000 years.	At second coming Christ inaugurates literal 1,000-year Millennium on earth.
Israel and The Church	Church is the new Israel. No distinction between Israel and church	Church is the new Israel. No distinction between Israel and church	Some distinction between Israel and church. Future for Israel but church is spiritual Israel.	Complete distinction between Israel and church. Distinct program for each.

Enns, P. P. "Eschatology: Doctrine of Last Things— Controversial Factors In Eschatology" *The Moody Handbook of Theology*. Chicago, Ill.: Moody Press, 1997, c1989.

The variances between these systems of theology, as Enn's chart suggests, are very well defined. Note again how interdependent each of the aspects of each particular theological system is.

Again, the focus of this chapter will be narrowed to the following three: (1) amillennialism, (2) postmillennialism, and (3) dispensational premillennialism. (The reader is reminded of the fact that *dispensational premillennialism* may well be described as merely a further development of *historic premillennialism*). These three major views are described and summarized below.

Amillennialism.

The history of amillennialism can be traced to the church fathers, particularly to the allegorical interpretive approaches to the Scriptures of Origen and Clement of Alexandria. Augustine adopted and further developed this allegorical method of interpretation, especially applying it to the interpretation of prophecy. "As a result of this methodology of Augustine, the Roman Catholic Church was amillennial. Although the Reformers did reassert the truth of several great Biblical doctrines, they did not really deal with eschatology. Thus Reformed theology as a whole has been amillennial."[377] From a *conservative* protestant standpoint, covenant theology, systematized only within the last 350 years, continues to lend support to amillennialism. The views presented in this chapter concerning amillennialism are primarily according to the predominant eschatological views of Reformed theology, since the *liberal* theologians, while holding "to a form of amillennialism... are for the most part unconcerned with eschatology."[378]

Amillennialism simply means *no* millennium. Hence, the "amillennialist asserts that the Bible does not teach that there will be a physical kingdom on the earth over which Christ will reign. Hence, Israel will not experience fulfillment of the Old Testament promises

---

[377] Karleen, P. S., *The Handbook to Bible Study: With a Guide to the Scofield Study System*. New York: Oxford University Press, 1987. Karleen notes: "For a brief summary of this area, see Robert G. Clouse, *The Meaning of the Millennium* (Downers Grove, IL: InterVarsity, 1977), 9–10."
[378] Enns, P. P., *The Moody Handbook of Theology*. 26 ESCHATOLOGY: DOCTRINE OF LAST THINGS: CONTROVERSIAL FACTORS IN ESCHATOLOGY. Chicago, Ill.: Moody Press, 1997, c1989.

of national blessing."[379] The term, however, does not precisely identify the amillennialists' position, since amillennialists adhere to the view that we are now abiding in a *millennium* of sorts in this current Church age. Hence, some amillennialists prefer to use the term *realized millennium* to describe this present age.

Gordon Lewis provides the following description of amillennialism:

> That there is to be a future sociopolitical kingdom is opposed primarily by amillennialists. However, amillennialists agree that Christ's return to defeat the hosts of wickedness (Rev. 19:11) is to be literally interpreted. Since Christ literally returns, why should He not literally reign (Rev. 20:1–7)? But amillennialists do not interpret Revelation 19 and Revelation 20 in chronological succession. Rather, they hold that we have a series of progressively parallel passages, each beginning with the start of the present dispensation, and each culminating at its end with the battle of Armageddon, the final judgment, and the eternal state. The events of Revelation 20, on this showing do not follow those of Revelation 19, but start at the beginning of our age.
>
> …
>
> In order to deny a future millennium, Kromminga argues, the amillennialists disrupt the story of Satanic deception as it unfolds in Revelation 12–20 and shift his activity from accusing the brethren in Christ's heavenly presence to the earth and its inhabitants.
>
> …
>
> Amillennialists often stress a single judgment of the righteous and the unrighteous.[380]

Postmillennialism.

"Postmillennialism is actually a fairly recent system, having been formulated after the Protestant Reformation."[381] For several decades

---

[379] Karleen, P. S., *The Handbook to Bible Study: With a Guide to the Scofield Study System*. New York: Oxford University Press, 1987.

[380] Lewis, Gordon R., "Theological Antecedents of Pretribulationism: III. Premillennialism," *Bibliotheca Sacra*. Dallas TX: Dallas Theological Seminary, 1996, c1955-1995.

prior to World Wars I and II, many enjoyed a period of unprecedented optimism. Due to sharp upward trends in scientific advancements, standard of living, etc., postmillennialism became increasingly popular. The optimism, of course, declined rapidly with the advents of the World Wars.

As the term implies, postmillennialists believe that Christ will return at the end of the millennium (which is not necessarily taken to mean a literal thousand-year period). Christ's return is expected as the grand climax of the perceived moral and spiritual advancements purported to be occurring in this present age; these positive developments are seen as issuing-in the millennial age.

Postmillennialism may be defined as "that view of the last things which holds that the Kingdom of God is now being extended in the world through the preaching of the Gospel and the saving work of the Holy Spirit in the hearts of individuals, that the world eventually is to be Christianized, and that the return of Christ is to occur at the close of a long period of righteousness and peace commonly called the 'Millennium.'"[382]

In other words, though not adopting the doctrine of universalism, postmillennialists are optimistic about the moral direction of the inhabitants of the world; that is, they adhere to the idea that the world is becoming a better place with the passing of time.

P. S. Karleen describes the postmillennial view as follows:

> The postmillennialist holds that there will be an earthly kingdom, but without the visible presence of Christ. This view sees Scripture as teaching that Christ will return to earth after the kingdom has been inaugurated by human beings and has run its course. This kingdom is to be equated roughly with some period of blessing in the present age between the two advents of Christ.[383]

---

[381] Karleen, P. S., *The Handbook to Bible Study: With a Guide to the Scofield Study System*. New York: Oxford University Press, 1987.
[382] Loraine Boettner, *The Millennium* (Philadelphia: Presbyterian & Reformed, 1966), p. 14. See pp. 3–105 for the definitive, representative position of postmillennialism. Cited by P. P. Enns, *The Moody Handbook of Theology*. ESCHATOLOGY: DOCTRINE OF LAST THINGS: CONTROVERSIAL FACTORS IN ESCHATOLOGY. Chicago, Ill.: Moody Press, 1997, c1989.
[383] Karleen, P. S., *The Handbook to Bible Study: With a Guide to the Scofield Study System*. New York: Oxford University Press, 1987.

Somewhat of a revised form of postmillennialism is currently gaining again in popularity under the doctrine of *theonomy*. Referencing this connection Robert Lighter writes:

> Theonomists usually acknowledge that since World War I, postmillennialism has not been a popular eschatological view. They hold that its unpopularity is totally unjustified and insist that all who adhere to Reformed Christianity must take postmillennialism seriously.[384]

Postmillennialists—especially the *theonomic* variety—expect to issue in a Christianized form of thinking and law, making it the norm rather than the exception.[385] This view sees the carrying out of the Great Commission in Matthew 28:18-20 as an increasingly successful endeavor, culminating in an eventual broad reception of the gospel. Robert Lightner, quoting Greg L. Bahnsen, sets forth this position in clear contrast to both amillennialism and premillennialism:

> In particular what sets off contemporary postmillennialism from amillennialism and premillennialism? As Bahnsen explains, "The thing that distinguishes the biblical postmillennialist then from amillennialism and premillennialism is his belief that Scripture teaches *the success of the great commission in this age of the church*."[21] Theonomists have an "optimistic confidence" that the nations of the world "will become disciples of Christ, and [that] the church will grow to fill the earth, and that Christianity will become the dominant principle."[22] "The gospel... shall convert the vast majority of the world to Christ and bring widespread obedience to His kingdom rule."[23] [386]

Dispensationalists (and amillennialists, on this point), on the other hand, stand in stark contrast, and see instead a growing animosity and

---

[384] Lightner, Robert P., "Theological Perspectives on Theonomy Part I: Theonomy and Dispensationalism: Postmillennialism," *Bibliotheca Sacra*. Dallas TX: Dallas Theological Seminary, 1996, c1955-1995.

[385] The subject of *Theonomy* is covered in greater detail in a later chapter.

21 21. Greg L. Bahnsen, "The Prima Facie Acceptability of Postmillennialism," *Journal of Christian Reconstruction* 3 (Winter 1976–77), p. 68.

22 22. Ibid.

23 23. Ibid.

[386] Lightner, Robert P., "Theological Perspectives on Theonomy Part I: Theonomy and Dispensationalism: Postmillennialism," *Bibliotheca Sacra*. Dallas TX: Dallas Theological Seminary, 1996, c1955-1995.

rejection of the gospel (i.e., apostasy). This position, which instead implies a narrowing remnant, is somewhat akin (a repeat, of sorts) to Israel's broad rejection of her Messiah at His first advent; at that time only a few (i.e., a small "sect") recognized Him, loved the truth, and became His faithful followers.

As for the historical aspects of postmillennialism in relation to the premillennial views held by the early church, Walvoord (making a distinction "between biblical postmillennialism and evolutionary postmillennialism as illustrated in Charles Hodge and James H. Snowden") writes as follows:

> Postmillennialism is traced to Tyconius, a fourth-century African Donatist. ... The Alexandrian school of theology (represented by Clement of Alexandria, Origen, Gaius, and others)... introduced views contrary to premillennialism as early as a century before Tyconius. ... Augustine [was] the first orthodox theologian to present antipremillennial views.[387]

Dispensational Premillennialism.

The term *premillennialism* signifies that Christ will literally return to this earth *before* the millennium and reign for a thousand years. Hence, "The premillennialist believes that there will be a physical kingdom on the earth, involving the fulfillment of national promises to Israel, with Christ present as King."[388]

From its beginning the early Church was premillennial in its belief. As previously noted, *dispensational* premillennialism differs from the premillennialism of the early church in two primary areas: (1) in its strong distinction between Israel and the Church, and (2) in maintaining a consistent literal interpretive method of the Scriptures. Both views, however, are consistent concerning the *chronological* and the *futuristic* view. "On the chronological and the futuristic view we have (1) the binding of Satan, (2) the first resurrection, (3) Christ's reigning for a thousand years, (4) the second resurrection, (5) the loosing and final doom of Satan, (6) the great white throne judgment,

---

[387] Walvoord, John F. A review of *Contemporary Options in Eschatology: A Study of the Millennium* by Millard J. Erickson. Grand Rapids: Baker Book House, 1977. 197 pp. *Bibliotheca Sacra.* Dallas TX: Dallas Theological Seminary, 1996, c1955-1995.

[388] Karleen, P. S., *The Handbook to Bible Study: With a Guide to the Scofield Study System.* New York: Oxford University Press, 1987.

(7) the new heaven and the new earth."[389] What allows for the consistency between the two is the fact that none of these points require either the preeminence of Israel during the millennial kingdom or that Christ reign from Jerusalem.

Norman Geisler notes the following:

> The Gnostics were the first to reject the premillennial view. They were followed by Caius, Origen, and Dionysius, all of whom engaged in allegorical interpretation of the Bible.[390]

Gordon Lewis summarizes this theological position in regards to its significance on the pretribulational view of the rapture as follows:

> In sum, we have found that: 1) dispensationalism (and so pretribulationalism) teaches that individual salvation in any age is always by God's grace through faith on the basis of Christ's atonement, (2) dispensationalism (and pretribulationalism) affirm that in different periods of time believers collectively accomplish distinct temporal purposes through institutions as different as national Israel and local churches, (3) local churches, however, are not the last institution God employs, for after Christ's return He will rule a sociopolitical kingdom, (4) Christ's rule on the throne of David will be headquartered in Jerusalem and give an instrumental prominence to the Jewish people.
>
> These four doctrines do not render a pretribulational view of the rapture logically necessary, but they are its usual antecedents. Given these tenets, the pretribulational rapture of the church is a meaningful possibility. So we have reasons to examine evidence indicating whether or not it will be a future actuality.[391]

Considered next is:

---

[389] Lewis, Gordon R., "Theological Antecedents of Pretribulationism: III. Premillennialism," *Bibliotheca Sacra.* Dallas TX: Dallas Theological Seminary, 1996, c1955-1995.

[390] Geisler, Norman L., "A Premillennial View of Law and Government," *Bibliotheca Sacra.* Dallas TX: Dallas Theological Seminary, 1996, c1955-1995.

[391] Lewis, Gordon R., "Theological Antecedents of Pretribulationism: IV. Dispensational Premillennialism," *Bibliotheca Sacra.* Dallas TX: Dallas Theological Seminary, 1996, c1955-1995.

A BRIEF OVERVIEW OF AFFECTED AND
RELATED DOCTRINES

APOSTASY IN THIS PRESENT AGE

Amillennialism.

Amillennialists, like dispensational premillennialists, believe this world is progressively becoming more and more sinful, and the condition of the Church is becoming more and more apostate.

Postmillennialism.

Postmillennialists, unlike both amillennialists and dispensational premillennialists, believe that this world, and the condition of the Church, is progressively getting better.

Dispensational Premillennialism.

(See above under "Amillennialism.")

COVENANTS

Amillennialism.

Amillennialists, like postmillennialists, see the covenants given to Israel in the Old Testament as now spiritually applying to the Church instead.

Postmillennialism.

(See above under "Amillennialism.")

Dispensational Premillennialism.

P. P. Enns identifies the covenants as the foundation of dispensational premillennialism:

> Although Revelation 20:4–6 confirms dispensational premillennialism, that is not the foundation of it; the foundation of dispensational premillennialism is found in the covenants of the Old Testament.[79] These covenants were *literal, unconditional,* and *eternal.*[392]

---

79 79. For a detailed discussion of these covenants see J. Dwight Pentecost, *Things to Come*, Grand Rapids: Zondervan, 1958, pp. 65–128; Ryrie, *The Basis of the Premillennial Faith*, pp. 48–125; John F. Walvoord, *The Millennial Kingdom*, Grand Rapids: Zondervan, 1959, pp. 139–220; and Charles L. Feinberg, *Millennialism: The Two Major Views*, 3d ed., Chicago: Moody, 1980.

[392] Enns, P. P., *The Moody Handbook of Theology.* Eschatology: Doctrine of Last Things. Chicago, Ill. Moody Press, 1997, c1989.

The covenants, however, are hardly viewed by dispensational premillennialists as they are by amillennialists and postmillennialists. Dispensational premillennialists see the *Abrahamic* covenant as unconditionally guaranteeing to *Israel*, in an unequivocally literal sense, the Promised Land. This covenant will be fulfilled in the millennium. This promise is further developed in both the *Palestinian* covenant and the *Davidic* covenant. It further sees in the Davidic covenant, in the same literal sense to *Israel*, promises pertaining to lineage that places Christ upon the "throne" in order that He might rule forever. This covenant will be fulfilled when Christ returns and establishes His rule over believing *Israel*. It further sees the *New* Covenant as the future blessing that will come upon *Israel* when they recognize Christ as Messiah, and open their hearts to receive the forgiveness of God's grace through Him. This covenant also awaits the millennium for its fulfillment.

RAPTURE

Amillennialism.

The rapture is not a significant issue in amillennialism.

Postmillennialism.

The rapture is not a significant issue in Postmillennialism.

Dispensational Premillennialism.

Dispensational premillennialists distinguish the rapture from the second coming of Christ, believing that the Church will be raptured *prior to* the tribulation period (hence, the *pretribulational* point of view), and that Christ's second coming will occur *at the end of* the tribulation.

Dispensational premillennialists recognize three principle sections of Scripture to reveal the rapture: John 14:3, 1 Corinthians 15:51–52, and 1 Thessalonians 4:13–18. These verses have the following characteristics in common: (1) they state nothing of a preceding tribulation, (2) they state plainly that the immediate destination of the Church after the rapture is heaven, not the millennial kingdom on earth, and (3) there is no mention of Christ's earthly reign immediately following.

There is some disagreement among pretribulationists as to whether the Old Testament saints will be included in the rapture. While it is true that the followers of Darby have generally interpreted the rapture to include all saints, a very common alternative explanation is that *only* the Church, the saints of this present age, are raised at the rapture, and that the Old Testament saints are raised at the time of the occurrences described in Revelation 20:4.[393] In regards to this explanation, Walvoord comments as follows: "the fact is there is no Scriptural proof that the Old Testament saints are raised at the rapture."[394]

TRIBULATION

Amillennialism.

Amillennialists believe that believers will experience tribulation in this present time.

Postmillennialism.

Postmillennialists believe that believers will experience tribulation in this present time.

Dispensational Premillennialism.

Dispensational premillennialists believe the tribulation to be a seven-year period (the latter half being called the Great Tribulation) that begins with the signing of a pseudo-covenant by the beast falsely purporting to bring peace to Israel. This seven-year period involves judgments from God in which His wrath falls upon the unbelieving inhabitants of this earth. This dreadful period is described in Revelation 6 – Revelation 19. The seventieth week of Daniel's prophecy (cf. Dan 9:24-27) is seen to refer to this seven-year period (i.e., a *week-of-years*). There are two basic purposes for the tribulation: (1) bring about the conversion of rebellious Israel, and (2) judge unbelieving peoples and nations.

---

[393] Cf. Walvoord, John F., "A Review of The Blessed Hope by George E. Ladd," *Bibliotheca Sacra.* Dallas TX: Dallas Theological Seminary, 1996, c1955-1995.
[394] Walvoord, John F., "A Review of The Blessed Hope by George E. Ladd," *Bibliotheca Sacra.* Dallas TX: Dallas Theological Seminary, 1996, c1955-1995. On this point Walvoord attaches the following footnote: "For further discussion of this point, see *Bibliotheca Sacra*, 113:3–5, January, 1956."

CHRIST'S RETURN

Amillennialism.

"Amillennialists do not deny the literal return of Christ, but they reject a literal thousand-year reign of Christ on the earth."[395] "Amillennialists understand the second coming of Christ as a *single event*."[396] In contrast to postmillennialism, amillennialism and premillennialism teach that Christ returns to a world that is progressively getting more sinful. "Unlike premillennarians who teach that Christ's second coming is to establish His earthly kingdom, amillennialists teach that the purpose of Christ's return is for 'introducing the future age, the eternal state of things.'[33] This will be accomplished by the resurrection of the dead and the final judgment."[397]

Postmillennialism.

Postmillennialists believe that Christ will literally return to this earth in visible form following the millennium. The time of His coming is not known.

Dispensational Premillennialism.

In contrast to postmillennialism, dispensational premillennialism and amillennialism teach that Christ returns to a world that is progressively getting more sinful. In contrast to both amillennialism and postmillennialism, dispensational premillennialists understand Christ's coming to be in two phases. Dispensational premillennialists believe that Christ will physically return to this earth at the end of the tribulation to execute judgment and to inaugurate the millennial kingdom. At this time a number of things will occur: (1) the Old Testament and tribulation saints will inherit the kingdom, (2) the Jews will be judged and held accountable for their faithfulness (or unfaithfulness) as stewards of the Word of God, (3) saved Jews will enter the millennial kingdom, (4) the unsaved will be cast into outer darkness, and (5) unbelieving Gentiles will be judged, particularly regarding their treatment of the Jews.

---

[395] Enns, P. P., *The Moody Handbook of Theology*. Eschatology: Doctrine of Last Things. Chicago, Ill.: Moody Press, 1997, c1989.
[396] Enns, Ibid.
33 33. Berkhof in *Systematic Theology*, p. 707.
[397] Enns, Idem.

THE KINGDOM

Amillennialism.

Amillennialists consider this current Church age (the *millennium*, in their view) the same as the *kingdom of God*. In other words, "we are in the kingdom in some way right now."[398] "According to amillennialists, Revelation 20:4–6 [refers] to 'the present reign of the souls of deceased believers with Christ in heaven' while the kingdom of God 'is now present in the world as the victorious Christ is ruling his people by his Word and Spirit, though they also look forward to a future, glorious, and perfect kingdom on the new earth in the life to come.'[30]"[399]

Postmillennialism.

The following points characterize the postmillennialist's views on the millennium: (1) The millennium does not necessarily have to be a thousand years—it may, in fact, be longer than a thousand years. (2) An optimistic outlook on the Church's success in carrying out the great commission to preach the gospel to the entire world; this leads the inhabitants to become "Christianized," and the kingdom of God is in this manner extended throughout the world. (3) Moral and spiritual development of the earth's inhabitants occurs. As a result: (4) evil, in its many forms, is reduced to negligible proportions. (5) Jesus Christ returns after this long period of righteousness and peace has been established and maintained for a while, this period constitutes the *"millennium."*

In coming to understand the postmillennial view, it is also helpful to note the following: (1) the righteousness required, which will constitute the millennial kingdom, occurs gradually, (2) life will continue in its present form during the millennium, (3) postmillennialists do not adhere to the doctrine of universalism (universal salvation), and (4) Revelation 19:11–21 "is [seen as] a picture of the whole period between the first and the second advents, seen from the point of view of heaven. It is the period of advancing victory of the Son of God over the world, emphasizing, in harmony

---

[398] Karleen, P. S., *The Handbook to Bible Study: With a Guide to the Scofield Study System*. New York: Oxford University Press, 1987.

30 30. Anthony A. Hoekema, *The Bible and the Future* (Grand Rapids: Eerdmans, 1979), p. 174.

[399] Enns, Idem.

with its place at the end of the book, the completeness of the victory."[400]

Dispensational Premillennialism.

Dispensational premillennialists believe that the Church will be raptured *prior to* the tribulation period. At the *end of* the tribulation Christ will enter Jerusalem (the center of the world) as the long awaited king, sit upon the throne of David (with David as regent), and establish the millennial kingdom on earth. Israel will be gathered again from the nations (Mat 24:31), converted (Zec 12:10–14), and restored to the land. The *marriage supper* (distinguished from the *marriage*, which takes place between Christ and the Church during the tribulation) will occur at this time, as Israel is brought under the rulership of her Messiah with nobles and governors also ruling with Christ.

A perfect environment, both physical and spiritual, will exist during the millennium. Some of the prevailing features will be: peace, joy, righteousness, holiness, truth, comfort, no poverty, no sickness, perfect obedience, and fullness of the Holy Spirit.

RESURRECTION OF THE DEAD

Amillennialism.

"The amillennial understanding says that the Bible teaches a *bodily* resurrection at the end of the age (1 Cor. 15:35–49)."[401] "With respect to the time of the resurrection, the resurrection of believers and unbelievers occurs at the same time.[35] ... This resurrection... occurs at the second coming of Christ (1 Cor. 15:23; Phil. 3:20–21; 1 Thess. 4:16), and is also designated 'the last day' or the 'day of the Lord.' It is at the end of the age and at the advent of the eternal state."[402]

---

[400] Warfield, B. B., *Biblical Doctrines*. New York: Oxford U., 1929, p. 648.

[401] Enns, Idem.

35 35. Berkhof states: "All of these passages speak of the resurrection as a single event and do not contain the slightest indication that the resurrection of the righteous and that of the wicked will be separated by a period of a thousand years." Berkhof, *Systematic Theology*, p. 724; and Hoekema, *The Bible and the Future*, pp. 240–43.

[402] Enns, Idem.

Postmillennialism.

"Postmillennialists are in general agreement with amillennialists concerning the resurrection. There will be a general resurrection of both believers and unbelievers (Dan. 12:2; Matt. 25:31, 32; John 5:28, 29; Acts 24:15; Rev. 20:12–13) that will take place in conjunction with the return of Christ (1 Cor. 15:23, 24; 1 Thess. 4:16).[51],[403]

Dispensational Premillennialism.

Dispensational premillennialists believe that the Old Testament and tribulation saints will be raised at the Second Advent to inherit the kingdom (Rev 20:4).

John Walvoord, in response to George Ladd's categorical denial that the first resurrection can occur in more than one stage, writes:

> According to 1 Corinthians 15:23–24, there are three stages (*tagma*) of the resurrection of saints: Christ the first, those at His coming second, and those at the end third. Even Tregelles admits 1 Corinthians 15:24 is not the resurrection before the millennium—but the one after it.[13] Matthew 27:52–53 is another "stage" of the resurrection. That saints are not all raised at the same time is not "inference."[404]

Elsewhere Walvoord acknowledges that this "third resurrection [in 1Corinthians 15] can be debated, as it is not clear whether it refers to a resurrection of the saints at the end of the millennium or refers to the resurrection of the wicked."[405]

Walvoord presents the overall dispensational premillennial scheme on the resurrection as follows:

> Actually, the order of resurrections are Christ first, then the resurrection of Matthew 27, then the resurrection of the rapture, and then the resurrection of the tribulation dead. To this should be added the resurrection of Old Testament saints

---

51 51. See the discussion by Charles Hodge, *Systematic Theology*, 3 vols. (Reprint. London: Clarke, 1960), 3:838–44.

[403] Enns, Idem.

13 13. Ladd, *The Hope of Christ's Second Coming*, pp. 104–5.

[404] Walvoord, John F., "A Review of The Blessed Hope by George E. Ladd," *Bibliotheca Sacra*. Dallas TX: Dallas Theological Seminary, 1996, c1955-1995.

[405] Walvoord, John F., "Posttribulationism Today—Part IV: Futurist Posttribulational Interpretation," *Bibliotheca Sacra*. Dallas TX: Dallas Theological Seminary, 1996, c1955-1995.

which even pretribulationists place at the end of the tribulation.[406]

FINAL JUDGMENT

Amillennialism.

"The final judgment according to amillennialists is at the end of the age and is associated with the second coming of Christ, the resurrection of all people, and the inauguration of the eternal state. It will be a general judgment 'for the very purpose of judging the living and consigning each individual to his eternal destiny.'[36] ... The *objects* of judgment will be angels (1 Cor. 6:2–3) and all people (Matt. 25:32; Rom. 2:5–6; 2 Cor. 5:10[39]), which includes both believers and unbelievers."[407]

Postmillennialism.

"Postmillennialists are also in general agreement with amillennialists concerning the final judgment. At the second coming of Christ there will be a general resurrection and a general judgment of all people (Matt. 13:37–43; 25:32), as well as of angels (2 Pet. 2:4). There will be a judgment concerning the deeds done in the body and people will be judged according to the light they have received (Luke 12:47–48). Those who heard the gospel will be judged according to their attitude toward Christ.[52] "[408]

Dispensational Premillennialism.

Dispensational premillennialists see two judgments: (1) pertaining to the body of Church age believers called the *bema* judgment (2Co 5:10; cf. 1Co 3:12-15), and (2) the Great White Throne judgment (Rev 20:11-15). The former is not viewed as having to do with eternal destiny, but rather with rewards (or lack thereof) for faithfulness.

---

[406] Walvoord, Ibid.

36 36. Berkhof, *Systematic Theology*, p. 728.

39 39. No distinction is made between the judgment seat of Christ or the great white throne judgment in amillennialism.

[407] Enns, Idem.

52 52. Charles Hodge, *Systematic Theology*, 3 vols. (Reprint. London: Clarke, 1960), 3:849–50.

[408] Enns, Idem.

ETERNAL STATE

Amillennialism.

"According to amillennialism ... at the consummation of the present age, the eternal state is inaugurated without any intervening millennium.[28] [409] "Amillennialists teach that both believers and unbelievers will continue in conscious existence in eternity. ... The suffering of unbelievers will be *eternal*, just as believers will enjoy heaven for all eternity. ... The end of the age will issue in 'the regeneration' (Matt. 19:28), in which there will be a 'renewal of the present creation.'[43] [410]

Postmillennialism.

"The judgment by Christ, as postmillennialists teach, will result in the eternal disposition of the righteous to eternal life and the wicked to everlasting punishment."[411]

Dispensational Premillennialism.

The eternal state will immediately follow the millennium. The heavens and the earth, the domain of Satan's rebellion, are then judged (2Pe 3:10). Both believers and unbelievers will continue in conscious existence throughout all eternity. Heaven will become the abode of all the redeemed; their bliss will be *eternal*. "The lake which burneth with fire and brimstone" will become the abode of all unbelievers; their suffering will have no end. (Cf. Heb 12:22-24, Rev 21-22, Etc.)

~ ~ ~

(Note: a list of the adherents associated with each camp is charted on the following page.)

---

28 28. Berkhof, *Systematic Theology*, p. 708.
[409] Enns, Idem.
43 43. Berkhof, *Systematic Theology*, p. 737.
[410] Enns, Idem.
[411] Enns, Idem.

A List of Adherents			
Amillennialists	**Postmillennialists**	**Historic/Non-Dispensational Premillennialists**	**Dispensational Premillennialists**
Augustine	Charles Hodge	George E. Ladd	F. L. Chapell
Medieval Catholicism	A. A. Hodge	J. Barton Payne	James H. Brookes
Liberal Theologians	B. B. Warfield	Daniel Fuller	Lewis S. Chafer
Protestant Reformers	William G. T. Shedd	A. Reese	Isaac Watts
Reformed Eschatology	A. H. Strong	M. J. Erickson	John N. Darby
Luther	James H. Snowden	D. H. Kromminga	Arno C. Gaebelein
Calvin		Philip Mauro	Harry H. Ironside
Floyd Hamilton		R. Laird Harris	William Kelly
Dale Moody			C. H. Mackintosh
John H. Gerstner			C. I. Scofield
Vern S. Poythress			William L. Pettingill
Bruce K. Waltke			James M. Gray
Oswald T. Allis			J. Dwight Pentecost
Louis Berkhof			John F. Walvoord
G. C. Berkhouwer			Charles C. Ryrie
Gordon H. Clark			Thomas Ice
Stephen H. Travis			W. Graham Scroggie
Jesse Wilson Hodges			E. Schuyler English
Jay E. Adams			Frank E. Gaebelein
Anthony A. Hoekema			William Culbertson
Many Evangelicals, Lutherans, Roman Catholics, Presbyterians, and Southern Baptist			Charles L. Feinberg
			Allan A. Mac Rae
			Clarence E. Mason
			Alva J. McClain
			Rene Pache
			Wilbur M. Smith
			Moderates
			Erich Sauer
			Progressives
			Craig A. Blaisings
			Darrel L. Bock
			Robert L. Saucy
			Kenneth Barker

Addendum: The Church's History in Relation to Eschatological Issues

It is somewhat a monumental task to successfully sort through the doctrines of the past couple of millennia as they have evolved into today's contemporary mindsets having to do with views on the rapture, the millennium, and the many other various features of eschatology. It is the author's hope that the information provided above has assisted the reader in coming to a clearer understanding. The following quotes by Ryrie and Walvoord shed light on some of the reasons for the difficulties.

Ryrie writes:

> One of the evident features of the history of Christian doctrine is the fact that the church generally focused its discussions on one area of theology at a time. In our own day the area is eschatology, and discussions of eschatology are being heard in all groups. In conservative circles these discussions are raising questions in another field—dispensationalism.[412]

Walvoord, in "A Review of The Blessed Hope by George E. Ladd," writes:

> While the evidence supports the conclusion that some of the fathers were posttribulational, the discussion does not sufficiently account for the doctrine of imminency as it appeared so commonly in the early church. Pretribulationists who are familiar with the early fathers have never claimed that they were explicitly pretribulational. The fact is that the early fathers were not at all clear on many details of their eschatology and, though their premillennialism seems firmly established, most contemporary premillenarians would disagree with many features of the eschatology of the early church.
>
> A fair statement of the facts seems to be that some of the early fathers were explicitly posttribulational, that is, they regarded the tribulation as future and the coming of the Lord as following the tribulation. It seems also clear that none of

---

[412] Ryrie, Charles C., "The Necessity of Dispensationalism," *Bibliotheca Sacra.* Dallas TX: Dallas Theological Seminary, 1996, c1955-1995.

the early fathers were explicitly pretribulationists as there is no extant writing which develops this subject in the way it was later explained by Darby and his associates. In many respects, the theology of the early church was immature and it took centuries of controversy to settle the major points of theology. It should be obvious that a difficult matter like pretribulationism would not be settled in such a context. In the fifth century, when the early church had established its theological basis sufficiently to deal further with eschatology, there was already so much departure from premillennialism that there was no valid basis for such discussion. It remained for the Protestant Reformation to restore the authority of Scripture and for others later to restore premillennialism and futurism as a whole, including a proper doctrine of the church. This context was essential to the pretribulationism of the nineteenth century.

...

The teaching of the Plymouth Brethren on the pretribulation rapture was a refinement of the doctrine of the imminence of the Lord's return which had been held in one form or another from the beginning. ... It is certainly significant that pretribulationism is widespread today and is found particularly in those who have specialized in the study of the prophetic Word among premillenarians.[413]

~ ~ ~

The remaining chapters of this book focus upon another important theological outcome—how *Law* and *Grace* are to be perceived.

---

[413] Walvoord, John F., "A Review of The Blessed Hope by George E. Ladd," *Bibliotheca Sacra.* Dallas TX: Dallas Theological Seminary, 1996, c1955-1995.

FOR FURTHER STUDY ON MILLENNIALISM AND RAPTURISM

Enns, P. P., "26 ESCHATOLOGY: DOCTRINE OF LAST THINGS," in *The Moody Handbook of Theology*. Chicago, Ill.: Moody Press, 1997, c1989.

Feinberg, Charles L., *Millennialism: The Two Major Views*, 3d ed. (Chicago: Moody, 1980).

Lewis, Gordon R., "Theological Antecedents of Pretribulationism," *Bibliotheca Sacra*. Dallas TX: Dallas Theological Seminary, 1996, c1955-1995.

Pentecost, J. Dwight, *Things To Come*. (Grand Rapids, MI.: Zondervan publications) 1958.

Ryrie, Charles C., *Dispensationalism* (Chicago: Moody Press, 1995) pp. 12, 13, 38-39, 48, 62, 65, 74, 83-86, 89-90, 123-124, 128-133, 137-138, 146-149, 152-153, 156, 172, 177-178.

- - -. *The Basis of the Premillennial Faith* (Neptune, N.J.: Loizeaux, 1953).

Stanton, Gerald B., *Kept from the Hour* (Grand Rapids: Zondervan, 1956).

Walvoord, John F., "A Review of The Blessed Hope by George E. Ladd," *Bibliotheca Sacra*. Dallas TX: Dallas Theological Seminary, 1996, c1955-1995.

- - -. *The Millennial Kingdom* (Grand Rapids: Zondervan, 1959).

- - -. *The Rapture Question*, rev. ed. (Grand Rapids: Zondervan, 1979).

- - -. "Posttribulationism Today—Part IV: Futurist Posttribulational Interpretation," *Bibliotheca Sacra*. Dallas TX: Dallas Theological Seminary, 1996, c1955-1995.

~ ~ ~

P. P. Enns, at the bottom of his article entitled "Eschatology: Doctrine of Last Things,"[414] recommends the following reading on the subjects of...

LAST EVENTS

* Emery H. Bancroft. *Christian Theology*, 2d ed., revised by Ronald B. Mayers. Grand Rapids: Zondervan, 1976. pp. 345–410.

---

[414] Enns, P. P., *The Moody Handbook of Theology*. Eschatology: Doctrine of Last Things. Chicago, Ill.: Moody Press, 1997, c1989.

** Louis Berkhof. *Systematic Theology*. Grand Rapids: Eerdmans, 1941. pp. 661–738.

** J. Oliver Buswell, Jr. Systematic Theology of the Christian Religion , 2 vols. Grand Rapids: Zondervan, 1962. 2:285–538.

** Millard J. Erickson. *Christian Theology*, 3 vols. Grand Rapids: Baker, 1985. 3:1149–1247.

* Charles C. Ryrie. *Basic Theology*. Wheaton: Victor, 1986. pp. 439–522 .

* Henry C. Thiessen. *Lectures in Systematic Theology*, revised by Vernon D. Doerksen. Grand Rapids: Eerdmans, 1979. pp. 331–99.

AMILLENNIALISM

** Oswald T. Allis. *Prophecy and the Church*. Philadelphia: Presbyterian and Reformed, 1945.

* Louis Berkhof.*Summary of Christian Doctrine*. Grand Rapids: Eerdmans, 1938. pp. 181–98.

** - - -. *Systematic Theology*. Grand Rapids: Eerdmans, 1938. pp. 661–738.

** G. C. Berkouwer. *The Return of Christ*. Grand Rapids: Eerdmans, 1972.

* William E. Cox. *Amillennialism Today*. Phillipsburg, N.J.: Presbyteri an & Reformed, 1966. pp. 57–135.

* Anthony A. Hoekema. "Amillennialism." In Robert G. Clouse, ed., *The Meaning of the Millennium: Four Views*. Downers Grove, Ill.: InterVarsity, 1977. pp. 155–87.

** - - -. *The Bible and the Future*. Grand Rapids: Eerdmans, 1979.

POSTMILLENNIALISM

* Loraine Boettner. *The Millennium*. Philadelphia: Presbyterian & Reformed, 1966. pp. 3105.

* - - -. "Postmillennialism." In Robert G. Clouse, ed., *The Meaning of the Millennium: Four Views*. Downers Grove, Ill.: InterVarsity, 1977. pp. 47–54, 95–103, 117–41, 199–208.

** John Jefferson Davis. *Christ's Victorious Kingdom: Postmillennialism Reconsidered*. Grand Rapids: Baker, 1986. This is an important and recent work on postmillennialism.

** Charles Hodge. *Systematic Theology*. Reprint. London: Clarke, 1960. 3:771–880.

** William G. T. Shedd. *Dogmatic Theology*, 3 vols. Reprint. Nashville: Nelson, 1980. 2:641–754.

** A. H. Strong. *Systematic Theology.* Valley Forge, Pa.: Judson, 1907. pp. 1003–56.

"HISTORIC" PREMILLENNIALISM

** Robert H. Gundry. *The Church and the Tribulation.* Grand Rapids: Zondervan, 1973. Gundry actually identifies himself as a dispensationalist. However, he holds to a posttribulational rapture, a tenet of "historic premillennialism."

* George E. Ladd. *The Blessed Hope.* Grand Rapids: Zondervan, 1956.

** - - -. *Crucial Questions About the Kingdom of God.* Grand Rapids: Eerdmans, 1952.

* - - -. "Historic Premillennialism." In Robert G. Clouse, ed., *The Meaning of the Millennium: Four Views.* Downers Grove, Ill.: InterVarsity, 1977. pp. 17–40.

** - - -. *Jesus and the Kingdom.* New York: Harper, 1964.

* - - -. *The Presence of the Future.* Grand Rapids: Eerdmans, 1974.

* Douglas J. Moo. "The Case for the Posttribulation Rapture Position." In *The Rapture: Pre-, Mid-, or Post- Tribulational?* Grand Rapids: Zondervan, 1984.

** J. Barton Payne. *Encyclopedia of Biblical Prophecy.* New York: Harper, 1973.

** Alexander Reese. *The Approaching Advent of Christ.* Reprint. Grand Rapids: Grand Rapids International, 1975.

DISPENSATIONAL PREMILLENNIALISM

** Charles L. Feinberg. *Millennialism: The Two Major Views.* Chicago: Moody, 1980.

* Rene Pache. *The Return of Jesus Christ.* Chicago: Moody, 1955.

** J. Dwight Pentecost. *Prophecy for Today.* Grand Rapids: Zondervan, 1961.

* - - -. *Things to Come.* Grand Rapids: Zondervan, 1958. This is the most important work on the subject detailing the chronology of prophecy. This work also compares the differing interpretive positions: premillennialism, postmillennialism, amillennialism, pre-, mid-, post-, and partial rapture views. This is a comprehensive work that ought to be consulted by every serious student of prophecy.

* Charles C. Ryrie. *The Basis of the Premillennial Faith.* Neptune, N.J .: Loizeaux, 1953. This work is particularly important in establishing the foundations of premillennialism.

** Paul Lee Tan. *The Interpretation of Prophecy.* Rockville, Md.: Assurance, 1974. This work is significant in discussing the hermeneutical principles of premillennialism.

* John F. Walvoord. *Israel,the Nations,and the Church in Prophecy.* Grand Rapids: Zondervan, 1988. This is a valuable study delineating the distinctives of Israel, the nations, and the church, showing God's particular purpose for each. This volume is a compilation of three works that were previously published separately.

** - - -. *The Millennial Kingdom.* Grand Rapids: Zondervan, 1959. This work discusses the different millennial views, tracing their historical developments and their hermeneutical systems.

* - - -. *The Rapture Question*, rev. & enlarged ed. Grand Rapids: Zondervan, 1979. This work explains the biblical basis of the pretribulational view and also interacts with the other tribulational views.

~ ~ ~

FOR ADDITIONAL STUDY[415] ON MILLENNIALISM AND RAPTURISM

Adams, Jay E., *The Time Is at Hand* (Philadelphia: Presbyterian & Reformed, 1970).

Bahnsen, Greg L., "The Prima Facie Acceptability of Postmillennialism," *Journal of Christian Reconstruction* 3 (Winter 1976–77).

Berkhof, *Systematic Theology* (Grand Rapids: Wm. B. Eerdmans Publishing Co., 1941).

Bethune, J. F.-Baker, *An Introduction to the Early History of Christian Doctrine* (London: Methuen & Co., 1942).

Bibliotheca Sacra, on "Posttribulationism," 112:289–303, October, 1955, and 113:1–15, January, 1956.

Boettner, Loraine, *The Millennium* (Philadelphia: Presbyterian & Reformed, 1966).

- - -. "Postmillennialism," in *The Meaning of the Millennium.*

---

[415] Note: it is not to be assumed that ALL works suggested by the author for review have been written from a dispensational standpoint.

Brookes, *Maranatha.*

- - -. *"Till He Come."*

Brown, David, *Christ's Second Coming.*

Chilton, *Paradise Restored.*

Clouse, Robert G., *The Meaning of the Millennium* (Downers Grove, IL: InterVarsity, 1977).

Culver, Robert D., *Daniel and the Latter Days.*

Hendriksen, William, *More Than Conquerors* (Grand Rapids: Baker, 1939).

Hoehner, Harold W., *Chronological Aspects of the Life of Christ* (Grand Rapids: Zondervan, 1977).

Hoekema, Anthony A., "Amillennialism," in Robert G. Clouse, ed., *The Meaning of the Millennium: Four Views* (Downers Grove, Ill.: InterVarsity, 1977).

- - -. *The Bible and the Future* (Grand Rapids: Eerdmans, 1979).

Hook, H. Phillip, "The Doctrine of the Kingdom in Covenant Premillennialism" (unpublished Th. D. diss., Dallas Theological Seminary, 1959).

Kline, "Comments on an Old-New Error."

Kromminga, D. H., *The Millennium.*

Ladd, George E., *Crucial Questions about the Kingdom of God* (Grand Rapids: Eerdmans, 1952).

- - -. "Historic Premillennialism," in *The Meaning of the Millennium.*

- - -. *The Blessed Hope* (Grand Rapids: Wm. B. Eerdmans Publishing Co., 1956).

- - -. *The Hope of Christ's Second Coming.*

Lord, David N., *The Coming and Reign of Christ.* New York, 1808.

McClain, Alva J., *Daniel's Prophecy of the Seventy Weeks* (Grand Rapids: Zondervan, 1940).

McDougall, Duncan, *The Rapture of the Saints* (Blackwood, NJ: O.F.P.M. Publishers, 1970).

Montgomery, John W., *Where Is History Going?* (Minneapolis: Bethany Fellowship, 1969).

Pache, Rene, *The Return of Christ.*

Reese, Alexander, *The Approaching Advent of Christ* (Reprint. Grand Rapids: Grand Rapids International, 1975).

Rushdoony, R. J., "Postmillennialism versus Impotent Religion," *Journal of Christian Reconstruction* 3 (Winter 1976–77).

Payne, J. Barton, *The Imminent Appearing of Christ* (Grand Rapids: Wm. B. Eerdmans Publishing Co., 1962).

Scofield Reference Bible.

Seiss, Joseph A., *The Last Times and the Great Consummation.* (Philadelphia and London, 1860).

*Smith, Wilbur M., *The Biblical Doctrine of Heaven* (Chicago: Moody, 1968).

- - - . "Heaven," in *The Zondervan Pictorial Encyclopedia of the Bible.*

Walvoord, John F., "Does the Church Fulfill Israel's Program? - Part 1," *Bibliotheca Sacra.* Dallas TX: Dallas Theological Seminary, 1996, c1955-1995.

- - - . "Premillennialism and the Tribulation," *Bibliotheca Sacra* 112 (April 1955).

- - - . *The Rapture Question* (Grand Rapids: Dunham, 1957).

Weber, Timothy, *Living in the Shadow of the Second Coming, 1875– 1982* (Grand Rapids: Zondervan Publishing House, 1983).

Witmer, John A., ed., *Bibliotheca Sacra.* Dallas TX: Dallas Theological Seminary, 1996, c1955-1995. A review of "The Revival of Apocalyptic in the Churches," George Eldon Ladd, Review and Expositor 72 (Summer 1975): 263–70. "The Eschatology of Hal Lindsey," Dale Moody, Review and Expositor 72 (Summer] 975): 271 -78.

- - -, ed., *Bibliotheca Sacra.* Dallas TX: Dallas Theological Seminary, 1996, c1955-1995. A review of "Principles of Interpretation in Regard to Prophecy with Special Reference to Millennialism," C. Kuehne, *The Journal of Theology* 21 (December 1981): 2–28.

~ ~ ~

See also all resources under the Bibliography identified by a <%> mark at the beginning of the reference.

CHAPTER TWENTY SIX

—LAW-GRACE TENSION

Amillennialists, postmillennialists, non-dispensational premillennialists, and to some degree, progressive dispensationalists, as a result of not employing the consistent literal method of interpreting the Scriptures, fail to arrive at a consensus on a number of major theological issues (e.g., making a clear distinction between Israel and the Church; the millennium; the rapture; etc.). While none of the above listed camps are willing to openly forsake the *unity* of Scripture, various degrees of theological confusion nevertheless abound (the major highlights of which having already been brought under consideration). Another prevalent difficulty which deserves serious consideration is how the **Law** is to be viewed in relation to the **Gospel** (or **Grace**). This issue has proven to be somewhat of a challenge for many non-dispensational systems of theology. The question has been posed as follows: Is the relationship between Law and Grace to be considered a *conflict, counterpart, contrast, contradiction,* or *continuum?*

Unlike the systems of theology listed above, dispensationalism, as a result of making clear distinctions between Israel and the Church, enjoys a number of theological benefits. One of the chief benefits is the ease of which the *unity* of the Scriptures can be maintained concerning **Law** and **Grace**, when viewed in light of the recognized dispensations. Examined in this chapter is what is meant by "Law-Grace tension" and how it relates to the above mentioned opposing (and/or semi-opposing) eschatological mindsets. In coming to understand this dilemma, it will be helpful to first briefly present an overview of the unfortunate history of *forced conformity* as can be found in the history of Christendom.

A BRIEF OVERVIEW OF THE HISTORY OF FORCED CONFORMITY IN CHRISTENDOM.[416]

Constantine.

A mindset of forced conformity can be found early-on in the history of orthodox Christianity. This mindset first showed up early in the fourth century immediately following the brilliant strategic maneuverings, both military and political, of the pagan Emperor

---

[416] For a more complete explanation, see Dave Hunt, *What Love is This?* (Bend, Oregon: The Berean Call, 2004), pp. 67-85.

Constantine. Constantine feignedly converted to Christianity and proceeded to demand that his entire army join him in his false conversion. He then set out to conquer his enemies in the name of Jesus instead of in the name of the pagan gods. This compromise has had an enormous impact upon Christianity down through the centuries.

At this point, in addition to the military advantages gained by such a maneuver, and through the guise of so-called Christian "unity," Constantine established an internal beachhead whereby he was able to begin systematically corrupting (i.e., spreading his paganism throughout) Christianity. All who refused to go along with this newly mandated official state-sponsored form of Christianity, suffered persecution at his hand. State-sponsored persecution of the Church was nothing new. What was novel about this movement was that *now* the persecution was inflicted upon true Christians (such as the Donatists of North Africa, e.g.,) in the name of *Jesus* instead of in the name(s) of the pagan gods. This, unfortunately, became the often-followed pattern.

Augustine.

Augustine followed Constantine's example, thus prompting the continued killing of the so-called "heretics" (i.e., true Christians, such as the Donatists and others) as he set about to cement the Emperor's state-church. Of Augustine it has been said that:

> The very greatness of his name has been the means of perpetuating the grossest errors which he himself propagated. More than anyone else, Augustine has encouraged the pernicious doctrine of salvation through the sacraments of an organized earthly Church, which brought with it priestcraft with all the evil and miseries that has entailed down through the centuries.[417]

The idea of forced conformity became a common characteristic in developing Christendom as evidenced later by the Crusaders. Both Muslims and Jews were slaughtered in order to retake the Holy Land during the reign of Pope Urban II. Similar to Muhammad's and the Quran's promise to Muslims, full forgiveness of sins was offered to those who died fighting such "holy wars."

---

[417] John W. Kennedy, *The Torch of the Testimony* (Christian Books Publishing House, 1963), 68, as cited by Dave Hunt in *What Love is This?* (Bend, Oregon: The Berean Call, 2004), p. 69.

Calvin.

Though John Calvin is often ranked and admired among the faithful Reformers, he nevertheless clearly picked up the Augustinian error of state enforced orthodoxy. Calvin developed an extreme view of God's sovereignty and envisioned a society in which all of mankind would conform to the righteousness of God. Capitalizing on his legal training, he was able to establish a partnership of sorts with the church and the civil authorities in Geneva, Switzerland early in the 16th century. He then set out to establish and enforce his envisioned form of Calvinistic Christianity.

Calvin's first move was to banish the Anabaptists. Then the burden of his misguided intentions fell upon the remaining inhabitants of Geneva, whether Christian or not. By April of 1537, rigid house-to-house inspections were launched in order to enforce conformity to the newly constructed "Confession of Faith" (derived by Guillaume Farel and John Calvin). After undergoing a few initial setbacks, by the end of 1541 Calvin's plan began to take shape. As the *new protestant pope* (as he is now, in retrospect, referred to by some), Calvin was well on his way to establishing his envisioned kingdom of God upon this tiny segment of the earth (Geneva had a population of approximately 20,000 at the time of Calvin's experiment). Geneva, Calvin hoped, according to Stefan Zweig,[418] would become "the New Jerusalem, a center from which the salvation of the world would radiate."[419] The punishment for violations, insubordinations, etc., included: floggings, imprisonments, torture, banishments, and, in many cases, burning at the stake. In one case, "four who failed to escape were beheaded and quartered, and their body parts were hung in strategic locations as a warning."[420] Speaking of such punishments, Durant reports the following:

> Fornication was to be punished with exile or drowning; adultery, blasphemy, or idolatry, with death... a child was beheaded for striking its parents. In the years 1558-59 there were 414 prosecutions for moral offenses; between 1542 and

---

[418] "Zweig [Dave Hunt writes]... pored over the official records of the City Council for Calvin's day." (Hunt, Dave, *What Love is This?* [Bend, Oregon: The Berean Call, 2004], p. 73.)

[419] Stefan Zweig, Eden Paul and Cedar Paul, trans., *The Right to Heresy* (London: Cassell and Company, 1936), 57; cited in Henry R. Pike, *The Other Side of John Calvin* (Head to Heart, n. d.), 21-22.

[420] Wendel, *Calvin*, 100; Cottret, *Calvin*, 198-200, as cited by Dave Hunt in *What Love is This?* (Bend, Oregon: The Berean Call, 2004), p. 71.

1564 there were seventy-six banishments and fifty-eight executions.[421]

In one sense, the good name of the Reformation was hi-jacked by Calvin's renegade variation of Protestantism, and "'Geneva became the symbol and incarnation of that 'other' Reformation...,'[23] but which [some] Calvinists today claim was *the* Reformation."[422] Hence, Calvin's endeavors in Geneva became responsible for sparking the term "Reformed Theology."

What occurred in Geneva can perhaps be better understood by understanding Calvin's views on the millennial kingdom. Dave Hunt writes the following:

> Of those who believed in a thousand-year reign of Christ upon earth, Calvin said their "fiction is too puerile to need or to deserve refutation."[15] As far as Calvin was concerned, Christ's kingdom began with His advent upon earth and had been in process ever since. Rejecting the literal future reign of Christ upon the earth through His Second Coming to establish an earthly kingdom upon David's throne in Jerusalem, Calvin apparently felt obliged to establish the kingdom by his own efforts in Christ's absence.[423]

A BRIEF DESCRIPTION OF THE PROBLEM

By the extreme example which the Geneva experiment provides, it is easy to see how critical one's view on the millennium turns out to be. Much aberrant theology results from the failure to clearly distinguish Israel from the Church. It is difficult, if not impossible, to come to a proper view of either *Law* or *Grace*, if the Church is viewed as nothing more than "*spiritual* Israel"—i.e., a continuation of the Old Testament body of believers. (It is interesting to note that believers during the time *prior* to Israel's existence are almost never given due consideration by non-dispensationalists.)

---

[421] Durant, *Civilization*, III: 474, as cited by Dave Hunt in *What Love is This?* (Bend, Oregon: The Berean Call, 2004), pp. 72-73.
23 23. Bernard Cottret, *Calvin: A Biography*, tr. M. Wallace McDonald (Grand Rapids, MI: William B. Eerdmans Publishing Company, 2000) 250.
[422] Hunt, Dave, *What Love is This?* (Bend, Oregon: The Berean Call, 2004), p. 72
15 15. John Calvin, *Institutes of the Christian Religion*, trans. Henry Beveridge (Grand Rapids, MI: Wm. B. Eerdmans Publishing Company, 1998 ed.), III: xxv, 5.
[423] Hunt, Idem., p. 70.

CONSIDERING THE PROBLEM AS IT
RELATES TO AMILLENNIALISM

It stands to reason that covenant theologians (of the amillenarian variety) are going to view the *Law* differently than do dispensationalists. After all, to refresh the reader's memory, they refer to the dispensation of *Law* as the time prior to Adam's fall, and the dispensation of *Grace* as the present time (i.e., a time beginning with the fall of Adam and extending until the end of this age, a point at which the eternal state begins). Thus, according to them, the giving of the Law at Sinai falls into this present age, and is in many ways, the degree of which is often blurry, directly applicable to the Church today. Again, they do not distinguish a difference between Israel and the Church.

Even though both Augustine and Calvin were amillennialists, it appears that today's amillennialists are not as prone to make such gross errors as that which occurred in their day-in-time—as the Geneva experiment portrays. This is, no doubt, at least partially attributable to the fact that amillennialists share the same view as do dispensationalists concerning apostasy—believing that apostasy will increase more and more as this age progresses. In this sense, the Geneva experiment appears to be somewhat of a peculiar anomaly.

CONSIDERING THE PROBLEM AS IT
RELATES TO POSTMILLENNIALISM

Today, when it comes to the *Law-Grace* issue, the greater potential for another Geneva-type experiment, except on a much grander scale, is more likely to arise from those adhering to the *postmillennial* point of view, especially the *theonomic* variety. *Postmillennialism* is gaining in popularity today. As mentioned earlier, Charles Hodge often writes in dispensationalist-like language, so much so that he might even, at times, be mistaken for a dispensationalist. Hodge, however, is far from being a dispensationalist; he is a covenant theologian and a postmillenarian. It is to be noted, however, that he often strikes a commendable balance on the Law-Grace issue in his writings.[424] On the other hand, a number of vestigial hints, the likes of which have led his antecedents to commit such horrible atrocities as those described above, can also

---

[424] Cf., e.g.: Hodge, C. *Systematic Theology*. Oak Harbor, WA: Logos Research Systems, Inc., 1997. Vol. II, pp. 375-6, 561, Etc.

be detected in his writings. For example, in his work entitled *Systematic Theology*, Hodge writes as follows:

> So long as we are in the body, religion cannot be exclusively a matter of the heart. It must have its institutions and ordinances...[425]
>
> ...
>
> It is to be remembered, that adultery is a crime in the sight of man as well as in the sight of God, and as such it ought to be punished. Under the old dispensation it was punished by death; under the new, it may be punished by imprisonment, or by prohibition of any future marriage. Christ leaves the punishment of this, as of other crimes, to be determined by his disciples in their civil capacity.[426]

The key phrase to ponder here is: "Christ leaves the punishment of this, as of other crimes, to be determined *by his disciples* in their civil capacity" (emphasis added). This obviously envisions Christ's "disciples" as having advanced to the point, via success of the Gospel, no doubt, of becoming the authoritative magistrates in the land—those judicially responsible for the administration of such "punishment." This aligns well with those views currently espoused by Theonomists (neopostmillenarians) who evidently interpret Paul's comments in Romans 13:1-7 to be equating "powers" and "rulers" with Christ's "disciples"; a view which assumes the state as being based on the Bible. Such a conquered state is exactly what Greg L. Bahnsen envisions as he writes: "the doctrine of the state presented by Paul in Romans 13 is a *reaffirmation of the essential Older Testament conception of the civil magistrate.*"[427] Although amillennialists, as previously pointed out, have proven themselves quite capable of getting twisted up on this matter, this view is not held today by many, if any, outside of the postmillennial, particularly the theonomic, persuasion (note: the subject of *theonomy* is taken up in the next chapter).

Anyone familiar with Hodge realizes that his writings, which are typically commendable, obviously originate from a pure heart. One would never suppose that Hodge would coalesce with any party intent upon committing such atrocities as those previously described.

---

[425] Hodge, Vol. III, p. 333.
[426] Hodge, Vol. III, p. 393.
[427] Bahnsen, Greg L., *Theonomy in Christian Ethics* (Nutley, NJ: Craig Press, 1979), p. 398, as cited by Norman L. Geisler, "A Premillennial View of Law and Government." *Bibliotheca Sacra.* Dallas TX: Dallas Theological Seminary, 1996, c1955-1995.

However, also detectable in his writings is that all-too-familiar blur which cannot help but arise from his failure to make a clear distinction between Israel and the Church. An inevitable byproduct of this fundamental error is the associated failure to properly discriminate between the mandates imposed under the Mosaic code and the *heaven-high* instructions presented to the Christian under the economy of grace.

CONCLUSION

An important question must be asked when attempting to determine how applicable the Law is for believers today, namely: How are the laws that *do* apply to today's believers to be *enforced?* The answer to this question, it appears, has been that which amillennialists, and more recently, postmillennialists, have grappled with down through the centuries. Concerning this *Law-Grace* tension there appears to be three possible positions:[428]

(1) The position taken by covenant theologians who are amillennialist

(2) A similar (but potentially more aggressive) position taken by covenant theologians who are postmillennialist (especially the theonomists variety)

(3) The dispensational position

It is not likely that we, in our day-in-time, will witness the promotion of another Geneva-type experiment at the hands of contemporary amillennialists. It does not appear, however, that the same can be said of modern postmillennialists (currently referred to by some as *neo*-postmillennialists). These, it appears, have the potential, should the right (or wrong) circumstances arise, to reproduce another Geneva-type experiment, but on a much grander scale. The following related comments by a number of authors are to be carefully considered:

Brinsmead writes:

---

[428] A more moderate position on "a law-gospel continuum," as held by Fuller, might also be listed. Fuller suggests that "a 'work of faith' or the 'obedience of faith' presupposes an inseparable connection between faith and resulting works." Since they are inseparable and since genuine faith always produces works, "there is no need for establishing an elaborate division in Scripture as is done in covenant theology and dispensationalism" (Fuller, *Gospel and Law,* p. 113) as noted by Wayne G. Strickland in "Preunderstanding and Daniel Fuller's Law-Gospel Continuum," *Bibliotheca Sacra.* Dallas TX: Dallas Theological Seminary, 1996, c1955-1995.

Puritan-Reformed theology has a tendency to construct its ethical system from the written code of Moses. We suggest that this is why so much Puritan-Reformed ethics looks suspiciously like a system of Christian Judaism. Some covenantal theologians are so anxious to stress the continuity between the Old and New Testaments (which is valid) that they do not do justice to the really new thing God has done in Christian.[429]

Strickland draws very near to the heart of the problem when he writes:

The Mosaic Law is not binding on believers today, but the law of Christ is. This is summed up in the principle of love for one's neighbor. The Mosaic Law provided external motivation for sanctification, but the fulfillment of the law of Christ is made possible by the permanent indwelling ministry of the Holy Spirit. By not presenting believers with a rigid, concrete codification of laws, but merely presenting love for their neighbor as the law of Christ, the focus is on dependence on the Holy Spirit. Also legalism is avoided.[430]

Though some, as Strickland notes, perceive it necessary to compound this with "more... legislation":

Some argue for a more concrete law of Christ, which, though not complete and detailed like the Mosaic Law, nevertheless is more specific than merely loving one's neighbor. Those arguing for a more specific body of legislation would look to the many principles set forth by the epistles as being an unofficial codification for the New Testament believer.[431]

As a concluding thought to this chapter, the author would suggest the following for the reader's contemplation: there could hardly be a greater difference between that form of morality which emerges from *imposed* legislation and that form of legislation which emerges from true morality!

---

[429] Brinsmead, R. D., "The Basis of New Testament Ethics," *Verdict* 4 (1981), pp. 21-22, as cited by Wayne G. Strickland in "Preunderstanding and Daniel Fuller's Law-Gospel Continuum," *Bibliotheca Sacra*. Dallas TX: Dallas Theological Seminary, 1996, c1955-1995.

[430] Strickland, Wayne G., "Preunderstanding and Daniel Fuller's Law-Gospel Continuum," *Bibliotheca Sacra*. Dallas TX: Dallas Theological Seminary, 1996, c1955-1995.

[431] See, e.g., Charles C. Ryrie, *The Grace of God*, Chicago: Moody Press, 1963, pp. 63–71.

Chapter Twenty Seven

—Theonomy

Introduction to Theonomy

With such glaring atrocities imposed in times past upon the people of God as well as upon some non-Christians, as the history of forced conformity exhibits (see the previous chapter), it is difficult to understand why some continue to insist that it is God's will that systems after the same or similar sort be established and enforced today. This, however, is exactly what one finds as he investigates the currently rising movement known as *theonomy* (or *neopostmillennialism*). The purpose of this chapter is to provide the reader with a general overview of what is meant by the term *theonomy* in today's theological circles.

Defining Theonomy

As previously stated, covenant theology comes in two basic forms: (1) postmillennialism, (2) and amillennialism. Two divisions are to be further noted within the former: (a) classic postmillennialism, and (b) theonomic (or Chalcedon) postmillennialism. *Theonomists* may therefore be described as a slightly revised postmillennial variety of covenant theology which, while being quite distinguishable from amillennialism, also stands as a direct antithesis to premillennial dispensationalism.

On the subject of "theonomy" Robert Lightner writes as follows:

> Until recently the word "theonomy" has been used comparatively little. But it is now becoming common in theological circles. The English word comes from two Greek words—θεός [*Theos*] ("God") and νόμος [*nomos*] ("law"). Its broadest meaning therefore is "law of God."[432]

---

[432] Lightner, Robert P., "Theological Perspectives on Theonomy Part I: Theonomy and Dispensationalism," *Bibliotheca Sacra.* Dallas TX: Dallas Theological Seminary, 1996, c1955-1995. See also Meredith G. Kline, "Comments on an Old-New Error," *Westminster Theological Journal* 41 [1978]: 172–73.

DISTINGUISHING THEONOMY FROM CLASSIC POSTMILLENNIALISM

On the contemporary scene today, it is a well-established reality that theonomy and postmillennialism go hand-in-hand; the one advocating the other. However, the kind of postmillennialism advanced by theonomists (or Chalcedon) spokesmen is to be distinguished from *classic* postmillennialism. The differences appear to lie more in the *extremity* and/or degree of *development* of their views rather than in *substance*.

Lightner, while explaining theonomists' views, quotes Bahnsen as follows:

> Theonomists have an "optimistic confidence" that the nations of the world "will become disciples of Christ, and [that] the church will grow to fill the earth, and that Christianity will become the dominant principle."[22] "The gospel *f* shall convert the vast majority of the world to Christ and bring widespread obedience to His kingdom rule."[23] [433]

Lightner later explains the difference as follows:

> Along with its interpretation of Matthew 5:17–19, theonomy's view of judicial law and its interpretation of "general equity" in the Westminster Confession constitute the most serious differences with mainstream covenant-Reformed thinking. It is in these areas that the greatest conflict arises.[434]

DISTINGUISHING THEONOMY FROM DISPENSATIONALISTS

Besides those positions previously discussed, there are at least two other major issues which distinguish theonomists from dispensationalists: (1) "the view that Christ's sufferings in His life were as substitutionary as His suffering on the cross"[435] (held by

---

22 22. Greg L. Bahnsen, "The Prima Facie Acceptability of Postmillennialism," *Journal of Christian Reconstruction* 3 (Winter 1976–77):68.

23 23. Ibid.

[433] Lightner, Idem.

[434] Lightner, Robert P., "Theological Perspectives on Theonomy Part II: Nondispensational Responses to Theonomy," *Bibliotheca Sacra*. Dallas TX: Dallas Theological Seminary, 1996, c1955-1995.

[435] Lightner, Robert P., "Theological Perspectives on Theonomy Part I: Theonomy and Dispensationalism," *Bibliotheca Sacra*. Dallas TX: Dallas Theological

covenant-reformed thinkers);[436] and (2) views concerning the *enforcement* of the Mosaic Law. The primary focus at hand is upon the latter.

AMILLENNIALISTS REFUTE BOTH
THEONOMY AND DISPENSATIONALISM

It is interesting to note that some amillennialists, though sharing the same covenental views as those held by postmillinnialists and theonomists, refute theonomy even more aggresively than they do dispensationalism. In fact, due to theonomy's claim to resolve the long-standing dispute concerning the Law of Moses—intimating its full application for today's believer—amillennarians consider themselves far more threatened by theonomy's rise in popularity than do dispensationalists.

Meredith Kline, a committed amillennialist, in his review of Greg L. Bahnsen's *Theonomy in Christian Ethics,* expresses criticism of theonomy's purpose concerning the "Mosaic law" as follows:

> Their [theonomists'] special thesis is that the Mosaic law, more or less in its entirety, constitutes a continuing norm for mankind and that it is the duty of the civil magistrate to enforce it, precepts and penalties alike. To put the matter in a comparative perspective, this theory of theonomic politics stands at the opposite end of the spectrum of error from dispensationalism. The latter represents an extreme of failure to do justice to the continuity between the old and new covenants. Chalcedon's [theonomy's] error, no less extreme or serious, is a failure to do justice to the discontinuity between the old and new covenants.[437]

Seminary, 1996, c1955-1995. See Lightner, "The Savior's Sufferings in Life," *Bibliotheca Sacra* 127 (/128) (January-March 1970):26–37 for further discussion of this position.

[436] Hodge also connected Jesus' life-sufferings with "propitiation." He writes: "He was to bear our sins, to be a curse for us, offering Himself as a sacrifice, or propitiation to God in expiation of the sins of men. This involved his whole life of humiliation, sorrow, and suffering, and his ignominious death upon the cross under the hiding of his Father's countenance" (Hodge, C., "Covenant Of Redemption: The Work assigned to the Redeemer," *Systematic Theology.* Oak Harbor, WA: Logos Research Systems, Inc., 1997.)

[437] Meredith G. Kline, "Comments on an Old-New Error," *Westminster Theological Journal* 41 (1978):172–73, as cited by Robert P. Lightner, "Theological Perspectives

Lightner notes that:

> Theonomy has been under considerable study and attack from those of nondispensational persuasion. In fact they have been far more vociferous in their opposition than have dispensationalists.... But this is not much of a surprise.
>
> After all, theonomists have been more critical of traditional Reformed theology than of dispensational theology. The criticisms have been directed against the inconsistencies in covenant theology's and amillennialism's failure to conform to and be consistent with the Westminster Confession of Faith, to which they purport to give full allegiance.[438]

Amillenarians are therefore often described as standing somewhere between postmillennialism and dispensationalism. (Note: the manner in which the Westminster Confession of Faith is to be interpreted and applied is contested by both theonomists as well as amillenarians.)

THEONOMY AND MODERN-DAY MOVEMENTS

There are a number of movements which have emerged which are in one manner or another based upon (and/or associated with) theonomic (neopostmillenarian) theology. These movements include: Kingdom [Now/Now but Not-Yet] Theology; Dominion Theology (Dominionists); Prosperity Theology; Positive-confession; The "Social Gospel"; Reconstructionism;[439] The Christian Reconstruction Movement (CRM); Etc. Notable proponents associated with such movements include: Rousas John Rushdoony, Gary North, Earl Paulk, and Tommy Reid.[440]

---

on Theonomy Part I: Theonomy and Dispensationalism," *Bibliotheca Sacra*. Dallas TX: Dallas Theological Seminary, 1996, c1955-1995.

[438] Lightner, Robert P., "Theological Perspectives on Theonomy Part II: Nondispensational Responses to Theonomy," *Bibliotheca Sacra*. Dallas TX: Dallas Theological Seminary, 1996, c1955-1995.

[439] On this connection Ryrie writes: "*Theonomy* is associated with *reconstructionism* though perhaps it is only one aspect of it." See Ryrie, Charles C., *Dispensationalism*. Chicago: Moody Press, 1995. p. 13.

[440] See Bruce Barron book entitled *Heaven on Earth?* Grand Rapids: Zondervan Publishing House, 1992 and Robert P. Lightner's review of this work, *Bibliotheca Sacra*. Dallas TX: Dallas Theological Seminary, 1996, c1955-1995.

SOME THEONOMISTS MAKE COMMENTS THAT LEAVE THE IMPRESSION THAT THEY VIEW THE MOSAIC LAW AS A MEANS OF ATTAINING ETERNAL LIFE

In addition to, and perhaps stemming from the notion that Christ's life-sufferings were in some manner substitutionary, theonomists also hold views concerning the role of the Mosaic Law in regards to a person's salvation that sets them at the extreme opposite end of the spectrum from dispensationalism. Roy L. Aldrich quotes a couple of the more extreme comments as follows:

> "Christians should recite the commandments (as their creeds) to keep in memory what they must do to enter into life."[441]

> "The law is a rule of life for believers, reminding them of their duties and leading them in the way of life and salvation."[442]

It is difficult, at least in this author's view, to interpret such comments, particularly the former, as anything other than the setting forth of "another gospel."

THEONOMISTS INTEND A RETURN TO MOSAIC LAW

In light of such views it's a bit easier to understand, as Lighner points out below, Rushdoony's intention to return to the Mosaic Law:

> [The intention of theonomists, as Rushdoony plainly states, is to] mandate... dominion in Christ's name over every area of life and thought.... also to work for a Christian state and school.[443]

---

[441] Pope, William B., *A Compendium* of *Christian Theology*, III, 174, as cited by Roy L. Aldrich, "Causes for Confusion of Law and Grace." *Bibliotheca Sacra.* Dallas TX: Dallas Theological Seminary, 1996, c1955-1995.

[442] Berkhof, L., *Systematic Theology*, p. 615, as cited by Roy L. Aldrich, "Causes for Confusion of Law and Grace," *Bibliotheca Sacra.* Dallas TX: Dallas Theological Seminary, 1996, c1955-1995.

[443] R. J. Rushdoony, "Postmillennialism versus Impotent Religion," *Journal of Christian Reconstruction* 3 (Winter 1976–77):126, as cited by Robert P. Lightner, "Theological Perspectives on Theonomy Part I: Theonomy and Dispensationalism," *Bibliotheca Sacra.* Dallas TX: Dallas Theological Seminary, 1996, c1955-1995.

Lighner further notes:

> They are postmillennial, insisting that the Mosaic Law in
> its entirety is just as much God's rule of life, His *modus
> operandi*, for the world today as it was in the days of
> Moses.[444]

Lightner again writes:

> Of course Christians have always honored God's Law
> given through Moses. It is indeed a revelation of Himself.

> But the word [*theonomy*] is now being used to designate a
> new idea gaining ground in some circles, particularly those
> emphasizing Reformed doctrine, that the governments of the
> world today should be guided in their judicial decisions by all
> the legislation of the Old Testament and, in particular, should
> assess the Old Testament penalties for any infraction to those
> laws, whether civil or religious.[3] [445]

In regards to the practice of "assess[-ing] the Old Testament
penalties for any infraction," Norman Geisler points out that:

> Bahnsen carries through consistently Rushdoony's idea of
> theonomy and concludes that Christians should still practice
> the Old Testament law today, including capital punishment
> for homosexuals, drunkards, and rebellious children....[21] [446]

Bahnsen, citing Calvin, Warfield, and Honeyman, insists that
Jesus in Matthew 5:15–20 is teaching that the law is to be observed in
this age in its most minute prescription and detail, and there is no
suggestion of any limit in time to its observance.

---

[444] Lightner, Robert P., "Theological Perspectives on Theonomy Part I: Theonomy
and Dispensationalism," *Bibliotheca Sacra*. Dallas TX: Dallas Theological
Seminary, 1996, c1955-1995.
3 3. R. Laird Harris, "Theonomy in Christian Ethics," *Covenant Seminary Review* 5
(1979):l.
[445] Lightner, Robert P., "Theological Perspectives on Theonomy Part I: Theonomy
and Dispensationalism," *Bibliotheca Sacra*. Dallas TX: Dallas Theological
Seminary, 1996, c1955-1995. See also Meredith G. Kline, "Comments on an Old-
New Error," *Westminster Theological Journal* 41 [1978]: 172–73.
21 21. Greg L. Bahnsen, *Theonomy in Christian Ethics* (Nutley, NJ: Craig Press,
1979), p. 398.
[446]Geisler, Norman L., "A Premillennial View of Law and Government." *Bibliotheca
Sacra*. Dallas TX: Dallas Theological Seminary, 1996, c1955-1995.

Again, Lightner notes that their goal reaches to "the entire world":

> Besides insisting that the entire Mosaic Law is operative for believers, theonomists also hold that the church is obligated to promote and enforce obedience to God's Law in society as well.[447]

This view is not peculiar to Bahnsen. Chilton stated that Matthew 5:13–16 "is nothing less than a mandate for the complete social transformation of the entire world."[9] [448]

Their agenda is therefore clear, namely: a "world takeover" with the intentions of imposing God's (Mosaic) Law upon every citizen of the world.

Theonomists rely heavily upon Matthew 5:17[449] where the word "fulfil" is interpreted to mean "to confirm" (as it indeed is sometimes used—see Rom 15:19; 2Co 10:6; Jam 2:23; and Rev 3:2). Lightner, however, asserts that the word "fulfil" is in this case to be understood in its more common usages, that is, "the accomplishment of prophecies"; which leads him to conclude that:

> Rather than using πληρῶσαι [pleroo] in Matthew 5:17–19 to argue that the Mosaic Law is still operative today as a rule of life, it is better to understand Christ's words as teaching the inerrancy of Scripture.[450]

Lightner goes on to quote Chilton as follows:

> Our goal is world dominion under Christ's Lordship, a "world takeover" if you will; but our strategy begins with reformation, reconstruction of the church. From that will flow

---

[447] Lightner, Robert P., "Theological Perspectives on Theonomy Part I: Theonomy and Dispensationalism," *Bibliotheca Sacra.* Dallas TX: Dallas Theological Seminary, 1996, c1955-1995.

[9] 9. David Chilton, *Paradise Restored: An Eschatology of Dominion* (Tyler TX: Reconstruction Press, 1985), p. 12.

[448] Lightner, Robert P., "Theological Perspectives on Theonomy Part I: Theonomy and Dispensationalism," *Bibliotheca Sacra.* Dallas TX: Dallas Theological Seminary, 1996, c1955-1995.

[449] Note: Matthew 5:17-19 is referred to as the "golden text" of theonomy.

[450] Lightner, Robert P., "Theological Perspectives on Theonomy Part III: A Dispensational Response to Theonomy," *Bibliotheca Sacra.* Dallas TX: Dallas Theological Seminary, 1996, c1955-1995.

social and political reconstruction, indeed a flowering of Christian civilization (Hag. 1:1–15, 2:6–9, 18–23).[451]

In accord with Chilton's view, Rushdoony adopts the position that "the saints must prepare to take over the world's governments and its courts."[452] This amazingly aggressive view, which would make every state a theocracy, or perhaps better stated, a Christocracy, is strongly promoted by those who are of theonomic pursuasion.[453]

According to Chilton, the Great Commission of Matthew 28:19–20:

> ...does not end with simply *witnessing* to the nations. Christ's command is that we *disciple* the nations—*all* the nations. The kingdoms of the world are to become the kingdoms of Christ. They are to be discipled, made obedient to the faith. This means that every aspect of life throughout the world is to be brought under the lordship of Jesus Christ: families, individuals, business, science, agriculture, the arts, law, education, economics, psychology, philosophy, and every other sphere of human activity.[454]

In response to Chilton's position, Thomas Ice defends the dispensational position as follows:

> Why is this passage [Matthew 28:19–20] not talking about evangelism, as most understand it? Premillennialists certainly believe that all those things Chilton mentioned will occur, but they disagree with the postmillennialists on *timing* (these changes will occur after Christ returns, not before) and *agency* (just as in creation, the Flood, the Exodus, and salvation,

---

[451] David Chilton, *Paradise Restored: An Eschatology of Dominion* (Tyler TX: Reconstruction Press, 1985), p. 214 (italics his), as cited by Robert P. Lightner, "Theological Perspectives on Theonomy Part I: Theonomy and Dispensationalism," *Bibliotheca Sacra.* Dallas TX: Dallas Theological Seminary, 1996, c1955-1995.

[452] R. J. Rushdoony, "Government and the Christian," *The Rutherford Institute* 1 (July/August 1984):6, p. 7, as cited by Robert P. Lightner, "Theological Perspectives on Theonomy Part I: Theonomy and Dispensationalism," *Bibliotheca Sacra.* Dallas TX: Dallas Theological Seminary, 1996, c1955-1995.

[453] See, for example, Paul B. Fowler, "Theonomy: An Assessment of Its Implications for Church and Society" (unpublished paper)

[454] Chilton, *Paradise Restored,* p. 213, as cited by Thomas D. Ice, "An Evaluation of Theonomic Neopostmillennialism," *Bibliotheca Sacra.* Dallas TX: Dallas Theological Seminary, 1996, c1955-1995.

Christ will accomplish this directly, not through secondary means).[455]

So, as Ice points out, the difference simply comes down to a matter of *timing* and *agency*. Theonomists see themselves as issuing in the kingdom, by force, if necessary; whereas dispensationalists believe that Christ will Himself accomplish this directly.

COMPARING THEONOMY'S VIEWS ON LAW WITH THOSE OF DISPENSATIONALISTS

In the final analysis, the most dynamic comparison comes down to the extreme views held by theonomists concerning the *Law* against the views of the *Law* as they are held by the proponents of dispensationalism. Robert Lightner makes this comparison by first citing Rushdoony's theonomic views of "the Law's purpose" as follows:

> The law thus has a position of centrality in man's indictment (as a sentence of death against man the sinner), in man's redemption (in that Christ died, who although the perfect lawkeeper as a new Adam, died as man's substitute), and in man's sanctification (in that man grows in grace as he grows in lawkeeping, for the law is the way of sanctification) ʃ man's justification is by the grace of God in Jesus Christ; man's sanctification is by means of the law of God ʃ the law then first asserts principles, second it cites cases to develop implications of these principles, and third, the law has as its purpose and direction the restitution of God's order.[456]

Aside from the hint that Christ's sufferings in His life were as substitutionary as His suffering on the cross, the more disputed portions of Rushdoony's assertions here are: (1) that "man's sanctification is by means of the law of God" and (2) the law's role in "the restitution of God's order."

---

[455] Ice, Thomas D., "An Evaluation of Theonomic Neopostmillennialism," *Bibliotheca Sacra.* Dallas TX: Dallas Theological Seminary, 1996, c1955-1995.
[456] Rushdoony, *The Institute of Biblical Law*, pp. 3–4, 12, as cited by Lightner, Robert P., "Theological Perspectives on Theonomy Part III: A Dispensational Response to Theonomy," *Bibliotheca Sacra.* Dallas TX: Dallas Theological Seminary, 1996, c1955-1995.

Lightner lists five contrasting dispensational views concerning "the Law's purpose" as follows:

1. *To reveal God's holiness.* (Lev 11:44; cf. 1Pe 1:16)

2. *To unify and distinguish Israel as a nation.* (cf. Exo 19:5–8; 31:13)

3. *To provide a basis for Israel's walk with and worship of God.* (cf. Lev 1–7; 23)

4. *To expose the sinfulness of man.* (Rom 3:19, 20; 5:20; 7:8, 8-13; Gal 3:19)

5. *To reveal Christ.*[457]

Dispensationalists further adhere to the Biblical teaching that the Law of Moses as "a rule of life" has been "done away" (see next chapter).

ADHERENTS OF THEONOMY

"Reconstructionism of the 'dominion' variety is... traced [by Bruce Barron] to Cornelius Van Til and Abraham Kuyper."[458] Thomas Ice refers to Rousas John Rushdoony as "The patriarch of the movement."[459]

Lightner lists the expressions/adherents of *theonomy* as follows:

> Postmillennial theonomy finds current expression in the *Journal of Christian Reconstruction*, the Chalcedon Ministries, Christianity and Civilization, and the Geneva Divinity School Press of Tyler, Texas. Some significant contributors to the movement are Greg L. Bahnsen, James B. Jordan, Gary North [Rushdoony's son-in-law], Rousas John Rushdoony, and Norman Shepherd.[460]
>
> ...

---

[457] Cf. Lightner, Robert P., "Theological Perspectives on Theonomy Part III: A Dispensational Response to Theonomy," *Bibliotheca Sacra.* Dallas TX: Dallas Theological Seminary, 1996, c1955-1995.

[458] Lightner, Robert P. Rev. of *Heaven on Earth?* by Bruce Barron. Grand Rapids: Zondervan Publishing House, 1992. 238 pp. *Bibliotheca Sacra.* Dallas TX: Dallas Theological Seminary, 1996, c1955-1995. (Jul 1994).

[459] Ice, Thomas D., "An Evaluation of Theonomic Neopostmillennialism," *Bibliotheca Sacra.* Dallas TX: Dallas Theological Seminary, 1996, c1955-1995.

[460] Lightner, Robert P., "Theological Perspectives on Theonomy Part I: Theonomy and Dispensationalism," *Bibliotheca Sacra.* Dallas TX: Dallas Theological Seminary, 1996, c1955-1995, f. n. # 1.

The most important recent contribution to theonomy is Bahnsen's *Theonomy in Christian Ethics*, published by the Presbyterian and Reformed Publishing Company in 1977 with a second and enlarged edition published in 1984.[461]

There are a number of others who are in one manner or another listed in the connection.[462]

~ ~ ~

This brief but sobering examination of *Theonomy* accentuates just how critical one's view of the role of the Mosaic Law is in our day-in-time. The goal of the remaining portion of this book is to provide clarity to the extremely important issue of *Law* and *Grace* from a dispensational (Biblical) standpoint.

---

[461] Lightner, Ibid.

[462] Thomas Ice notes these additional adherents as follow: "Chalcedon has an expanding staff and board of affiliates which include Samuel L. Blumenfeld (an expert on the history of public education), John Lofton (a columnist for the Washington, DC *Times,* and television commentator), Mark R. Rushdoony (R. J.'s son), Otto J. Scott, and the investment counselor R. E. McMaster, Jr. Chalcedon also has representatives in Europe and other parts of the world. The *Chalcedon News* (1986) reported, "*The Conservative Digest,* now published from Colorado, has as senior editor Otto Scott, and as contributing editors John Lofton and R. J. Rushdoony" (Ice, Thomas D., "An Evaluation of Theonomic Neopostmillennialism," *Bibliotheca Sacra.* Dallas TX: Dallas Theological Seminary, 1996, c1955-1995. fn. 8). Ice adds to this list the "Tyler group... The ICE (Institute for Christian Economics)... and the sister organization Geneva Ministries [which] followed." Ice notes the involvement of a number of others as well: David Chilton, Francis Schaeffer [It should be pointed out, however, that Schaeffer, although his son Franky has abandoned the position, was a premillennialist], Ray Sutton, James Jordan, George Grant, Michael Gilstrap, James Michael Peters, Lewis E. Bulkeley, Joseph C. Morecraft III, Gary DeMar, Francis Nigel Lee, Joe Kickasola, and Robert Tilton.

FOR FURTHER STUDY ON THE THEONOMY

Barron, Bruce, *Heaven on Earth?* Grand Rapids: Zondervan Publishing House, 1992. 238 pp

Geisler, Norman L., "A Premillennial View of Law and Government." *Bibliotheca Sacra.* Dallas TX: Dallas Theological Seminary, 1996, c1955-1995.

Ice, Thomas D., "An Evaluation of Theonomic Neopostmillennialism," *Bibliotheca Sacra.* Dallas TX: Dallas Theological Seminary, 1996, c1955-1995.

Lightner, Robert P., "Theological Perspectives on Theonomy Part I: Theonomy and Dispensationalism," *Bibliotheca Sacra.* Dallas TX: Dallas Theological Seminary, 1996, c1955-1995.

- - -. "Theological Perspectives on Theonomy Part II: Nondispensational Responses to Theonomy," *Bibliotheca Sacra.* Dallas TX: Dallas Theological Seminary, 1996, c1955-1995.

- - -. "Theological Perspectives on Theonomy Part III: A Dispensational Response to Theonomy," *Bibliotheca Sacra.* Dallas TX: Dallas Theological Seminary, 1996, c1955-1995.

Richard, Ramesh P., "Methodological Proposals for Scripture Relevance—Part IV: Application Theory in Relation to the Old Testament," *Bibliotheca Sacra.* Dallas TX: Dallas Theological Seminary, 1996, c1955-1995.

Witmer, John A., "A Review of Wrongly Dividing the Word of Truth—Part 1," *Bibliotheca Sacra.* Dallas TX: Dallas Theological Seminary, 1996, c1955-1995.

- - -. "A Review of Wrongly Dividing the Word of Truth—Part 2," *Bibliotheca Sacra.* Dallas TX: Dallas Theological Seminary, 1996, c1955-1995.

CHAPTER TWENTY EIGHT

—LAW DESCRIBED AND DEFINED

INTRODUCTION

The Church's history is replete with doctrinal confusion, misunderstanding, and misuse of the Law of God. Even today, many Christians seem to have the general idea that they are somehow *free* from the Law, but fail to understand exactly how, in what manner, to what degree, etc. It is clear that the New Testament teaches that Christ has for the Christian become "the end of the law" (Rom 10:4), but some find it confusing that the New Testament repeats, and apparently endorses, nearly all of the Laws from which we as Christians are said to have been made free (the New Testament makes reference to nine of the Ten Commandments). What are Christians to conclude? Are New Testament believers bound to some sort of New Testament reconstruction of Old Testament Law (i.e., in some edited, truncated, and/or otherwise altered form)? ... Or, are New Testament Christians perhaps *directly* responsible to abide by the Old Testament Law itself? Has Old Testament Law been slightly, moderately, or completely abrogated? ... Or has it been abrogated at all? And if the Old Testament Law has been *done away*, how are their frequent reiterations in the New Testament to be explained?

It is hoped that the content of this and the following chapter will help clear these somewhat-confusing paradoxical dilemmas. (The reader is also advised to study the contents of the **Appendix**.) Throughout history, a number of efforts have been made to define, describe, and explain the *Law* and its relationship to *Grace*.

TYPICAL CHRISTIAN EXPLANATIONS OF THE LAW-GRACE DILEMMA

The Love Solution

One attempt to resolve the Law-Grace dilemma involves somewhat of a blind-to-all-else focus on the New Testament's teaching that *love* is the fulfillment of the Law (Rom 13:9; Jam 2:8). This view would have Christians believe that in order to fulfill "their duty in terms of the law... The Christian is under the evangelical obligation of love and the written law becomes his guide, a rule of gratitude." [463] Thus, by re-identifying the role of the Old Testament Law as merely a "guide" to the greater New Testament obligation to "love," only the condemning power of the Law is considered to have ended.

The Categorical Divisions Solution

A common effort to resolve the dilemma comes in the form of dividing the Old Testament Law into categories. Along this line of thought Ryrie notes the following typical description of the law:

> The law is generally divided into three parts—the moral, the ceremonial, and the judicial. The moral part is termed "the words of the covenant, the ten words" (Exod. 34:28) from which Greek equivalent we derive the label *decalogue*. The judgments begin at Exodus 21:2 and determine the rights between man and man with attendant judgments on offenders. The ceremonial part, which commences at Exodus 25:1, regulated the worship life of Israel. [464]

Paul Enns outlines this three-category view of the Old Testament Law as follows:

> The Law can be divided into three categories: the civil, ceremonial, and the moral laws. [3]

THE MORAL LAW

> The moral law is found principally in the Ten Commandments (Ex. 20:2–17; Deut. 5:6–21), although not restricted to them. The Ten Commandments are listed in two categories: man's relationship to God, covering the first four commandments (Ex. 20:2–11), and man's relationship to man, covering the last six commandments (Ex. 20:12–17). The moral law begins with the statement, "I am the Lord your God, who brought you out of the land of Egypt" (Ex. 20:2), hence, "the standard of moral measurement in deciding what

---

[463] Johnston, O. Raymond, "Law," *Baker's Dictionary of Theology*, p. 319, as cited by Charles C. Ryrie, "The End of the Law." *Bibliotheca Sacra*. Dallas TX: Dallas Theological Seminary, 1996, c1955-1995.

[464] Ryrie, Charles C., "The End of the Law." *Bibliotheca Sacra*. Dallas TX: Dallas Theological Seminary, 1996, c1955-1995.

3 3. Kaiser, Walter C. Jr., *Toward an Old Testament Theology* (Grand Rapids: Zondervan, 1978), pp. 114–18; and Leon Wood, *A Survey of Israel's History* (Grand Rapids: Zondervan, 1970), pp. 148–50.

was right or wrong, good or evil, was fixed in the unwavering and impeccably holy character of Yahweh, Israel's God. His nature, attributes, character, and qualities provided the measuring stick for all ethical decision."[4]

THE CIVIL LAW

The civil law involves many of the laws appearing in Exodus 21:1–24:18, as well as in Leviticus and Deuteronomy. These laws reflect social concerns whereby the Israelites would live with proper concern for their neighbors in the mediatorial kingdom. The laws have reference to slaves, injury to others, property rights, oppression of widows and orphans, money lending, and many other concerns.

THE CEREMONIAL LAW

The ceremonial law, described mainly in Exodus 25:1–40:38 (as well as in Leviticus and Deuteronomy), involves the tabernacle, the clothing and function of the priests, and the sacrifices and offerings.

It should be noted that these categories are intermingled in the text of Exodus–Deuteronomy; within a given context, all three aspects of the law may be described. Nor is it always a simple matter to distinguish between the three aspects of the law.[465]

At first glance, these divisions certainly do appear helpful. However, it is the opinion of this author and others that they fall short of providing an adequate explanation. As George Stevens points out:

It is common to make a distinction between the ceremonial and the moral parts of the law, and to suppose that, while the former are done away, the latter are still binding upon Christians. But this distinction is recognized neither in the Old Testament nor in the New; it is a modern division of the law which is quite convenient and natural for

---

4 4. Kaiser, *Toward an Old Testament Theology*, p. 114.

[465] Enns, Paul P., *The Moody Handbook of Theology*, "Chapter 6 – THEOLOGY OF THE MOSAIC ERA: CONSTITUTION OF THE NATION." Chicago, Ill.: Moody Press, 1997, c1989.

us to make, but one of which a quite unwarrantable use is commonly made.[466]

Roy Aldrich explains:

It is common to divide the Mosaic law into three parts: the Ten Commandments (often called the moral law), the ordinances, and the judgments. The ordinances are the laws governing Israel's religious life while the judgments are the civil laws. These divisions are sometimes helpful for analysis and study but actually have no Scriptural authority.

...

As a matter of fact both the Old and New Testaments regard the law of Moses as an indivisible unit (Jas. 2:10; Gal. 5:3; Josh. 1:8).[467]

Aldrich goes on to mention a number of other authors who reject the idea of this three-part division.[468] He also emphasizes the significant point that in "the Jewish conscience," the law is taken "as a divine unity" and not in divisions.

The Reformed Tradition (Calvin) Solution

As indicated previously, John Calvin obviously had distorted views as to how the Law was to be applied in either the Christian community and/or in society. Nevertheless, in seeking to resolve the Old Testament–New Testament/Law–Grace dilemma, many have adopted Calvin's views on the Law (which is somewhat of a combination of various aspects of the above two mentioned solutions). Ryrie describes Calvin's views as follows:

A more usual solution is that of Calvin, which is followed by many in the Reformed tradition. Calvin taught that the abrogation of the law had reference to liberating the conscience from fear and to discontinuing the ancient Jewish

---

[466] Stevens, George B., *The Theology of the New Testament*, footnote, p. 24, as cited by Roy L. Aldrich, "Has the Mosaic Law Been Abolished?" *Bibliotheca Sacra*. Dallas TX: Dallas Theological Seminary, 1996, c1955-1995.

[467] Aldrich, Roy L., "Has the Mosaic Law Been Abolished?" *Bibliotheca Sacra*. Dallas TX: Dallas Theological Seminary, 1996, c1955-1995.

[468] Godet, *Commentary on Romans*, p. 14–4; A. S. Peake, *The Expositor's Greek New Testament*, III, 525; Erich Sauer, *The Dawn* of *World Redemption*, p. 194; and Patrick Fairbairn, *The Revelation of Law in Scriptures*, p. 466. (Aldrich, Roy L., "Has the Mosaic Law Been Abolished?" *Bibliotheca Sacra*. Dallas TX: Dallas Theological Seminary, 1996, c1955-1995.)

ceremonies. He then distinguishes between the moral law, which he said was abrogated only in its effect of condemning men, and the ceremonial law, which was abrogated both in effect and in its use. In discussing 2 Corinthians 3 he only distinguishes the general differences of death and life in the old and new covenants.[5]... Thus Calvin, as many who have followed him, considered part but not all of the law as ended and the Ten Commandments as binding on the church today (although the fourth commandment concerning the Sabbath had to be interpreted nonliterally).[469]

Ryrie notes, however, that:

> This still does not solve the dilemma or relieve the tension between the law as a unit being done away and some commandments being retained.[470]

JEWISH EXPLANATIONS/DESCRIPTIONS OF THE LAW

As mentioned above, this three-fold division of the Law, as presented by many Christians today (i.e., the moral, the ceremonial, and the judicial), was not a position held by the Jews. They instead saw the Law as a *unit*. Ryrie notes the following Jewish description of the law:

> Although this threefold division of the law is quite popularly accepted in Christian theology, the Jews either did not acknowledge it or at least did not insist on it. They first counted all the particular precepts; then divided them into families of commandments. By this method they counted 613 total laws and twelve families of commandments. "The numeral letters of torah denote six hundred and eleven of them; and the other two, which, as they say, are the first words of the decalogue, were delivered by God himself to the people, and so come not within the compass of the word Torah in that place: whence they take this important consideration, namely, Deut. 33:4, 'Moses commanded us the law,' that is, of six hundred and eleven precepts; two being

---

5 5. John Calvin, *Institutes*, II, XI, 4.

[469] Ryrie, Charles C., "The End of the Law." *Bibliotheca Sacra*. Dallas TX: Dallas Theological Seminary, 1996, c1955-1995.

[470] Ryrie, Ibid.

given by God himself, completes the number of six hundred and thirteen."[1]

These 613 individual laws were further divided into negative and positive commands, and it was said that there were 365 negative ones and 248 positive ones. This meant that there was one command for each day of the year, in order to keep man from temptation, and one command for each member of the body of man to remind him to obey God with his whole being.

...

The twelve families into which the law was categorized were according to the number of the twelve tribes of Israel. These were further subdivided into twelve families of affirmative and twelve of negative commands. The affirmative families concerned: (1) God and His worship, (2) the sanctuary and priesthood, (3) sacrifices, (4) cleanness and uncleanness, (5) alms and tithes, (6) things to be eaten, (7) passover and other feasts, (8) rule and judgment, (9) truth and doctrines, (10) women and matrimony, (11) criminal judgments and punishments, and (12) judgments in civil causes. The negative families concerned: (1) false worship, (2) separation from the heathen, (3) things sacred, (4) sacrifices and priests (5) meats, (6) fields and harvest, (7) house of doctrines, (8) justice and judgment, (9) feasts, (10) chastity, affinity and purity, (11) marriages, and (12) the kingdom. The total number of the commandments, which is far above the usual ten that the average person remembers when he thinks of the law, and the intricate dividing of them, easily and effectively illuminates several New Testament passages which speak of the detail and burden of the law (cf. Heb. 9:1, 10; Acts 15:10; Eph. 2:15).[471]

In arguing for this "indivisible unit [of] the Law of Moses," Aldrich writes:

According to orthodox Jewish tradition, there are 613 commandments in the law of Moses. These are divided into

---

1 1. *The Works of John Owen,* ed., William H. Goold, XVIII, 481.
[471] Ryrie, Charles C., "The End of the Law." *Bibliotheca Sacra.* Dallas TX: Dallas Theological Seminary, 1996, c1955-1995.

248 affirmative laws and 365 negative laws. Moses Margoliouth, who was one of the translators of the English Revised Version, published a catalog of the 613 commandments in English in 1743. In this list the Ten Commandments are not placed first and there is no indication of special emphasis or importance above the others. In fact, the usual Ten Commandments are expanded into thirteen laws. This is done by dividing Exodus 20:4–5 into three separate injunctions against idolatry and making two laws out of the fourth commandment concerning the Sabbath. These thirteen laws are serially numbered from twenty-six to thirty-eight in the long list of 613 laws. There is no attempt to separate or classify different kinds of laws. The listing is on the basis of the order of the occurrence of the laws from Genesis through Deuteronomy. All of this shows that orthodox Judaism believes the Mosaic laws constitute a unified system and that all the laws are equally binding.[472]

DEFINING THE LAW

Failure to adequately define the terms is a major reason for misunderstanding Law (and Grace). In the Old Testament, the word *law* is primarily translated from the Hebrew word *tôrāh* (*towrah*—law, instruction, teaching, a precept or statute). *Tôrāh* (Strong's # 8451) is found 219 times, appearing in 212 verses. The term carries with it a wide range of meanings within Judaism. Its most common use by far has to do with references to the Mosaic code. Included among its many other usages are: (1) when speaking of "The lives of outstanding rabbis," and (2) "The whole of the Old Testament... particularly the Pentateuch."[473] Other related terms include: *hōq* (statute, decree); *mišpāt* (judgment, legal decision); *dābār* (word); and *miṣwāh* (command [-ment]). The English word *law* (*laws, lawful, lawgiver*) is also translated from a number of other Hebrew words in the Old Testament:[474]

---

[472] Aldrich, Roy L., "Has the Mosaic Law Been Abolished?" *Bibliotheca Sacra.* Dallas TX: Dallas Theological Seminary, 1996, c1955-1995.

[473] Ryrie, Charles C., "The End of the Law." *Bibliotheca Sacra.* Dallas TX: Dallas Theological Seminary, 1996, c1955-1995.

[474] Definitions taken from Bible Research Systems, Version 6.2, Revision A. (Austin TX.) 1996.

chathan(1) ([# 2859] *law* 32 times) – "to give (a daughter) away in marriage; hence (gen.) to contract affinity by marriage"

chathan(2) ([# 2860] *law* 5) – "a relative by marriage (espec. through the bride); fig. a circumcised child (as a species of religious espousal)"

kallah ([# 3618] *law* 17) – "a bride (as if perfect); hence a son's wife"

chamowth ([# 2545] *law* 11) – "a mother-in-law"

dath(1) ([# 1882] *law* 9, *laws* 2) – "decree, law"

dath(2) ([# 1881] *law* 6, *laws* 3) – "a royal edict or statute"

mishpat ([# 4941] *lawful* 7, *law* 2) – "prop. a verdict (favorable or unfavorable) pronounced judicially, espec. a sentence or formal decree"

chaqaq ([# 2710] *lawgiver* 6, *law* 1) – "prop. to hack, i.e. engrave... (laws being cut in stone or metal tablets in primitive times)"

cham ([# 2524] *law* 4) – "a father-in-law (as in affinity)"

choq ([# 2706] *law* 4) – "an enactment; hence an appointment (of time, space, quantity, labor or usage)"

yebemeth ([# 2994] *law* 2) – "a sister-in-law"

mitzvah ([# 4687] *law* 1) – "a command, whether human or divine (collect. the Law)"

tsaddiyq ([# 6662] *lawful* 1) – "just"

shalliyt ([# 7990] *lawful* 1) – "mighty; abstr. permission; concr. a premier"

timmahown ([# 8541] *laws* 1) – "consternation"

In the New Testament, the word *law* is primarily translated from the Greek word *nomos* (Strong's # 3551). *Nomos* is found 197 times, appearing in 158 verses. It is "from a primary *nemo* (to parcel out, especially food or grazing to animals.)" *Nomos* carries with it the following meanings:

(1) anything established, anything received by usage, a custom, a law, a command

(1.a) of any law whatsoever

(1.a.1) a law or rule producing a state approved of God

(1.a.1.a) by the observance of which is approved of God

(1.a.2) a precept or injunction

(1.a.3) the rule of action prescribed by reason

(1.b) of the Mosaic law, and referring, acc. to the context. either to the volume of the law or to its contents

(1.c) the Christian religion, the law demanding faith, the moral instruction given by Christ, esp. the precept concerning love

(1.d) the name of the more important part (the Pentateuch), is put for the entire collection of the sacred books of the OT

The English word *law* (*laws, lawful, lawgiver, unlawful, lawless*) is also translated from a number of other Greek words in the New Testament:

exesti ([# 1832] *lawful* 29 times, *may* 2, *let* 1) – "it is lawful"

nomikos ([# 3544] *lawyer[s]* 8, *about the law* 1) – "pertaining to the law, one learned in the law; an interpreter and teacher of the Mosaic law"

nomimos ([# 3545] *lawfully* 2) – "lawfully, agreeable to the law, properly"

nomodidaskalos ([# 3547] *doctor of the law* 2, *teacher of the law* 1) – "a teacher and interpreter of the law, among the Jews; of those who among Christians went about as champions and interpreters of the Mosaic law"

nomothesia ([# 3548] *giving of the law* 1) – "law giving, legislation"

nomotheteo ([# 3549] *receive the law* 1, *establish* 1) – "to enact laws; [to be] furnished with laws; to sanction by law, enact"

nomothetes ([# 3550] *lawgiver* 1) – "a lawgiver"

numphe ([# 3565] *bride* 5, *daughter in law* 3) – "a betrothed woman, a bride; a recently married woman, young wife; a young woman; a daughter-in-law"

anomos(1) ([# 0459] *without law* 4, *transgressor* 2, *wicked* 2, *lawless* 1, *unlawful* 1) – "destitute of (the Mosaic) law;

of the Gentiles; departing from the law, a violator of the law, lawless, wicked"

anomos(2) ([# 0460] *without law* 2) – "without the law, without the knowledge of the law; to sin in ignorance of the Mosaic law; live ignorant of law and discipline"

anomia ([# 0458] *iniquity* 12, *unrighteousness* 1, *transgress the law+4160* 1, *transgression of the law* 1) – "the condition of without law: because ignorant of it, because of violating it; contempt and violation of law, iniquity, wickedness"

penthera ([# 3994] *mother in law* 3, *wife's mother* 3) – "mother-in-law, a wife's mother"

pentheros ([# 3995] *father in law* 1) – "father-in-law, a wife's father"

krino ([# 2919] *judge* 88, *determine* 7, *condemn* 5, *go to law* 2, *call in question* 2, *esteem* 2, misc 8) – "(1) to separate, put asunder, to pick out, select, choose; to approve, esteem, to prefer; to judge; to pronounce an opinion concerning right and wrong; to dispute; to go to law, have suit at law; etc."

krima ([# 2917] *judgment* 13, *damnation* 7, *condemnation* 5, *be condemned* 1, *go to law+2192* 1, *avenge+2919* 1) – "a decree, judgments; condemnation of wrong; the sentence of a judge; a matter to be judicially decided, a lawsuit, a case in court; etc."

agoraios ([# 0060] *baser sort* 1, *law* 1) – "in, of or belonging to the market place; frequenting the market place; hucksters, petty traffickers, retail dealers; idlers, loungers, the common sort, low, mean vulgar"

athemitos ([# 0111] *unlawful thing* 1, *abominable* 1) – "contrary to law and justice, prohibited by law, illicit, criminal"

ennomos ([# 1772] *lawful* 1, *under law* 1) – "bound to the law; bound by the law, lawful; regular"

paranomeo ([# 3891] *contrary to the law* 1) – "to act contrary to the law, to break the law"

~ ~ ~

Roy Aldrich points out a major reason for the confusion that exists in coming to a good understanding of *law*:

> Much of the confusion over law and grace is caused by the failure to distinguish the moral law from the Mosaic law—especially from the Ten Commandments. When so many commentators and theologians say that the Ten Commandments have never been repealed or abrogated they really mean that the moral law of God is eternal. This conclusion no one would question. But the moral law of God is not identical with the Mosaic Ten Commandments.[475]

Note: the distinction Aldrich makes here between "the moral law" and "the Mosaic Ten Commandments" is extremely critical to grasp. It is to be pointed out that Aldrich's use here of the term "moral law" is not to be understood as a part of the three-fold division described above, but is rather, as shall be seen shortly, to be interpreted in the same sense as that of *inherent* or *intrinsic* law.

Even though some of the divisions in the following list by Robert McQuilkin are only aspects of the Mosaic Law and probably could be combined, they are taken from the twelve different uses of the word *law* in the New Testament:

> (1) The Pentateuch (Lk. 24:44); (2) The Old Testament (John 12:34; John 15:25); (3) The Mosaic Law (Matt. 22:37–40); (6) Some Particular Precept or Regulation of the Law (John 19:7); (7) The Ceremonial Law (Heb. 7:28; Heb. 8:4; Heb. 9:22); (8) Law as Principle (Rom. 3:37; Rom. 8:2); (9) Law in General (Rom. 7:1, 2); (10) Law as Penalty (Rom. 4:15; Gal. 3:10); (11) Law as Contrasted with Grace (Gal. 3:11; Matt. 23:23); (12) The Law of Christ (Gal. 6:2; Jas. 1:25; Jas. 2:12).[476]

---

[475] Aldrich, Roy L., "Causes for Confusion of Law and Grace." *Bibliotheca Sacra.* Dallas TX: Dallas Theological Seminary, 1996, c1955-1995.

[476] McQuilkin, Robert, *Law and Grace*, p. 9f, as cited by Roy L. Aldrich, "Causes for Confusion of Law and Grace." *Bibliotheca Sacra.* Dallas TX: Dallas Theological Seminary, 1996, c1955-1995.

Lewis Sperry Chafer defines and divides the Bible's use of the term *law* as follows:

> *Law* is a term used about 200 times in the Bible, meaning a rule which regulates human conduct. Six subdivisions of the Bible doctrine of law follow:
>
> 1. NATURAL, INHERENT, OR INTRINSIC. That which God requires of every creature because of His own character, as it is written: "Be ye holy; for I am holy" (Lev. 11:44; 1 Pet. 1:16). This law was binding upon all, from Adam to Moses (cf. Gen. 26:5; Rom. 2:14-15; 5:12-14).
>
> 2. PRESCRIBED BY MAN. (Gen. 9:6; Matt. 20:15; Luke 20:22; Acts 19:38; 1 Tim. 1:8-10; 2 Tim. 2:5). That which human government requires of its subjects.
>
> 3. OF MOSES. A rule divinely given through Moses to govern Israel in the land of promise. It was commended to them because they were a covenant people. Thus it defined the manner of their daily life. It was itself a covenant of works (Ex. 19:5-6). This covenant they soon broke. It will yet be superseded by the New Covenant (Jer. 31:31-34; Heb. 8:8-13). This agreement will include the former Law of Moses (Deut. 30:8).
>
> The Law of Moses is recorded in three parts:
>
> > a. COMMANDMENTS. Embrace the moral government of Israel (Ex. 20:1-17). They are condensed and summarized in Matthew 22:36-40; fulfilled by love (Rom. 13:10; Gal. 5:14; James 2:8); proved to be law in character (Rom. 7:7-14).
> >
> > b. JUDGMENTS. Embrace the social requirements (Ex. 21:1-23:33).
> >
> > c. ORDINANCES. Regulate the worship (Ex. 25:1-31:18).
>
> These three forms of law satisfied all of Israel's requirements before God. But the entire system, including the commandments as a rule of life, ceased with the death of Christ (John 1:17; Rom 10:4). The Law of Moses, to be sure, was an ad interim dealing in effect only until Christ should come. For the time being it gave to sin the character of

transgression (Rom. 5:13; Gal 3:19). It was preceded (Ex. 19:4) and followed (John 1:17) by grace.

4. REVEALED WILL OF GOD IN ANY FORM. That which has been disclosed in addition to law codes. Observe the definite article with *law* in Romans 7:15-25 because thus Paul may refer to something besides the Law of Moses. The law as the will of God includes all His revealed orders for any people at any time. The word *law* in Romans, then, is used nine times without the article and many more times with the article (cf. Rom. 8:4), and not always referring to Moses.

5. MESSIANIC RULE OF LIFE FOR THE KINGDOM. That which governs the millennium (Matt. 5:1-7:29). Proof that the Messianic rule is pure law may be gained in the following test: (1) any action is legal which aims to secure merit (Matt. 6:14-15); (2) any action is legal which has been wrought in reliance upon the flesh (Rom. 6:14).

6. OF CHRIST. That which now governs the Christian (1 Cor. 9:20-21; Gal. 6:2). Observe the term "my commandments" which was used by Christ only in the upper room (Joh. 14:15, etc.). This form of life-direction includes all the teachings of grace addressed to the Christian, who is not himself under law since grace has provided all the merit that ever could be required (John 1:16; Rom. 5:1; 8:1; Col. 2:10). The saved one is "inlawed to Christ" (1 Cor. 9:20-21, lit. rendering). The believer is not without law to govern his conduct when "inlawed" to Christ.[477]

McQuilkin, as does Aldrich above, uses the term "moral law" in the same sense as Chafer (above) uses the terms "natural, inherent, or intrinsic law":

> The moral law is not equivalent to the Mosaic Law. However, the Mosaic law, which was "added" because of transgressions, included the moral law. It included also the ceremonial law, civil law, criminal law, sanitary law,

---

[477] Chafer, Lewis Sperry, *Systematic Theology*, Grand Rapids, MI: Kregel Publications, 1993, VII, 225–26.

governmental law. But the moral law existed before Moses, and continues after the Cross.[478]

Finally, Wood-Marshall contributes the following:

> Given the OT background, it is not surprising that the term "law" (nomos) in the NT usually refers to the law of Moses. In most cases the focus is on Sinaitic legislation, i.e. the commands and prescriptions of the law (*e.g.* Lk. 2:22–24, 27, 39; Rom. 2:12–27; 1 Cor. 9:8–9). The phrase "the law and the prophets" also occurs (*e.g.* Mt. 5:17; 7:12; 22:40; Lk. 16:16; Jn. 1:45; Acts 13:15; Rom. 3:21; *cf* Lk. 24:44), denoting the OT scriptures as a whole. "Law" in these cases refers to the Pentateuch, while "prophets" designates the rest of the OT. The term "law" also occasionally refers to the OT as Scripture and yet does not denote the Pentateuch, for Paul cites passages from Psalms, Proverbs and Isaiah and labels them as "law" (*cf.* Rom. 3:10–19; 1 Cor. 14:21). There are a few other instances in which the term "law" may not refer to the law of Moses.[479]

NON-BIBLICAL PARALLELS OF LAW

The reader may be surprised to hear that about half of the laws contained in the Book or Code of the Covenant (cf. Exo 24:7) are also found in the law-codes of a number of non-Biblical Near-Eastern sources.

These sources include:

> The laws of Lipit-Ishtar *c.* 2100 BC, the laws of Eshnunna and Hammurapi *c.* 1750 BC, the Hittite laws and the Middle Assyrian laws. There are also thousands of legal documents dealing with marriage, wills, sale, and disputes spanning nearly three millennia, from Sumer to Egypt, which shed light on Israelite legal practice. ... Certainly legal texts from very

---

[478] McQuilkin, Robert, *Law and Grace*, pp. 9 f., as cited by Roy L. Aldrich, "Causes for Confusion of Law and Grace." *Bibliotheca Sacra.* Dallas TX: Dallas Theological Seminary, 1996, c1955-1995.

[479] Wood, D. R. W., D. R. W. Wood, & I. H. Marshall. *New Bible Dictionary,* "LAW." electronic ed. of 3rd ed. Downers Grove: InterVarsity Press, 1996, c1982, c1962. pp. 672-77.

different times and places have contributed to elucidating biblical law.[480]

Wood-Marshall go on to note:

> This suggests we are dealing with collections of traditional case law... presupposing at many points the normal legal practices of the Near East.
>
> ...
>
> It is widely recognized that the Israelite covenant roughly follows the pattern of Near Eastern vassal treaties made between great kings and their underlings. In the OT setting, the Lord is the great king and Israel is his vassal, pledged to total loyalty.[481]

Once one realizes the nature of the concept of *law*, however, such discoveries present no problem. Confusion is completely averted by properly viewing the Mosaic code as another sequential expression of *intrinsic* truth (law) rather than as a primary source of it. Again, it is critical that a distinction be made between "the moral law" (i.e., *inherent* or *intrinsic* law/truth) and "the Mosaic code." It is the author's wish that the reader keep this very important point in mind as he proceeds on to the next chapter.

---

[480] Wood, D. R. W., D. R. W. Wood, & I. H. Marshall. Ibid.
[481] Wood, D. R. W., D. R. W. Wood, & I. H. Marshall. Ibid.

CHAPTER TWENTY NINE

—LAW-GRACE EXPLAINED

INTRODUCTION

It is hoped that the information provided in the preceding chapters has prepared the way for further revelation concerning the *Law-Grace* issue. The purpose of this chapter is to further clear a number of the prevalent and somewhat confusing paradoxical dilemmas that have arisen in relation to this important subject.

THE CONCEPT OF LAW

Laws of Aerodynamics

The content of this section may seem a bit out of place, but the author seeks to convey certain concepts of *law* by briefly examining the principles of aerodynamics. (The contemplations prompted by this illustration shall be clarified shortly.)

First, a description of aerodynamics: aerodynamics is a "branch of [theoretical] physics that deals with the motion of air and other gaseous fluids and with the forces acting on bodies passing through such a fluid."[482] It finds its application in a number of fields: (1) aircraft, rockets, and missiles, (2) automobiles, high-speed trains, and ships, and (3) structures such as bridges, tall buildings, etc. to determine their resistance to high winds. Looking over history, man's experience with the *laws* of aerodynamics can be divided into at least seven stages:

1. **Unsophisticated Observation/Contemplation**.
    Observation by the ancients of the flight of birds obviously stirred speculation, even though they had no clue of the physical properties of the principles pondered. Observation, of course, leads to contemplation. At some point along the way, it entered into the mind of man to begin considering the possibility that man might one-day be able to fly.

2. **Lift off**. Man first got off the ground (as far as history records) in 1783. This was done by way of a hot air balloon designed by the French brothers Joseph-Michel and Jacques-Étienne Montgolfier. Benjamin Franklin envisioned putting a

---

[482] Britannica 2002 Deluxe Edition, CD-ROM

motor on such a vehicle, and by the year 1852 a Frenchman by the name of Henri Gifford invented the first power driven balloon.

3. **Gliders**. Following along an entirely independent line of development than the lighter-than-air vehicles (balloons), the first successful glider (i.e., motorless aircraft) was built by Sir George Cayley in 1849.

4. **Motor propelled aircraft**. Our modern era of aerodynamic engineering then began to emerge; this era was profoundly marked by the first Wright brother's flight in 1903.

5. **Jet Flight**. The advent of turbo-powered technology dramatically changed the air transportation industry. The first jet flight was made on August 27, 1939; subsequent jet aircraft were introduced into service in 1944. This phase of development opened the door for a new era of knowledge concerning supersonic flight. Enormous technological improvements in propulsion, avionics, materials, stability, controls, onboard microcomputers, digital electronics, alternative fuels and weight reduction have since emerged to meet the new demands.

6. **Supersonic Aircraft**. The development of rocket engines for aircraft propulsion made supersonic air travel possible. The first successful liquid-propellant rocket developed and built by Robert H. Goddard flew on March 16, 1926. At this point flight began to exceed the speed of sound. The first manned supersonic aircraft was flown by U.S. Air Force captain Charles E. Yeager in 1947. This opened a whole new spectrum and introduced new challenges in high-speed aeroelasticity, and transonic, supersonic, and hypersonic aerodynamics. The knowledge and data associated with these flights revealed new and vital information concerning the upper atmosphere.

7. **Space Travel**. In the late 1950s and early 1960s intense astronautical growth and development occurred, resulting in the landing on the moon on July 20, 1969. Since then, unmanned voyages to Jupiter, Saturn, and other planets have occurred. Such ventures have opened the minds of man to that which was before thought of as unimaginable impossibilities.

What's the point? Consider the fact that the *inherent* truth of *all* laws pertaining to aerodynamics has remained **unaltered since the beginning**. They existed fully in tact from before the time they were first contemplated as man observed the birds in flight. Each stage of development has been accompanied by ignorance. That which is now considered basic was once-upon-a-time severe stumblingblocks. For example, the idea of air as a resistant force evaded those early contemplators. Hence, a number of other related concepts also eluded them: the compressibility of air, the proportional relationship of air resistance to velocity, etc. And even more perplexing, who would have ever dreamed that the lift responsible for causing a bird to fly came primarily from the low pressures produced upon the top of the wings instead of some phenomenon having to do with the bottom of the wings?

Discovery of the **applicable laws** were critical for successful development of the principles. But the laws associated with many of the upcoming stages often had no applicable value whatsoever in the current stage, due to the nature of that particular stage. Hence, if one were to write the laws for one particular stage of development, they might read much differently than the laws written for another stage of development. For example, in one stage the following law might be appropriately submitted: "thou shalt not spread thine arms like the wings of an eagle and dive off a cliff." In a later stage a different law might be better suited, for example: "thou shalt not dive off a cliff with your hang-glider without having undergone proper training and being properly equipped." While the former law can in no way be considered untrue, the second law is directly applicable to its time. The second law, however, would not so easily apply during the time in which the first law was written.

It is also true that should one form of flight be entirely "done away," the laws that apply to that particular technology, though there may be nothing at all untrue about the *principles*, may hardly be directly applicable to the next particular technology. For example, the laws applicable to hot air balloon travel, though true, hold little to no value when applied to supersonic air travel, at least not in the same sense.

It might also be noted that independent lines of development are entirely possible. The glider, for example (note point # 3 above), was developed concurrent with the lighter-than-air vehicles, but entirely independent of it. Entirely different laws applied.

Again, every law pertaining to aerodynamics *already existed* and was as completely valid from *before* the very first venture as they are *now*. Even today, no matter how much more remains to be discovered, all *true* laws will remain fully in tact, although many will not be applicable in the same sense. All true scientific discoveries that have emerged from the past have only been further enhanced by subsequent scientific discoveries—never are they nullified. A progressive development of knowledge is the result. It might also be noticed that as developments and new discoveries emerge, definitions need to be updated occasionally to match the new discoveries. One might also expect that the language from any given era cannot but reflect certain degrees of ignorance of the yet undiscovered information. These unknowns might be classified as "mysteries."

In summary, the author would be hard-pressed to come up with a better description of the concept of *law* than that of Ryrie's:

> The solution proposed in this essay is basically one which distinguishes between a code and the commandments contained therein. The Mosaic law was one of several codes of ethics which God has given throughout history. That particular code contained, as we have seen, 613 specific commandments. But there have been other God-given codes. The laws under which Adam's life was governed combine to form what might be called a code for the Garden of Eden. There were at least two commandments in that code—dress the Garden and avoid eating the fruit of one tree. Noah was given commandments which included, after the Flood, the permission to eat meat (Gen. 9:3). God revealed many commandments, statutes, and laws to Abraham which guided his life; together these may be called the Abrahamic code of conduct. The laws through Moses were codified formally and fearfully by being handed down from Mount Sinai. The New Testament speaks of the "law of Christ" (Gal. 6:2) and the "law of the Spirit of life" (Rom. 8:2). In the law of Christ are the hundreds of commandments of the New Testament epistles, and together these form a new and distinct code of ethics.

The Mosaic law has been done away in its entirety as a code. God is no longer guiding the life of man by this particular code. In its place He has introduced the law of Christ. Many of the individual commands within that law are new, but some are not. Some of the ones which are old were also found in the Mosaic law and they are now incorporated into the law of Christ. As a part of the Mosaic law they are completely and forever done away. As part of the law of Christ they are binding on the believer today. There are also in the law of Christ commandments from pre-Mosaic codes, as, for instance, the permission to eat meat (1 Tim 4:3). But the inclusion of this one, for example, does not mean that it is necessary to go through theological contortions in order to retain a part of the Mosaic code, so that that particular permission may be retained in this New Testament era. Likewise, it is not necessary to resort to nonliteral exegesis of 2 Corinthians 3 or Hebrews 7 or the fourth commandment in order to understand that the code is ended and familiar commandments are included in the new code.

May this procedure not be likened to the various codes in a household with growing children? At different stages of maturity new codes are instituted but some of the same commandments appear often. To say that the former code is done away and all its commandments is no contradiction. It is as natural as growing up. So it is with the Mosaic law and the law of Christ.[483]

THE MOSAIC LAW "DONE AWAY"

In light of the above, it is not difficult to understand the clear New Testament declaration that the Mosaic Law has been *"done away"* in its *entirety*, no part in any sense applicable to the New Testament believer. Of course, the moral principles *inherent* in the Mosaic Law still apply today, just as they applied *prior to* the giving of the Law at Mt. Sinai. It is helpful to understand that the Mosaic code was never presented to Israel as a means of salvation. Obedience to it was, however, expected, in response to God's grace in delivering Israel from Egypt (cf. Exo 20:2). Obedience incurred blessings.

---

[483] Ryrie, Charles C., "The End of the Law." *Bibliotheca Sacra*. Dallas TX: Dallas Theological Seminary, 1996, c1955-1995.

Disobedience assured all sorts of disasters and calamities. Listed below are a number of comments by a number of authors who hold similar positions.

Charles Ryrie writes:

> The evidence of the New Testament forces to the conclusion that the law—all of it, including the Ten Commandments—has been done away.[484]

Wayne Strickland writes:

> This Mosaic Law naturally ended when God suspended His program with Israel (Rom. 9:11; 10:4; 2 Cor. 3:6–7).
>
> …
>
> Since the Holy Spirit ministers in the life of New Testament believers on behalf of Christ, there is no need for any lengthy, detailed, codified, external means of restraint or rule such as the Mosaic Law.[38]
>
> …
>
> The concept of the law of Christ explains why Paul could say the Mosaic Law had ceased while at the same time saying that one could still fulfill the law. … Since both the Mosaic Law and the law of Christ are founded on God's moral law, one who fulfills the law of Christ is in essence fulfilling the heart of the Mosaic Law.[485]

Having these concepts in mind, the comments of a number of other authors are now considered.

Pfeiffer-Harrison write as follows:

> The Law is not properly thought of as opposing the promises of God, for it operated in a different sphere. Life could not come by the Law. Those who enjoyed spiritual life in the legal dispensation had it not because of the Law but because of the grace of God, which forgave the sins committed against the Law. Such OT passages as promise life

---

[484] Ryrie, Ibid.

38 38. On this point Strickland refers to R. D. Brinsmead, "The Basis of New Testament Ethics," *Verdict* 4 (1981), p. 21.

[485] Strickland, Wayne G., "Preunderstanding and Daniel Fuller's Law-Gospel Continuum," *Bibliotheca Sacra*. Dallas TX: Dallas Theological Seminary, 1996, c1955-1995.

in connection with keeping the commandments of God (e.g., Deut 8:1), are properly interpreted as referring to life in a temporal sense, the enjoyment of God's favor and blessing in this earthly existence. **Righteousness** (a righteous standing before God) was no more possible in terms of law in Moses' day than in Paul's. Further, the Law cannot be opposed to the promises, since it aids their fulfillment by shutting men up to their need of grace and showing them that they must put their trust in Christ (cf. Gal 3:19).[486]

Roy Aldrich writes as follows:

The Mosaic law was of the nature of a covenant made with Israel alone. ... (Ex. 19:3b, 5). This covenant in no sense superseded or canceled the earlier Abrahamic covenant of promise (Gal. 3:14–18). It was added as a temporary institution until Christ should come. ... (Gal. 3:19).

It needs to be emphasized that the end of the Mosaic law, including the Ten Commandments, does not cancel or detract one iota from the eternal moral law of God. The moral principles of the ten laws did not begin with Sinai but are as eternal and immutable as the character of God. To understand this should dispel the fears of those who think the abolition of the Mosaic law leaves only a state of lawlessness. The moral principles embodied in the law of Moses Paul calls "the righteousness of the law" (Rom. 8:4), and shows that such principles are the goal of the Spirit-directed life in the same context in which he teaches the believer is not under the Mosaic law (Rom. 6—Rom. 8).

This should be no more difficult to understand than the fact that a citizen of the United States is not under the laws of Canada, even though the moral principles underlying the laws of the two countries are the same. When a citizen of the United States becomes a citizen of Canada he does not remain under ten of the best laws of the United States. Nor does the fact that some of the laws of the United States are quite similar to some of the laws of Canada confuse or compromise his new exclusive responsibility to Canada. So the believing

---

[486] Pfeiffer, C. F., & E. F. Harrison. *The Wycliffe Bible Commentary: New Testament*. Chicago: Moody Press, 1962. Ga 3:21.

Jew of the first century moved entirely from the Mosaic economy of law into the new economy of grace instituted by Jesus Christ (John 1:17).[487]

Along the same line of thought, Aldrich again writes:

> To avoid confusion and legalism a careful distinction should be made between the moral law and the Mosaic Ten Commandments. When so many say that the Ten Commandments apply to Christians as fully as they ever did to Israel they mean that the moral principles of the law are still binding. But this is not what they have expressed. If the Ten Commandments of the law are still binding then all of the penalties must remain the same. The death penalties should be imposed for Sabbath-breaking, idolatry, adultery, rebellion against parents, etc. To change the penalty of a law means to abolish that law. A law without a penalty is an anomaly. A law with its penalty abolished becomes only good advice. That all of this is not pointless hair-splitting is as evident as the difference between life and death. It is just this difference that is indicated by Paul's description of the Ten Commandments as "the ministration of death, written and engraven in stones" (2 Cor. 3:7a).
>
> ...
>
> The temporary institution of the Mosaic economy embodied the moral law but did not initiate it, and certainly the termination of the Mosaic law did not terminate the moral law.[488]

George Barker Stevens eloquently frames the matter as follows:

> But when it is said the Old Testament system is abrogated in the new, it is of capital importance to observe that the new replaces the old, not by destruction, but by fulfillment. The new does not reject and discard the old; it preserves and embodies it... the new comes out of the old by a natural and orderly process of development. In that process what is essential and permanently useful is taken up into Christianity,

---

[487] Aldrich, Roy L., "Has the Mosaic Law Been Abolished?" *Bibliotheca Sacra.* Dallas TX: Dallas Theological Seminary, 1996, c1955-1995.
[488] Aldrich, Roy L., "Causes for Confusion of Law and Grace." *Bibliotheca Sacra.* Dallas TX: Dallas Theological Seminary, 1996, c1955-1995.

more completely developed and applied, and reinforced by higher motives on the plane of broader principles.

Christ did not fulfill a part of the law merely, but the whole of it. He did not complete the ritual part of the Old Testament alone, but all its moral parts as well. ... If he fulfills the system in all its parts, then must the system *as such* pass away.

...all its elements of permanent value and validity have been made part and parcel of the gospel. To the old system *as such* we have no need to go back, because the gospel is its completion, and we have no occasion to supplement Christianity by additions from Judaism. But the Old Testament has not thereby been *destroyed*, but *fulfilled*. ... The fulfillment is, by its very nature, a conserving process; it rejects nothing which it can use, but embodies it in its perfect result. All the essentials of the Old Testament are preserved in the New, and it is as parts of the gospel of Christ that they are binding upon the Christian man. He is not under the Old Testament system, or, to state the case more fully, he is under only so much of it as has been taken up and incorporated into Christianity, and he is under that because it is a part of Christianity, not because it is a part of the Old Testament religion. If it is asked, Is not the Christian under the authority of the ten commandments? the reply is, In their Old Testament form and as part of that system, he is not. The essential substance of the ten commandments consists of changeless principles of righteousness, and is therefore a part of Christianity; in that sense the Christian is under the commandments, and in no other.

...Christianity is complete and sufficient in itself as a guide to faith and action. The whole philosophy of the subject is in that most expressive figure of Jesus to which we have referred: His gospel is not a patch to be sewed on the old garment of Judaism, but a wholly new garment.[489]

---

[489] Stevens, George Barker, *The Theology of the New Testament*, pp. 23–25, as cited by Roy L. Aldrich, "Has the Mosaic Law Been Abolished?" *Bibliotheca Sacra*. Dallas TX: Dallas Theological Seminary, 1996, c1955-1995.

In reference to the continuation of "the moral principles" contained in the old "Mosaic economy," Aldrich writes:

> Only a theocracy could enforce such laws. No government, or denomination, or society even pretends to enforce them today. This is as it should be for they were given only to Israel and have long been abolished.

> However, it is not only conceded but emphatically insisted that the moral principles of the ten laws are abiding and eternal.[490]

Carl Henry concurs:

> The eternal moral law is binding not on the believer in its Mosaic form, but the Old Testament moral law rather retains its force because it is a part of the righteous will of the immutable God.[491]

Lightner, when presenting his case that "the Law of Moses [has been] Done Away as a Rule of Life," does so by listing from a Biblical (dispensational) standpoint "Six passages [which] address the relationship of the Law of Moses to the present age":[492]

1. ***Acts 15:1–29*** (esp. vv. 1-5, 10-11, 19–21, 24–29). The issue before the Jerusalem Council was how circumcision and the Law of Moses related to the salvation of Gentiles and their Christian walk. Note the use of the term, "yoke upon the neck" in v. 10.

2. ***Galatians 3:17–25*** (esp. 17, 19, 21-22, 25; cf. vv. 2-16, esp. v. 11). There is little doubt that Paul was here discussing the whole Mosaic system. The entire Law, not just the Ten Commandments, Paul argued, was temporary and served as a tutor or a schoolmaster until Christ came.

3. ***Galatians 5:18*** (cf. vv. 1-14, 22-24; Rom 6:14). Deliverance from the Law is related to living the Christian

---

[490] Aldrich, Roy L., "Has the Mosaic Law Been Abolished?" *Bibliotheca Sacra.* Dallas TX: Dallas Theological Seminary, 1996, c1955-1995.

[491] Henry, Carl F. H., *Christian Personal Ethics*, p. 353, as cited by Roy L. Aldrich, "Has the Mosaic Law Been Abolished?" *Bibliotheca Sacra.* Dallas TX: Dallas Theological Seminary, 1996, c1955-1995.

[492] Cf. Lightner, Robert P., "Theological Perspectives on Theonomy Part III: A Dispensational Response to Theonomy," *Bibliotheca Sacra.* Dallas TX: Dallas Theological Seminary, 1996, c1955-1995.

life, and not to attaining salvation. The same is true of Paul's conduct (cf. 1Co 9:20). The fruit of the Spirit are a result of salvation and not the condition of it, thus contradicting the theonomists' claim.

4. **_Romans 6:14_** (cf. 1–10 & 11–23). Living the Christian life is clearly in view. In the first part of the chapter Paul is referring to the relationship the believer has with God through justification; in the last half of the chapter he was writing about the need of progressive sanctification... which is based on Christ's death, rather than on the deeds of the Law. The Law is no more a means of sanctification than it is a means of justification.

5. **_2 Corinthians 3:6–13_** (esp. v. 7; cf. vv. 1–5, 14–18). Here a clear distinction may be seen between the moral law, which is eternal and eternally binding, and the Ten Commandments, which, in contradistinction to the views of theonomists, was temporary and has passed away as a rule of life. (Note v. 7, where the Law is referred to as "the ministration of death.")

6. **_Hebrews 7:11–12_** (cf. vv. 1–10, 13–28, esp. v. 19). Here a comparison is made between the legal and the spiritual priesthoods. The Levitical priesthood was to be superseded by the priesthood of Christ. This meant disannulling not only the Levitical priesthood but also the whole Mosaic system of law.

From these six passages may be gleaned a number of astonishingly direct descriptions and statements concerning the Mosaic Law. These, when compiled, have the potential to surprise even the most well seasoned Bible student. For example, in them the Mosaic Law is described as and/or spoken of in relation to:

- "A yoke upon the neck of the disciples, which neither our fathers nor we were able to bear" (Act 15:10)

- That which would impose "trouble" upon Gentile believers (Act 15:19)

- Seeking justification or sanctification via the Law of Moses is likened unto:

  - Disobedience to the truth (Gal 3:1; 5:7)

- Foolishness (Gal 3:1, 3)

- Becoming "bewitched" (Gal 3:1)

- Attempting to be "made perfect by the flesh" (Gal 3:3)

- Suffering "in vain" (Gal 3:4)

- Being "hindered" (Gal 5:7)

- Something not conducive to the ministry of the Holy Spirit (Gal 3:5)

- Being "under the curse" (Gal 3:10, 13)

- To become justified before God by "the works of the law" requires that one commit to "all things which are written in the book of the law to do them" (Gal 3:10; cf. v. 12)

- "But that no man is justified by the law in the sight of God... is evident" (Gal 3:11)

... "[For] the law is not of faith" (Gal 3:12)

- "The inheritance [is not] of the law" (Gal 3:18)

- "[The law] was added because of transgressions" (Gal 3:19)

- No law can give life (Gal 3:21)

- It was "written... with ink" (2Co 3:3)

- It is "the letter [which] killeth" (2Co 3:6)

- It is "the ministration of death" (2Co 3:7)

- It was "written and engraven in [tables of] stones" (2Co 3:3,7)

- "[Its] glory was to be done away" (2Co 3:7)

- It is "the ministration of condemnation" (2Co 3:9)

- It "had no glory in this respect, by reason of the glory that excelleth" (2Co 3:10)

- It "is done away" (2Co 3:11)

- "Moses... put a vail over his face, [so that] ... That the children of Israel could not stedfastly look to the end of [it]" (2Co 3:13)

- It "is abolished" (2Co 3:13)

- Israel's "minds were blinded" (2Co 3:14)

- "Even unto this day, when Moses is read, the vail is upon their [Israel's] heart" (2Co 3:14-15)

- Christians are not to "be... entangled again with the yoke of bondage" (Gal 5:1)

- "If ye be circumcised, Christ shall profit you nothing" (Gal 5:2)

- "Every man that is circumcised... is a debtor to do the whole law" (Gal 5:3)

- "Christ is become of no effect unto you, whosoever of you are justified by the law" (Gal 5:4)

- "Whosoever of you are justified by the law; ye are fallen from grace" (Gal 5:4)

- To seek to be justified by the law is a "persuasion" that does not come from God (Gal 5:8)

- It is likened unto "a little leaven" which, if allowed, will "leaveneth the whole lump" (Gal 5:9)

- He who "troubleth" the Lord's disciples with such "leaven... shall bear his judgment, whosoever he be" (Gal 5:10; cf. v. 12)

- "The works of the flesh are manifest"; and such vices "cannot" be overcome by human will (Gal 5:17, 19-21)

- "Ye are not under the law, but under grace" (Rom 6:14; cf. v. 15)

- "Perfection" does not come "by the Levitical priesthood," else there would be no "further need... that another priest should rise" (Heb 7:11)

- The "Priesthood [has] changed" (Heb 7:12)

... "There is made of necessity a change also of the law" (Heb 7:12)

- As priest, Jesus did not arise "after the law of a carnal commandment" (Heb 7:15-16)

- There "is verily a disannulling" of the law (Heb 7:18)

- The law has been "abolished" (2Co 3:13) due to "the weakness and unprofitableness thereof" (Heb 7:18)

- "The law made nothing perfect" (Heb 7:19)

~ ~ ~

Note, in Acts 15 and Galatians 3 the Mosaic Law is presented antithetically in regards to "faith"/ "belief." For example:

- "Hear the word of the gospel, and believe" (Act 15:7)
- "Purifying their hearts by faith" (Act 15:9)
- "We believe that through the grace of the Lord Jesus Christ we shall be saved" (Act 15:11)
- "This only would I learn of you, Received ye the Spirit by the works of the law, or by the hearing of faith?" (Gal 3:2)
- "Abraham believed God, and it was accounted to him for righteousness" (Gal 3:6)
- "They which are of faith, the same are the children of Abraham" (Gal 3:7)
- "God would justify the heathen through faith" (Gal 3:8)
- "They which be of faith are blessed with faithful Abraham" (Gal 3:9)
- "The just shall live by faith" (Gal 3:11)
- "We... receive the promise of the Spirit through faith" (Gal 3:14)
- "The promise by faith [is] given to them that believe [in Jesus Christ]" (Gal 3:22)
- After "faith" comes, the believer is no longer "under the law" (Gal 3:23-25)
- The believer is "justified by faith" (Gal 3:24)
- "Ye are all the children of God by faith in Christ Jesus" (Gal 3:26)
- "By faith in Christ Jesus... are ye Abraham's seed, and heirs according to the promise" (Gal 3:26-29)
- "For we through the Spirit wait for the hope of righteousness by faith" (Gal 5:5)
- "Faith [availeth]" (Gal 5:6)

In 2 Corinthians 3, the focus is primarily upon the contrasts between the Mosaic Law and that which Christ ministers by "the Spirit of the living God." For example:

- It causes ministers not to "commend" themselves (v. 1)

- It causes ministers not to "need" the commendation of others (v. 1)

- It results in people "...manifestly declared to be the epistle of Christ ministered by us, written not with ink, but with the Spirit of the living God; not in tables of stone, but in fleshy tables of the heart [known and read of all men]" (vv. 2, 3)

- It causes ministers to "trust... through Christ to God-ward" (v. 4)

- It causes ministers to realize that they "are [not] sufficient of themselves" (v. 5)

- It causes ministers "to [not] think any thing... of [them]selves" (v. 5)

- It causes ministers to rely solely upon the "sufficiency... of God" (v. 5)

- It makes us "able ministers of the new testament; not of the letter, but of the spirit: for the letter killeth, but the spirit giveth life" (v. 6)

- This "ministration of the spirit [is] rather glorious" (v. 8)

- This "ministration of righteousness [doth much more] exceed in glory" (v. 9)

- This "ministration of righteousness... excelleth in glory" (v. 10)

- And this glory doth "much more... remaineth glorious" (v. 11)

- Its ministers "have such hope" (v. 12)

- Its ministers "use great plainness of speech" (v. 12)

- Its ministers do not have "blinded" minds, for the "vail is done away in Christ" (v. 14)

- Where this ministration is (i.e., "the Spirit of the Lord"), "there is liberty" (v. 17)

In Galatians 5, the focus is primarily upon the contrasts between the Mosaic Law and liberty, freedom, profit, and "the fruit of the Spirit." For example:

- "Stand fast therefore in the liberty wherewith Christ hath made us free" (v. 1)

- "Christ shall profit you" (v. 2)

- "Brethren, ye have been called unto liberty" (v. 13)
- "By love serve one another" (vv. 13, 14)"
- "All the law is fulfilled in one word... love" (v. 14)
- "The fruit of the Spirit is love..." (v. 22)
- "They that are Christ's have crucified the flesh with the affections and lusts" (v. 24)

In Romans 6, the primary focus is upon the contrasts between the Mosaic Law and the *freedom* "from sin" that comes through Christ's death, burial, and resurrection:

- "For he that is dead is freed from sin" (v. 7; cf. vv. 1-7)
- "Likewise reckon ye also yourselves to be dead indeed unto sin, but alive unto God through Jesus Christ our Lord" (v. 11)
- "Being then made free from sin, ye became the servants of righteousness [and]... servants to God" (v. 18; cf. v 22)
- Hence, "eternal life through Jesus Christ" is referred to as "the gift of God" (v. 23)

In Hebrews 7, the focus is primarily upon the contrasts between the Mosaic Law and the power that attains unto perfection—namely, the "endless life" of Jesus Christ:

- "It is yet far more evident: for that after the similitude of Melchisedec there ariseth another priest, [16]Who is made, not after the law of a carnal commandment, but after the power of an endless life" (vv. 15-16)
- Jesus is "a better hope" than that of "the law" (v. 19)
- Only by Jesus can one be made "perfect" (v. 19)
- Only by Jesus can one "draw nigh unto God" (v. 19)
- "Jesus [was] made a surety of a better testament" (v. 22)
- Jesus "continueth ever" (v. 24)
- Jesus "hath an unchangeable priesthood" (v. 24)
- Jesus "is able also to save them to the uttermost that come unto God by him" (v. 25)
- Jesus "ever liveth to make intercession for them" (v. 25)
- Jesus is "holy, harmless, undefiled, separate from sinners" (v. 26)

- Jesus is "made higher than the heavens" (v. 26)

- Jesus has no need "to offer up sacrifice... for his own sins" (v. 27)

- Jesus "offer[-ed] up sacrifice... for the people's [sins]... when he offered up himself" (v. 27)

~ ~ ~

PARTICULARLY RELEVANT VERSES FOUND IN THE CONTEXT OF THE SIX ABOVE - MENTIONED PASSAGES INCLUDE:

❖ "Forasmuch as we have heard, that certain which went out from us have troubled you with words, subverting your souls, saying, Ye must be circumcised, and keep the law: to whom we gave no such commandment" (Act 15:24)

❖ "He therefore that ministereth to you the Spirit, and worketh miracles among you, doeth he it by the works of the law, or by the hearing of faith?" (Gal 3:5)

❖ "For as many as are of the works of the law are under the curse" (Gal 3:10)

❖ "Christ hath redeemed us from the curse of the law, being made a curse for us: for it is written, Cursed is every one that hangeth on a tree" (Gal 3:13)

❖ "And this I say, that the covenant [to Abraham], that was confirmed before of God in Christ, the law, which was four hundred and thirty years after, cannot disannul, that it should make the promise of none effect. [18]For if the inheritance be of the law, it is no more of promise: but God gave it to Abraham by promise. [19]Wherefore then serveth the law? It was added because of transgressions, till the seed should come to whom the promise was made; and it was ordained by angels in the hand of a mediator" (Gal 3:17-19)

❖ "Is the law then against the promises of God? God forbid: for if there had been a law given which could have given life, verily righteousness should have been by the law" (Gal 3:21)

❖ "The scripture hath concluded all under sin, that the promise by faith of Jesus Christ might be given to them that believe [23]But before faith came, we were kept under the law, shut up unto the faith which should afterwards be revealed. [24]Wherefore the law was our schoolmaster to bring us unto Christ, that we might be justified by faith. [25]But after that faith is come, we are no longer under a schoolmaster" (Gal 3:22-25)

❖ "But we all, with open face beholding as in a glass the glory of the Lord, are changed into the same image from glory to glory, even as by the Spirit of the Lord" (2Co 3:18)

❖ "Christ is become of no effect unto you, whosoever of you are justified by the law; ye are fallen from grace" (Gal 5:4)

❖ "For in Jesus Christ neither circumcision availeth any thing, nor uncircumcision; but faith which worketh by love" (Gal 5:6)

❖ "And I, brethren, if I yet preach circumcision, why do I yet suffer persecution? then is the offence of the cross ceased" (Gal 5:11)

❖ "For all the law is fulfilled in one word, even in this; Thou shalt love thy neighbour as thyself" (Gal 5:14)

❖ "This I say then, Walk in the Spirit, and ye shall not fulfil the lust of the flesh" (Gal 5:16)

❖ "If ye be led of the Spirit, ye are not under the law" (Gal 5:18)

❖ "But the fruit of the Spirit is love, joy, peace, longsuffering, gentleness, goodness, faith, [23]Meekness, temperance: against such there is no law" (Gal 5:22-23)

❖ "If therefore perfection were by the Levitical priesthood, (for under it the people received the law,) what further need was there that another priest should rise after the order of Melchisedec, and not be called after the order of Aaron? [12]For the priesthood being changed, there is made of necessity a change also of the law" (Heb 7:11-12)

❖ "And it is yet far more evident: for that after the similitude of Melchisedec there ariseth another priest, [16]Who is made, not after the law of a carnal commandment, but after the power of an endless life" (Heb 7:15-16)

❖ "For the law made nothing perfect, but the bringing in of a better hope did; by the which we draw nigh unto God" (Heb 7:19)

❖ "For the law maketh men high priests which have infirmity; but the word of the oath, which was since the law, maketh the Son, who is consecrated for evermore" (Heb 7:28)

Other passages to note under these considerations include: Joh 1:17; Act 13:39; Rom 3:19–31; 4:1-25 (esp. vv. 5, 13–16, 23–24); 5:20–21; 7:1–6, 8, 12; 8:1–4; 9:11; 10:1–9; 11:5–7; 1Co 15:56; Gal 2:16, 21; 3:3, 23–25; 4:19–31; 5:1, 16, 18, 22, 23, 25; Eph 2:15; Phi 3:8-9; Col 2:13-14; Heb 10:1-18; Jam 2:10.

Note: an exhaustive study-outline on the subject of "**LAW in the Bible**" is provided in the **Appendix**.

GRACE

This subject of *grace* obviously deserves much more attention than will be given it in this section, but it would certainly be a mistake to risk leaving the impression that grace did not exist the in the Old Testament when God's people were under the Mosaic Law. It would be equally incongruous to assume that since the Mosaic Law has been "done away," that "law" does not exist in the New Testament.

Having these concerns in mind, Paul Enns writes as follows:

> *Grace.* Although dispensationalists emphasize that the present church age is an age of grace (John 1:17; Rom. 6:14), that emphasis is not to imply that grace did not exist in previous dispensations. The approach to God in salvation is always through grace, and grace was also manifested in the dispensation of law.[15] God chose Israel but passed over the Gentiles. He promised the people of Israel a land, peace, victory over enemies, and blessing. Despite Israel's repeated failure, God continued to deal with the nation in grace—the period of the judges and the monarch were a display of such grace. Amid Israel's failure God promised the nation a new covenant whereby He would forgive her sins. God provided divine enablement through the display of His grace and the ministry of the Spirit.
>
> While God's grace is uniquely displayed in the present age through the advent of Jesus Christ, grace was also displayed under the law.

---

15 15. Charles C. Ryrie, *The Grace of God* (Chicago: Moody, 1963), pp. 101–9.

...

...Dispensationalism has sometimes erred in stressing grace as restricted to the church age while ignoring or minimizing grace in other dispensations. God's grace has been displayed in every age.

...Dispensationalism has also at times projected a negative attitude toward God's law as though it were opposed to God's grace. God's law is present in one or several forms throughout every dispensation for healthy and necessary divine reasons. ...[493]

Along this same line of thought, Pfeiffer-Harrison write:

The new dispensation of free grace brought men the first opportunity, historically speaking, to put faith in Christ. ... The age of law was a time of discipline, the Law serving as a **schoolmaster** (not teacher; in fact, only a teacher's aid, usually a slave whose task it was to insure the safe arrival of the child at the school). Christ is the real teacher, who takes us in hand and shows us the way of God in terms of grace. ... The disciplinary function of the Law, in the historic sense, ceased with the coming of Christ. But the Law may still operate in an individual life to create a sense of sin and need, thus preparing the heart to turn to Christ.[494]

CONCLUSION

God's person and character are perfect and divine, far beyond the description of mere written words. Any and all codes of law, in whatsoever economy they have been given, can only be considered a *partial* reflection/revelation of His indescribable *glory* and His eternal principles of righteousness. Regardless of which of these codes one is speaking about, "all have sinned, and come [fallen] short of the glory of God" (Rom 3:23). Hence, Chafer describes sin as "any want of conformity to the character of God."[495]

---

[493] Enns, P. P., *The Moody Handbook of Theology*. Chicago, Ill.: Moody Press, 1997, c1989.

[494] Pfeiffer, C. F., & E. F. Harrison. *The Wycliffe Bible Commentary: New Testament*. Chicago: Moody Press, 1962. Ga 3:23.

[495] Chafer, Lewis Sperry, *Systematic Theology*, Grand Rapids, MI: Kregel Publications, 1993, II, 260.

The *"glory"* of the Mosaic code of the Old Testament pales in comparison to the *"glory"* of the New (2Co 3:10). The New Testament, far from negating or contradicting the eternal moral principles contained in the Mosaic code, is found to be in perfect harmony with the principles of their expression, even though the Mosaic code has been clearly "done away." In fact, the New Testament, far from opening the way for license and/or antinomianism, demands a morality more excellent than that of the former code.

The eternal *principles* represented by these codes of law given by God, however, are timeless, reaching far beyond any particular dispensation in which they may have been issued, in whatever form. This is true when speaking of the code that was given during the time when Adam and Eve walked with God in the garden, the time of Abraham, the Mosaic economy, the pre-flood era, the post-flood era, this current Christian dispensation, and/or any other period contemplated. In fact, the *principles* represented by *all* of them exceed the boundaries of time itself, and are inseparably linked to the Everlasting Father throughout the stretch of eternity past, present, and future; dominions of which, even at this very moment, are inhabited by Him (a depth of revelation outside the scope of this book). In other words, it was just as wrong to steal, kill, commit adultery, covet, curse, etc. before man was ever created as it is now; this will also be true when all of creation enters the eternal realm. The absolute pure nature of God's moral principles, in whatever form they have been revealed, will remain true in the coming millennial kingdom and beyond, even into the upcoming eternal state.

In each economy a progressive revelation of God's glory has been meted out in various measures/manners to humankind in the form of codes expressing the eternal moral law of God. Unfortunately, men possess minds of extremely limited capacity and hearts even more desperate. God has expressed Himself to us in written form in the *infallible* and *absolutely inerrant* Word of God—the Bible. These expressions are *perfect* and *pure* in every sense of the word. They are also, in their current form, *complete*—in the sense that nothing is to be added to them or taken away from them—*ever!* (Cf. Deu 4:2; 12:32; Pro 30:5-6; Mat 5:18; Rev 22:18-19.)

It may also be stated that no book, not even the Bible, is capable of fully revealing *all* there is to know and understand about God.[496] It would be impossible to conceive of 10 laws (or 613, or a thousand, or a million), most of which are negatively framed (8 ½ of the 10 commandments are negatively framed), adequately representing the standard ideal for human behavior, since this ideal is nothing less than the character of God Himself. Much less would any form of code be able to adequately convey the much more incomprehensible demands of God to "be ye holy, for I am holy" (1Pe 1:16) and to "Be… perfect, even as your Father which is in heaven is perfect" (Mat 5:48). (Some earnestly take aim at the former [i.e., via the Mosaic code] foolishly thinking they might somehow be able to attain such virtue after their own efforts.) But the demands of the Law, as Wood-Marshall cleverly state, "[rather] represent the floor below which no one should fall."[497] To frame it another way, the former (1Pe 1:16) basically states what it is we're to DO and/or not DO! The latter (Mat 5:48) states what we're to BE! Such a true standard of the glory and righteousness of God can *only* be found in one person—Jesus Christ (Joh 5:39; 2Co 4:4; 2Th 2:14; Etc.).

Throughout the annals of time, God has unfolded a marvelous display of His *glory* in the manner in which He has orchestrated the dispensations. His *glory* is uniquely expressed in this current Church Age, also called the dispensation of grace, by the permanent indwelling of the Holy Spirit in every believer. This unprecedented dispensational distinctive makes it possible for Christ's life to be produced *apart from the Law* because the standard—"to be conformed to the image of his Son" (Rom 8:29)—is now attainable by the indwelling work of the Spirit in the believer who will walk in ever-dependent relationship with Him. As in every other dispensation, failure to *glorify* God with His all-sufficient provision of *grace* leads into the next dispensation. In the millennium, the final dispensation as laid out in **Table One** on page 26, the full display of *grace* is the Person of the resurrected Christ. He reigns upon the earth removing

---

[496] Cf. Deu 29:29; Job 9:2, 10; 26:14; Psa 40:5; 77:19; Ecc 3:11; Isa 40:26-28; Joh 20:30-31; 21:25; Act 1:7; Rom 11:33-36; Eph 3:8, 10, 14-21; Col 2:2-3. See also: Psa 36:6, 9; 71:15; 92:5; 97:2; Dan 2:22; 4:34-35; Mat 11:27; 13:11,35; Rom 16:25-27; 1Co 2:6-16; Eph 2:7; 3:14-21.

[497] Wood, D. R. W., D. R. W. Wood, & I. H. Marshall. *New Bible Dictionary,* "LAW." electronic ed. of 3rd ed. Downers Grove: InterVarsity Press, 1996, c1982, c1962. pp. 672-77.

every excuse (bad environment, unchecked sin, etc.) for man's failure to fulfill his responsibilities and give all *glory* to God. In every dispensation throughout all of Scripture, God's marvelous display of *grace* is the revelation of His Son—the *only* One Who could ever perfectly *fulfill* the Law of God (Mat 5:17)—establishing *grace* as the means of man's participation in God's *glory* in every age and for all eternity.

A degree of understanding by *grace* has been granted us unworthy fallen creatures. As we permit ourselves to become enlightened by the power of the Holy Spirit, God opens our understanding of His Word. Thirsty hearts are somehow guided by His Spirit to gaze through this glass darkly (1Co 13:12), as He moves us to search out the wondrous depths of His *glory* and become partakers of the riches of His *grace*. Such *glory* has been the primary purpose of God throughout all ages. The privileges of *grace* are available to *all* who respond to God by putting their faith in Jesus Christ—that Name above all names—and thereby become recipients of His blessed redemption. This divine gift has been made possible by one means and one means only: the sacrifice of the Father's only begotten Son—Jesus Christ—who died upon Calvary's tree in our stead.

FOR FURTHER STUDY ON LAW-GRACE

Aldrich, Roy L., "Has the Mosaic Law Been Abolished?" *Bibliotheca Sacra.* Dallas TX: Dallas Theological Seminary, 1996, c1955-1995.

- - -. "Causes for Confusion of Law and Grace." *Bibliotheca Sacra.* Dallas TX: Dallas Theological Seminary, 1996, c1955-1995.

Chafer, Lewis Sperry, *Systematic Theology* (Dallas: Dallas Seminary Press, 1947–48), Vol. 3, pp. 76-86, 240-244, 342 -345; Vol. 7, pp. 225-6.

Hunt, Dave, *What Love is This?* (Bend, Oregon: The Berean Call, 2004), pp. 67-85.

McClain, Alva J., *Law And The Christian Believer In Relation To The Doctrine Of Grace* (Winona Lake, Indiana: The Brethren Missionary Herald Company, Inc., 1954.)

Ryrie, Charles C., *Dispensationalism* (Chicago: Moody Press, 1995) pp. 13, 37, 56, 58, 69, 101, 105-121, 176.

- - -. "The End of the Law." *Bibliotheca Sacra.* Dallas TX: Dallas Theological Seminary, 1996, c1955-1995.

Strickland, Wayne G., "Preunderstanding and Daniel Fuller's Law-Gospel Continuum." *Bibliotheca Sacra.* Dallas TX: Dallas Theological Seminary, 1996, c1955-1995.

—LAW IN THE BIBLE

Note: this section contains an exhaustive study of *every* use of the words *law(s), lawful, etc.* in both the Old and the New Testament.

Index

I.   Moses: His Birth, Life, Call, Ministry, etc.
II.   The Mosaic Covenant; Given to Israel Only
III.   Non-Mosaic Laws, Penalties, Covenants, Testimonies, etc. (e.g., Pre-Mosaic (i.e., Pre-Sinai); of the Persians, Medes; etc.)
IV.   Justified Disobedience to Non-Mosaic Law (civil, authorities, pagan laws, etc.)
V.   Law Sometimes Spoken of in Connection with Egypt (e.g., Israel's deliverance from, etc.)
VI.   In-Laws
VII.   Lawgiver
VIII.   Israel w/o law
IX.   Strivings over/about the Law
X.   The Law [to be] Taught [to Children], Learned, Known, Written, Remembered, Studied; The Law teaches; etc.
XI.   Law was for "Strangers" (non-Israelites) too (i.e., those who chose to "sojourn" with Israel)
~
XII.   Characteristics of the Law
XIII.   Under Cov., Israel's Obedience was Commanded, Demanded, Required, Expected, Etc.
XIV.   Israel's Obedience Resulted in Blessings
XV.   Israel's Disobedience Resulted in Curses; Defeat; Death; Etc. (with similar results applicable to this Age as well)
XVI.   Examples of Obedience to Law
XVII.   Old Testament Salvation by Faith/Mercy/Grace, Not by Works of Law
XVIII. Obedience to Law Prompted by Grace, Gift, Rebuke, Chastisement from God
XIX.   Holiness, Sanctification, Encouragement, etc. Involved
~
XX.   The [Fiery] Law Proves, Test, Convicts, Judges, Makes Sin Exceedingly Sinful, Etc.
XXI.   Man Fails to, Refuses to Keep, Reject, Corrupts, Hypocritically Keeps, Transgresses, Etc. God's laws
XXII.   The Heart (Laws in; Circumcised; Prepared; not right; matters of; etc.)
XXIII. Repentance Required
XXIV.   Forgiveness Required, Granted thru Christ

~ ~ ~

I.   Moses: His Birth, Life, Call, Ministry, etc.

Exo 2:1-22; 3:1-22; 4:1-12,18-31; 5:1-23; 6:1-13,20; 7; 8:1-32; 9:1-35; 10:1-29; 11:1-10; 12:1-51; 13; 14; 15; 16:2-3,7-8; 17:2-3,16; 18:1-26; 19:3-9; 32:19,22-23,30; 33:8,11; 34:29-35; 40:16-38; Lev 9:23; 10:16-20; Num 10:29,35-36; 11:10-30; 12; 14:2-4,12-20; 16; 20:2-5,10; 21:4-6; 27:12-14,22-23; 31:2,14; 36:13; Deu 1:3,9-18,26-28,37; 5:5,27-28,31; 9:1-3,13-29; 18:15-18; 31:2,7-8,14,23-29; 32:48-52; 33; 34:1-12; Hos 12:13; Mat 17:3-4; Mar 7:9-10; 9:4; Luk 9:30; Act 3:22; 7:20-45; 2Co 3:13; Heb 11:23-28; Jud 1:9.

Selected Passage(s):

❖ "And he said, Hear now my words: If there be a prophet among you, I the LORD will make myself known unto him in a vision, and will speak unto him in a dream. ⁷My servant Moses is not so, who is faithful in all mine house. ⁸With him will I speak mouth to mouth, even apparently, and not in dark speeches; and the similitude of the LORD shall he behold..." (Num 12:6-8)

❖ "And there arose not a prophet since in Israel like unto Moses, whom the LORD knew face to face..." (Deu 34:10).

Commentary: None.

II. The Mosaic Covenant; Given to Israel Only.

Exo 19:3,5-6,11-13,20-24; 20:1-19; 21:22-25; 24:12; 34:28; Lev 6:9,14,25; 7:1,7,11,37; 11:46; 12:7; 13:59; 14:2,32; 14:54,57; 15:32; 26:46; Num 5:29-30; 6:13,21; 19:2,14; 31:21; 36:13; Deu 1:1-5; 4:1-14,44-45; 5:1-2,6-21; 10:5; 22:30; 27:8; 28:1; 31:9,11-12,24,26; 33:4,10; Jos 8:31-32,34; 24:26; 2Ki 14:6; 1Ch 16:17; 2Ch 25:4; 35:12; Ezr 7:26; Neh 9:13-14; Psa 78:1,5; 81:4-5; 105:10; 147:20; Isa 8:16; Jer 31:32; 32:11; Mar 12:24-27; Luk 2:21-24; Joh 7:19; 8:5-7,17; 10:34; 18:31-32; 19:6-7; Act 28:23-24; Rom 9:4-5; 15:8; 1Co 9:8-9; Heb 7:5; 8:3-5; 9:1,10,19,22.

Selected Passage(s):

❖ "And Moses brought forth the people [Israel] out of the camp to meet with God; and they stood at the nether part of the mount. [18]And mount Sinai was altogether on a smoke, because the LORD descended upon it in fire: and the smoke thereof ascended as the smoke of a furnace, and the whole mount quaked greatly. [19]And when the voice of the trumpet sounded long, and waxed louder and louder, Moses spake, and God answered him by a voice. ... [20:1]And God spake all these words, saying..." (Exo 19:17-19, 20:1).

❖ "Keep therefore and do them [the commandments of the LORD your God]; for this is your wisdom and your understanding in the sight of the nations, which shall hear all these statutes, and say, Surely this great nation is a wise and understanding people. [7]For what nation is there so great, who hath God so nigh unto them, as the LORD our God is in all things that we call upon him for? [8]And what nation is there so great, that hath statutes and judgments so righteous as all this law, which I set before you this day? ... [11]And ye came near and stood under the mountain; and the mountain burned with fire unto the midst of heaven, with darkness, clouds, and thick darkness. [12]And the LORD spake unto you out of the midst of the fire: ye heard the voice of the words, but saw no similitude; only ye heard a voice. [13]And he declared unto you his covenant, which he commanded you to perform, even ten commandments; and he wrote them upon two tables of stone. [14]And the LORD commanded me at that time to teach you statutes and judgments, that ye might do them in the land whither ye go over to possess it. ... [44]And this is the law which Moses set before the children of Israel: ..." (Deu 4:6-8, 11-14, 44).

❖ "And it came to pass, when Moses had made an end of writing the words of this law in a book, until they were finished,... [26]Take this book of the law, and put it in the side of the ark of the covenant of the LORD your God, that it may be there for a witness against thee." (Deu 31:24,26)

❖ "[These are the] Israelites; to whom pertaineth the adoption, and the glory, and the covenants, and the giving of the law, and the service of God, and the promises; [5]Whose are the fathers, and of whom as concerning the flesh Christ came, who is over all, God blessed for ever. Amen." (Rom 9:4-5).

Commentary:

The Mosaic Law was issued to Israel (Exo 19:3,6; Lev 26:46; etc.) as a "covenant" (Exo 19:5). The threat of death loomed over all who dared approach the mount from which it was issued (Exo 19:12-13). However, when the children of Israel saw "the thunderings, and the lightnings, and the noise of the trumpet, and the mountain smoking," they feared greatly and dared not approach. They requested that Moses tell them what God was saying rather than hearing God's voice directly themselves (Exo 20:18-19).

The Decalogue (Exo 20:1-17) is often thought of as a summary of the Mosaic Law. Exact and sometimes compound (multiple) restitutions were required (e.g., Exo 21:22-25; 22:1-15). Death was the penalty for many violations. The most common example illustrating the severity of the Mosaic Law is that of a man who "gathered sticks upon the Sabbath day" and was "put to death" for doing so (Num 15:32-36).

III. Non-Mosaic Laws, Penalties, Covenants, Testimonies, etc. (e.g., Pre-Mosaic; Persians, Medes; Mother's; etc.)

Gen 2:15-17; 4:24; 8:15-9:6; 11:31-12:3; 15:6; 17:1-9; 19:12,14; 26:5; 47:26; Exo 6:2-8; 16:4; 18:14-20,24,27; Est 1:8,13,15,19; 3:8; 4:11,16; Pro 1:8; 3:1; 6:20-21; Dan 6:5-10,12,15; Mat 19:8; Mar 10:2-6; Act 14:15-18; 22:25; Rom 1:20; 2:12-16,26-27; 4:9-18; 5:12-15; 13:1-7; 1Co 6:1,6-7; 2Co 12:4; Gal 3:15-19; Jam 4:17; 1Pe 2:13.

Selected Passage(s):

❖ "Because that Abraham obeyed my voice, and kept my charge, my commandments, my statutes, and my laws" (Gen 26:5).

❖ "When they have a matter, they come unto me [Moses]; and I judge between one and another, and I do make them know the statutes of God, and his laws" (Exo 18:16).

❖ "My son, keep thy father's commandment, and forsake not the law of thy mother" (Pro 6:20).

❖ "Now, O king [Darius], establish the decree, and sign the writing, that it be not changed, according to the law of the Medes and Persians, which altereth not" (Dan 6:8).

❖ "He saith unto them, Moses because of the hardness of your hearts suffered you to put away your wives: but from the beginning it was not so" (Mat 19:8).

❖ "For the invisible things of him from the creation of the world are clearly seen, being understood by the things that are made, even his eternal power and Godhead; so that they are without excuse" (Rom 1:20).

❖ "For when the Gentiles, which have not the law, do by nature the things contained in the law, these, having not the law, are a law unto themselves: ^{15}Which shew the work of the law written in their hearts, their conscience also bearing witness, and their thoughts the mean while accusing or else excusing one another;) ^{16}In the day when God shall judge the secrets of men by Jesus Christ according to my gospel" (Rom 2:14-16).

❖ "Wherefore, as by one man sin entered into the world, and death by sin; and so death passed upon all men, for that all have sinned: ^{13}(For until the law sin was in the world: but sin is not imputed when there is no law. ^{14}Nevertheless death reigned from Adam to Moses, even over them that had not sinned after the similitude of Adam's transgression, who is the figure of him that was to come" (Rom 5:12-14).

❖ "Let every soul be subject unto the higher powers. For there is no power but of God: the powers that be are ordained of God. ^{2}Whosoever therefore resisteth the power, resisteth the ordinance of God: and they that resist shall receive to themselves damnation" (Rom 13:1-2).

Commentary: None.

IV. Justified Disobedience to Non-Mosaic Law (e.g., civil authorities, pagan laws, etc.)

Exo 1:22-2:10; Est 3:1-8; 4:11-16; Dan 3:1-20; 6:5-10.

Selected Passage(s):

❖ "And Pharaoh charged all his people, saying, Every son that is born ye shall cast into the river, and every daughter ye shall save alive. $^{2:1}$And there went a man of the house of Levi, and took to wife a daughter of Levi. ^{2}And the woman conceived, and bare a son: and when she saw him that he was a goodly child, she hid him [Moses] three months" (Exo 1:22-2:2).

❖ "And Haman said unto king Ahasuerus, There is a certain people scattered abroad and dispersed among the people in all the provinces of thy kingdom; and their laws are diverse from all people; neither keep they the king's laws: therefore it is not for the king's profit to suffer them" (Est 3:8).

❖ "Nebuchadnezzar the king made an image of gold, whose height was threescore cubits, and the breadth thereof six cubits: he set it up in the plain of Dura, in the province of Babylon. [4]Then an herald cried aloud, To you it is commanded, O people, nations, and languages, [5]That at what time ye hear the sound of the cornet, flute, harp, sackbut, psaltery, dulcimer, and all kinds of musick, ye fall down and worship the golden image that Nebuchadnezzar the king hath set up: [6]And whoso falleth not down and worshippeth shall the same hour be cast into the midst of a burning fiery furnace. ... [12]There are certain Jews whom thou hast set over the affairs of the province of Babylon, Shadrach, Meshach, and Abednego; these men, O king, have not regarded thee: they serve not thy gods, nor worship the golden image which thou hast set up. ... [16]Shadrach, Meshach, and Abednego, answered and said to the king, O Nebuchadnezzar, we are not careful to answer thee in this matter. ... [18]Be it known unto thee, O king, that we will not serve thy gods, nor worship the golden image which thou hast set up. (Dan 3:1,4-6,12,16,18)

❖ "Then said these men, We shall not find any occasion against this Daniel, except we find it against him concerning the law of his God. ... [7]All the presidents of the kingdom, the governors, and the princes, the counsellors, and the captains, have consulted together to establish a royal statute, and to make a firm decree, that whosoever shall ask a petition of any God or man for thirty days, save of thee, O king, he shall be cast into the den of lions. [9]Wherefore king Darius signed the writing and the decree. [10]Now when Daniel knew that the writing was signed, he went into his house; and his windows being open in his chamber toward Jerusalem, he kneeled upon his knees three times a day, and prayed, and gave thanks before his God, as he did aforetime" (Dan 6:5,7,9-10).

Commentary: None.

V. Law Sometimes Spoken of in Connection with Egypt (e.g., Israel's deliverance from, etc.)

Exo 6:2-8; 13:9; Lev 11:44-45; 19:35-37; Deu 4:45; 5:5-7,15; 28:27,68; 2Ki 17:7; Psa 81:4-5; Jer 31:32; Mat 2:15.

Selected Passage(s):

❖ "And it shall be for a sign unto thee upon thine hand, and for a memorial between thine eyes, that the LORD'S law may be in thy mouth: for with a strong hand hath the LORD brought thee out of Egypt" (Exo 13:9).

❖ "And [the young child] was there until the death of Herod: that it might be fulfilled which was spoken of the Lord by the prophet, saying, Out of Egypt have I called my son" (Mat 2:15).

Commentary: None.

VI. In-Laws

Gen 19:12,14; 38:11,13,16,24-25; Exo 3:1; 4:18; 18:1-2,5-8,12,14-15; Lev 18:15; 20:12; Num 10:29; Jdg 1:16; 4:11; 15:6; 19:4-5,7,9; Rth 1:6-8,14-15,22; 2:11,18-20,22-23; 3:1,6,16-17; 4:15; 1Sa 4:19; 4:21; 18:18,21-23,26-27; 22:14; 2Ki 8:27; 1Ch 2:4; Neh 6:18; 13:28; Eze 22:11; Mic 7:6; Mat 10:35; Luk 12:53; Joh 18:13.

Selected Passage(s): None.

Commentary: None.

VII. Lawgiver

Num 21:18; Deu 33:21.

Selected Passage(s): None.

Commentary: None.

VIII. Israel Without Law

2Ch 15:3; Lam 2:9; Eze 7:26.

Selected Passage(s):

❖ "Now for a long season Israel hath been without the true God, and without a teaching priest, and without law" (2Ch 15:3).

Commentary: None.

IX. Strivings Over/About the Law

Act 19:38-39; 1Ti 1:3-4,7; Tit 3:9.

Selected Passage(s):

❖ "But avoid foolish questions, and genealogies, and contentions, and strivings about the law; for they are unprofitable and vain" (Tit 3:9).

Commentary: None.

X. The Law [to be] Taught [to Children], Learned, Known, Written, Remembered, Studied; Publicly Read; The Law Teaches; etc.

Exo 18:16,20; 24:12; Lev 14:54,57; Deu 4:1-2,5,9-10,14,44; 6:5-7; 11:19; 17:11,18-19; 30:2; 31:10-13; 32:46; 33:10; Jos 8:34-35; 2Ch 17:9; Ezr 7:6,10; 7:25; Neh 8:1-3,7-9,13; Psa 78:1,5; 94:12; 119:18, 102; Pro 31:26; Isa 2:2-5; Mic 4:2; Hag 2:11; Mal 2:6-7; 4:4; Mat 5:19; 23:2; Mar 12:14,17; Luk 2:46; Act 13:15; 15:21; 22:3; 28:23-24; Eph 6:4; Heb 8:11.

Selected Passage(s):

❖ "Only take heed to thyself, and keep thy soul diligently, lest thou forget the things which thine eyes have seen, and lest they depart from thy heart all the days of thy life: but teach them thy sons, and thy sons' sons" (Deu 4:9).

❖ "And thou shalt teach them diligently unto thy children, and shalt talk of them when thou sittest in thine house, and when thou walkest by the way, and when thou liest down, and when thou risest up" (Deu 6:7).

❖ "Give ear, O my people, to my law: incline your ears to the words of my mouth.... ⁵For he established a testimony in Jacob, and appointed a law in Israel, which he commanded our fathers, that they should make them known to their children" (Psa 78:1,5).

❖ "Blessed is the man whom thou chastenest, O LORD, and teachest him out of thy law" (Psa 94:12).

❖ "And when they were come, they say unto him, Master, we know that thou art true, and carest for no man: for thou regardest not the person of men, but teachest the way of God in truth: Is it lawful to give tribute to Caesar, or not?" (Mar 12:14).

❖ "And when they had appointed him a day, there came many to him into his lodging; to whom he expounded and testified the kingdom of God, persuading them concerning Jesus, both out of the law of Moses, and out of the prophets, from morning till evening. ²⁴And some believed the things which were spoken, and some believed not" (Act 28:23-24).

Commentary: None.

XI. Law was for "Strangers" (non-Israelites) Too (i.e., those who chose to "sojourn" with Israel)

Exo 12:49; Lev 24:22; Num 15:16,29; Deu 5:14.

Selected Passage(s):

❖ "Ye shall have one manner of law, as well for the stranger, as for one of your own country: for I am the LORD your God" (Lev 24:22).

Commentary: None.

XII. Characteristics of the Law

Deu 4:8; Psa 19:7; 119:96,103,142; Pro 13:14; Rom 7:12,14,16, 22; 1Ti 1:8; Jam 1:25.

Selected Passage(s):

❖ "The law of the LORD is perfect, converting the soul: the testimony of the LORD is sure, making wise the simple" (Psa 19:7).

Commentary:

From these verses, the following characteristics of the Law may be gleaned:
- Perfect (Psa 19:7; 119:96; Jam 1:25)
- Exceeding Broad (Psa 119:96)
- Sweet (Psa 119:103)
- Righteous (Deu 4:8)
- True (Psa 119:142)
- Fountain of Life (Pro 13:14)
- Holy (Rom 7:12)
- Just (Rom 7:12)
- Good (Rom 7:12,16; 1Ti 1:8)
- Spiritual (Rom 7:14)
- Delightful (Rom 7:22)
- After the Inward Man (Rom 7:22)

XIII. Under Cov., Israel's Obedience was Commanded, Demanded, Required, Expected, Etc.

Lev 26:2; Deu 4:6; 6:2; 10:12-13; 29:29; 33:4; Jos 1:7-8; 22:5; 23:6; 1Ki 2:3; 2Ki 17:13,37; 23:24-25; 1Ch 16:40; 2Ch 6:16; 14:4; 19:10; Job 22:22; Psa 78:1; Pro 4:2; Isa 1:10; 2:2-5; Eze 43:11-12; 44:5; Mic 6:7-8; Mal 4:4; Joh 2:23; 7:2,10; Act 15:1,5; Rom 2:13,25; 1Co 7:19,39; 9:8-9,20; 14:34; Jam 4:17.

See also, in regards to this Age: Rom 6:6,15-16,19-22; 7:6-7; 8:4-5,11-13; 12:1-2; 1Co 6:15-18; 2Co 6:14; 10:5; Col 3:1; 1Th 1:3,8; 2Ti 2:5; Heb 2:1-4; Jam 1:25; 2:12; 1Jo 2:1; 3:22-24.

Selected Passage(s):

❖ "And now, Israel, what doth the LORD thy God require of thee, but to fear the LORD thy God, to walk in all his ways, and to love him, and to serve the LORD thy God with all thy heart and with all thy soul" (Deu 10:12).

❖ "Only be thou strong and very courageous, that thou mayest observe to do according to all the law, which Moses my servant commanded thee: turn not from it to the right hand or to the left… [8]This book of the law shall not depart out of thy mouth; but thou shalt meditate therein day and night, that thou mayest observe to do according to all that is written therein…" (Jos 1:7-8).

❖ "But take diligent heed to do the commandment and the law, which Moses the servant of the LORD charged you, to love the LORD your God, and to walk in all his ways, and to keep his commandments, and to cleave unto him, and to serve him with all your heart and with all your soul" (Jos 22:5).

❖ "Be ye therefore very courageous to keep and to do all that is written in the book of the law of Moses, that ye turn not aside therefrom to the right hand or to the left" (Jos 23:6).

❖ "And the statutes, and the ordinances, and the law, and the commandment, which he wrote for you, ye shall observe to do for evermore; and ye shall not fear other gods" (2Ki 17:37).

❖ "For I give you good doctrine, forsake ye not my law" (Pro 4:2).

❖ "For not the hearers of the law are just before God, but the doers of the law shall be justified" (Rom 2:13).

❖ "For circumcision verily profiteth, if thou keep the law: but if thou be a breaker of the law, thy circumcision is made uncircumcision" (Rom 2:25).

❖ "Therefore to him that knoweth to do good, and doeth it not, to him it is sin" (Jam 4:17).

Commentary:

It would be absurd to believe that God's Law is perfect, just, holy, good, etc., and fail to realize that it is God's will for man to live in accordance to it. Anything otherwise would be to classify God as an irresolute *softy*, and to degrade the purity of His character. It is God's will that men live in *perfect* accordance to His Law, and He does not grade on the curve. Nothing short of pristine performance and unblemished conformity will satisfy His call for obedience and His demands for righteousness and holiness. Even a *single* violation renders one guilty of the entire

Law (Jam 2:10. cf. Deu 27:26; Mat 5:18-19; Gal 3:10). Furthermore, as noted above, such demands are not even slightly relinquished for the New Testament Christian (see the passages listed above under "See also, in regards to this Age"); thus leaving "all the world guilty before God" (Rom 3:19). The good news may be stated as follows: Jesus is the *only* person who has ever perfectly satisfied the demands of the Law. Only by becoming a recipient of His righteousness (cf. Rom 4:6; 5:19; 1Co 1:30; 2Co 5:21; Phi 3:9; 2Pe 1:1; etc.) can a believer meet God's demands for true righteousness and perfect holiness.

XIV. Israel's Obedience Resulted in Blessings

Lev 18:5; 26:3-12, 46; Deu 4:1-8; 5:10,16; 8:1; 10:13; 17:18-20; 27:3; 28:1-14; 30:1-16,19-20; 33:4; Jos 1:7-8; 23:14-15; 1Ki 2:3; 2Ki 21:8; 2Ch 31:20-21; Neh 9:29; Psa 1:1-3; 37:31; 94:12; 111:10; 119:1,70,72,77, 92,98-100,104,165,174; Pro 7:2; 28:7; 29:18; Eze 18:5-9,19-21,27; 33:14-19; Dan 3:21-30; Rom 10:5; Eph 6:1-3; Jam 1:25. cf. 1Jo 3:22-24.

Selected Passage(s):

❖ "To keep the commandments of the LORD, and his statutes, which I command thee this day for thy good?" (Deu 10:13).

❖ "And it shall come to pass, if thou shalt hearken diligently unto the voice of the LORD thy God, to observe and to do all his commandments which I command thee this day... [2]all these blessings shall come on thee, and overtake thee, if thou shalt hearken unto the voice of the LORD thy God" (Deu 28:1-2).

❖ "Blessed is the man that walketh not in the counsel of the ungodly, nor standeth in the way of sinners, nor sitteth in the seat of the scornful. [2]But his delight is in the law of the LORD; and in his law doth he meditate day and night" (Psa 1:1-2).

❖ "Blessed are the undefiled in the way, who walk in the law of the LORD" (Psa 119:1).

❖ "The law of thy mouth is better unto me than thousands of gold and silver" (Psa 119:72).

❖ "Keep my commandments, and live; and my law as the apple of thine eye" (Pro 7:2).

Commentary:

Many blessings/benefits were promised unto all among Israel who would obey God's Law. Listed below are a number of these blessing/benefits as they are found in (or in close proximity to) the verses that speak of God's Law:

A. God will Establish His Covenant with You (Lev 26:9)
B. God will establish His Tabernacle among You (Lev 26:11)
C. Possession of [Blessings in, Returned Unto, Established in] the Land [that floweth with milk and honey] (Lev 26:5; Deu 4:1-2,5; 5:16; 8:1; 27:3; 28:8,11; 30:1-5,16,20; 2Ki 21:8)
D. [Long] Life (Lev 18:5; Deu 4:1-2,4; 5:16; 8:1; 17:18-20; 30:6,15-16,19-20; Neh 9:29; Psa 119:77; Pro 7:2; Eze 18:5-9,19-21,27; 33:14-16,19; Rom 10:5)
E. [Long] Life for Children (Deu 17:18-20; Eze 18:19-20; Eph 6:1-3)
F. Chasing, Victory over [Wiser than, God destroying, putting curses upon, etc.] your Enemies (Lev 26:7-8; Deu 28:7; 30:7; Psa 119:98)
G. Wisdom and Understanding [Learning] (Deu 4:6; Psa 94:12; 111:10; 119:98-100,104; Pro 28:7)
H. Being a Good Testimony unto [Feared by] other Nations (Deu 4:6-8; 28:10)
I. Nearness to [Request Granted by] God [in all that He is Called upon for] (Deu 4:7; cf. 1Jo 3:22-24)
J. God will have respect unto you (Lev 26:9)
K. God's Soul shall not Abhor you (Lev 26:11)
L. God shall walk among you (Lev 26:12)
M. God will be your God (Lev 26:12)
N. Ye shall be God's People (Lev 26:12)
O. God's Mercy (Deu 5:10)
P. That it May Go Well With Thee (Deu 5:16)
Q. Multiply [above thy fathers] (Lev 26:9; Deu 8:1; 30:5,16)
R. Good [Success] (Deu 10:13; 30:5,9,15; Jos 1:7-8)
S. Learning to Fear the Lord (Deu 17:18-19)
T. Set on High Above All Nations of the Earth (Deu 28:1)
U. Blessed in the City (Deu 28:3)
V. Blessed in the Field (Deu 28:3)
W. God will make you fruitful (Lev 26:9)
X. Blessed Fruit of Body (Deu 28:4,11; 30:9)
Y. Blessed Fruit of Ground/Land (Lev 26:4; Deu 28:4,11; 30:9)
Z. Your threshing shall reach unto the vintage, and the vintage shall reach unto the sowing time (Lev 26:5)
AA. Blessed Fruit of Cattle (increased kine, sheep) (Deu 28:4,11; 30:9)
BB. Blessed Basket and Store (Lev 26:10; Deu 28:5)
CC. Ye shall eat your bread to the full (Lev 26:5)
DD. Blessed Coming in and Going out (Deu 28:6)
EE. Blessed Storehouses (Deu 28:8)
FF. Blessed, Fruitful, Prosperous In Deed(s) (Deu 28:8,12; 30:9; 1Ki 2:3; 2Ch 31:20-21; Psa 1:1-3; Jam 1:25)

GG. Blessed, Fruitful, Prosperous In "Thy Way" (Going[s]) (Jos 1:7-8; 1Ki 2:3; Psa 1:1-3)

HH. Established as a Holy People unto the Lord (Deu 28:9)

II. Plenteous in Goods/Good Things (Deu 28:11; Jos 23:14-15)

JJ. Good Treasures of Heaven (Rain in his Season) Opened by God (Lev 26:4; Deu 28:12)

KK. Lend [unto many Nations] and not Borrow (Deu 28:12)

LL. Made the Head and not the Tail (Deu 28:13)

MM. Placed Above Only, and Not Beneath (Deu 28:13)

NN. Captivity Turned (Deu 30:1-3)

OO. God's Compassion (Deu 30:1-3)

PP. Circumcised Heart (Deu 30:6)

QQ. Love For God (Deu 30:6)

RR. God's Rejoicing (Deu 30:9)

SS. Inheritance (Deu 33:4)

TT. Not a Single Failure "of all the good things which the LORD your God spake concerning you" (Jos 23:14-15)

UU. Delight(s) (Psa 1:1-2; 119:70,77,92,174)

VV. Like a Tree Planted by the Rivers of Water (Fruit in Season, Leaf not Withering) (Psa 1:1-3)

WW. No Steps Sliding (Psa 37:31)

XX. Undefiled in the Way (e.g., Purged From, Hatred of Every False) (Deu 4:3; Psa 119:1,104)

YY. Great Peace (Lev 26:6; Psa 119:165)

ZZ. Protection from the sword (Lev 26:6)

AAA. Ye shall lie down, and none shall make you afraid (Lev 26:6)

BBB. Rid [of] evil beasts out of the land (Lev 26:6)

CCC. Offended in/by Nothing (Psa 119:165)

DDD. Vision (Pro 29:18)

EEE. Crowned (2Ti 2:5)

FFF. Happiness (Pro 29:18)

GGG. No Sins Mentioned (Eze 33:14-16)

These clearly focus on *earthly* promises! Considering the emphasis some put on achieving salvation by/through the law, the reader might be surprised to observe how glaringly absent from the above Scriptures are any references to *eternal life, salvation, redemption, heaven,* etc. (A reminder: this list emerged from a comprehensive study of *all* the Biblical verses that contain the words *law(s), lawful, etc.*) What is instead found is the following truth: "obey... *that it may be well unto you*" (e.g., Jer 7:23). This should come as a very liberating truth to all who may have formerly been bound by the clutches of certain traditional religions: religions which promote the idea that men are somehow able to attain righteousness, eternal life, etc. by obeying God's Law.

XV. Israel's Disobedience Resulted in Curses; Defeat; Death; Etc. (with similar results applicable to this Age as well).

Lev 10:1-7; 20:12; 26:14-39, 46; Num 5:29-30; 15:29, 32-36; Deu 4:1-3, 9; 5:1, 11; 17:11-13; 22:13-29; 27:15-26; 28:14-68; 29:21; 30:1,15,17-19; Exo 21:22-25; 22:1-15; Jos 8:34; 23:15-16; 2Ki 14:6; 17:15-23; 2Ch 19:10; 25:4; Ezr 7:26; Psa 78:1,5,10,33-37; 89:30-32; 119:92; Pro 28:7,9; 29:18; Isa 5:24; 24:5; 42:24; 49:24; Jer 6:19; 8:7-13,16-17; 9:13-16,19,21-22; 25:11; 26:4-6; 32:23-24; 44:21-23; Lam 2:9; Eze 18:10-13,20; 22:26-31; Dan 9:10-11,13; Hos 4:6; 8:1; Amo 2:4; Zec 7:12; Mal 2:7-9; 3:7-10; Mat 5:19; Mar 12:24-27; Luk 11:42-52; Joh 5:14; 8:5; 19:6-7; Act 13:40-41; Rom 4:15; 5:9,12-18,20-21.

See also, in regards to this Age: Rom 6:15-16; 7:5,8-13,23-24; 8:6,10,13; 13:1-7; 14:23; 1Co 6:12; 2Co 11:14-15; Gal 3:10; Col 2:14; 2Th 2:8-10; Heb 2:1-4; 10:28-31; Jam 4:11-12; 1Jo 5:16; Rev 3:16.

Selected Passage(s):

❖ "Cursed be he that confirmeth not all the words of this law to do them. And all the people shall say, Amen" (Deu 27:26).

❖ "And thou shalt not go aside from any of the words which I command thee this day, to the right hand, or to the left, to go after other gods to serve them. [15]But it shall come to pass, if thou wilt not hearken unto the voice of the LORD thy God, to observe to do all his commandments and his statutes which I command thee this day; that all these curses shall come upon thee, and overtake thee" (Deu 28:14-15).

❖ "Moreover all these curses shall come upon thee, and shall pursue thee, and overtake thee, till thou be destroyed; because thou hearkenedst not unto the voice of the LORD thy God, to keep his commandments and his statutes which he commanded thee: [46]And they shall be upon thee for a sign and for a wonder, and upon thy seed for ever. [47]Because thou servedst not the LORD thy God with joyfulness, and with gladness of heart, for the abundance of all things" (Deu 28:45-47).

❖ "If thou wilt not observe to do all the words of this law that are written in this book, that thou mayest fear this glorious and fearful name, THE LORD THY GOD; [59]Then the LORD will make thy plagues wonderful, and the plagues of thy seed, even great plagues, and of long continuance, and sore sicknesses, and of long continuance" (Deu 28:58-59).

❖ "I call heaven and earth to record this day against you, that I have set before you life and death, blessing and cursing: therefore choose life, that both thou and thy seed may live" (Deu 30:19).

❖ "And what cause soever shall come to you of your brethren that dwell in your cities, between blood and blood, between law and commandment, statutes and judgments, ye shall even warn them that they trespass not against the LORD, and so wrath come upon you, and upon your brethren: this do, and ye shall not trespass" (2Ch 19:10).

❖ And they came in, and possessed it; but they obeyed not thy voice, neither walked in thy law; they have done nothing of all that thou commandedst them to do: therefore thou hast caused all this evil to come upon them" (Jer 32:23).

❖ "Beware therefore, lest that come upon you, which is spoken of in the prophets" (Act 13:40).

❖ "For as many as are of the works of the law are under the curse: for it is written, Cursed is every one that continueth not in all things which are written in the book of the law to do them" (Gal 3:10).

Commentary:

Though *many* blessings, benefits, etc. were promised to the soul that *obeyed* God's Law, Israel was warned that *many more* curses, evils, etc. would befall the soul that *disobeyed* the Laws of God. And, as will be noted below, death loomed as a threat unto the New Testament Christian as well. Listed below are a number of penalties found in (or in close proximity to) such passages, that threaten to befall any person who commits violations against God's Law. Observe again how glaringly absent from the list, even from the New Testament passages, are references to *eternal damnation, hell,* etc.

A. Scattered, Taken, Plucked From, Cast out from/Loss of Possession of the Land (that floweth with milk and honey); Land Shall Become a Desolation/Astonishment; Banishment (Lev 26:32-39; Deu 28:21,25,63-64; 30:17-18; Jos 23:15-16; 2Ki 17:22-23; Ezr 7:26; Jer 9:13-16,19; 25:11; 44:21-23; Lam 2:9)

B. Destroyed, Perish [Quickly]; Shortened Life; [Fruit Unto] Death [without Mercy]; Devoured; As Rottenness, Consumed; Go up as Dust; Etc.(Lev 10:1-7; 20:12; Num 15:29, 32-36; Deu 4:3; 17:11-13; 22:20-27; 28:20-22,24,48,51,61,63; 30:15,17-19; Jos 23:15; 2Ki 14:6; 2Ch 25:4; Ezr 7:26; Psa 78:10,34; 119:92; Pro 29:18; Isa 5:24; Jer 8:8,13; 9:13,16, 21-22; Eze 18:10-13,20; 22:26-31; Hos 4:6; Joh 8:5; 19:6-7; Act 13:40-41; Rom 5:12-15,17,21. Cf.: Rom 6:15-16; 7:5,8-13, 23-24; 8:6,10,13; 2Th 2:8-10; Heb 10:28-31; Jam 4:11-12; 1Jo 5:16)

C. No Opportunity to Enjoy Children; Children Taken Captive; [Death of] Children [Passed Through the Fire]; Etc. (Deu 28:41; 2Ki 17:15-17; Jer 9:13,21-22)

D. Defeated/ Overtaken/ Distressed/ Captivated/ Slain By, Serve, Driven Unto, Delivered into the Hand of, Etc. the Enemy, Other Nations, Spoilers, Robbers; Captivity; Imprisonment (Lev 26:17,25; Deu 28:25,36,41,48-57,68; 30:1; 2Ki 17:15; 2Ki 17:19-23; Ezr 7:26; Isa 42:24; 49:24; Jer 8:7-10,16-17; 25:11; 32:23-24; Hos 8:1. Cf.: Rom 7:23)

E. Destroy you with your idols, images, high places (Lev 26:30)

F. Uncertainty, No Assurance of Life, Dismayed, Confounded, No Understanding, Void of Knowledge, Deceived, Become Forgetful (Deu 4:8-9; 28:66; Jer 8:7-9; 9:13,19; Dan 9:10-11,13; Luk 11:52. Cf.: 2Th 2:8-10)

G. Shameful Testimony, Contemptible and Base Before Other Nations/People (Deu 28:37,45-46; Jer 26:4-6; Mal 2:7-9)

H. Removed From God's Sight (2Ki 17:18-20, 22-23)

I. Not Multiplied, Diminished (Deu 28:62-63; 2Ki 17:18)

J. Cursed (Deu 27:15-26; 28:20; 29:21; 30:1,19; Jos 8:34; Jer 26:4-6; 44:21-23; Dan 9:10-11; Gal 3:10)

K. Cursed in the City (Deu 28:16)

L. Cities made waste (Lev 26:31,33)

M. Cursed in the Field (Deu 28:16,38)

N. Cursed Fruit of Body (Deu 28:18,32)

O. Cursed Fruit of Ground/Land (Deu 28:18,33,38-40,42,51; Jer 8:8,13)

P. Sow seed in vain, for your enemies shall eat it (Lev 26:16)

Q. Cursed Increase of Kine, Flocks of Sheep, Etc. (Deu 28:18,31,51)

R. Cursed Coming in and Going out (Deu 28:19)

S. Cursed Basket, Store (Deu 28:17,30)

T. Eat, and not be Satisfied (Lev 26:26)

U. Cursed, Unfruitful, Not Prosperous In Deed(s) (Deu 28:20)

V. Not Prosperous, Not Plenteous in Goods/Good Things (Deu 28:29)

W. Confiscation of Goods (Ezr 7:26)

X. Powder and Dust For Rain (Deu 28:24)

Y. Borrow [from many Nations] and not Lend (Deu 28:44)

Z. Made the Tail and not the Head (Deu 28:44)

AA. Placed Beneath (low), and Not Above (high) (Deu 28:43)

BB. They that hate you shall reign over you (Lev 26:17)

CC. Ye shall flee when none pursueth you (Lev 26:17)

DD. God's Displeasure/Anger Kindled; [Fire of God's/Great] Wrath (Lev 10:1-7; Jos 23:15-16; 2Ki 17:15-18; 2Ch 19:10; Eze 22:26-31; Zec 7:12; Mat 3:7; Rom 4:15; 5:9; 13:1-7)

EE. God will set His face against you (Lev 26:17)

FF. God will also walk contrary unto you [in fury] (Lev 26:24,28)

GG. God will break the pride of your power (Lev 26:19)

HH. God will make your heaven as iron, and your earth as brass (Lev 26:19)

II. Your strength shall be spent in vain (Lev 26:20)

JJ. Your land shall not yield her increase (Lev 26:20)

KK. Trees of the land shall not yield their fruits (Lev 26:20)

LL. God will even appoint over you terror, consumption, and the burning ague, that shall consume the eyes, and cause sorrow of heart (Lev 26:16)

MM. Punished/Plagued/Chastened seven times [more] for your sins (Lev 26:18,21,24,28)

NN. Become as Graves (Luk 11:44)

OO. No Peace, Ease or Rest; Discontent; Trouble; Etc. (Deu 28:65,67; Psa 78:10,33)

PP. No Vision (Lam 2:9)

QQ. Guilt, Condemnation, Damnation (Deu 5:11; Rom 5:16,18,20. Cf.: Rom 13:1-7; 14:23)

RR. Chastised and/or Fined (Deu 22:13-19, 28-29)

SS. Vexation (Deu 28:20)

TT. Rebuke (Deu 28:20)

UU. Incurable/Cleaving/Great Pestilence [of Long Continuance], Plague, Botch/Disease [of Egypt], Emerods, Scab, Itch, Etc. (Lev 26:25; Deu 28:21,27, 35,58-61; Jer 32:23-24)

VV. Fever (Deu 28:22)

WW. Inflammation (Deu 28:22)

XX. Extreme Burning (Deu 28:22)

YY. Sword (Lev 26:25,33; Deu 28:22; Jer 32:23-24. Cf.: Rom 13:1-7)

ZZ. Blasting (Deu 28:22)

AAA. Mildew (Deu 28:22)

BBB. Brass Heaven (Deu 28:23)

CCC. Defiled/Iron Earth (Deu 28:23; Isa 24:5)

DDD. Carcass for meat unto all fowls of air and beast of earth (Deu 28:26)

EEE. Madness (Deu 28:28,34)

FFF. Blindness (Deu 28:28-29)

GGG.   Astonishment of/Trembling/Fearful/ Faintness of Heart (Lev 26:36; Deu 28:28,65,67)

HHH.   Oppression (Deu 28:29,33)

III.   Spoiled (Deu 28:29; Isa 42:24; Jer 9:13,19)

JJJ.   Beyond the Help of [Any] Man (Deu 28:26,29,31,68; Jer 9:13,22)

KKK.   Pine away in your [fathers'] iniquities (Lev 26:39)

LLL.   Broken Betrothals/Marriages (Deu 28:30; Jer 8:7-10)

MMM.   Houses Overtaken/Inhabited by Others (Deu 28:30)

NNN.   Powerless (Deu 28:32)

OOO.   Crushed Away (Deu 28:33)

PPP.   Hewn Down [Axed], and Cast into the Fire (Mat 3:7-10)

QQQ.   Cast Down (Jer 8:8,11-12)

RRR.   [Turned Over to] Idolatry/Other gods (Deu 28:36,64; 2Ki 17:15-17)

SSS.   Hunger (Deu 28:48)

TTT.   Thirst (Deu 28:48)

UUU.   Famine (Jer 32:23-24)

VVV.   Nakedness (Deu 28:48)

WWW.   Yoked of Iron Upon Neck (Deu 28:48)

XXX.   Eat Children (i.e., Sons & Daughters) (Lev 26:29; Deu 28:53-57)

YYY.   Brought to Nought (Deu 28:63)

ZZZ.   Failing Eyes (Deu 28:65)

AAAA.   Sorrow of Mind (Deu 28:65)

BBBB.   Fear Day and Night (Deu 28:66-67)

CCCC.   Flee at the sound of a shaken leaf (Lev 26:36)

DDDD.   Fall when none pursueth (Lev 26:36-37)

EEEE.   No power to stand before your enemies (Lev 26:37)

FFFF.   Evil (Deu 30:15; Jos 23:15; 2Ki 17:16-17; Jer 6:19; 32:23; 44:21-23; Dan 9:10-11,13)

GGGG.   Vanity; Become Vain (2Ki 17:15; Psa 78:10,33)

HHHH.   Rejected/Spued By God (From Being a Priest) (2Ki 17:19-20; Hos 4:6. Cf.: Rev 3:16)

IIII.   Afflicted By God (2Ki 17:19-20)

JJJJ.   Rent From the House of David (2Ki 17:21-22)

KKKK.   Restitution (sometimes multifold); Punishment; Fined; Have Own Way/Works Recompensed Upon One's Own Head; "Eye for an Eye"; etc. (Exo 21:22-25; 22:1-15; Num 5:29-30; Eze 22:26-31; Amo 2:42. Cf.: 2Co 11:14-15; Heb 2:1-4)

LLLL.   Indignation (Eze 22:26-31)

MMMM.   The Rod; Stripes (Psa 89:30-32)

NNNN.   Shame (Pro 28:7; Jer 8:7-9)

OOOO. Error (Amo 2:4; Mar 12:24-27)
PPPP. Desolate Sanctuaries (Lev 26:31)
QQQQ. Even Prayer Shall Be Abomination (Pro 28:9)
RRRR. God will not smell the savour of your sweet odours (Lev 26:31)
SSSS. God will send wild beasts among you, which shall rob you of your children, and destroy your cattle, and make you few in number (Lev 26:22)
TTTT. Biting Serpents/Cockatrices (Jer 8:8,17. cf. Mat 3:7)
UUUU. Fed With Wormwood (Jer 9:13-15)
VVVV. Water of Gall to Drink (Jer 9:13-15)
WWWW. Your high ways shall be Desolate (Lev 26:22)
XXXX. Children Forgotten by the Lord (Hos 4:6)
YYYY. Called Least in the Kingdom of Heaven (Mat 5:19)
ZZZZ. Woe (Luk 11:42-47,52)
AAAAA. Become Hypocrites (Luk 11:44)
BBBBB. Have Law "Depart from thy Heart All the Days of thy Life" (Deu 4:8-9)
CCCCC. Held Responsible for the Blood of all the Prophets (Luk 11:47-51)
DDDDD. Held Responsible for Hindering Others from Entering into Knowledge (Luk 11:52)

In addition to these which can be *directly* derived from the Scriptures, the following, by way of *deduction* (since their antithesis was promised to those who *obeyed* the Law of God), may also be derived:

A. Fear of Other Nations/People
B. Rendering Void God's Mercy
C. Not Well
D. No Good [Success]
E. Failing to Learn to Fear the Lord
F. Set Below All Nations of the Earth
G. Cursed, Unfruitful, Not Prosperous In "Thy Way" (Going[s])
H. Not Established as a Holy People unto the Lord
I. Rendering Void God's Compassion
J. Uncircumcised Heart
K. No Love For God
L. No Inheritance
M. Sadness
N. Steps Sliding
O. Defiled in the Way
P. Offended in/by Everything
Q. No Happiness
R. Tormented By Sins

Again, these speak exclusively of *earthly* matters! The reader will note, as he reviews these passages, how often it is explicitly stated that the Lord Himself is responsible for bringing on the curse, calamity, wrath, evil, etc. It may also be noted, by comparing the number of passages found in this list to the number of those in the previous section, that the Bible *emphasizes the negative* when it comes to the Law; there are approximately twice as many negative references as there are positive. This negative emphasis holds true in the Decalogue as well (8 ½ of the Ten Commandments are framed negatively). Paul aptly identified these "handwriting of ordinances" as "against us" and "contrary to us" (Col 2:14); that is, in our fallen condition.

Also, as in the case above of God's demands for obedience, such threats of punishment are not at all lightened for this current Age; this even applies, perhaps especially, to Christians. Paul himself recognized the danger of being *"brought under the power of any"* (1Co 6:12) and of becoming *"a castaway"* (1Co 9:27). Clearly revealed in the New Testament is the fact that severe consequences, even *"unto death,"* are subject to befall those who severely/willfully transgress. Below are only a few examples:

❖ "But a certain man named Ananias, with Sapphira his wife, sold a possession, ²And kept back part of the price, his wife also being privy to it, and brought a certain part, and laid it at the apostles' feet. ⁵And Ananias... fell down, and gave up the ghost... ¹⁰Then fell she [Sapphira] down straightway at his feet, and yielded up the ghost: and the young men came in, and found her dead, and, carrying her forth, buried her by her husband. ¹¹And great fear came upon all the church, and upon as many as heard these things." (Act 5:1-11)

❖ "But Peter said unto him [Simon], Thy money perish with thee, because thou hast thought that the gift of God may be purchased with money... ²⁴Then answered Simon, and said, Pray ye to the Lord for me, that none of these things which ye have spoken come upon me" (Act 8:20,24)

❖ "He that eateth and drinketh [the Lord's supper] unworthily, eateth and drinketh damnation [a condemnatory sentence] to himself, not discerning the Lord's body. ³⁰For this cause many are weak and sickly among you, and many sleep" (1Co 11:29-30)

❖ "Therefore we ought to give the more earnest heed to the things which we have heard, lest at any time we should let them slip. ²For if the word spoken by angels was stedfast, and every transgression and disobedience received a just recompence of reward; [3]How shall we escape, if we neglect so great salvation; which at the first began to be spoken by the Lord, and was confirmed unto us by them that heard him; [4]God also bearing them witness, both with signs and wonders, and with divers miracles, and gifts of the Holy Ghost, according to his own will?" (Heb 2:1-4)

❖ "There is one lawgiver, who is able to save and to destroy: who art thou that judgest another?" (Jam 4:12)

❖ "If any man see his brother sin a sin which is not unto death, he shall ask, and he shall give him life for them that sin not unto death. There is a sin unto death: I do not say that he shall pray for it" (1Jo 5:16).

XVI. Examples of Obedience to Law

2Ki 23:24-25; 2Ch 23:18; 25:4; 30:16; 31:3,20-21; 35:6,11-12,26; Ezr 3:2; 6:18; 7:14,21,24; 10:3; Neh 8:14,18; 10:28-29,34,36; 13:1,3,5; Psa 119:51,55,61,97,101,102,109; Dan 3:18,21-30; Luk 2:21-24,27,39; Joh 7:50-51; Act 21:20,24,28; 22:3,12; Rom 2:26-27. Cf. Rom 6:17-18.

Selected Passage(s):

❖ "And thus did Hezekiah throughout all Judah, and wrought that which was good and right and truth before the LORD his God. [21]And in every work that he began in the service of the house of God, and in the law, and in the commandments, to seek his God, he did it with all his heart, and prospered" (2Ch 31:20-21).

❖ "I have remembered thy name, O LORD, in the night, and have kept thy law" (Psa 119:55).

❖ "But if not, be it known unto thee, O king, that we will not serve thy gods, nor worship the golden image which thou hast set up…" (Dan 3:18 [cf. vv. 21-30]).

Commentary:

Biblical examples of obedience to the Law include:
A. Putting Away/Not Worshipping Idols (2Ki 23:24-25; Dan 3:18,21-30)
B. Offerings [with Rejoicing and Singing] (2Ch 23:18; 31:3; 35:6,11-12; Ezr 3:2; Neh 10:34,36; 13:1,3,5; Luk 2:21-24,27,39)
C. Not Slaying Children for the Sins of the Fathers (2Ch 25:4)
D. Circumcising Children (Luk 2:21)
E. Standing "in their place after the manner" (2Ch 30:16)
F. Sprinkled the Blood (2Ch 30:16)

G. Celebrating/Honoring Holy Days (Passover, Booths, etc.) (2Ch 31:3; 35:6,11-12; Neh 8:14,18; 10:34,36; Luk 2:21-24,27,39)

H. Doing Good, Right, and Truth (2Ch 31:20-21; 35:26)

I. [Preparing/Appointing/etc. those for the] Service of/in the House of God (2Ch 31:20-21; 35:6; Ezr 6:18; 7:14,21,24; Act 22:3)

J. Separating from Heathen/Strange Wives/etc.; Sanctifying/Purifying Self; etc. (2Ch 35:6; Ezr 10:3; Neh 10:28; 13:1,3; Act 21:20,24,28)

K. Building the Altar of God (Ezr 3:2)

L. Not Imposing Toll, Tribute, or Custom (Ezr 7:14,21,24)

M. Trembling at the Commandment of God (Ezr 10:3)

N. Entered Into a Curse, and Into an Oath (Neh 10:28-29)

O. Not Declining/Departing From the Law (Psa 119:51,102)

P. Remembering the Name of the Lord (Psa 119:55)

Q. Not Forgetting the Law (Psa 119:61,109)

R. Keeping the Law (Psa 119:55,101; Act 21:24)

S. Loving the Law (Psa 119:97)

T. Meditating on the Law (Psa 119:97)

U. Refraining Feet From Every Evil Way (Psa 119:101)

V. Hearing the Accused (Joh 7:50-51)

W. Shaving Head (Act 21:20,24,28)

X. Walking Orderly (Act 21:20,24,28)

Y. Being Devout (Act 22:12)

XVII. Old Testament Salvation by Faith/Mercy/Grace, Not by Works of Law

Gen 15:6; Psa 103:1-14; 119:40-41,44; Isa 33:22; 38:17; 55:1-2,7-9; Mic 6:7-8; Hab 2:4; Rom 4:6-8; 9:4-11; 9:31-32; 10:1-3; 11:5-7; 1Co 7:19.

Selected Passage(s):

❖ "And he [Abram] believed in the LORD; and he counted it to him for righteousness" (Gen 15:6).

❖ "Behold, for peace I had great bitterness: but thou hast in love to my soul delivered it from the pit of corruption: for thou hast cast all my sins behind thy back" (Isa 38:17).

❖ "Ho, every one that thirsteth, come ye to the waters, and he that hath no money; come ye, buy, and eat; yea, come, buy wine and milk without money and without price. ²Wherefore do ye spend money for that which is not bread? and your labour for that which satisfieth not? hearken diligently unto me, and eat ye that which is good, and let your soul delight itself in fatness. ... ⁷Let the wicked forsake his way, and the unrighteous man his thoughts: and let him return unto the LORD, and he will have mercy upon him; and to our God, for he will abundantly pardon. [8]For my thoughts are not your thoughts, neither are your ways my ways, saith the LORD. [9]For as the heavens are higher than the earth, so are my ways higher than your ways, and my thoughts than your thoughts" (Isa 55:1-2,7-9).

❖ "Will the LORD be pleased with thousands of rams, or with ten thousands of rivers of oil? shall I give my firstborn for my transgression, the fruit of my body for the sin of my soul? [8]He hath shewed thee, O man, what is good; and what doth the LORD require of thee, but to do justly, and to love mercy, and to walk humbly with thy God? (Mic 6:7-8).

❖ "The just shall live by his faith" (Hab 2:4).

❖ "Even as David also describeth the blessedness of the man, unto whom God imputeth righteousness without works, [7]Saying, Blessed are they whose iniquities are forgiven, and whose sins are covered. [8]Blessed is the man to whom the Lord will not impute sin" (Rom 4:6-8).

❖ "Who are Israelites; to whom pertaineth the adoption, and the glory, and the covenants, and the giving of the law, and the service of God, and the promises; [5]Whose are the fathers, and of whom as concerning the flesh Christ came, who is over all, God blessed for ever. Amen. [6]Not as though the word of God hath taken none effect. For they are not all Israel, which are of Israel: [7]Neither, because they are the seed of Abraham, are they all children: but, In Isaac shall thy seed be called. [8]That is, They which are the children of the flesh, these are not the children of God: but the children of the promise are counted for the seed. [9]For this is the word of promise, At this time will I come, and Sarah shall have a son. [10]And not only this; but when Rebecca also had conceived by one, even by our father Isaac; [11](For the children being not yet born, neither having done any good or evil, that the purpose of God according to election might stand, not of works, but of him that calleth;)" (Rom 9:4-11).

❖ "But Israel, which followed after the law of righteousness, hath not attained to the law of righteousness. [32]Wherefore? Because they sought it not by faith, but as it were by the works of the law. For they stumbled at that stumblingstone" (Rom 9:31-32).

❖ "Brethren, my heart's desire and prayer to God for Israel is, that they might be saved. [2]For I bear them record that they have a zeal of God, but not according to knowledge. [3]For they being ignorant of God's righteousness, and going about to establish their own righteousness, have not submitted themselves unto the righteousness of God" (Rom 10:1-3).

❖ "Even so then at this present time also there is a remnant according to the election of grace. ⁶And if by grace, then is it no more of works: otherwise grace is no more grace. But if it be of works, then it is no more grace: otherwise work is no more work. ⁷What then? Israel hath not obtained that which he seeketh for; but the election hath obtained it, and the rest were blinded" (Rom 11:5-7).

❖ "Circumcision is nothing…" (1Co 7:19).

Commentary: None.

XVIII. Obedience to Law Prompted by Grace, Gift, Rebuke, Chastisement from God

1Ch 22:12; 2Ch 33:8; Neh 9:29; Psa 18:19; 40:4,6; 51:14-15; 105:41-45; 115:3; 119:18; 29,34-44,77,153; 174; Pro 3:11-12; Isa 42:21; 51:4; Jer 31:33; Act 14:15; Col 3:1; Heb 12:5-13.

Selected Passage(s):

❖ "Only the LORD give thee wisdom and understanding, and give thee charge concerning Israel, that thou mayest keep the law of the LORD thy God" (1Ch 22:12).

❖ "He opened the rock, and the waters gushed out; they ran in the dry places like a river. ⁴²For he remembered his holy promise, and Abraham his servant. ⁴³And he brought forth his people with joy, and his chosen with gladness: ⁴⁴And gave them the lands of the heathen: and they inherited the labour of the people; ⁴⁵That they might observe his statutes, and keep his laws. Praise ye the LORD" (Psa 105:41-45).

❖ "Open thou mine eyes, that I may behold wondrous things out of thy law" (Psa 119:18).

❖ "Remove from me the way of lying: and grant me thy law graciously" (Psa 119:29).

❖ "Give me understanding, and I shall keep thy law; yea, I shall observe it with my whole heart. ³⁵Make me to go in the path of thy commandments; for therein do I delight. ³⁶Incline my heart unto thy testimonies, and not to covetousness" (Psa 119:34-36).

❖ "My son, despise not the chastening of the LORD; neither be weary of his correction: ¹²For whom the LORD loveth he correcteth; even as a father the son in whom he delighteth" (Pro 3:11-12).

Commentary: None.

XIX. Holiness, Sanctification, Encouragement, etc. Involved

Exo 28:36-38; Lev 10:1-7; 11:44-45; 19:2; 20:7; Num 6:13,21; 2Ch 31:4; Psa 119:1,29,101,104,113,163; Pro 13:14; Isa 8:20; Rom 3:31; 6:19-22; 8:18,23; 1Co 6:19-20; 2Co 6:14; 7:1; Col 3:1; 2Ti 1:3; Heb 12:9-11,14-17; Jam 1:27; 3:17; 1Pe 1:15-15.

Selected Passage(s):

❖ "Blessed are the undefiled in the way, who walk in the law of the LORD" (Psa 119:1).

❖ "To the law and to the testimony: if they speak not according to this word, it is because there is no light in them" (Isa 8:20).

❖ "Do we then make void the law through faith? God forbid: yea, we establish the law" (Rom 3:31).

Commentary: None.

XX. The [Fiery] Law Proves, Test, Convicts, Judges, Makes Sin Exceedingly Sinful, Etc.

Exo 16:4; Deu 33:2; 2Ki 22:8,11; 2Ch 34:14-15,19-21; Neh 8:9-18; 9:3; Psa 94:12; Pro 6:20-23; Mal 2:6; Mat 14:4-5; Mar 3:4-6; 6:18-19; Joh 5:45-47; 8:8-9; Act 7:52-54; 24:24-25; 28:23-24; Rom 2:12; 3:19-20; 5:20-21; 7:7-13; 1Co 15:56; 2Co 3:6-9; Gal 3:19; 1Ti 1:8-11; Heb 12:18-21; Jam 2:9-11.

Selected Passage(s):

❖ "Then said the LORD unto Moses, Behold, I will rain bread from heaven for you; and the people shall go out and gather a certain rate every day, that I may prove them, whether they will walk in my law, or no" (Exo 16:4)

❖ "And he said, The LORD came from Sinai, and rose up from Seir unto them; he shined forth from mount Paran, and he came with ten thousands of saints: from his right hand went a fiery law for them" (Deu 33:2)

❖ "And when they brought out the money that was brought into the house of the LORD, Hilkiah the priest found a book of the law of the LORD given by Moses. [15]And Hilkiah answered and said to Shaphan the scribe, I have found the book of the law in the house of the LORD. ... [19]And it came to pass, when the king had heard the words of the law, that he rent his clothes. [20]And the king commanded... [21]Go, enquire of the LORD for me, and for them that are left in Israel and in Judah, concerning the words of the book that is found: for great is the wrath of the LORD that is poured out upon us, because our fathers have not kept the word of the LORD, to do after all that is written in this book" (2Ch 34:14-15,19-21; 2Ki 22:8,11).

- ❖ "All the people wept, when they heard the words of the law" (Neh 8:9).
- ❖ "And they stood up in their place, and read in the book of the law of the LORD their God one fourth part of the day; and another fourth part they confessed, and worshipped the LORD their God" (Neh 9:3).
- ❖ "Blessed is the man whom thou chastenest, O LORD, and teachest him out of thy law" (Psa 94:12).
- ❖ "For the commandment is a lamp; and the law is light; and reproofs of instruction are the way of life" (Pro 6:23).
- ❖ "Do not think that I will accuse you to the Father: there is one that accuseth you, even Moses, in whom ye trust" (Joh 5:45)
- ❖ "He stooped down, and wrote on the ground. [9]And they which heard it, being convicted by their own conscience, went out one by one, beginning at the eldest, even unto the last" (Joh 8:8-9).
- ❖ "Which of the prophets have not your fathers persecuted? and they have slain them which shewed before of the coming of the Just One; of whom ye have been now the betrayers and murderers: [53]Who have received the law by the disposition of angels, and have not kept it. [54]When they heard these things, they were cut to the heart, and they gnashed on him with their teeth" (Act 7:52-54).
- ❖ "As many as have sinned in the law shall be judged by the law" (Rom 2:12).
- ❖ "Now we know that what things soever the law saith, it saith to them who are under the law: that every mouth may be stopped, and all the world may become guilty before God. [20]Therefore by the deeds of the law there shall no flesh be justified in his sight: for by the law is the knowledge of sin" (Rom 3:19-20).
- ❖ "Moreover the law entered, that the offence might abound" (Rom 5:20).
- ❖ "What shall we say then? Is the law sin? God forbid. Nay, I had not known sin, but by the law: for I had not known lust, except the law had said, Thou shalt not covet. [8]But sin, taking occasion by the commandment, wrought in me all manner of concupiscence. For without the law sin was dead. [9]For I was alive without the law once: but when the commandment came, sin revived, and I died. [10]And the commandment, which was ordained to life, I found to be unto death. [11]For sin, taking occasion by the commandment, deceived me, and by it slew me. [12]Wherefore the law is holy, and the commandment holy, and just, and good. [13]Was then that which is good made death unto me? God forbid. But sin, that it might appear sin, working death in me by that

which is good; that sin by the commandment might become exceeding sinful" (Rom 7:7-13).

❖ "The sting of death is sin; and the strength of sin is the law" (1Co 15:56).

❖ "Who also hath made us able ministers of the new testament; not of the letter, but of the spirit: for the letter killeth, but the spirit giveth life. [7]But if the ministration of death, written and engraven in stones, was glorious, so that the children of Israel could not stedfastly behold the face of Moses for the glory of his countenance; which glory was to be done away: [8]How shall not the ministration of the spirit be rather glorious? [9]For if the ministration of condemnation be glory, much more doth the ministration of righteousness exceed in glory" (2Co 3:6-9).

❖ "Wherefore then serveth the law? It was added because of transgressions, till the seed should come to whom the promise was made" (Gal 3:19).

❖ "But we know that the law is good, if a man use it lawfully; [9]Knowing this, that the law is not made for a righteous man, but for the lawless and disobedient, for the ungodly and for sinners, for unholy and profane, for murderers of fathers and murderers of mothers, for manslayers, [10]For whoremongers, for them that defile themselves with mankind, for menstealers, for liars, for perjured persons, and if there be any other thing that is contrary to sound doctrine; [11]According to the glorious gospel of the blessed God, which was committed to my trust" (1Ti 1:8-11).

❖ "For ye are not come unto the mount that might be touched, and that burned with fire, nor unto blackness, and darkness, and tempest, [19]And the sound of a trumpet, and the voice of words; which voice they that heard intreated that the word should not be spoken to them any more: [20](For they could not endure that which was commanded, And if so much as a beast touch the mountain, it shall be stoned, or thrust through with a dart: [21]And so terrible was the sight, that Moses said, I exceedingly fear and quake:)" (Heb 12:18-21).

❖ "But if ye have respect to persons, ye commit sin, and are convinced of the law as transgressors. [10]For whosoever shall keep the whole law, and yet offend in one point, he is guilty of all. [11]For he that said, Do not commit adultery, said also, Do not kill. Now if thou commit no adultery, yet if thou kill, thou art become a transgressor of the law" (Jam 2:9-11).

Commentary:

The passages listed under this section reveal a number of important functions of the Law:

A. Proves Those Who Will Walk in God's Way or Not (Exo 16:4; Act 28:23-24)
B. Described as "Fiery" (Deu 33:2; Heb 12:18)
C. Brings About Conviction, Trembling, Fear and Quaking (2Ch 34:14-15,19-21; 2Ki 22:8,11; Joh 8:8-9; Act 7:52-54; 24:24-25; Heb 12:18-21)
D. Makes Aware of God's Forthcoming Wrath Due to Disobedience (2Ch 34:14-15,19-21)
E. A Means of National Reformation (2Ch 34:14-15,19-21; Neh 8:9-18)
F. Causes Some to Weep (Neh 8:9)
G. Brings Some to Hours (e.g., "one fourth part of the day") of Confessing Sins and Worshipping God (Neh 9:3)
H. Chastens, Reproves, Instructs (Psa 94:12; Pro 6:23)
I. Turns Many Away From Iniquity (Mal 2:6)
J. Invokes the Murderous Intentions of Some (Mat 14:4-5; Mar 3:4-6; 6:18-19; Act 7:52-54)
K. Causes Every Mouth to be Stopped (Rom 3:19)
L. Convinces Transgressors (Jam 2:9-11)
M. Causes All the World to Become Guilty Before God (Rom 3:19; Jam 2:9-11)
N. Brings About the Knowledge of Sin (Rom 3:20; 7:7)
O. Causes the Offence to Abound (Rom 5:20)
P. Causes Sin to Reign Unto Death (Rom 5:20-21; 7:9-13; 1Co 15:56; 2Co 3:6-7)
Q. Gives Sin an Occasion [e.g., to Deceive] (Rom 7:8,11)
R. Brings Sin to Life (Rom 7:8-9)
S. Brings Sin to Light [i.e., "that it might appear sin"] (Rom 7:12-13)
T. Causes Sin to Become "Exceeding Sinful" (Rom 7:12-13)
U. Strengthens Sin (1Co 15:56)
V. Causes to Surface All manner of Concupiscence (desire, craving, longing, desire for what is forbidden, lust) in Us (Rom 7:8)
W. "The Letter [that] Killeth" (2Co 3:6)
X. "The Ministration of Death" (2Co 3:7)
Y. "The Ministration of Condemnation" (2Co 3:9)
Z. Came With a Glory that could not be Steadfastly Beheld (2Co 3:7-9)
AA. "Added Because of Transgressions" (Gal 3:19)
BB. "Not Made For a Righteous Man" (1Ti 1:8-9)
CC. "Made For": (1Ti 1:8-11)
1. Lawless and disobedient
2. Ungodly and for sinners
3. Unholy and profane

4. Murderers of fathers and murderers of mothers
5. Manslayers
6. Whoremongers
7. Them that defile themselves with mankind
8. Menstealers
9. Liars
10. Perjured persons
11. Any other thing that is contrary to sound doctrine
DD. Could Not Be Heard/Endured (Heb 12:18-21)
EE. Death Unto All Who Touch the Mount (Heb 12:20)

~ ~ ~

At this point, the author suggests that the reader contemplate the following four verses:

❖ "Now we know that what things soever the law saith, it saith to them who are under the law" (Rom 3:19).

❖ "But we know that the law is good, if a man use it lawfully" (1Ti 1:8).

❖ "The law is not made for a righteous man, but for the lawless and disobedient..." (1Ti 1:9).

❖ "For whosoever shall keep the whole law, and yet offend in one point, he is guilty of all" (Jam 2:10).

XXI. Man Fails, Refuses to Keep, Hypocritically Keeps, Rejects, Corrupts, Transgresses, Sins Against, Etc. God's Laws

Gen 8:21; Exo 16:28; 20:18-19; 2Ki 10:31; 17:7-23,34; 2Ch 12:1; Neh 9:26,29,34; Psa 78:1,5,10,33-37; 94:20; 119:53,70,85,126, 136,150; Pro 1:7; 28:4,7,9; 31:5; Isa 5:24; 24:5; 30:9; 42:24; Jer 2:8; 6:19; 8:5-12; 9:13-14; 16:11; 18:18; 26:4-5; 32:23-24; 44:10,21-23; Eze 22:26-30; Dan 7:25; 9:10-11,13; Hos 4:6; 8:1,12; Amo 2:4; Hab 1:4; Zep 3:4; Zec 7:12; Mal 2:7-9; Mat 14:4-5; 15:7-9; 23:3,23-28; 27:6; Mar 6:18-19; 7:8,13; 12:24-27; Luk 7:30; 11:37-52; 18:9-14; Joh 5:44-45; 7:19,48-49; 18:31-32; 19:6-7; Act 6:11-14; 7:52-54; 13:27-29; 15:5; 23:3; 28:23-27; Rom 2:12,17-27; 3:10-20,23; 5:12-19; 7:5,14-25; 8:5-8; 9:31-32; 10:1-3; 1Co 14:21; 2Co 11:14-15; Gal 3:20-25; 4:21; 5:1-14,18-24; 6:13; Eph 2:1-3,11-12; Phi 3:2-8; Col 2:13-14; 2Th 2:8-10; 1Ti 1:5-7,9-11; 4:1-3; Heb 7:28; 8:7-9; 12:18-21; Jam 2:9-11; 4:11-12; 2Pe 2:8; 1Jo 1:6-10; 3:4.

Selected Passage(s):

❖ "For their heart was not right with him, neither were they stedfast in his covenant" (Psa 78:37).

❖ "Horror hath taken hold upon me because of the wicked that forsake thy law" (Psa 119:53).

❖ "It is time for thee, LORD, to work: for they have made void thy law" (Psa 119:126).

❖ "Rivers of waters run down mine eyes, because they keep not thy law" (Psa 119:136).

❖ "This is a rebellious people, lying children, children that will not hear the law of the LORD" (Isa 30:9).

❖ "Hear, O earth: behold, I will bring evil upon this people, even the fruit of their thoughts, because they have not hearkened unto my words, nor to my law, but rejected it" (Jer 6:19).

❖ "I have written to him the great things of my law, but they were counted as a strange thing" (Hos 8:12).

❖ "Thus saith the LORD; For three transgressions of Judah, and for four, I will not turn away the punishment thereof; because they have despised the law of the LORD, and have not kept his commandments, and their lies caused them to err, after the which their fathers have walked" (Amo 2:4).

❖ "But the scripture hath concluded all under sin..." (Gal 3:22).

❖ "Whosoever committeth sin transgresseth also the law: for sin is the transgression of the law" (1Jo 3:4).

Commentary:

It is interesting to note that there are about twice as many New Testament references denoting sin, transgression, etc. as there are Old Testament references. The passages listed under this section reveal a number of manners in which God's Laws/Commandments have been and/or can be violated, transgressed against, sinned against, etc.:

A. Wickedness, Evil, Evil Thoughts, Evil Heart [from youth], Abomination, Etc. (Gen 8:21; 2Ki 17:11,13,17; Psa 78:37; 119:70; Jer 6:19; 8:6; 44:21-23; Mat 15:7-9)

B. Refuse to hear, obey, do, walk in, return, turn, repent, etc. (Exo 16:28; 2Ki 17:14,34; Neh 9:26,29; Psa 78:10; Isa 30:9; 42:24; Jer 8:5-6; 9:13-14; 32:23; 44:10,21-23; Dan 9:10-11,13; Zec 7:12; Gal 5:7)

C. Withdraw, Remove, Leave, Forsake, Turn aside (Exo 20:18-19; 2Ki 17:16; 2Ch 12:1; Psa 119:53,150; Pro 28:4; Jer 9:13-14; 16:11; Eph 2:1-3; 1Ti 1:5-7)

D. Sin, Depart Not from Sins, Transgress, Trespass, Corrupt, Infirmity, Be at fault, Violate, Done Violence to, Profane, Depart From Law, Be Contrary to, Be Guilty, Offend, Etc. (2Ki 10:31; 17:7,21; Neh 9:29; Isa 24:5; 42:24; Jer 2:8; 44:21-23; Eze 22:26; Dan 9:11; Hos 8:1,12; Hab 1:4; Zep 3:4; Mal 2:7-9; Act 23:3; Rom 2:12, 27; 3:10, 19-20, 23;

5:12-19; 7:5, 14-25; Gal 3:20-25; Eph 2:1-3; Col 2:13-14; Heb 7:28; 8:7-9; Jam 2:9-11; 1Jo 3:4)

E. Harden Necks (2Ki 17:14; Neh 9:29)

F. Reject (2Ki 17:15; Jer 6:19; 8:9; Hos 4:6; Luk 7:30)

G. Rebel (Neh 9:26; Isa 30:9)

H. Heed Not, Hear Not, Hearken Not, Turn away ear (2Ki 10:31; Neh 9:29,34; Pro 28:9; Jer 6:19; 18:18; 26:4-5; 1Co 14:21; Gal 4:21; Heb 12:18-21)

I. Keep/Kept Not (2Ki 17:19; Neh 9:34; Psa 78:10; 119:136; Jer 16:11; Amo 2:4; Mal 2:7-9; Joh 7:19; Act 7:52-54)

J. Despise [Wisdom, Instruction, God's Law, Etc.] (Pro 1:7; Isa 5:24; Jer 8:9 Amo 2:4)

K. Violate, Be not steadfast in, Break, Transgress His Covenant (Psa 78:37; Isa 24:5; Hos 8:1)

L. Cast Away; Cast God's Law behind back (Neh 9:26; Isa 5:24)

M. Make Void God's Law (Psa 119:126; Mar 7:8, 13)

N. Count God's Law as a Strange Thing (Hos 8:12)

O. Forget (Pro 31:5; Hos 4:6)

P. Know Not, Understand Not the Truth, Pass over the Judgment of the Lord, Etc. (Jer 8:7; Dan 9:13; Hos 4:6; Mar 12:24-27; Luk 11:42-43; Act 13:27-29; Rom 3:11; 1Ti 1:5-7)

Q. Fear, Walk After other gods (2Ki 17:7; Jer 16:11)

R. Go After, Walk in the Statutes of, Etc. the Heathen, things that do not profit, One's own course, the imagination of one's on heart, Out of the way, Etc. (2Ki 17:8,11,15,18; Jer 2:8; 8:6; 9:13-14; Rom 3:12, 16)

S. Do secretly those things that are not right (2Ki 17:9)

T. Witchcraft, Idolatry (e.g., [graven] images, groves, high places, green trees, [burn] incense, golden calf, worship all the host of heaven, prophesy by, walk after, serve Baal, divination and enchantments, etc.) (Lev 26:1; 2Ki 17:9-12, 16-17; Jer 2:8; 9:13-14; 44:21-23; Gal 5:19-21; 1Ti 4:1-3)

U. Believe Not, Fear Not [God] (2Ki 17:14,34; Jer 44:10; Act 28:23-24; Rom 3:18; 1Ti 1:5-7; 4:1-3)

V. Follow Vanity, Become Vain, Vain Glory, Etc. (2Ki 17:15; Jer 8:8; Eze 22:28; Mat 15:7-9; Gal 6:13)

W. Follow Mischief (Psa 119:150)

X. Cause sons, daughters to pass through fire (2Ki 17:17)

Y. Slay God's Prophets and Apostles (Neh 9:26; Luk 11:47-51; Act 7:52-54)

Z. Wrought Great Provocations (Neh 9:26)

AA.   Pride, Lofty [opinion of one's self], Not Humble, Self-Exaltation (Neh 9:29; Jer 8:8; 18:18; 44:10; Dan 7:25; ; Luk 18:9-14)

BB.   Self-righteousness, Works (Luk 18:9-14; Rom 9:31-32; 10:1-3)

CC.   Withdraw the shoulder (Neh 9:29)

DD.   Flatter God (Psa 78:36)

EE.   Profane, Dishonor, Blaspheme God (Eze 22:26; Rom 2:23-24)

FF.   [Divine] Lie(s) [Unto God], Deceive, Deal Falsely, Etc. (Psa 78:36; Isa 30:9; Jer 8:5,10; Eze 22:28; Amo 2:4; 2Co 11:14-15; 1Ti 1:9-11; 4:1-3; 1Jo 1:6-8)

GG.   Speak Not Right [against the Most High] (Jer 8:6,11; Dan 7:25; Joh 7:46-49)

HH.   Prophesy Falsely (Eze 22:28)

II.   Smite, Deceive with the tongue (Jer 18:18; Rom 3:13; 2Co 11:14-15)

JJ.   Frame Mischief (Psa 94:20)

KK.   Dig Pit for, Devise Devices against, Compass about the righteous (Psa 119:85; Jer 18:18; Hab 1:4)

LL.   Be a Companion of Riotous men (Pro 28:7)

MM.   Drink Wine (Pro 31:5)

NN.   Pervert Judgment (Pro 31:5; Hab 1:4)

OO.   [Think to] Change the Ordinance, Times and Laws (Isa 24:5)

PP.   Backslide (Jer 8:5)

QQ.   Covetousness (Jer 8:10)

RR.   No Shame, Unable to Blush (Jer 8:12)

SS.   Put not difference between holy and profane, unclean and clean, Etc. (Eze 22:26)

TT.   Hide eyes from God's Sabbaths (Eze 22:26)

UU.   Destroy, Persecute, Wear out Souls/Saints (Eze 22:27-29; Dan 7:25; Act 7:52-54)

VV.   Vex the Poor and Needy (Eze 22:29)

WW.   Lade men with burdens grievous to be borne (Luk 11:45-46)

XX.   Rob, Get Dishonest Gain (Eze 22:27,29)

YY.   Daub with untempered morter (Eze 22:28)

ZZ.   Use Oppression, Oppress the Stranger wrongfully, Etc. (Eze 22:29)

AAA.   Not Stand in the Gap (Eze 22:30)

BBB.   Prayerlessness (Dan 9:13)

CCC.   Cause many to stumble (Mal 2:7-9)

DDD.   Partiality in the law (Mal 2:7-9)

EEE.   Illicit marriages (Mat 14:4-5; Mar 6:18-19)

FFF.   Substitute, Usurp God's Law with the Traditions/ Commandments of men (Mat 15:7-9; Mar 7:8, 13)

GGG.   Follow God with mere lip-service (Mat 15:7-9; 23:3)

HHH.   Hypocrisy (Mat 15:7-9; 23:3, 23-24; 23:25-28; Luk 11:37-41, 44; 2Co 11:14-15; Gal 6:13; 1Ti 4:1-3)

III.   Omission (Mat 23:3, 23-24)

JJJ.   Misc (Mat 27:6; Luk 7:30; Joh 18:31-32; Act 15:1,5)

KKK.   Love the uppermost seats in the synagogue (Luk 11:42-43)

LLL.   Love Greetings in the Markets (Luk 11:42-43)

MMM.   Love the praise and honor of men (Joh 5:44-45. Cf. 12:43; Rom 2:29)

NNN.   Enter not into knowledge, peace (Luk 11:52; Act 13:27-29; 28:25-27; Rom 2:17-27; 3:17; 10:1-3)

OOO.   Take away the key of knowledge from others (Luk 11:52)

PPP.   Hinder those entering into knowledge (Luk 11:52; Joh 7:46-49; Rom 2:17-27; 1Ti 4:1-3)

QQQ.   Despise others (Luk 18:9-14)

RRR.   Hatred (Gal 5:19-21)

SSS.   Murder (Joh 7:19; 19:6-7; Act 7:52-54; 13:28; Rom 3:15; Gal 5:19-21; 1Ti 1:9-11)

TTT.   Falsely Accuse (Joh 7:46-49; Act 6:11-14)

UUU.   Seek not after God (Rom 3:11)

VVV.   Be Unprofitable (Rom 3:12)

WWW.   Do Not Good (Rom 3:12)

XXX.   Cursing (Rom 3:14)

YYY.   Bitterness (Rom 3:14)

ZZZ.   Destruction and Misery (Rom 3:16)

AAAA.   Works of the Flesh, Be Carnal [-ly minded], Be in the Flesh (Rom 7:5, 14-25; 8:5-8; Gal 5:1-24; Eph 2:11-12; Phi 3:2-8)

BBBB.   Pretend to be the ministers of Christ (2Co 11:14-15)

CCCC.   Not Loving (Gal 5:6-7, 13-14; 1Ti 1:5-7)

DDDD.   Adultery, Fornication, Homosexuality, Whoremonger, etc. (Gal 5:19-21; 1Ti 1:9-11)

EEEE.   Uncleanness, Lasciviousness, Wantonness, etc. (Gal 5:19-21)

FFFF.   Variance, Emulations (strive, contention, jealousy) (Gal 5:19-21)

GGGG.   Wrath (Gal 5:19-21)

HHHH.   Strife (self-seeking pursuits) (Gal 5:19-21)

IIII.   Seditions, Heresies, Divisions (Gal 5:19-21)

JJJJ.   Envyings (Gal 5:19-21)

KKKK.   Drunkenness, Revellings (Gal 5:19-21)

LLLL.   Affections and Lust (Gal 5:22-24; Eph 2:1-3)
MMMM.   Walking according to the course of this world/in darkness (Eph 2:1-3; 1Jo 1:6-8)
NNNN.   Receive not the love of the truth, doing not the truth (2Th 2:8-10; 1Jo 1:6-10)
OOOO.   Ungodly, Unholy (1Ti 1:9-11)
PPPP.   Speak evil of others (Jam 4:11-12)
QQQQ.   Being judgmental towards others (Jam 4:11-12)
RRRR.   Unwise associations (2Pe 2:8; cf. 1Co 15:33)

XXII.   The Heart (Laws in; Circumcised; Prepared; not right; matters of; etc.)

Deu 4:9; 6:6; 10:12; 11:18; 17:20; 28:47; 30:2,6,8,10-14,17-18; 32:46; Jos 23:14; 2Ki 23:25; 2Ch 31:20-21; Ezr 7:10; Psa 37:31; 40:8; 51:17; 78:10,37; 119:34-36; Pro 6:20-21; Isa 51:7; Jer 31:33; 32:39-42; Eze 36:26-27; Mat 5:21-30,38-42; 15:7-9,18-20; 18:21-22,35; 23:25-28; Mar 3:4-6; 7:8,13-19; 12:28-34; Luk 11:37-41,44; Act 28:25-27; Rom 2:14-16,28-29; 6:17; 10:6-9; Gal 4:6; 1Ti 1:5; Heb 8:10; 10:15-18; 13:9; Jam 1:26.

Selected Passage(s):

❖ "And now, Israel, what doth the LORD thy God require of thee, but to fear the LORD thy God, to walk in all his ways, and to love him, and to serve the LORD thy God with all thy heart and with all thy soul" (Deu 10:12)

❖ "Set your hearts unto all the words which I testify among you this day, which ye shall command your children to observe to do, all the words of this law" (Deu 32:46)

❖ "It is a good thing that the heart be established with grace" (Heb 13:9)

Commentary:

The Bible has much to say about the heart. The following selected passages reveal how the heart is often spoken of in connection, contrast, etc. with the Law:

A. Things that are to be done with *all* thy heart and soul:
    a. Hearken unto the voice of the LORD (Deu 30:10)
    b. Keep his commandments and his statutes (Deu 30:10; Pro 6:20; Eze 36:26-27)
    c. Observe the Law (Psa 119:34)
    d. Obey, Do His voice (Deu 30:2, 8, 10-14; 32:46; Eze 36:26-27; Rom 6:17)
    e. Turn unto the LORD (Deu 30:10; 2Ki 23:25)
    f. Seek God (2Ch 31:20-21)

g. Wrought that which is good and right and truth before the LORD (2Ch 31:20-21)

h. Love the LORD thy God (Deu 30:6; Mar 12:28-34; 1Ti 1:5)

i. Walk in His ways and serve Him... (Deu 10:12; 2Ch 31:20-21; Psa 119:35; Eze 36:26-27)

(Note: God determines with His whole heart and soul to plant Israel in the land [Jer 32:41])

B. The heart may:

a. Be lifted up (Deu 17:20)

b. Be circumcised (Deu 30:6; Rom 2:28-29)

c. Depart from the righteous statutes and judgments of God (Deu 4:9)

d. Turn away [from hearing] God and, or God's command-ments (Deu 30:17-18; Mar 7:8,13-19; Act 28:25-27)

e. Be Set to observe to do all the words of this law (Deu 32:46)

f. Have the [work of the] Law of God written in it (See "E." below)

g. Be Prepared to seek and do and teach (Ezr 7:10)

h. Know (Jos 23:14; Isa 51:7)

i. Understand (Psa 119:34; Act 28:25-27)

j. Believe (Rom 10:9)

k. Say (Rom 10:6-9)

l. Be broken and contrite (Psa 51:17)

m. Be Pure (1Ti 1:5)

n. Love (1Ti 1:5)

o. Have the Spirit of God cry "Abba, Father" from within (Gal 4:6)

p. Be not right (Psa 78:37)

q. Be Inclined unto God's testimonies (Psa 119:36)

r. Be one (Jer 32:39)

s. Be new (Eze 36:26)

t. Be "established with grace" (Heb 13:9)

u. Be stony (Eze 36:26)

v. Be hard (Mar 3:4-6)

w. Be of flesh (Eze 36:26)

x. Wax Gross (Act 28:25-27)

y. Be deceived [by one's own self] (Jam 1:26)

z. Commit adultery by merely looking lustfully upon a woman (Mat 5:27-30)

aa. Be hypocritical (Mat 15:7-9; 23:25-28; Luk 11:37-41,44)

bb. Be far from God (Mat 15:7-9)

cc. Be a grief to God when not in a right condition (Mar 3:4-6)

dd. Defile a man by that which proceeds out of it (Mat 15:18-20; Mar 7:8,13-19)

C. The Law may:
  a. Be not kept (Psa 78:8, 10)
  b. Be refused (Psa 78:8, 10)
  c. Be Forsaken (Pro 6:20-21)
  d. Be Vainly substituted by the commandments, traditions of men (Mat 15:7-9; Mar 7:8,13-19)

D. God is to be served with:
  a. Joyfulness and gladness of heart (Deu 28:47)
  b. Delight (Psa 40:8; 119:35)

E. The Law, Word of God to be [bound within, laid up in, written in] the heart [and mind] [and tied about thy neck] (Deu 30:10-14; Psa 37:31; 40:8; Pro 6:21; Isa 51:7; Jer 31:33; Rom 2:14-16; 10:6-9; Heb 8:10; 10:15-18)

F. The fear of God in the heart (Jer 32:39-40)

G. From the heart trespasses are to be forgiven (Mat 18:21-22,35)

H. A man must first be cleansed/circumcised within (Mat 23:25-28; Luk 11:37-41,44; Rom 2:14-16,28-29)

XXIII. Repentance Required

Psa 51:14; Mat 3:7-10; 4:17; Act 17:30-31.

Selected Passage(s):

❖ "Bring forth therefore fruits meet for repentance" (Mat 3:8)

❖ "From that time Jesus began to preach, and to say, Repent: for the kingdom of heaven is at hand" (Mat 4:17)

❖ "And the times of this ignorance God winked at; but now commandeth all men every where to repent" (Act 17:30)

Commentary: None.

XXIV. Forgiveness Required, Granted thru Christ

Mat 18:21-22, 35; Luk 17:4; Act 13:38; 2Co 5:19, 21; Col 1:14; 2:13; Heb 9:19, 22; 1Jo 1:9.

Selected Passage(s):

❖ "Be it known unto you therefore, men and brethren, that through this man is preached unto you the forgiveness of sins" (Act 13:38)

❖ "In whom we have redemption through his blood, even the forgiveness of sins" (Col 1:14)

❖ "And you, being dead in your sins and the uncircumcision of your flesh, hath he quickened together with him, having forgiven you all trespasses" (Col 2:13)

❖ "If we confess our sins, he is faithful and just to forgive us our sins, and to cleanse us from all unrighteousness" (1Jo 1:9)

Commentary:

A distinction is to be noted between the forgiveness that is granted at the moment of one's translation into the kingdom of God's dear Son, which completely alters his *relationship* with God (e.g., Act 13:38; Col 1:14; 2:13), and that forgiveness which is granted to a Christian in order that he or she might be restored again unto *fellowship* with God (e.g., 1Jo 1:9).

XXV. Scribes, Doctors of, Lawyers, Pharisees, Chief Priests, the Concision, etc.

2Ki 22:8; 2Ch 34:15; Ezr 7:6, 12, 21; Neh 8:1; 12:44; Jer 8:8; Mat 3:7; 5:20; 12:2; 19:3; 22:35; 23:3, 23-28; 27:6; Mar 2:23-27; 3:4-6; 10:2; Luk 5:17; 6:2; 7:30; 10:25; 11:37-46, 52; 14:3; 18:9-14; Joh 7:48-49; 19:6; Act 5:34; 6:12; Phi 3:2-3; Tit 3:13.

Selected Passage(s):

❖ "How do ye say, We are wise, and the law of the LORD is with us? Lo, certainly in vain made he it; the pen of the scribes is in vain" (Jer 8:8)

❖ "But when he saw many of the Pharisees and Sadducees come to his baptism, he said unto them, O generation of vipers, who hath warned you to flee from the wrath to come?" (Mat 3:7)

❖ "Except your righteousness shall exceed the righteousness of the scribes and Pharisees, ye shall in no case enter into the kingdom of heaven" (Mat 5:20)

❖ "But when the Pharisees saw it, they said unto him, Behold, thy disciples do that which is not lawful to do upon the sabbath day. ... [5]But he [Jesus] said unto them, Have ye not read in the law, how that on the sabbath days the priests in the temple profane the sabbath, and are blameless?" (Mat 12:2-8; cf. Mar 2:23-27)

❖ "Ye blind guides, which strain at a gnat, and swallow a camel" (Mat 23:24)

❖ "Woe unto you, lawyers! for ye have taken away the key of knowledge: ye entered not in yourselves, and them that were entering in ye hindered" (Luk 11:52)

❖ "And he spake this parable unto certain which trusted in themselves that they were righteous, and despised others: [10]Two men went up into the temple to pray; the one a Pharisee, and the other a publican. [11]The Pharisee stood and prayed thus with himself, God, I thank thee, that I am not as other men are, extortioners, unjust, adulterers, or even as this publican. [12]I fast twice in the week, I give tithes of all that I possess. [13]And the publican, standing afar off, would not lift up so much as his eyes unto heaven, but smote upon his breast, saying, God be merciful to me a sinner. [14]I tell you, this man went down to his house justified rather than the other: for every one that exalteth himself shall be abased; and he that humbleth himself shall be exalted" (Luk 18:9-14)

❖ "Beware of dogs, beware of evil workers, beware of the concision. [3]For we are the circumcision, which worship God in the spirit, and rejoice in Christ Jesus, and have no confidence in the flesh" (Phi 3:2-3)

Commentary:

Though the Bible makes it clear that *faith* is/was the only means of attaining salvation, even under the old economy (cf. Rom 4:1-25), for some reason those who were of "the concision" failed to discern the futility of their legalistic efforts to attain "the righteousness of God" (cf. Rom 9:30–10:13).

XXVI. Law under New Covenant clearly stated to be different than it was under Old Covenant.

Jer 31:33; 32:37-42; Eze 36:24-28; 44:24; Mat 3:7-10; 11:13; 12:2-5; Luk 6:2-4; 16:16; Joh 1:17; 7:23; 8:5-7, 17; 10:34; 15:25; Act 10:28; 16:20-22; Rom 11:30-31; 1Co 6:19-20; 9:20-21; Gal 1:18; 2:14-21; 3:11-12; 4:30; 5:18; Col 2:16-17, 20; 3:1; Heb 1:1-2; 7:5, 9-12, 16-19, 28; 8:3-13; 9:1, 10; 10:1-2; 12:18-24; 13:9-10; Jam 2:12.

Selected Passage(s):

❖ "But this shall be the covenant that I will make with the house of Israel; After those days, saith the LORD, I will put my law in their inward parts, and write it in their hearts; and will be their God, and they shall be my people" (Jer 31:33)

❖ "A new heart also will I give you, and a new spirit will I put within you: and I will take away the stony heart out of your flesh, and I will give you an heart of flesh. [27]And I will put my spirit within you, and cause you to walk in my statutes, and ye shall keep my judgments, and do them" (Eze 36:26-27)

❖ "For all the prophets and the law prophesied until John" (Mat 11:13)

❖ "The law and the prophets were until John: since that time the kingdom of God is preached, and every man presseth into it" (Luk 16:16)

❖ "For the law was given by Moses, but grace and truth came by Jesus Christ" (Joh 1:17)

❖ "Now Moses in the law commanded us, that such should be stoned: but what sayest thou? [6]This they said, tempting him, that they might have to accuse him. But Jesus stooped down, and with his finger wrote on the ground, as though he heard them not. [7]So when they continued asking him, he lifted up himself, and said unto them, He that is without sin among you, let him first cast a stone at her" (Joh 8:5-7)

❖ "Ye know how that it is an unlawful thing for a man that is a Jew to keep company, or come unto one of another nation; but God hath shewed me that I should not call any man common or unclean" (Act 10:28)

❖ "Unto the Jews I became as a Jew, that I might gain the Jews; to them that are under the law, as under the law, that I might gain them that are under the law; [21]To them that are without law, as without law, (being not without law to God, but under the law to Christ,) that I might gain them that are without law" (1Co 9:20-21)

❖ "After three years I went up to Jerusalem to see Peter,... [2:14]But when I saw that they walked not uprightly according to the truth of the gospel, I said unto Peter before them all, If thou, being a Jew, livest after the manner of Gentiles, and not as do the Jews, why compellest thou the Gentiles to live as do the Jews? [15]We who are Jews by nature, and not sinners of the Gentiles, [16]Knowing that a man is not justified by the works of the law, but by the faith of Jesus Christ, even we have believed in Jesus Christ, that we might be justified by the faith of Christ, and not by the works of the law: for by the works of the law shall no flesh be justified. ... [19]For I through the law am dead to the law, that I might live unto God. [20]I am crucified with Christ: nevertheless I live; yet not I, but Christ liveth in me: and the life which I now live in the flesh I live by the faith of the Son of God, who loved me, and gave himself for me. [21]I do not frustrate the grace of God: for if righteousness come by the law, then Christ is dead in vain" (Gal 1:18; 2:14-16, 19-21)

❖ "But that no man is justified by the law in the sight of God, it is evident: for, The just shall live by faith. [12]And the law is not of faith: but, The man that doeth them shall live in them" (Gal 3:11-12)

❖ "Nevertheless what saith the scripture? Cast out the bondwoman [i.e., the 'covenant... from the mount Sinai'] and her son: for the son of the bondwoman shall not be heir with the son of the freewoman [i.e., 'Jerusalem which is above']" (Gal 4:30)

❖ "But if ye be led of the Spirit, ye are not under the law" (Gal 5:18)

❖ "God, who at sundry times and in divers manners spake in time past unto the fathers by the prophets, [2]Hath in these last days spoken unto us by his Son, whom he hath appointed heir of all things, by whom also he made the worlds" (Heb 1:1-2)

❖ "If therefore perfection were by the Levitical priesthood, (for under it the people received the law,) what further need was there that another priest should rise after the order of Melchisedec, and not be called after the order of Aaron? [12]For the priesthood being changed, there is made of necessity a change also of the law.... [16]Who is made, not after the law of a carnal commandment, but after the power of an endless life.... [18]For there is verily a disannulling of the commandment going before for the weakness and unprofitableness thereof. [19]For the law made nothing perfect, but the bringing in of a better hope did; by the which we draw nigh unto God.... [28]For the law maketh men high priests which have infirmity; but the word of the oath, which was since the law, maketh the Son, who is consecrated for evermore" (Heb 7:11-12, 16, 18-19, 28)

❖ "But now hath he obtained a more excellent ministry, by how much also he is the mediator of a better covenant, which was established upon better promises. [7]For if that first covenant had been faultless, then should no place have been sought for the second. [8]For finding fault with them, he saith, Behold, the days come, saith the Lord, when I will make a new covenant with the house of Israel and with the house of Judah: [9]Not according to the covenant that I made with their fathers in the day when I took them by the hand to lead them out of the land of Egypt; because they continued not in my covenant, and I regarded them not, saith the Lord. [10]For this is the covenant that I will make with the house of Israel after those days, saith the Lord; I will put my laws into their mind, and write them in their hearts: and I will be to them a God, and they shall be to me a people: ... [13]In that he saith, A new covenant, he hath made the first old. Now that which decayeth and waxeth old is ready to vanish away" (Heb 8:6-10, 13)

❖ "Then verily the first covenant had also ordinances of divine service, and a worldly sanctuary.... [10]Which stood only in meats and drinks, and divers washings, and carnal ordinances, imposed on them until the time of reformation" (Heb 9:1, 10)

❖ "For the law having a shadow of good things to come, and not the very image of the things, can never with those sacrifices which they offered year by year continually make the comers thereunto perfect. [2]For then would they not have ceased to be offered?

because that the worshippers once purged should have had no more conscience of sins" (Heb 10:1-2)

❖ "For ye are not come unto the mount that might be touched, and that burned with fire, nor unto blackness, and darkness, and tempest, [19]And the sound of a trumpet, and the voice of words; which voice they that heard intreated that the word should not be spoken to them any more: [20](For they could not endure that which was commanded, And if so much as a beast touch the mountain, it shall be stoned, or thrust through with a dart: [21]And so terrible was the sight, that Moses said, I exceedingly fear and quake:) [22]But ye are come unto mount Sion, and unto the city of the living God, the heavenly Jerusalem, and to an innumerable company of angels, [23]To the general assembly and church of the firstborn, which are written in heaven, and to God the Judge of all, and to the spirits of just men made perfect, [24]And to Jesus the mediator of the new covenant, and to the blood of sprinkling, that speaketh better things than that of Abel" (Heb 12:18-24)

❖ "We have an altar, whereof they have no right to eat which serve the tabernacle" (Heb 13:10)

❖ "So speak ye, and so do, as they that shall be judged by the law of liberty" (Jam 2:12)

Commentary:

The above listed "Selected Passages" make this point so very clear, commentary is unnecessary.

XXVII. The New Testament Presents a Much Higher Standard (i.e., Perfection Required; etc.)

Mat 5:20, 48; 7:12; Luk 10:25-28; Act 24:5-6, 12-14; Rom 8:18, 23; 12:1-2; 1Co 6:1, 6-7; 2Co 3:6-12; Col 3:1; Heb 2:1; 8:6, 13; 13:9-12; 1Pe 1:15-16.

Selected Passage(s):

❖ "Except your righteousness shall exceed the righteousness of the scribes and Pharisees, ye shall in no case enter into the kingdom of heaven" (Mat 5:20)

❖ "Be ye therefore perfect, even as your Father which is in heaven is perfect" (Mat 5:48)

❖ "Brethren, by the mercies of God... present your bodies a living sacrifice, holy, acceptable unto God, which is your reasonable service. [2]And be not conformed to this world: but be ye transformed by the renewing of your mind, that ye may prove what is that good, and acceptable, and perfect, will of God" (Rom 12:1-2)

❖ "[God] hath made us able ministers of the new testament; not of the letter, but of the spirit: for the letter killeth, but the spirit giveth life.... [9]For if the ministration of condemnation be glory, much more doth the ministration of righteousness exceed in glory. [10]For even that which was made glorious had no glory in this respect, by reason of the glory that excelleth. [11]For if that which is done away was glorious, much more that which remaineth is glorious. [12]Seeing then that we have such hope, we use great plainness of speech" (2Co 3:6, 9-12)

❖ "If ye then be risen with Christ, seek those things which are above, where Christ sitteth on the right hand of God" (Col 3:1)

❖ "Therefore we ought to give the more earnest heed to the things which we have heard" (Heb 2:1)

❖ "But now hath he obtained a more excellent ministry, by how much also he is the mediator of a better covenant, which was established upon better promises" (Heb 8:6)

❖ "But as he which hath called you is holy, so be ye holy in all manner of conversation; [16]Because it is written, Be ye holy; for I am holy" (1Pe 1:15-16)

Commentary:

This, far from having an *earthly* focus (as was the case with Israel's relation to the Law), presents a *heaven-high* standard, attainable *only* by one putting his faith in Christ!

XXVIII. Man Cannot Keep God's Laws

Gen 8:21; Jer 13:23; Act 15:10; Rom 3:19-20; 7:5, 14-25; 8:5-8; Gal 3:20-25; 4:21; 6:13; Eph 2:1-3, 11-12; Phi 3:2-8; Col 2:13-14; Heb 12:18-21; Jam 2:9-11; 2Pe 2:14; 1Jo 1:8, 10.

Selected Passage(s):

❖ "The imagination of man's heart is evil from his youth" (Gen 8:21)

❖ "Can the Ethiopian change his skin, or the leopard his spots? then may ye also do good, that are accustomed to do evil" (Jer 13:23)

❖ "Why tempt ye God, to put a yoke upon the neck of the disciples, which neither our fathers nor we were able to bear?" (Act 15:10)

❖ "Now we know that what things soever the law saith, it saith to them who are under the law: that every mouth may be stopped, and all the world may become guilty before God. [20]Therefore by the deeds of the law there shall no flesh be justified in his sight: for by the law is the knowledge of sin" (Rom 3:19-20)

❖ "For we know that the law is spiritual: but I am carnal, sold under sin.... [18]For I know that in me (that is, in my flesh,) dwelleth no good thing: for to will is present with me; but how to perform that which is good I find not" (Rom 7:14, 18)

❖ "Because the carnal mind is enmity against God: for it is not subject to the law of God, neither indeed can be" (Rom 8:7)

❖ "Neither they themselves who are circumcised keep the law" (Gal 6:13)

❖ "And you... were dead in trespasses and sins; [2]...In time past ye walked according to the course of this world, according to the prince of the power of the air, the spirit that now worketh in the children of disobedience: [3]...fulfilling the desires of the flesh and of the mind; and were by nature the children of wrath" (Eph 2:1-3)

❖ "We... have no confidence in the flesh" (Phi 3:3)

❖ "They could not endure that which was commanded" (Heb 12:20)

❖ "For whosoever shall keep the whole law, and yet offend in one point, he is guilty of all" (Jam 2:10)

❖ "Having eyes full of adultery, and that cannot cease from sin" (2Pe 2:14)

❖ "If we say that we have no sin, we deceive ourselves, and the truth is not in us.... [10]If we say that we have not sinned, we make him a liar, and his word is not in us" (1Jo 1:8, 10)

Commentary:

It might seem a bit confusing to state in this section that man is *utterly unable to keep* the Law, in light of the fact that the Bible sets forth examples of some *keeping* the law (see section XVI. Cf. also Section XIV, XVIII and XIX). Perhaps the best Biblical text to consult in order to resolve this dilemma is where Paul claimed to be, as far as "touching the righteousness which is in the law, *blameless*" (Phi 3:6; cf. Act 22:3); yet he recognized his utter failure to meet God's perfect standard of righteousness (see Rom 7:5-25). He could not have expressed a more extreme difference between these two positions as he classified his exemplary/ impeccable/*"blameless"* record as nothing more than *"dung"* (Phi 3:8). He obviously saw a big difference between that which could be considered *acceptable compliance* with the obligations of the Mosaic Law (e.g., ceremonial, etc.), and *meeting the standards* of righteousness and true holiness before God. It is also interesting to note that Paul elsewhere referred to himself at the "chief [of] sinners" (1Ti 1:15). The Bible's testimony is unmistakably plain: "The scripture hath concluded all under sin, that the promise by faith of Jesus Christ might be given to them that believe" (Gal 3:22; cf. Eph 2:1; Col 2:13; etc.)

XXIX. Jesus is The lawgiver; Law to/of Christ; Jesus Abrogates, amends, makes exception to OT Law

Gen 49:10; Psa 60:7; 108:8; 110:4; Isa 2:2-5; 33:22; 42:1,4; 51:4; Mic 4:2; Mat 5:21-48; 7:12; 12:2-5, 10-12; 19:3,8-9; 20:15-16; 22:17, 21; Mar 2:24-26; 3:4-6; 10:2,3-6,11-12; 12:14,17; Luk 6:2-4, 9; 14:3-5; 20:22,25; Joh 5:10-11; Rom 7:4; 1Co 9:20-21; 15:28; 2Co 10:5; Gal 1:18; 2:14-21; 6:2; Jam 4:11-12.

Selected Passage(s):

❖ "Out of Zion shall go forth the law, and the word of the LORD from Jerusalem" (Isa 2:3)

❖ "The Jews therefore said unto him that was cured, It is the sabbath day: it is not lawful for thee to carry thy bed. [11]He answered them, He that made me whole, the same said unto me, Take up thy bed, and walk" (Joh 5:10-11)

❖ "There is one lawgiver, who is able to save and to destroy" (Jam 4:12)

Commentary:

Since Jesus is the "Lawgiver," He has power to abrogate, modify, amend, etc. the Law, as He sees fit under any dispensation. This by no means implies, however, far from what might be the bent perceptions of a sinister mind, that He ever *diminished* or undermined the *principles* of the Laws which pertained to any previous economy. He clearly set forth *a higher moral standard* for this Age of Grace (cf. Mat 5:48; 7:12; 19:3, 8-9; etc.). Jesus introduced these added revelations with words such as: "Ye have heard that it was said of them of old time... But I say unto you..." (cf. Mat 5:21-47). Topics addressed or amended included obligations in regards to: murder; anger; offenses; adultery; oaths; legal matters; forbearance of wrongs; love for, prayers for, and treatment of one's enemies and/or persecutors; etc.

XXX. Law is a Schoolmaster to turn/bring us to the Lord

Neh 9:26; Rom 3:19-20; 7:7-11, 13, 21-24; Gal 3:22-25; Heb 9:1, 10.

Selected Passage(s):

❖ "Now we know that what things soever the law saith, it saith to them who are under the law: that every mouth may be stopped, and all the world may become guilty before God" (Rom 3:19)

❖ "I had not known lust, except the law had said, Thou shalt not covet.... [13]that sin by the commandment might become exceeding sinful" (Rom 7:7,13)

❖ "Wherefore the law was our schoolmaster to bring us unto Christ, that we might be justified by faith" (Gal 3:24)

Commentary: None.

XXXI. Law [Has been, Is, Will be] Fulfilled (By, Unto Jesus)

Psa 40:4, 6-8; Deu 21:23; Mat 1:22-23; 2:15, 17-18, 23; 4:14-17; 5:17-20; 7:12; 8:17; Luk 16:17; 24:44; Joh 1:45; 3:16; 12:34-36; 15:25; 18:31-32; Act 10:38; 13:25-39; 17:30-31; Rom 3:21-22, 24-31; 4:23-25; 5:16-19; 6:4-10; 7:1-6; 8:3-4, 9-11; 10:4; 1Co 1:23, 30; 6:17; 2Co 4:4-5; Gal 3:13-14, 26-28; 4:1-7; Eph 2:4-7, 10, 13-16; Phi 3:2-3, 8-11; Col 2:11-15; 3:1; 2Th 2:14; Heb 7:5, 9-12, 16-19, 28; 9:8,11-14; 10:1-18; 13:9-15.

Selected Passage(s):

❖ "Lo, I come: in the volume of the book it is written of me, [8]I delight to do thy will, O my God: yea, thy law is within my heart" (Psa 40:7-8)

❖ "Now all this was done, that it might be fulfilled which was spoken of the Lord by the prophet, saying, [23]Behold, a virgin shall be with child, and shall bring forth a son, and they shall call his name Emmanuel, which being interpreted is, God with us" (Mat 1:22-23)

❖ "Think not that I am come to destroy the law, or the prophets: I am not come to destroy, but to fulfil. [18]For verily I say unto you, Till heaven and earth pass, one jot or one tittle shall in no wise pass from the law, till all be fulfilled" (Mat 5:17-18)

❖ "These are the words which I spake unto you, while I was yet with you, that all things must be fulfilled, which were written in the law of Moses, and in the prophets, and in the psalms, concerning me" (Luk 24:44)

❖ "Philip findeth Nathanael, and saith unto him, We have found him, of whom Moses in the law, and the prophets, did write, Jesus of Nazareth, the son of Joseph" (Joh 1:45)

❖ "For they that dwell at Jerusalem, and their rulers, because they knew him not, nor yet the voices of the prophets which are read every sabbath day, they have fulfilled them in condemning him. [28]And though they found no cause of death in him, yet desired they Pilate that he should be slain. [29]And when they had fulfilled all that was written of him, they took him down from the tree, and laid him in a sepulcher" (Act 13:27-29)

❖ "For what the law could not do, in that it was weak through the flesh, God sending his own Son in the likeness of sinful flesh, and for sin, condemned sin in the flesh: [4]That the righteousness of the law might be fulfilled in us, who walk not after the flesh, but after the Spirit" (Rom 8:3-4)

❖ "For Christ is the end of the law for righteousness to every one that believeth" (Rom 10:4)

❖ "Christ hath redeemed us from the curse of the law, being made a curse for us: for it is written, Cursed is every one that hangeth on a tree: [14]That the blessing of Abraham might come on the Gentiles through Jesus Christ; that we might receive the promise of the Spirit through faith" (Gal 3:13-14)

❖ "But when the fulness of the time was come, God sent forth his Son, made of a woman, made under the law, [5]To redeem them that were under the law, that we might receive the adoption of sons" (Gal 4:4-5)

❖ "And you, being dead in your sins and the uncircumcision of your flesh, hath he quickened together with him, having forgiven you all trespasses; [14]Blotting out the handwriting of ordinances that was against us, which was contrary to us, and took it out of the way, nailing it to his cross" (Col 2:13-14)

❖ "[There ariseth another priest] who is made, not after the law of a carnal commandment, but after the power of an endless life" (Heb 7:16)

❖ "For the law having a shadow of good things to come, and not the very image of the things, can never with those sacrifices which they offered year by year continually make the comers thereunto perfect.... [4]For it is not possible that the blood of bulls and of goats should take away sins. [5]Wherefore when he cometh into the world, he saith, Sacrifice and offering thou wouldest not, but a body hast thou prepared me: [6]In burnt offerings and sacrifices for sin thou hast had no pleasure. [7]Then said I, Lo, I come (in the volume of the book it is written of me,) to do thy will, O God.... [10]By the which will we are sanctified through the offering of the body of Jesus Christ once for all.... [14]For by one offering he hath perfected for ever them that are sanctified" (Heb 10:1-14)

❖ "We have an altar, whereof they have no right to eat which serve the tabernacle.... [12]...Jesus... suffered without the gate. [13]Let us go forth therefore unto him without the camp, bearing his reproach. [14]For here have we no continuing city, but we seek one to come. [15]By him therefore let us offer the sacrifice of praise to God continually, that is, the fruit of our lips giving thanks to his name" (Heb 13:10-15)

Commentary:

Again, the plainness of these passages makes commentary unnecessary.

XXXII. Mosaic Law "Done Away"; [Works] Cannot Justify. A Person is Rather Saved/Justified by/thru Faith, Grace, the Cross, etc.

Psa 40:4, 6-8; 51:14-17; Act 13:39; 15:5, 10-11, 19, 24, 28-29; 16:29-31; 18:13-15; 21:28; Rom 1:2, 5, 17; 3:19-31; 4:1-25; 5:9, 11, 15-21; 6:1-23; 7:24-25; 8:1-2; 10:1-9; 11:5-7, 30-31; 14:23; 16:25-26; 1Co 15:56; 2Co 3:1-18; 5:17-21; Gal 1:18; 2:14-21; 3:2-28; 4:1-7; 5:1-14, 18, 22-24; Eph 1:7, 13-14; 2:1-10, 13-16; 4:5, 30; Phi 3:2-11; Col 1:14; 2:11-15; 1Ti 1:3-5; Heb 7:1-28; 8:3-13; 9:1, 10, 19, 22; 10:1-18; 1Jo 1:7; 2:1-2.

Selected Passage(s):

❖ "And by him all that believe are justified from all things, from which ye could not be justified by the law of Moses" (Act 13:39)

❖ "Therefore we conclude that a man is justified by faith without the deeds of the law" (Rom 3:28)

❖ "Knowing that a man is not justified by the works of the law, but by the faith of Jesus Christ, even we have believed in Jesus Christ, that we might be justified by the faith of Christ, and not by the works of the law: for by the works of the law shall no flesh be justified.... [21]I do not frustrate the grace of God: for if righteousness come by the law, then Christ is dead in vain" (Gal 2:16, 21)

... Etc. ... (See below under "Commentary.")

Commentary:

For Commentary and additional Selected Verses, go to the Chapter entitled "Law-Grace Explained" and begin reading at the sub-section entitled "The Mosaic Law 'Done Away.'"

XXXIII. Blinded Minds, Veiled Hearts, Seared Consciences

Joh 5:45-47; 7:19,45-49; 9:28-29; 19:7; Act 6:11-14; 21:28; Rom 2:23; 9:31-33; 2Co 3:13-16; 4:4; 2Th 2:10-11; 1Ti 4:1-3; Heb 12:14-17; Jam 1:26; 1Jo 2:7-11.

Selected Passage(s):

❖ "The children of Israel could not stedfastly look to the end of that which is abolished: [14]But their minds were blinded: ... [15]Even unto this day, when Moses is read, the vail is upon their heart. [16]Nevertheless when it shall turn to the Lord, the vail shall be taken away" (2Co 3:13-16)

❖ "In whom the god of this world hath blinded the minds of them which believe not, lest the light of the glorious gospel of Christ, who is the image of God, should shine unto them" (2Co 4:4)

❖ "And with all deceivableness of unrighteousness in them that perish; because they received not the love of the truth, that they might be saved. [11]And for this cause God shall send them strong delusion, that they should believe a lie" (2Th 2:10-11)

❖ "Now the Spirit speaketh expressly, that in the latter times some shall depart from the faith, giving heed to seducing spirits, and doctrines of devils" (1Ti 4:1)

❖ "Again, a new commandment I write unto you … [10]He that loveth his brother abideth in the light, and there is none occasion of stumbling in him. [11]But he that hateth his brother is in darkness, and walketh in darkness, and knoweth not whither he goeth, because that darkness hath blinded his eyes" (1Jo 2:8-11)

Commentary: None.

XXXIV. Found Innocent in Regards to the Law; Delivered/ Free From/Dead to the Law; Clear Conscience

Psa 51:14; Act 23:29; 24:5-6, 12-14; 25:8; 28:22; Rom 2:26-27; 6:6-7, 11-23; 7:1-6, 17, 20, 25; 8:1-2; 1Co 6:12; 7:39; 9:20-21; 10:23; 2Co 3:17-18; Gal 2:19-21; 5:1-14, 18, 22-24; Col 2:16-17, 20; 1Ti 4:3-5; Heb 10:1-2; 2Pe 2:8; 1Jo 3:24.

Selected Passage(s):

❖ "Neither can they prove the things whereof they now accuse me. [14]But this I confess unto thee, that after the way which they call heresy, so worship I the God of my fathers, believing all things which are written in the law and in the prophets" (Act 24:13-14)

❖ "Neither against the law of the Jews, neither against the temple, nor yet against Caesar, have I offended any thing at all" (Act 25:8)

❖ "Knowing this, that our old man is crucified with him, that the body of sin might be destroyed, that henceforth we should not serve sin. [7]For he that is dead is freed from sin…. [11]Likewise reckon ye also yourselves to be dead indeed unto sin, but alive unto God through Jesus Christ our Lord…. [14]For sin shall not have dominion over you: for ye are not under the law, but under grace" (Rom 6:6-7, 11, 14)

❖ "Know ye not, brethren, (for I speak to them that know the law,) how that the law hath dominion over a man as long as he liveth? … [4]Wherefore, my brethren, ye also are become dead to the law by the body of Christ; that ye should be married to another, even to him who is raised from the dead, that we should bring forth fruit unto God…. [6]But now we are delivered from the law, that being dead wherein we were held; that we should serve in newness of spirit, and not in the oldness of the letter." (Rom 7:1,4, 6)

❖ "There is therefore now no condemnation to them which are in Christ Jesus, who walk not after the flesh, but after the Spirit. [2]For the law of the Spirit of life in Christ Jesus hath made me free from the law of sin and death" (Rom 8:1-2)

❖ "Now the Lord is that Spirit: and where the Spirit of the Lord is, there is liberty. [18]But we all, with open face beholding as in a glass the glory of the Lord, are changed into the same image from glory to glory, even as by the Spirit of the Lord" (2Co 3:17-18)

❖ "I through the law am dead to the law, that I might live unto God. [20]I am crucified with Christ: nevertheless I live; yet not I, but Christ liveth in me: and the life which I now live in the flesh I live by the faith of the Son of God, who loved me, and gave himself for me. [21]I do not frustrate the grace of God: for if righteousness come by the law, then Christ is dead in vain" (Gal 2:19-21)

❖ "Stand fast therefore in the liberty wherewith Christ hath made us free, and be not entangled again with the yoke of bondage.... [13]For, brethren, ye have been called unto liberty; only use not liberty for an occasion to the flesh, but by love serve one another" (Gal 5:1, 13)

❖ "But if ye be led of the Spirit, ye are not under the law.... [22]But the fruit of the Spirit is love, joy, peace, longsuffering, gentleness, goodness, faith, [23]Meekness, temperance: against such there is no law. [24]And they that are Christ's have crucified the flesh with the affections and lusts" (Gal 5:18, 22-24)

❖ "For the law having a shadow of good things to come, and not the very image of the things, can never with those sacrifices which they offered year by year continually make the comers thereunto perfect. [2]For then would they not have ceased to be offered? because that the worshippers once purged should have had no more conscience of sins" (Heb 10:1-2)

Commentary: None.

XXXV. Love Fulfils the Law

Lev 19:18; Deu 30:16, 20; Jos 22:5; Mat 5:43-48; 22:35-40; Mar 12:28-34; Luk 10:25-28; Rom 13:8-10; 1Co 13:1-3; Gal 5:14; 6:2; 1Th 1:3; Heb 12:5-8; Jam 2:8; 1Jo 2:7-11; 3:23.

Selected Passage(s):

❖ "Thou shalt love thy neighbour as thyself: I am the LORD" (Lev 19:18)

❖ "I command thee this day to love the LORD thy God, to walk in his ways, and to keep his commandments and his statutes and his judgments..." (Deu 30:16)

- ❖ "But I say unto you, Love your enemies…" (Mat 5:44)
- ❖ "Master, which is the great commandment in the law? [37]Jesus said unto him, Thou shalt love the Lord thy God with all thy heart, and with all thy soul, and with all thy mind. [38]This is the first and great commandment. [39]And the second is like unto it, Thou shalt love thy neighbour as thyself. [40]On these two commandments hang all the law and the prophets" (Mat 22:36-40)
- ❖ "Owe no man any thing, but to love one another: for he that loveth another hath fulfilled the law. [9]For this, Thou shalt not commit adultery, Thou shalt not kill, Thou shalt not steal, Thou shalt not bear false witness, Thou shalt not covet; and if there be any other commandment, it is briefly comprehended in this saying, namely, Thou shalt love thy neighbour as thyself. [10]Love worketh no ill to his neighbour: therefore love is the fulfilling of the law" (Rom 13:8-10)
- ❖ "Though I speak with the tongues of men and of angels, and have not charity, I am become as sounding brass, or a tinkling cymbal. [2]And though I have the gift of prophecy, and understand all mysteries, and all knowledge; and though I have all faith, so that I could remove mountains, and have not charity, I am nothing. [3]And though I bestow all my goods to feed the poor, and though I give my body to be burned, and have not charity, it profiteth me nothing" (1Co 13:1-3)
- ❖ "All the law is fulfilled in one word, even in this; Thou shalt love thy neighbour as thyself" (Gal 5:14)
- ❖ "Bear ye one another's burdens, and so fulfil the law of Christ" (Gal 6:2)
- ❖ "If ye fulfil the royal law according to the scripture, Thou shalt love thy neighbour as thyself, ye do well" (Jam 2:8)
- ❖ "He that loveth his brother abideth in the light, and there is none occasion of stumbling in him" (1Jo 2:10)
- ❖ "And this is his commandment, That we should believe on the name of his Son Jesus Christ, and love one another, as he gave us commandment" (1Jo 3:23)

Commentary:

Though the New Testament reveals that "love is the fulfilling of the law," this doctrine has mistakenly been used by some to incorporate certain portions of the Mosaic Law into this Age of Grace (for explanation, see the Chapter entitled "Law Described and Defined," esp. the sub-section entitled "Typical Christian Explanations of the Law-Grace Dilemma").

BIBLIOGRAPHY

In the below selected bibliography, the resources marked by the <~> symbol indicate that they are suggested by the author as additional study material in regards to the "Definition of Dispensationalism"; the resources marked by the <#> symbol indicate that they are suggested as additional study material in regards to "Israel and the Church"; and the resources marked by the <%> symbol indicate that they are suggested as additional study material in regards to "Millennialism and Rapturism." It must again be pointed out, however, that *not all* works suggested by the author for review have been written from a dispensational standpoint.

~Aldrich, Roy L., "A New Look at Dispensationalism," *Bibliotheca Sacra.* Dallas TX: Dallas Theological Seminary, 1996, c1955-1995.

~ - - -. "An Apologetic for Dispensationalism," *Bibliotheca Sacra.* Dallas TX: Dallas Theological Seminary, 1996, c1955-1995.

~ - - -. "An Outline Study on Dispensationalism," *Bibliotheca Sacra.* Dallas TX: Dallas Theological Seminary, 1996, c1955-1995.

- - -. "Causes for Confusion of Law and Grace." *Bibliotheca Sacra.* Dallas TX: Dallas Theological Seminary, 1996, c1955-1995.

- - -. "Has the Mosaic Law Been Abolished?" *Bibliotheca Sacra.* Dallas TX: Dallas Theological Seminary, 1996, c1955-1995.

Allis, Oswald T., *Prophecy and the Church.*

Angus, Joseph, and Green, Samuel G., *The Bible Handbook.*

Bailey, Mark L. Rev. of *Basic Bible Interpretation,* by Roy B. Zuck. Wheaton, IL: Victor Books, 1991. 324 pp. *Bibliotheca Sacra. Dallas TX: Dallas Theological Seminary, 1996, c1955-1995.*

Bass, Clarence B., *Backgrounds to Dispensationalism* (Grand Rapids: Baker Book House, 1960).

Berkhof, Louis, *Principles of Biblical Interpretation.*

- - -. *Systematic Theology* (Grand Rapids: Eerdmans, 1941).

Bethune, J. F.-Baker, *An Introduction to the Early History of Christian Doctrine* (London: Methuen & Co., 1942).

Bible, King James Version.

~ # % Blaising, Craig A., "Development of Dispensationalism by Contemporary Dispensationalists," *Bibliotheca Sacra,* Dallas TX: Dallas Theological Seminary, 1996, c1955-1995.

- - -. "Doctrinal Development in Orthodoxy." *Bibliotheca Sacra.* Dallas TX: Dallas Theological Seminary, 1996, c1955-1995.

- - -. Ibach, Robert D., Jr., Ed. Rev. of "Revelation and the Hermeneutics of Dispensationalism," by William H. Shepherd, Jr., *Anglican Theological Review* 71 (1989). *Bibliotheca Sacra.* Dallas TX: Dallas Theological Seminary. 1996, c1955-1995.

% Blum, Edwin A., "Augustine: The Bishop and Theologian," *Bibliotheca Sacra.* Dallas TX: Dallas Theological Seminary, 1996, c1955-1995.

Bock, Darrell L., "The Son of David and the Saints' Task: The Hermeneutics of Initial Fulfillment," *Bibliotheca Sacra.* Dallas TX: Dallas Theological Seminary. 1996, c1955-1995.

- - -. Rev. of *The Uses of the Old Testament in the New,* by Walter C. Kaiser, Jr. Chicago: Moody Press, 1985; *Bibliotheca Sacra.* Dallas TX: Dallas Theological Seminary. 1996, c1955-1995—Jul 1986.

Bowers, Russell H., Jr., "Dispensational Motifs in the Writings of Erich Sauer." *Bibliotheca Sacra,* Dallas TX: Dallas Theological Seminary. 1996, c1955-1995.

Briggs, Charles Augustus, *General Introduction to the Study of Holy Scripture.*

Britannica 2002 Deluxe Edition CD-ROM

~ Brown, R. E., J. A. Fitzmyer, & R. E. Murphy. *The Jerome Biblical Commentary.* Englewood Cliffs, N.J.: Prentice-Hall, 1996, c1968.

Burns, J. Lanier. Rev. of *Evangelical Dictionary of Theology.* Edited by Walter A. Elwell. Grand Rapids: Baker Book House, 1984. xxi + 1204 pp. *Bibliotheca Sacra.* Dallas TX: Dallas Theological Seminary, 1996, c1955-1995.

Case, Shirley Jackson, *The Millennial Hope.*

Chafer, Lewis Sperry, *Systematic Theology,* 8 Vols. [Dallas, TX: Dallas Seminary Press, 1948; reprint (8 vols. in 4), Grand Rapids: Kregel, 1992].

Chafer, Rollin T., *The Science of Biblical Hermeneutics.*

Chapell, F. L., *Biblical and Practical Theology.*

Combs, Jim, *What on Earth is a Dispensation?* (Springfield, MO.: Tribune Publishers, 1994).

% Cook, Stuart S. Rev. of *Looking Both Ways: Exploring the Interface between Christianity and Sociology* by Richard Perkins. Grand Rapids: Baker Book House, 1987. 189 pp. *Bibliotheca Sacra.* Dallas TX: Dallas Theological Seminary. 1996, c1955-1995.

Crenshaw, Curtis, *Dispensationalism Today, Yesterday, and Tomorrow* (Memphis: Footstool, 1989).

Crutchfield, Larry V., "Ages and Dispensations in the Ante-Nicene Fathers," *Bibliotheca Sacra.* Dallas TX: Dallas Theological Seminary, 1996, c1955-1995.

- - -. "Israel and the Church in the Ante-Nicene Fathers," *Bibliotheca Sacra,* Dallas TX: Dallas Theological Seminary, 1996, c1955-1995.

- - -. "The Doctrine of Ages and Dispensations as Found in the Published Works of John Nelson Darby (1800–1882)" (PhD diss., Drew University, 1985).

Decker, Rodney J., "The Church's Relationship to the New Covenant," *Bibliotheca Sacra.* Dallas TX: Dallas Theological Seminary, 1996, c1955-1995.

% Deibler, E. C., Rev. of *Evangelicalism and Anabaptism.* Edited by C. Norman Kraus. Scottdale, PA: Herald Press, 1979, 190 pp. *Bibliotheca Sacra.* Dallas TX: Dallas Theological Seminary, 1996, c1955-1995.

Demy, Timothy J. and Ice, Thomas D., "The Rapture and an Early Medieval Citation," *Bibliotheca Sacra.* Dallas TX: Dallas Theological Seminary, 1996, c1955-1995.

Denton, R.C. as cited by Enns, P. P. (1997, c1989). *The Moody handbook of theology.* Chicago, Ill.: Moody Press. 29.

~ # % Dollar, George W., "Early American Dispensationalist:—The Reverend F. L. Chapell," *Bibliotheca Sacra.* Dallas TX: Dallas Theological Seminary, 1996, c1955-1995.

Easton, M. *Easton's Bible Dictionary*. Oak Harbor, WA: Logos Research Systems, Inc., 1996, c1897.

Ehlert, Arnold D. *A Bibliographic History of Dispensationalism* (Grand Rapids: Baker Book House, 1966).

~ # Enns, P. P. *The Moody Handbook of Theology*. Chicago, Ill.: Moody Press, 1997, c1989.

Erickson, Millard J., *Christian Theology*, 3 vols. (Grand Rapids: Baker, 1985).

% Evans, W., & S. M. Coder. The Great Doctrines of the Bible. Enl. ed. /. Chicago: Moody Press, 1998, c1974.

Farrar, F. W., *History of Interpretation*.

Feinberg, Charles L., *Millennialism: The Two Major Views*, 3d ed. (Chicago: Moody, 1980).

- - -. *Premillennialism or Amillennialism*.

Feinberg, John, "Salvation in the Old Testament," in *Tradition and Testament*, ed. John S. Feinberg and Paul D. Feinberg (Chicago: Moody, 1981).

Feinberg, J. S., P. D. Feinberg, & A. Huxley. *Ethics for a Brave New World*. Wheaton, Ill.: Crossway Books, 1996, c1993.

Fritsch, Charles T., "Biblical Typology," *Bibliotheca Sacra*, 104:216, April, 1947.

Funk and Wagnalls New Standard Dictionary, s.v.

% Geisler, Norman L., "A Premillennial View of Law and Government," *Bibliotheca Sacra*. Dallas TX: Dallas Theological Seminary, 1996, c1955-1995.

Gilbert, George Holley, *The Interpretation of the Bible*.

Girdlestone, R. B., *The Grammar of Prophecy*.

Glenny, W. Edward, "The 'People of God' in Romans 9:25–26," *Bibliotheca Sacra*. Dallas TX: Dallas Theological Seminary, 1996, c1955-1995.

Graber, John, "Ultra-Dispensationalism," unpublished Doctor's dissertation, Dallas Theological Seminary, Dallas, Texas, 1949.

Hamilton, Floyd, E., *The Basis of Millennial Faith* (Grand Rapids: Eerdmans, 1942).

% Hannah, John D., "A Review of The Incredible Scofield and His Book," *Bibliotheca Sacra*. Dallas TX: Dallas Theological Seminary, 1996, c1955-1995.

- - -. "The Early Years of Lewis Sperry Chafer," *Bibliotheca Sacra* 144 (January-March 1987).

~ # % Harbin, Michael A., "The Hermeneutics of Covenant Theology," *Bibliotheca Sacra*. Dallas TX: Dallas Theological Seminary, 1996, c1955-1995.

Hodge, Charles, *Systematic Theology*. Oak Harbor, WA: Logos Research Systems, Inc., 1997.

Horne, Thomas Hartwell, *An Introduction to the Critical Study and Knowledge of the Holy Scriptures*.

Hospers, Gerrit H., *The Principle of Spiritualization in Hermeneutics*.

Houghton, George G., "Lewis Sperry Chafer, 1871–1952," *Bibliotheca Sacra*. Dallas TX: Dallas Theological Seminary, 1996, c1955-1995.

Howe, Fred R., F. Duane Lindsey, Ed. Rev. of *Christian Theology*. Vol. 3. by Millard J. Erickson. Grand Rapids: Baker Book House, 1985. 444 pp.

Bibliotheca Sacra. Dallas TX: Dallas Theological Seminary, 1996, c1955-1995.

Hughes, Archibald, *A New Heaven and a New Earth* (London: Marshall, Morgan & Scott, 1958).

Hullinger, Jerry M., "The Problem of Animal Sacrifices in Ezekiel 40–48," *Bibliotheca Sacra.* Dallas TX: Dallas Theological Seminary, 1996, c1955-1995.

Hunt, Dave, *What Love is This?* (Bend, Oregon: The Berean Call, 2004).

Ice, Thomas D., "An Evaluation of Theonomic Neopostmillennialism," *Bibliotheca Sacra.* Dallas TX: Dallas Theological Seminary, 1996, c1955-1995.

Ironside, H.A., Unpublished Class Notes, Dallas Theological Seminary.

- - -. *Wrongly Dividing the Word of Truth.*

Jamieson, R., A. R. Fausset, A. R. Fausset, D. Brown, & D. Brown. *A Commentary, Critical and Explanatory, on the Old and New Testaments.* Oak Harbor, WA: Logos Research Systems, Inc., 1997.

Johnson, Elliott E., "Hermeneutical Principles and the Interpretation of Psalm 110," *Bibliotheca Sacra.* Dallas TX: Dallas Theological Seminary, 1996, c1955-1995.

Johnson, S. Lewis., Jr., Rev. of *The Book Of Acts*, by F. F. Bruce. Wm. B. Eerdmans Publishing Company, Grand Rapids, Michigan, 1954. 555 pp. *Bibliotheca Sacra.* Dallas TX: Dallas Theological Seminary, 1996, c1955-1995.

% Karleen, P. S., *The Handbook to Bible Study: With a Guide to the Scofield Study System.* New York: Oxford University Press, 1987.

Kline, Meredith G., "Comments on an Old-New Error," *Westminster Theological Journal* 41 (1978).

Kraus, C. Norman, *Dispensationalism in America* (Richmond, VA: John Knox Press, 1958).

Ladd, *The Hope of Christ's Second Coming.*

% Lewis, Gordon R., "Theological Antecedents of Pretribulationism: (esp. 'III. Premillennialism,' and 'IV. Dispensational Premillennialism')," *Bibliotheca Sacra.* Dallas TX: Dallas Theological Seminary, 1996, c1955-1995.

Lightner, Robert P. Rev. of *Essentials of Evangelical Theology,* Vol. 2. By Donald G. Bloesch. San Francisco: Harper & Row, 1979. *Bibliotheca Sacra.* Dallas TX: Dallas Theological Seminary, 1996, c1955-1995. (Jul 1980A).

- - -. Rev. of *Heaven on Earth?* By Bruce Barron. Grand Rapids: Zondervan Publishing House, 1992. 238 pp. *Bibliotheca Sacra.* Dallas TX: Dallas Theological Seminary, 1996, c1955-1995. (Jul 1994).

- - -. Rev. of *Israelology: The Missing Link in Systematic Theology,* by Arnold G. Fruchtenbaum. Tustin, CA.: Ariel Ministries Press, 1989. *Bibliotheca Sacra.* Dallas TX: Dallas Theological Seminary, 1996, c1955-1995. (Jan 1994A).

- - -. Rev. of *The Origins of Dispensationalism,* by Larry Crutchfield. Lanham, MD: University Press of America, 1992. 236 pp. *Bibliotheca Sacra.* Dallas TX: Dallas Theological Seminary, 1996, c1955-1995. (Oct 1992A).

~ # % - - -. "Theological Perspectives on Theonomy Part I: Theonomy and Dispensationalism: [Postmillennialism]," *Bibliotheca Sacra.* Dallas TX: Dallas Theological Seminary, 1996, c1955-1995.

- - -. "Theological Perspectives on Theonomy Part II: Nondispensational Responses to Theonomy," *Bibliotheca Sacra.* Dallas TX: Dallas Theological Seminary, 1996, c1955-1995.

- - -. "Theological Perspectives on Theonomy Part III: A Dispensational Response to Theonomy," *Bibliotheca Sacra.* Dallas TX: Dallas Theological Seminary, 1996, c1955-1995.

Lowith, Karl, *Meaning in History.*

Machen, J. Gresham, *The Origin of Paul's Religion.*

% Mason, Jr., Clarence E., "A Review of Dispensationalism by John Wick Bowman: Part I," *Bibliotheca Sacra.* Dallas TX: Dallas Theological Seminary, 1996, c1955-1995.

~ # - - -. "A Review of Dispensationalism by John Wick Bowman: Part II," *Bibliotheca Sacra.* Dallas TX: Dallas Theological Seminary, 1996, c1955-1995.

~ Merriam-Webster, I. *Merriam-Webster's Collegiate Dictionary.* 10th ed. Springfield, Mass., U.S.A.: Merriam-Webster, 1996, c1993.

Merrill F. Unger, "Dispensations," *Unger's Bible Dictionary.*

McClain, Alva J., "A Premillennial Philosophy of History," *Bibliotheca Sacra,*"3:113–14, April-June, 1956.

- - -. *Law and the Christian Believer In Relation To The Doctrine of Grace* (Winona Lake, Indiana: The Brethren Missionary Herald Company, Inc., 1954.)

Northrup, B. E. *True Evangelism : Paul's Presentation of the First Five Steps of the Soul-Winner in Romans,* 1997, c1996.

Oxford English Dictionary, s.v.

Oswald T. Allis, *Prophecy and the Church.*

Packer, J. I. *Concise Theology : A Guide to Historic Christian Beliefs.* "LAW: God Legislates, and Demands Obedience." Wheaton, Ill.: Tyndale House, 1995, c1993.

% Pentecost, J. Dwight, Rev. of *The First And Second Epistles To The Thessalonians.* The New International Commentary on the New Testament. By Leon Morris. Wm. B. Eerdmans Publishing Company, Grand Rapids, 1959. *Bibliotheca Sacra.* Dallas TX: Dallas Theological Seminary, 1996, c1955-1995. (Apr 1960).

- - -. "Salvation in the Tribulation," *Bibliotheca Sacra.* Dallas TX: Dallas Theological Seminary, 1996, c1955-1995.

- - -. "The Purpose of the Sermon on the Mount." *Bibliotheca Sacra.* Dallas TX: Dallas Theological Seminary, 1996, c1955-1995.

- - -. *Things to Come: A Study in Biblical Eschatology.* Grand Rapids, MI.: Zondervan Publications, 1958, 633 pp.

Pfeiffer, C. F., & E. F. Harrison. *The Wycliffe Bible Commentary: New Testament.* Chicago: Moody Press, 1962.

- - -. *The Wycliffe Bible Commentary: Old Testament.* Chicago: Moody Press, 1962.

Philip Schaff and Henry Wace, ed., *Nicene and Post-Nicene Fathers,* second series, 14 vols. (Grand Rapids: Wm. B. Eerdmans Publishing Co., n.d.).

Pyne, Robert A. and Nebeker, Gary L., Williams, Lin M., ed. Rev. of *Introducing Christian Doctrine*, by Millard J. Erickson. Edited by L. Arnold Hustad. Grand Rapids: Baker Book House, 1992, 423 pp. *Bibliotheca Sacra.* Dallas TX: Dallas Theological Seminary, 1996, c1955-1995.

- - -. Rev. of *Faith Works: The Gospel according to the Apostles.* By John F. MacArthur, Jr. Dallas, TX: Word Books, 1993, 272 pp. *Bibliotheca Sacra. Dallas TX: Dallas Theological Seminary, 1996, c1955-1995.*

- - -. Rev. of "The Law of Moses and the Christian: A Compromise," David A. Dorsey, *Journal of the Evangelical Theological Society* 34 (September 1991). *Bibliotheca Sacra.* Dallas TX: Dallas Theological Seminary, 1996, c1955-1995.

- - -. "The 'Seed,' the Spirit, and the Blessing of Abraham," *Bibliotheca Sacra.* Dallas TX: Dallas Theological Seminary, 1996, c1955-1995.

% - - -. Williams, Lin M., ed. Rev. of *The Case for Progressive Dispensationalism: The Interface Between Dispensational and Non-Dispensational Theology* by Robert L. Saucy. Grand Rapids: Zondervan Publishing House, 1993, 336 pp. *Bibliotheca Sacra.* Dallas TX: Dallas Theological Seminary, 1996, c1955-1995.

Radmacher, Earl D., "The Current Status of Dispensationalism and Its Eschatology," in *Perspectives on Evangelical Theology.*

Ramm, Bernard, *Protestant Biblical Interpretation.*

Rand, James F., ed. Rev. of "The Bible and Modern Religions. II. Dispensationalism, Interpretation," 10:170–87, by John Wick Bowman, April, 1956. *Bibliotheca Sacra.* Dallas TX: Dallas Theological Seminary, 1996, c1955-1995.

Richards, L., & L. O. Richards. *The Teacher's Commentary,* "Study Guide 11: Exodus 13-19—The Need for Law." Wheaton, Ill.: Victor Books, 1987.

Richard, Ramesh P., "Methodological Proposals for Scripture Relevance—Part I: Selected Issues in Theoretical Hermeneutics," *Bibliotheca Sacra.* Dallas TX: Dallas Theological Seminary, 1996, c1955-1995.

- - -. "Methodological Proposals for Scripture Relevance—Part III: Application Theory in Relation to the New Testament," *Bibliotheca Sacra.* Dallas TX: Dallas Theological Seminary, 1996, c1955-1995.

- - -. "Methodological Proposals for Scripture Relevance—Part IV: Application Theory in Relation to the Old Testament," *Bibliotheca Sacra.* Dallas TX: Dallas Theological Seminary, 1996, c1955-1995.

% - - -. "Premillennialism as a Philosophy of History—Part I: Non-Christian Interpretations of History," *Bibliotheca Sacra.* Dallas TX: Dallas Theological Seminary, 1996, c1955-1995.

% - - -. "Premillennialism as a Philosophy of History—Part II: Elements of a Biblical Philosophy of History," *Bibliotheca Sacra.* Dallas TX: Dallas Theological Seminary, 1996, c1955-1995.

% - - -. "Premillennialism as a Philosophy of History—Part III: The Premillennial Interpretation of History," *Bibliotheca Sacra.* Dallas TX: Dallas Theological Seminary, 1996, c1955-1995.

- - -. "Soteriological Inclusivism and Dispensationalism," *Bibliotheca Sacra.* Dallas TX: Dallas Theological Seminary, 1996, c1955-1995.

Ryrie, Charles C., "A Trilogy of Theology," *Bibliotheca Sacra.* Dallas TX: Dallas Theological Seminary, 1996, c1955-1995.

- - -. *Dispensationalism.* Chicago: Moody Press, 1995, 224 pp.

- - -. "The End of the Law." *Bibliotheca Sacra.* Dallas TX: Dallas Theological Seminary, 1996, c1955-1995.

~ # % - - -. "The Necessity of Dispensationalism," *Bibliotheca Sacra.* Dallas TX: Dallas Theological Seminary, 1996, c1955-1995.

- - -. Rev. of *A Bibliographic History Of Dispensationalism.* Compiled by Arnold D. Ehlert. Grand Rapids: Baker Book House, 1965. 110 pp. *Bibliotheca Sacra.* Dallas TX: Dallas Theological Seminary, 1996, c1955-1995.

% - - -. Rev. of *A Dispensational Theology* by Charles F. Baker. Grand Rapids: Grace Bible College Publication, 1971, 688 pp. *Bibliotheca Sacra.* Dallas TX: Dallas Theological Seminary, 1996, c1955-1995.

% - - -. Rev. of *Is The Rapture Next?* by Leon J. Wood. Zondervan Publishing House, Grand Rapids, 1956. 120 pp. *Bibliotheca Sacra.* Dallas TX: Dallas Theological Seminary, 1996, c1955-1995.

% - - -. Rev. of *The Church In God* by Harold J. Ockenga. Fleming H. Revell Company, Westwood, New Jersey, 1956. 350 pp. *Bibliotheca Sacra.* Dallas TX: Dallas Theological Seminary, 1996, c1955-1995.

- - -. *The Basis of the Premillennial Faith* (Neptune, N.J.: Loizeaux, 1953).

- - -. *The Grace of God* [Chicago: Moody Press, 1963].

Saucy, "Contemporary Dispensationalist Thought."

Schaff, Philip, *History of the Christian Church.*

% Scofield, C. I., Editor, *The Scofield Reference Bible.*

- - -. *Rightly Dividing the Word of Truth* (Grand Rapids: Zondervan Publishing House, 1965).

Scroggie, W. Graham, *Ruling Lines of Progressive Revelation.*

Smith, Wilbur M., *The Biblical Doctrine of Heaven* (Chicago: Moody, 1968).

Smock, C. McKay, *God's Dispensations.*

Souter, Alexander, *A Pocket Lexicon to the Greek New Testament.*

Sproul, R. C. *Essential Truths of the Christian Faith.* Wheaton, Ill.: Tyndale House, 1996, c1992.

Stedman, R. C., *Bibliotheca Sacra. Dallas TX: Dallas Theological Seminary, 1996, c1955-1995.* A review of *The Fundamentals Of Dispensationalism.* By Cornelius R. Stam. The Berean Searchlight, Chicago, 1951. 279 pp.

Stevens, George Barker, *The Theology of the New Testament,* pp. 23–25, as cited by Roy L. Aldrich, "Has the Mosaic Law Been Abolished?" *Bibliotheca Sacra.* Dallas TX: Dallas Theological Seminary, 1996, c1955-1995.

Strickland, Wayne G., "Preunderstanding and Daniel Fuller's Law-Gospel Continuum." *Bibliotheca Sacra.* Dallas TX: Dallas Theological Seminary, 1996, c1955-1995.

Terry, Milton, S. *Biblical Hermeneutics* (Grand Rapids: Zondervan Publishing House, 1974).

The American Heritage Dictionary, 3rd Ed., CD-Rom, Ver. 3.5, 1994.

The Moody handbook of theology. Chicago, Ill.: Moody Press.

Torrey, R. *The New Topical Text Book: A Scriptural Text Book for the Use of Ministers, Teachers, and All Christian Workers,* "The Law of Moses." Oak Harbor, WA: Logos research Systems, Inc., 1995, c1897.

Turner, David, "The Continuity of Scripture and Eschatology: Key Hermeneutical Issues," *Grace Theological Journal* 6 (Fall 1985).

Virkler, Henry A., *Hermeneutics: Principles and Processes of Biblical Interpretation* (Grand Rapids: Baker Book House, 1981).

Wallace, Roy, *Studies in Systematic Theology.* Shreveport, La.: LinWel, 2001. 422 pp.

Walvoord, John F., A review of *Acts Dispensationally Considered* by Cornelius R. Stam. Berean Bible Society, Chicago, Vol. I, 1954, 294 pp., Vol. II, 1955, 293 pp. *Bibliotheca Sacra.* Dallas TX: Dallas Theological Seminary, 1996, c1955-1995.

~ # % - - -. A review of *Backgrounds To Dispensationalism* by Clarence B. Bass. Wm. B. Eerdmans Publishing Company, Grand Rapids, Michigan, 1960, 184 pp. *Bibliotheca Sacra.* Dallas TX: Dallas Theological Seminary, 1996, c1955-1995.

% - - -. A review of *Christian Hope and the Future of Man* by Stephen H. Travis, Leicester: Inter-Varsity Press, 1980, 143 pp. *Bibliotheca Sacra.* Dallas TX: Dallas Theological Seminary, 1996, c1955-1995.

- - -. A review of *Dispensationalism Today* by Charles C. Ryrie. Chicago: Moody Press, 1965, 221 pp. *Bibliotheca Sacra.* Dallas TX: Dallas Theological Seminary, 1996, c1955-1995.

% - - -. A Review of *From Eternity To Eternity* by Erich Sauer. Wm. B. Eerdmans Publishing Company, Grand Rapids. 1954. 207 pp. *Bibliotheca Sacra.* Dallas TX: Dallas Theological Seminary, 1996, c1955-1995.

~ # % - - -. "A Review of The Blessed Hope by George E. Ladd," *Bibliotheca Sacra.* Dallas TX: Dallas Theological Seminary, 1996, c1955-1995.

- - -. A review of *The Greatness Of The Kingdom* by Alva J. McClain, Zondervan Publishing House, Grand Rapids, 1959, 556 pp. *Bibliotheca Sacra.* Dallas TX: Dallas Theological Seminary, 1996, c1955-1995.

- - -. A review of *The Hope Of Glory* by Dale Moody, Grand Rapids: William B. Eerdmans Publishing Company, 1964, 300 pp. *Bibliotheca Sacra.* Dallas TX: Dallas Theological Seminary, 1996, c1955-1995.

% - - -. A review of *The Last Things* by George Eldon Ladd, Grand Rapids: Wm. B.Eerdmans Publishing Co., 1978, 119 pp. *Bibliotheca Sacra.* Dallas TX: Dallas Theological Seminary, 1996, c1955-1995.

- - -. A review of *The Unity Of The Bible* by H. H. Rowley, The Westminster Press, Philadelphia, 1955, 201 pp. *Bibliotheca Sacra.* Dallas TX: Dallas Theological Seminary, 1996, c1955-1995.

% - - -. A review of *What Presbyterians Believe* by Gordon H. Clark. Presbyterian and Reformed Publishing Company, Philadelphia, 1956, 130 pp. *Bibliotheca Sacra.* Dallas TX: Dallas Theological Seminary, 1996, c1955-1995.

% - - -. "Does the Church Fulfill Israel's Program? - Part 1," *Bibliotheca Sacra.* Dallas TX: Dallas Theological Seminary, 1996, c1955-1995.

- - -. J. D. Pentecost, ed. Rev. of *Dispensationalism In America* by C. Norman Kraus. John Knox Press, Richmond, 1958, 156 pp. *Bibliotheca Sacra.* Dallas TX: Dallas Theological Seminary, 1996, c1955-1995.

% - - -. Rev. of *Christ's Kingdom And Coming* by Jesse Wilson Hodges. Wm. B. Eerdmans Publishing Co., Grand Rapids, 1957, 247 pp. with indexes. *Bibliotheca Sacra.* Dallas TX: Dallas Theological Seminary, 1996, c1955-1995.

% - - -. Rev. of *Contemporary Options in Eschatology: A Study of the Millennium* by Millard J. Erickson. Grand Rapids: Baker Book House, 1977, 197 pp. *Bibliotheca Sacra.* Dallas TX: Dallas Theological Seminary, 1996, c1955-1995.

% - - -. Rev. of *Dispensationalism Today* by Charles C. Ryrie. Chicago: Moody Press, 1965, 221 pp. *Bibliotheca Sacra.* Dallas TX: Dallas Theological Seminary, 1996, c1955-1995.

% - - -. Rev. of *Fundamentalism And The Missouri Synod* by Milton L. Rudnick. St. Louis, Missouri: Concordia Publishing House, 1956, 152 pp. *Bibliotheca Sacra.* Dallas TX: Dallas Theological Seminary, 1996, c1955-1995.

- - -. Rev. of *Jesus Christ And History* by George Eldon Ladd. Chicago: Inter-Varsity Press, 1963, 62 pp. *Bibliotheca Sacra.* Dallas TX: Dallas Theological Seminary, 1996, c1955-1995.

- - -. "Posttribulationism Today," *Bibliotheca Sacra* 132 (1975).

~ # % - - -. "Posttribulationism Today—Part IV: Futurist Posttribulational Interpretation," *Bibliotheca Sacra.* Dallas TX: Dallas Theological Seminary, 1996, c1955-1995.

Warfield, B. B., *Biblical Doctrines* (New York: Oxford U., 1929).

Wesley, J., *Sermons, on Several Occasions.* Oak Harbor, WA: Logos Research Systems, Inc., 1999.

Willson, Lloyd V., *The Fullness of Times.* Shreveport, La.: Linwel, 2000, 163 pp.

% Witmer, John A., "A Review of Wrongly Dividing the Word of Truth—Part 1," *Bibliotheca Sacra.* Dallas TX: Dallas Theological Seminary, 1996, c1955-1995.

% - - -. "A Review of Wrongly Dividing the Word of Truth—Part 2," *Bibliotheca Sacra.* Dallas TX: Dallas Theological Seminary, 1996, c1955-1995.

~ # - - -. A review of *Dispensationalism, Israel and the Church: The Search for Definition.* Edited by Craig A. Blaising and Darrell L. Bock. Grand Rapids: Zondervan Publishing House, 1992, 402 pp. *Bibliotheca Sacra.* Dallas TX: Dallas Theological Seminary, 1996, c1955-1995.

- - -. ed. A review of "The Revival of Apocalyptic in the Churches," George Eldon Ladd, Review and Expositor 72 (Summer 1975): 263–70. "The Eschatology of Hal Lindsey," Dale Moody, Review and Expositor 72 (Summer] 975). *Bibliotheca Sacra.* Dallas TX: Dallas Theological Seminary, 1996, c1955-1995.

~ - - -. ed. A review of "Trying The Spirits—Dispensationalism," R. C. Harbach, The Standard Bearer, XLII (April 1, 1966), 302. *Bibliotheca Sacra.* Dallas TX: Dallas Theological Seminary, 1996, c1955-1995.

- - -. ed. Rev. of "Dividing the Word of Truth: An Examination of Dispensationalism" by Stuart A. Frayne, Theodolite 7 (1984): 3–15. *Bibliotheca Sacra*, 1996, c1955-1995.

- - -. ed. Rev. of "Joachim of Fiore's Breakthrough to Chiliasm" by Robert E. Lemer, *Cristianesimo Nella Storia* 6 (October 1985): 489–512. *Bibliotheca Sacra.* Dallas TX: Dallas Theological Seminary, 1996, c1955-1995.

- - -. ed. Rev. of "Principles of Interpretation in Regard to Prophecy with Special Reference to Millennialism," C. Kuehne, *The Journal of Theology* 21

(December 1981): 2–28. *Bibliotheca Sacra.* Dallas TX: Dallas Theological Seminary, 1996, c1955-1995.

- - -. ed. Rev. of "Toward A Historical Interpretation Of The Origins Of Fundamentalism," Ernest R. Sandeen, *Church History,* March, 1967, pp. 66–83. *Bibliotheca Sacra.* Dallas TX: Dallas Theological Seminary, 1996, c1955-1995.

- - -. Ibach, Robert D., ed. A review of "Covenant Conditionality and a Future for Israel," Ronald W. Pierce, *Journal of the Evangelical Theological Society* 37 (March 1994). *Bibliotheca Sacra.* Dallas TX: Dallas Theological Seminary, 1996, c1955-1995.

- - -. Rev. of *The Johannine Logos* by Gordon H. Clark. Nutley, NJ: Presbyterian and Reformed Publishing Company, 1972. 90 pp. *Bibliotheca Sacra.* Dallas TX: Dallas Theological Seminary, 1996, c1955-1995.

Witsius, Hermann, *The Economy of the Covenants* (London: T. Tegg and Sons, 1837).

Wood, D. R. W., D. R. W. Wood, & I. H. Marshall. *New Bible Dictionary.* electronic ed. of 3rd ed. Downers Grove: InterVarsity Press, 1996, c1982, c1962.

Wuest, Kenneth S., "The Practical Use of the Greek New Testament—Part IV: The Greek Article in New Testament Interpretation," *Bibliotheca Sacra.* Dallas TX: Dallas Theological Seminary, 1996, c1955-1995.

[#] Wyrtzen, David B., "The Theological Center of the Book of Hosea," *Bibliotheca Sacra.* Dallas TX: Dallas Theological Seminary, 1996, c1955-1995.

[%] Zuck, Roy. B., A review of *Daniel: An Introduction and Commentary.* The Tyndale Old Testament Commentaries. By Joyce G. Baldwin. Downers Grove, IL: InterVarsity Press, 1978, 210 pp. *Bibliotheca Sacra.* Dallas TX: Dallas Theological Seminary, 1996, c1955-1995.

[# %] - - -. A review of *Dispensationalism* by Charles C. Ryrie. Chicago: Moody Press, 1995, 224 pp. *Bibliotheca Sacra.* Dallas TX: Dallas Theological Seminary, 1996, c1955-1995.

- - -. A review of *Hermeneutics: Principles and Processes of Biblical Interpretation* by Henry A. Virkler. Grand Rapids: Baker Book House, 1981, 255 pp. *Bibliotheca Sacra.* Dallas TX: Dallas Theological Seminary, 1996, c1955-1995.

[%] - - -. A review of *The Interpretation of Prophecy* by Paul Lee Tan. Winona Lake, IN: BMH Books, 1974, 435 pp. *Bibliotheca Sacra.* Dallas TX: Dallas Theological Seminary, 1996, c1955-1995.

- - -. A review of *The Psychology of Biblical Interpretation,* by Cedric B. Johnson. Grand Rapids: Zondervan Publishing House, 1983, 119 pp. *Bibliotheca Sacra.* Dallas TX: Dallas Theological Seminary, 1996, c1955-1995.

[#] - - -. Lindsey, F. Duane, Ed., A review of *Power Healing* by John Wimber with Kevin Springer. San Francisco: Harper & Row Publishers, 1987, 293 pp. *Bibliotheca Sacra.* Dallas TX: Dallas Theological Seminary, 1996, c1955-1995.